SUGAR CREEK

SUGAR CREEK

Life on the Illinois Prairie

John Mack Faragher

YALE UNIVERSITY PRESS
New Haven and London

Designed by Susan P. Fillion and set in Baskerville text
with Chisel and Clarendon Condensed display type by
The Composing Room of Michigan, Inc.
Printed in the United States of America by Murray
Printing Co., Westford, Mass.

Library of Congress Cataloging-in-Publication Data

Faragher, John Mack, 1945–
  Sugar Creek: life on the Illinois Prairie.

  Bibliography: p.
  Includes index.
  1. Sugar Creek Valley (Macoupin County and San-
gamon County, Ill.)—History. 2. Frontier and pi-
oneer life—Illinois—Sugar Creek Valley (Macoupin
County and Sangamon County, Ill.) 3. Sugar Creek
Valley (Macoupin County and Sangamon County,
Ill.)—Social conditions. 4. Sugar Creek Valley
(Macoupin County and Sangamon County, Ill.)—Eco-
nomic conditions.
F547.S94F37 1986 977.3'56 86-5622
ISBN 0-300-03545-4 (alk. paper)

10 9 8 7 6 5 4 3 2 1

To Michele Hoffnung
For the Good Times

Contents

Illustrations

Maps

Acknowledgments

Many people lent their assistance to this project. First, I depended upon the excellent staff and resources of several Illinois archives. At the Illinois State Historical Library in the Old Statehouse in Springfield, Cheryl Schnering guided me to mid-nineteenth-century farmers' accounts, family letters, reminiscences, plat maps, and photographs, and Roger Bridges was always quick to respond to my calls for help. At the Illinois State Archive, Wayne Temple introduced me to the original records of the federal land survey, tax lists, election returns, population and agricultural census materials, and taught me about surveying and Indian settlement patterns. At the Illinois Regional Archive Depository at the Archives of Sangamon State University, Nancy Hunt helped with the extant official records of Sangamon County dating from 1821, including the minutes and proceedings files of the county commissioner's court, the dockets and case files of the circuit court, land and probate records. Edward Hawes, John Knoefle, and Horace Q. Waggoner, also at Sangamon State, was each helpful in special ways.

This work would not have been possible without the work of local genealogists and historians. Special thanks go to the Sangamon County Genealogical Society, whose publications—including transcriptions of the manuscript schedules of the federal population census for Sangamon County for 1830 through 1860, federal land claim records, tax lists, marriage records, plat maps, probate materials, church records, and cemetery inventories—constitute an invaluable resource for the social historian. I want to especially thank Eileen Gochnanour and Joyce Stuper of the Society. I also learned from Mary Alice Dodds Bale, who knows the history of the Cumberland Presbyterian Church and its cemetery; from Father James Kondrath, who introduced me to the history of the local Catholic community and arranged for access to the diocese archives in Springfield; and from Walter Burtle, who inspired me with his knowledge of his neighborhood. Among many local people I am most indebted to Paul and Debbie Burtle, who helped me with local introductions, helped me to read deeds and property abstracts, and when the hour grew late provided me with a bed, and invited me to rise with the Sugar Creek sun and fog, to explore the timber and fields along the creek, and to share the fresh-slaughtered beeve.

Throughout the research and writing I depended on my friends and colleagues at Mount Holyoke College. The reference staff of Williston Memorial Library helped me with bibliographic problems and did their best to procure obscure titles and microfilm through interlibrary loan. My fellow historians urged me to broaden my perspectives, offered books and articles, and listened sympathetically. The college also provided research funds for several trips to Illinois and authorized leave time to complete the writing. My work was facilitated by a summer stipend from the National Endowment for the Humanities and by a fellowship from the American Council of Learned Societies.

A number of people took time out from their own busy schedules to read and comment on the manuscript. I want to thank Hal S. Barron, Daniel J. Czitrom, Donald H. Doyle, George B. Forgie, Robert V. Hine, Michele Hoffnung, Katheryn Marshal, and Nancy Grey Osterud. Their criticism was extremely helpful and provided me with the opportunity to see Sugar Creek through eyes other than my own. In several instances they saved me from significant errors. I must, of course, absolve them of any responsibility for those which remain. My editor Charles Grench gave me solid advice on the manuscript, as well as providing other necessary encouragement.

When I required quiet at home, Josh, Sarah, and Jesse complied by turning down the stereo or retreating to their rooms. When I was troubled with my work, they listened (or seemed to listen) politely, and on occasion suggested ways of proceeding that I found myself following with good results. Through both the good times and the bad, Michele combined the roles of supporter and critic, sustaining me through the research and writing. This book is for her.

Introduction

I began this project in order to understand more about Americans of the early-nineteenth-century West, the region now called the Midwest. In an earlier study, I followed western women and men onto the trails to California and Oregon. Afterward I found myself wondering how different their lives might look when rooted in the local soil that gave life to both corn and communities. Here I examine the settlers of a small section of rural Illinois, the first generation of a midwestern community, in the six decades before the American Civil War.

Some accounting of my intellectual debts is in order. I have long been fascinated with historical demography, for it opens to at least partial view the history of reproduction. Abstracting statistical data from census enumerations, vital records, and genealogical charts is tedious work, but the measurable aspects of reproductive life provide a base upon which social history must build. The technique of family reconstitution also allows historians to examine in outline the life histories of individual families. Linked with various other kinds of evidence, including reminiscence, and presented in the context of statistically sound generalizations, family history offers a way of bringing authentic, everyday actors, of both sexes, into the historical narrative.[1]

To be sure, both men and women constitute the integrated and indivisible web of everyday life. But simply writing women into the historical narrative does not suffice, for by an equally complex web of custom, law, and political economy women have been subjected to the individual and collective will of man. Demography does not, on its own, take up the "politics" of the family or household. We must also think about relationships, and they are not easily measured. History must elucidate the structures of power and dominance by which men have been able to exercise, protect, and perpetuate their control of the social order.[2]

Recently the productive system of early America has been the subject of a good deal of historical debate. Has American agriculture been fundamentally capitalist from its beginnings, or was it characterized by a different and distinctive mode of production that finally gave way to capitalism in the countryside? The debate over commercialism and self-sufficiency, although too narrowly framed, has challenged many old assumptions and raised new and important questions that have stimulated my work. Another important challenge is finding a way of linking the structures of the productive system to those of reproduction.[3]

The interrelationships between these subjects raise questions about the nature of community life in the American countryside and the American West. Over the past quarter-century, historians have devoted increasing attention to the study of community in American history, but despite the fact that until relatively recently the majority of Americans lived in the open country, those studies have generally focused on towns, villages, and cities. Sociologists have made fruitful suggestions about the nature of country communities, but we historians have only begun our study. As a fellow historian warns, "until we know as much about rural people as we do about townspeople, there is a danger that we will stress to excess the role of community in American history." Hopefully, my study of rural Illinois will help to fill this gap.[4]

An important dimension of local community is landscape. Geographer D. W. Meinig reminds us that "all human events *take place*." Moreover, in the process of acting out life's eventualities, men and women transform and reshape that place. I was attentive to questions of landscape in my archival work and incorporated "outdoor methods" by spending time tramping field and stream.[5]

From these diverse strands, several subjects came to hold particular interest for me: the dispossession of the Algonquin-speaking Indians and the establishment of Anglo-American settlements on the frontier; the creation of a distinctive rural landscape; the social relations between the sexes; the nature of western community life; and the transition to commercial agriculture. Respectively, these subjects constitute the focus of the five parts of this book. But believing in synthesis as well as analysis, in the art as well as the science of history, I wrote this book to be read as narrative, convinced that it is the layering of detail, the interrelation of subjects, and the mingling of abstract structure with conjuncture, that make up the gestalt of historical interpretation.

Histories of other communities from widely different times and places reminded me that there were some new and some old things about Sugar Creek. In America during the first half of the nineteenth century, the expansion of both the nation and the capitalist economy created special demands and opportunities. Westerners confronted the pressing realities of a settler society and an encroaching market. There were also the challenges of mass, democratic politics and religious diversity. But there was also much that was traditional. As they had been for centuries, the family and the household were the building blocks of society. The household was also the workplace, and the sexual division marked a line of great stratification in the ordering of work and authority. Endogamy resulted in kin relations that bound local households into what some have called "kinship communities." Religion and the local church were of overwhelming importance for the way people thought and acted. This is local history, but other works have helped me to keep Sugar Creek in a larger perspective.[6]

One hot, rainy summer day in 1978, I took refuge from my explorations of the steamy Sugar Creek timber in an air-conditioned tavern along the state highway. A young native struck up a conversation; we talked about the narrow opportunities for a young man in the local economy. He was moving to Dallas, he said, where he might find work with an uncle who built houses for midwestern migrants to the sun belt. Besides, he complained into his beer, "this place is nowhere!" Several years later, after the idea for this book had taken shape, my editor asked a historian to read and comment on my proposal. "I don't think that I had ever heard of Sugar Creek," the skeptical critic wrote back, "and I don't find it on maps of Sangamon County." On closer examination of the maps the creek may be found, running north from its prairie drainage into the Sangamon River, although after the 1930s much of its course disappeared into Lake Springfield, created when Sugar Creek was dammed as a municipal water supply for the nearby county seat and state capital of Springfield, Illinois. There was, however, a candid truth in the comments of both critics. It was precisely the commonplace character of the rural heritage of Sugar Creek that drew me to explore the twists and turns of its early history.

Timothy Flint, a missionary and intellectual transplanted from New England to western soil in the 1810s, believed that "a fair history of the society of a country village would be a thousand times more interesting than a novel"; but, he judged, "taste has not yet matured sufficiently to relish such a picture, and, perhaps, the historian does not yet exist who has the requisite discrimination and felicity to draw it." Yet the Sangamon Country, the "Land of Lincoln," has never wanted for historians. One of the first was Lincoln's law partner and biographer, William Henry Herndon. During his own time, Herndon was frequently castigated as a drunkard, a publicity-seeker, and a braggart; yet for all his faults, Herndon was a sensitive observer of his culture and a man who greatly stimulated the local interest in history. In 1842, at the age of just twenty-four, he requested the assistance of the Massachusetts Historical Society: "we here have no such thing as your institution," the young lawyer wrote, but "I wish to put such a thing in motion and I believe it can easily be done." After Lincoln's assassination, Herndon spent several years pursuing what we would now call "oral history" among the Sangamon men and women who had known his partner. As his carefully preserved, voluminous notes demonstrate, Herndon was as interested in the character of "pioneer society" as in that of his illustrious law partner.[7]

To his friend George Spears, Herndon assigned the task of interviewing men and women from the village of New Salem. After some time in the field, Spears expressed frustration that he could learn little from his interviews. "The Old Ladys would begin to count up what had happened in Salem when such a one of their children was born & such a one had a Bastard," he wrote, "but it all amounted to nothing." It escaped him, but Spears was on to something important here, the possibility of a different kind of history, something also remarked upon by the mid-nineteenth-century American novelist Caroline Kirkland during a trip through central Illinois just before the Civil War:

> Here and there, on these beautiful highlands, we find ancient ladies, bright-eyed and cheerful, who tell us they have occupied the self same house—built Kentucky-fashion, with chimney outside—for forty years or so. The legends these good dames tell are, no doubt, quite as interesting in their way as those which Sir Walter Scott used to thread the wilds of Scotland to gather up; but we value them not. By-and-by posterity will anathematize us for letting our old national stories die in blind contempt or sheer ignorance of their value.

Spears could little appreciate the stories of the "good dames" of the Sangamon, but Herndon served posterity well by dutifully recording them. "I have been with the People," he jotted while deep in his researches, "ate with them—slept with them & thought with them—cried with them too." Although such sentimentality colored nearly everything that Herndon wrote, he never lost the sense that what was commonplace could also be important.[8]

I researched this book in the libraries and archives of Sangamon County, but much of its sensibility developed in commonplace conversations over country kitchen tables. Many of today's residents of Sugar Creek are sensitive to the historic dimensions of the landscape of field and stream about them; others keep the history of their churches, cemeteries, and neighborhoods. Trained as an archival historian, I found my sense of Sugar Creek shaped not only by what I found in the historical record, not only by the questions provoked by reading community studies and social histories, but by the people of today's Sugar Creek as well. This book is in part a dialogue with local historians, past and present. We owe a debt to the men and women who have preserved the memory of the pioneers. We have an even greater obligation to restore to their history the depth and complexity of the times that gave birth to the American Midwest.

PART ONE

Howling Wilderness

THE ILLINOIS COUNTRY IN THE EARLY NINETEENTH CENTURY

1

The Pioneer
of Sugar Creek

In October of 1817, Robert Pulliam left his wife and children in southern Illinois and, accompanied by four men and one woman, led his string of cattle north into unsettled country. Moving at a grazer's pace, Pulliam's party spent at least ten days covering the hundred miles to Sugar Creek, and arrived there after autumn had set the prairie and timber ablaze with color. The herd grazed on the rich grass flourishing in the prairie meadows, while, a mile into the creek's timber in the midst of a large grove of sugar maple, the party built a rude log shelter to protect them from the winter. The men spent their winter days hunting and trapping the abundant small game of the river country; Mrs. Strickland, a sister of one of the hands, spent hers cooking over an open fire and tending to the domestic needs of camp. When snow covered the prairie, the drovers felled budding elm trees at the edge of the timber for the browsing cattle. Then, as spring approached, Pulliam set his men to work tapping the maples, rendering the sweet sap into sugar over the fire in the cabin. In April 1818, the party headed south, with fat stock, furs, and several hundred pounds of maple sugar to trade. Pulliam remained with his relations on the Kaskaskia River in St. Clair County until he and his family made a permanent move to Sugar Creek, in the spring of 1819.

Pulliam's story has provided the opening tale for the history of Sangamon County, Illinois, since 1859. That year a group of prominent local citizens formed an "Old Settlers' Society" and in order to

begin the task of writing their history, appointed a committee to inves-
tigate the competing claims of several families to the honor of being the
first to settle. The committee announced, after considerable delibera-
tion, that although other settlers had broken ground for planting a full
year before Pulliam brought his family in 1819, the 1817 sugarhouse
was the first "local habitation" of Americans in the country of the
Sangamon, so the committee awarded Pulliam the title "pioneer of
Sangamon County."[1]

Robert Pulliam typified his generation of pioneers. He was born in
Henry County, Virginia, on the eastern slope of the Blue Ridge near
the "dividing line" with North Carolina, in 1776. His father, John
Pulliam, the son of Scotch-Irish emigrants, had emigrated there in the
early 1770s after a childhood in the Shenandoah Valley, and there he
fought with the county militia during the Revolution. But when the
fighting ended, John led his wife (whose name was not recorded for
posterity) and three children through the Cumberland Gap in the
Appalachians into Kentucky, where Robert, his firstborn son, grew to
young manhood. John Reynolds, a neighbor of the Pulliam family in
Illinois and later governor of the state, described John as "a man of
good mind, and more energy and activity than ordinary."[2]

The Pulliam household and the Kentucky population grew apace.
By 1800 the new state counted nearly a quarter-million residents; for
her part, Mrs. Pulliam counted six more children. Poor settlers squatted on Kentucky land, hoping to accumulate the purchase price
through their own labor, but, caught in the inflation of land values that
accompanied development, many found themselves unable to raise the
necessary cash. Many emigrated once again, and John Pulliam was one
of these. After nearly two decades in Kentucky, he moved his family
northwest across the Ohio River into the Illinois Country in 1796.[3]

The Pulliams first settled at New Design, a community of Virginians
located on the bluffs overlooking "American Bottom," a narrow strip
of rich Mississippi floodplain running for a hundred miles along the
east side of the river, south of its confluence with the Missouri. At
American Bottom, French trappers and Jesuits built settlements in the
eighteenth century, and there Americans began to settle after their
conquest of the Illinois Country during the Revolution. There, in
1797, during an epidemic of what was probably malaria, Mrs. Pulliam
died, leaving her oldest daughter, Nancy, to mother the five youngest
children, while Robert and two half-grown brothers worked with their
father in the fields. Over the next several years, John Pulliam farmed
several sites both in Illinois and across the Mississippi in Spanish Missouri before finally settling his family at the outermost frontier of
American settlement in Illinois, on Kaskaskia River bottomland ten

miles above the Mississippi bluffs. In 1808 he sold his rights to the improvements on this place and followed the frontier of American settlement another ten miles upriver, where he spent the last years of his life operating "Pulliam's Ferry" across the Kaskaskia. Federal land sales did not begin in Illinois until 1815, so when John died in 1812 he had not secured title to the land he farmed along the river. It is likely, in fact, that John Pulliam had spent his whole life farming without ever owning land.[4]

Raised on the frontier, and often in transit, John Pulliam's oldest son, Robert, was no stranger to moving. The boy never attended school, never learned to read or write (although he did master his signature). "The circumstances of his life prevented his obtaining an education from books," his neighbor John Reynolds wrote. Instead, his "natural good sense" was trained in woodlore and weather sign, in the oral traditions of song and story, in the ways of backwoods farming, herding, hunting, and the ways of squeezing a small cash income from a subsistence economy. Addicted to the "rude sports of the time"— wrestling, animal baiting, and horse racing—young Pulliam achieved a wide reputation as a "pretty considerable" drinker and gambler. Along the banks of the Mississippi, folks told the tale of the time Pulliam won a two hundred-dollar bet by beating a bragging Missourian in a reckless horse race run on the frozen surface of the great river.[5]

When Robert left home for the first time at the age of twenty-six, he headed for the frontier, just as his father had. In the spring of 1804, not far from the base camp of the cross-continental expedition then being mounted by Merriwether Lewis and William Clark, Robert staked a claim along Wood River, a stream that feeds the Mississippi across from the mouth of the Missouri. In the American settlement there he met, courted, and wed Mary Stout, daughter of another frontier family. For the next twelve years Robert and Mary Pulliam squatted on the bluffs overlooking the confluence of the Missouri and Mississippi rivers, where they farmed, herded cattle, and raised three daughters and two sons.

Life on the frontier was pretty rugged. Local game, a patch or two of Indian corn and a few other vegetables, and a few hogs running wild in the woods living off the acorn and hickory nut mast supplied the family's subsistence. The nearest government authority was fifty miles south; the nearest mills, stores, and craftsmen were better than a day's ride away. In 1808, while on a hunting trip, Pulliam seriously injured his leg, and by the time he got to Cahokia, on American Bottom, it was so badly infected that his only hope was amputation. "The patient possessed such courage that he held his body as firm as a rock without assistance," wrote John Reynolds, who watched as an army surgeon

sawed through the bone, with no more anesthetic to ease the poor
man's pain than liberal doses of corn liquor. Robert Pulliam's peg-leg
stood as a lifetime symbol of frontier isolation.[6]

There were other dangers in Wood River. Kickapoo Indians had
been coming to the area for many years to garden, gather, and hunt. In
1804 explorer William Clark noted a camp of Kickapoo on the Illinois
side of the Mississippi, not five miles from Wood River, and just before
he and Clark set out with their exploring party, a Kickapoo tribal band
paid a visit to their base camp. When Americans moved into the area,
settlers and Kickapoo contended for the same ground, and the resulting violence continued for the next twelve years, finally culminating in
the struggle for the possession of Illinois during the War of 1812. In
1814, as part of that war, the Kickapoo murdered and scalped Mrs.
Reason Reagan and six children as they were walking through the
timber one sunny Sunday afternoon, just a mile from the Pulliam farm.
Pulliam's son Martin, seven years old at the time, remembered hearing
settlers' terrifying tales of American women tomahawked as they were
making soap in their farmyards, and their screaming babies hurled
into the boiling kettles by the Indians.[7]

After the war the United States opened a land office at Edwardsville,
county seat of newly established Madison County, and began the public
sale of Wood River lands. But Pulliam did not buy land in Wood River.
In 1816, after the crops were in, he and his family moved back to where
his relations were at the Kaskaskia ferry, where he bought a small herd
of American Bottom cattle. Settlers of American Bottom had raised
cattle for over half a century, and herders frequently preceded farmers, exploring new areas with their cattle and searching for a free
winter feed and a possible place for new settlement. Pulliam's 1817
reconnoiter of the possibilities one hundred miles north on Sugar
Creek was part of a family and social pattern, a move to the frontier to
stake out new lands ahead of the surveyors and land officers.[8]

In the historic lore of Sangamon County, however, Robert Pulliam
became something more than simply a typical frontiersman. At the
first gathering of the Old Settlers' Society, held in October 1859 on the
site of Pulliam's Sugar Creek homestead, James H. Matheny, a successful attorney, the best man at Abraham Lincoln's wedding, and a
recently defeated candidate for Congress on the new Republican party
ticket, described the pioneer of Sugar Creek as a latter-day Moses.

> Forty-two years ago the stillness of the unbroken forest was star-
> tled by the clangor of an axe in a strong man's hands. That day he
> had rested from a weary journey, but as he stood and gazed upon
> the beauty of the strange wild scene about him, there arose a
> longing in his heart to linger here. With that class of men to whom

HUSBAND MARTIN G. PULLIAM (1807–72), SON OF ROBERT PULLIAM, AND WIFE LUCY KNOTTS PULLIAM (1812–78), in photographs taken during the 1850s. Martin was born on his father's farm in Wood River, Illinois; Lucy, in southern Indiana. Both came to Sugar Creek with their parents in 1819 and settled on the east bank of the creek near the sugar camp. Married in 1827, Lucy bore seven sons and five daughters, two of whom died in infancy. In 1859, at the Old Settlers' meeting, Martin told the crowd that he had "not one unsound tooth in his head," had "never smoked a pipe or a cigar, or used a quid of tobacco," and had "not tasted a drop of intoxicating liquor for many years."

he belonged, to decide was to act. Soon his weary team was
loosened from their heavy load, . . . his axe rung out, wild and
clear, and some brave old tree that had stood the storms of a
hundred years, crashed headlong to the earth. We do not know
whether in that stilly hour, when all alone with nature and
nature's God, he formally kneeled down upon the green earth
and offered up a prayer for protection through the lonely hours
of that first night in the strange land to which he had come, but we
feel sure that there must have been in his heart a calm and un-
shaken trust that the guardian care of a kind Providence was
around about him, to shield and protect him from every harm.
This was a singularly marked characteristic of the early pioneers
of the West. They had "faith in God"—an unswerving trust in His
Providence . . . , an abiding faith that a kind Father is ever guard-
ing, with a sleepless watchfulness, the welfare of his wandering
children.

Matheny invoked the "God-is-on-our-side" sentiments that American
politicians and pioneers have traditionally used to justify their move
into other peoples' territories since the time of the Pilgrim fathers:

> We have a howling wilderness
> To Canaan's happy shore,
> A land of dearth and pits and snares
> Where chilling winds do roar.

> But Jesus will be with us,
> And guard us by the way;
> Though enemies examine us,
> He'll teach us what to say.

Matheny assigned Pulliam the part of discoverer and founder, forging
alone into the howling wilderness of central Illinois, beckoning the
chosen people to follow him and begin the course of history.[9]

Matheny's version of the American past ignored the context and the
setting for Pulliam's actions, substituting for them a mythic mission
that lay outside the scope of temporal events. He ignored the Indian
past, transforming everything that preceded Pulliam into natural history. Yet by setting out with his herds like some ancient patriarch,
Pulliam acted with apparent knowledge of good grazing to the north.
In packing the heavy kettles and other equipment necessary for sugaring, he seemed to anticipate the existence of a substantial stand of
maple. These clues suggest that this trailblazer followed a well-marked
path to the San-gam-ma Country (as Americans called the fertile land
of central Illinois in the first decades of the nineteenth century,) a trail
laid out by more than a century of human occupancy and history. The

peg-legged pioneer of Sugar Creek played but one role in a panorama of thousands—Indian and American, female and male—who made history. Robert Pulliam depended on the Indians and Europeans who came before him, and the timing of his exploration places the pioneer of Sugar Creek at the culminating point of a decades-long struggle for American control of these Indian lands.

2

Hunters and Sugar-Makers

What attracted Pulliam to Sugar Creek had attracted others before him. French Jesuits and fur traders of the eighteenth century first encountered the San-gam-ma Country as they coursed down the Illinois River on their way from Canada to their Mississippi missions and settlements; the banks of timber must have seemed apiece with the great forest that stretched eastward to the Atlantic. Along the banks of northward-flowing Sugar Creek, giant sycamores, some over fifteen feet in diameter, grew beside tall cottonwoods, hickories, and oaks, their foliage interwoven with a latticework of huge pea vines and an undergrowth of dense red elm, witch hazel, and other brush that made the forest nearly impenetrable from the river. Modern forest science classifies these woods as part of oak-hickory region of the great northeastern deciduous forest. "When the traveller enters the depths of these dark old woods," wrote an early visitor to the San-gam-ma, "a cool chill runs over his frame, and he feels as if he were entering the sepulcher."[1]

But the river view can be deceptive. Beginning at the banks, forest covered a mile or two of broken country but then thinned, giving way to an undulating expanse of prairie. The drainage system and associated timber of the Sangamon River lie in the southeastern section of the Prairie Peninsula, a great wedge of grassland extending from the Great Plains east as far as the Wabash River basin, thousands of square miles of prairie, upon which native grasses flourished. Before settlers plowed these grasses and introduced naturalized European varieties, native big bluestem, Indian grass, and Canadian wild rye grew a good deal taller than a man. On the prairie near Sugar Creek, south of the river, shallow drainage encouraged standing water and bogs, where slough grass and huge wildflowers grew, and mosquitoes and hard-biting horseflies bred in abundance.

With mean summer and winter temperatures of 75 and 30 degrees, respectively, and a frost-free growing season of over 180 days, central Illinois is climatically typical of the temperate American Midwest. But while in the woodlands to the east the heaviest rains occur in winter, over 60 percent of prairie rains fall from April to September. These summer rains fail regularly; then temperatures soar and drought scorches the land. Because grasses possess a superior ability to use subsoil moisture, periodic drought favored the persistence of prairie over forest and produced a succession of mixed grassland-timber balances until the contemporary environment emerged some seven thousand years ago: grasses on the shallowly drained uplands, timber on the dissected and sloping hills approaching the waterways. Occasionally a free-flowing spring produced a wooded grove in the midst of the prairie. Over many centuries these variations in flora created important corresponding differences in soil types; of the land drained by Sugar Creek, 15 percent of the soil is of woodland and bottomland type, 75 percent predominantly prairie, and another 10 percent characteristic of the transition between these two zones.[2]

The San-gam-ma Country encompassed a considerable range of environmental diversity with an abundance of life forms prospering amid the variations of soil and drainage, prairie and woodland. The autumn color that greeted Pulliam when he arrived in October 1817 was an indication of this variety. As summer faded, the bluestem prairies turned from green to tawny red and vermilion, tall goldenrod, sawtooth sunflowers, and black-eyed Susans stood proud in dense patches of bright yellow, and willow aster, prairie snakeroot, and tall ironweed added their touch of whites and violets. The foliage of broad-trunked white oaks turned orange and dull purple, red oaks took on their characteristic rich fall shades, sugar maples painted the landscape yellow, orange, and crimson, and sumac and poison ivy stained the forest floor a rich burgundy. Hickories tended to dead browns and dull yellows, but their rich harvest of nuts added to the abundant crop of acorns, walnuts, and ruby-tinged hawthorne pomes.

The great American forest contained more species of edible and nutritious nuts than any of the world's woodlands. Beeches, including the American chestnut, were heavy mast producers, and oaks offered up crops of acorns. Indians and Americans most valued the hickories. Indians used *Pawcohicora,* an Algonquian word for the oily food product removed from the steeped and pounded kernels of the nut, in the preparation of corn cakes and hominy; the pioneers renamed it "sweet hickory milk." The *pecan,* another Algonquian word meaning simply "nut," was the most prized of the hickories; Americans called these "Illinois nuts," because they first found them in the fertile bottomland of Illinois. The forest also produced a wide variety of fruit: in spring, raspberries, mulberries, may apples, and tiny, intensely sweet wild strawberries; in summer, blackberries and wild plums; and in fall, paw paw, persimmon, crab apple, wild cherry, red and black haws, and wild grapes.[3]

This cornucopia attracted a diverse community of animals. At the water's edge lived beaver, mink, muskrat, raccoon, and weasel. Deeper in the timber were bear, grey fox, squirrel, opossum, and skunk, as well as wild turkey, broad-winged hawk, owl, and woodpecker. The margin between forest and prairie provided the most prolific habitat, home to cottontail, red fox, coyote, wolf, white-tailed deer, and elk, as well as sandhill crane, prairie chicken, and hawk. Grazing the prairies, before Indians and Americans hunted them to extinction around 1800, were American bison. Catfish, carp, crappie, bass, and sucker inhabited the waterways and backwater ponds. The San-gam-ma, near the Great Mississippi Flyway for migratory waterfowl, was a place of rest and succor for over-flying ducks and geese. In the fall, when the beechnuts were ripe, passenger pigeons darkened the sky like thick passing clouds, roosting in the high forest trees.[4]

The heavy mast fattened man as well as beast. The first human settlers in the San-gam-ma practiced gathering, hunting, and fishing in seasonal cycles. From the study of the refuse of these settlers of several thousand years ago, archaeologists know that they fished with hooks; hunted for deer, turkey, small mammals, and migratory birds with sophisticated fluted stone-point projectiles; and prepared forest nuts in stone grinders. The diffusion of this technology from other parts of North America into the Illinois Country depended upon regional trade networks enabling distant peoples to share their learning. Archaeologists have recovered Gulf coast conch shells, Atlantic shark's teeth, and far western grizzly claws, among other imports, from several ancient sites in central Illinois.[5]

The importation of the bow and arrow in the eighth century A.D. intensified the human exploitation of these animal resources. Fall and winter hunting camps became more substantial; families moved to the woods together and set up bases from which local and long-range hunts took place. In the summer, whole villages moved to the prairie for the communal buffalo hunt. Men controlled hunting; they manufactured the weapons and were collectively responsible for providing meat and furs to the women of their lineage. So important was hunting to male identity, reported the first European observers of the Indians of the Illinois, that parents strapped minature bows and arrows to the cradle boards of sons, little boys were rarely seen without their arms, and young men could not marry before proving their hunting ability. Women, in their roles as gatherers, and later as cultivators, produced surpluses to outfit male hunting parties. Some of these parties ranged far from the base camp, but the abundance of animal life in forest and prairie permitted most hunting to take place within the customary territory of the village.

People calling themselves "Inoca," or "Ininiwek" in the plural, first greeted Louis Joliet and Father Jacques Marquette on their exploration of the Illinois Country in 1673. The French altered the name to a form they could pronounce more easily, "Illiniwek," then gradually substituted their own plural suffix to make "Illinois." The name stuck. But even before the Illinois encountered the French themselves, European forces had begun to transform their lives. The North American fur trade, a European importation, quickly captured the attention of most tribes, and the engrossment of large tracts for hunting grounds transformed traditional intertribal conflict into full-scale tribal warfare. Early in the seventeenth century, the Iroquois, based in upper New York, attempted to extend their control of the fur trade by establishing military dominance over the various tribes of the animal-rich Great Lakes and Ohio Valley regions. By the 1650s the Iroquois imperial reach extended all the way to the Mississippi, and in 1655 they began an assault on the villages of the Illinois that they continued for the next thirty years.[6]

The Illinois fought back but, no match for the powerful Iroquois, soon settled for a strategy of assimilation with the French, leaving central Illinois and relocating their villages near the Mississippi River trading posts and missions, practicing agriculture and livestock-raising, and intermarrying with soldiers and settlers. Gradually, disease, alcoholism, and cultural disintegration reduced the Illinois people to the pitiful existence of "trading-post Indians." By the close of the eighteenth century, the Illinois had all but lost a unique tribal identity.

The Illinois migration to American Bottom opened the Illinois river valleys to settlement by northern bands of Potawatomi, Chippewa, and Kickapoo. The Kickapoo settled the Sangamon Country. In 1612 Samuel de Champlain reported that the tribe was situated between the head of Lake Erie and Saginaw Bay on Lake Huron, but the Iroquois fur-trade wars drove them around the southern end of Lake Michigan to the Rock River region of Wisconsin, where the French encountered them again after 1665. They then moved south, into the drainage of the Illinois, Sangamon, and Wabash rivers, a move completed by the

1760s. For the next half-century the tribe occupied the rich prairies of
central Illinois and western Indiana. In the eighteenth century, the
Kickapoo were the settlers of Sugar Creek.[7]

Anthropologists once believed that in Algonquian the name
Kickapoo, the self-designation of the tribe, meant "he who moves
about, standing now here, now there." Scholars today dismiss this
translation as "linguistically impossible," as "folk etymology," but it had
the advantage of fitting the history of the Kickapoo well, since their
movements were frequent and extensive. They were the first of the
woodland Algonquian to integrate the horse into their economy, and
they quickly became superb handlers and judges of horseflesh;
mounted, Kickapoo men ranged widely in their hunting and raiding,
and this helps to explain the tribe's mobility.[8]

In their settlement of central Illinois, the Kickapoo were also assisted by their use of the long-barreled, small-caliber "Kentucky" rifle,
developed by skilled Pennsylvania-German gunsmiths in the mid-eighteenth century. All Indian tribes quickly adopted European weapons.
As early as Marquette and Joliet's explorations in the 1670s, the Illinois
were in possession of firearms, as well as other European trade goods,
and eighteenth-century British traders and Kickapoo hunters regularly exchanged Kentucky rifles for furs and meat. With its long-range
accuracy, this rifle effected a revolution in the way men exploited their
environment and guaranteed that the day would come when abundant
game was just a hunter's memory.[9]

In the early nineteenth century the hunting opportunities of the
San-gam-ma became well known to Americans as well. Elisha Kelly, a
Carolina frontiersman out seeking his fortune, wandered into central
Illinois in 1817 and spent one or two winters hunting along Sugar
Creek, south of Pulliam's camp. In the early mornings, he watched
deer leave the heavy timber near the creek and gingerly move up the
ravines to emerge onto the open prairies, where they spent the day
grazing amid the tall grasses. In rich lands like this, a head of household could kill a week's supply of game in half a day. Kelly returned
home with tales of the fabulous San-gam-ma, and, along with father,
brothers, friends, and families, emigrated in 1819. For Kelly and many
others, the prime criterion for evaluating new lands was the quality and
quantity of hunting. "Almost every citizen," Illinois settler John Reynolds recalled, "made hunting his main business in the fall, by which he
added considerable to the support of himself and family."[10]

The Kickapoo hunted communally, but the American hunter generally traveled alone with his horse, hound, and gun. The Kentucky
rifle had to be held steady and true as spark ignited powder, so men
like Kelly almost always shot from rest, hidden in a blind, downwind
from the game. Other times, however, when charged by a buck or elk

or surprised by an Indian war party, a frontier hunter loaded on the run: dumped powder in, poured bullets down the muzzle, primed pan heavy, turned and fired, a handful of bullets stuffed in the mouth in case the chance came to fire again. Entangled as they were in a continual struggle with Indians for land and hunting rights, warfare was ever on the minds of frontiersmen, who decorated their powder horns with carved figures of men and animals and inscriptions such as this one, found on a horn passed from Ohio Valley father to Sugar Creek son:

February 14, 1758.

I Powder with my Brother Ball,
A Herow like, I conquer all:
Drums a Beeting, colours flying,
Trumpets sounding, men a Dying
These are the bold Affects of WAR.[11]

The San-gam-ma was hunter's paradise enough to draw Kickapoo and American settlers from a distance, but the forests contained other resources as well. All trees manufacture sugar, but the sugar maple (*Acer saccharum*) produces sucrose as well as glucose. Warm, sunny fall days, followed by cool nights, trigger the end of sap production and transform the food still in the leaves into red pigment; then, in late winter, warm days and freezing nights signal the sap to run again. Everywhere within the range of the sugar maple, from Nova Scotia to North Carolina, west to the Mississippi Valley, and north to the Great Lakes, Indians harvested the sweet sap of the maple in February and March. Documentary evidence dates Indian harvests as early as the beginning of the seventeenth century, and the practice was almost surely pre-Columbian.[12]

The Indians first taught the art of tapping the maple to the French. A French traveler through the Mississippi Valley in the 1760s wrote that "the French who are settled at the Illinois have learnt from the Indians to make this syrup, which is an exceeding good remedy for colds, and rheumatisms." With brass or copper kettles, which allowed for much more efficient boiling, another visitor wrote, "the French make sugar better than the Indian women, from whom they have learned how to make it; but they have not yet been able to whiten or to refine it." But by enclosing the kettles in a rude shanty, straining the syrup through linen, and further clarifying it with eggs or milk, Europeans gradually learned to remove the impurities from the sap. The goal was sugar so fine that, in the words of a nineteenth-century farmer's manual, "the whole coloring matter is extracted, and the peculiar flavor of the maple sugar is completely eradicated, leaving the sugar fully equal to the double refined cane loaf." By the late-eighteenth century, farmers from northern New England to Kentucky were making a refined variety of maple sugar. The Indians found most European innovations helpful, and as early as the 1680s the Illinois had obtained and were using French kettles. But few tribes made an attempt to purify the syrup, arguing that in its unrefined state it tasted better, more like the forest.[13]

In late February, "Sap Moon" in the Algonquian calendar, Indian men and women set up camp in the sugar bush. In central Illinois, sugar maple thrives on the rough and somewhat steep slopes that descend to the waterways, and may dominate the forest there. These thick stands of hard maple are self-seeded. But a productive sugar grove requires human care and attention. Indians removed brush that impeded movement from tree to tree, girdled and burned out old trees, and tended replacement saplings. By piling snow around the base of producing maples, collectors could delay the bursting of the leaf buds and extend the sap season by a week or more.[14]

In established groves, Indian women tapped trees by making horizontal gashes in the trunks three or four feet above the ground and inserting cedar "spiles" at a downward angle, allowing the sap to drip into elm or birch bark buckets. Before the importation of kettles, they collected the sap in wooden troughs, boiled it by dropping hot stones into the sap, and stirred until granulation occurred. The sugar they stored in *mococks,* sewn birch bark bags. Men cut wood, made fires for heating the stones or kettles, and hunted and fished for camp. The integration of men's and women's work, the place of sugar-making in the seasonal round marking the end of winter, and the delightful, sweet product all lent a festive air to the occasion. Children loved to pour the boiling sap on the snow to cool into chewy candy.[15]

But maple sugar was more than simply a treat for youngsters. At sugar-making time, young and old alike delighted in drinking the partially rendered sap, and Americans agreed that this was a delicious and refreshing drink. Women used maple molasses as a sweetner in vegetables, fish, and meat, sometimes mixing the sugar with bear's grease for storage and using it later as a basting over roast venison or duck. Most important, sugar-making often came at the end of a hard winter, a time when food stores might be nearly depleted; then maple sugar, mixed with the remaining parched corn, might serve as the principal food until the first crops of the spring. The preparation of maple sugar was an important social and subsistence activity.[16]

Maple sugar was an important product for American frontier farmers as well. Loaves of cane sugar sold at fifty cents a pound in the early nineteenth century, so cash-poor farm families used locally produced maple sugar, along with wild honey, as the usual sweetening at table, as a preservative for crab apples, wild plums, and other sour fruit, and as a glaze for hams and game. For a sweet plug of tobacco, farmers cured their home-grown leaf with a liberal mix of maple sugar. When put up in corn shucks, families could barter the sugar at the rate of seven to thirteen cents a pound, so sugar-making could produce a small income. "Maple sugar was legal tender for all debts, public and private," one early San-gam-ma settler recalled. The equipment for making sugar, then, was part of the inventory of every household fortunate enough to have a grove of maple in their timber. Early settler C. B. Stafford remembered cradling and rocking his baby in a sugar trough.[17]

Sugaring time was also a holiday for Americans. The rising of the sap occurred when farm labor was not otherwise employed, and frequently all hands retreated to the sugar bush. John James Audubon, pursuing his bird-watching rambles through Kentucky about 1810, spied the glow of a fire in the woods. "As I approached it," he wrote, "I observed forms of different kinds moving to and fro before it, like spectres; and ere long, bursts of laughter, shouts, and songs apprised me of some merry-making. I thought at first that I had probably stumbled upon a camp-meeting; but I soon perceived that the mirth proceeded from a band of sugar-makers." "At times," he continued, "neighbouring families join, and enjoy the labour as if it were a pastime, remaining out day and night for several weeks; for the troughs and kettles must be attended to from the moment when they are first put in requisition until the sugar is produced. The men and boys perform the most labourious part of the business, but the women and girls are not less busy."[18]

In the sugar grove along Sugar Creek in March of 1818, sugar was made once again. This time, however, while the work proceeded in much the same traditional way, it was Pulliam and his hands, not the Kickapoo, who collected the sap, while Mrs. Strickland tended the kettles. Pulliam was just another hunter and sugar-maker attracted to the abundance of the San-gam-ma. But his occupation of the sugar grove marked a turning point in the history of Sugar Creek.

3

Defenders of
the Manitou

$\mathbb{S}$ugar Creek became known to Americans during their struggle to possess central Illinois. The name for the creek first appeared in 1815 on a manuscript map prepared for Governor Ninian Edwards of Illinois Territory that summarized the geographical intelligence gathered during the northwestern Indian campaigns of the War of 1812. This was the most accurate and detailed mapping of central Illinois accomplished to date. Since the Kickapoo regularly made sugar, identifying their sugar groves became a matter of military necessity. The maker of Edward's wartime maps marked many creeks and groves "Sugar," and others, the site of salt licks, "Saline" or "Salt." The map also indicated the location of a "Kickapoo Town," north of the Sangamon River, on what is now called Kickapoo Creek. Other summer villages lay to the northeast at the headwaters of the river and north at Peoria Lake, where the Kickapoo, Potawatomi, Chippewa, and Ottawa all founded towns in the early eighteenth century. Sugar Creek, and the grove of productive maples that supplied its name, were clearly within the territory of the Sangamon Kickapoo. The data from Edward's surveys provided the basis for John Melish's *Map of Illinois,* printed in Philadelphia in 1819, the first published notice of Sugar Creek.[1]

The Kickapoo were great hunters, but like their Algonquian neighbors they practiced a subsistence strategy that combined women's horticulture and food gathering with male hunting. Maize horticulture, imported into the woodlands from the American southwest in the tenth century A.D., encouraged a sedentary pattern of settlement and transformed temporary Indian summer camps into granary villages surrounded by bottomland fields. The Indian villages of the upper Mississippi Valley consisted of hundreds of lodges, each lodge large enough to house several related families. "I took pleasure in observing the situation of this village," Marquette wrote in his journal after visiting a Kickapoo town in southern Wisconsin in 1673. "It is beautiful and very pleasing, for, from an eminence upon which it is placed, one beholds on every side prairies, extending farther than the eye can see, interspersed with groves or with lofty trees. The soil is very fertile, and yields much Indian corn. The savages gather quantities of plums and grapes, wherewith much wine could be made if desired." A Frenchman's comment, to be sure.[2]

The exchange of men's and women's products formed the central relationship of the Kickapoo economy, and these relations of production structured other aspects of Kickapoo culture. Women produced most of the food for the Indian diet. With wooden or stone hoes they worked sandy river-bottom soils to produce beans, squash, and their staple crop, maize or Indian corn. In late spring immature ears were picked and eaten whole, cob and all, but most harvesting awaited the "green" corn stage, when kernels were full but still "in the juice." Staggered plantings could lengthen green corn season, and for as many as two or three months Kickapoo men and women feasted on roasted or boiled ears. Since they had to store a surplus for winter, however, women "parched" large quantities for later boiling. In the fall, women picked the mature hard ears, soaked the otherwise inedible kernels, pounded them in a mortar to remove the tough skins or pericarps, and served them boiled with salt or maple sugar. Algonquian-speaking peoples called this dish *rockahominie,* shortened by Americans, who often survived on it, to "hominy." Women dried the remaining hard corn, beat it into meal as needed, then used it to thicken the soups or stews they habitually prepared. When women had finished the harvest, they pulled, piled, and burned the stalks in preparation for the next season's planting.[3]

Kickapoo women also gathered vegetable food. In addition to seasonal harvests of nuts, berries, and wild fruits, they regularly spent several hours each day collecting nutritious and tasty tubers, an activity that demanded great skill in surveying the dense ground cover for the appropriate flowering tops. The most popular root was the ground nut or wild potato known in Algonquian as *macopine,* but women also gathered the edible roots of wild artichoke, milkweed, arrowhead, and wild dill, which they either boiled or roasted. They also collected plants believed to have medicinal properties: whorled milkweed, used to treat snake or insect bites; tall ironweed, for stomach ailments; culver's root, used as a powerful emetic and cathartic; prairie snakeroot, widely believed to be a general curative; and Solomon's Seal, which nearly every Kickapoo, man, woman, and child carried for protection from evil manitous and witches.[4]

Despite the importance of women's labor to their diet, however, the Kickapoo considered the men's hunting their single most important economic activity. Their cuisine depended on meat, bone, and fat. When heavy competition from American hunters limited their own hunting, the Kickapoo invariably complained of "starvation," despite their garden crops. Moreover, fur, hide, and hair were essential for fiber, clothing, cover, and the foreign exchange that paid for imported trade goods. Men also cleared the land by girdling trees, stripping branches, and burning out the brush, only then turning fields over to women. Since Indians cropped their fields until they exhausted the soil's fertility, new land constantly needed clearing. Palisade construction around the village and the manufacture of wooden implements— cradle boards, ladles, bowls, traps, bows and arrows, deer calls, lacrosse sticks, snowshoes, and toboggans—were also men's responsibility.

So men cleared the fields, women worked them. Men returned from the hunt to distribute meat and pelts to the women of their lineage; women supplied the surpluses of corn that fed the hunters for most of their time in the woods. "Sap Moon" began a round of activities in which men and women worked closely together, first in the sugar bush, then in the fields. In the fall, men's labor took them into the woods again, where they encountered men from other tribes and returned, not only with furs and meat, but trade goods. During these long male absences, women took reponsibility for social continuity and cohesion in the village. The Kickapoo believed in a reciprocal division of labor according to gender.

In fact, the Kickapoo notion of reciprocity structured most personal relationships. Compare, for example, the contrasting ideas of American and Kickapoo about parent-child relations. The Judeo-Christian commandment is simply stated: Honor thy father and thy mother. But for the Kickapoo the role of father, *no'sa*, implied both parental authority and the duty to indulge the child's whims; son, *nekwisa*, included the obligation to honor parents and to care for them in old age, but also the obligation of determining one's own course. Mothers nursed Kickapoo babies on demand, and children continued to take the breast as late as age four or five; parents seemed little concerned about children's toilet habits. When children got into trouble, rather than punishing the offending offspring, parents were more likely to make good the damage. Adults who felt compelled to punish a child would do so by ignoring him, for refusal to recognize mutual obligations was the ultimate social sanction; to the Kickapoo, "withdrawal" from contact was the greatest of all possible insults. In other words, kinship relations were less command structures, as they were in American culture, than two-way connections.[5]

Moreover, the Kickapoo extended kinship relations well beyond the immediate family. The word *no'sa* stood not only for the biological father but also for the father's brothers, the husbands of all women in the mother's lineage, and the sons of all women in the father's mother's lineage. Mother, *nekya,* referred only to one's biological mother, but the diminutive form, *neki'ha,* was used to designate almost all the women of mother's lineage as well as the wives of all "fathers." The network of kin terms placed an individual in a complex of reciprocal relationships with a great number of other people. "In a small community of less than five hundred in which each member is probably related to at least one-fourth of the other members," two contemporary anthropologists of the Mexican Kickapoo write, "behavior toward the entire community is governed by strict rules requiring that everyone be polite, friendly and helpful to others." The reciprocal nature of kinship relations facilitated cooperation. The Kickapoo generally perceived all their personal relationships in terms of kinship: members of the same clan addressed each other as "brother" and "sister," everyone addressed old people as "grandfather" or "grandmother," and the whole community thought of even supernatural forces in kin terms.[6]

In Kickapoo cosmology, the universe operates as a grand metaphor for these reciprocal principles. "The earth is an individual," a clan leader told one anthropologist; "so are the rocks, the trees, the clouds, and the night. They are put here as witnesses for the behavior of man. The Spirit is watching man always through his witnesses or messengers. All of his actions are noticed." These many spirits, or manitous, watch to see that men and women comply with the reciprocal order of things. The hunter foregoes the first deer he sees, the gatherer passes over the first plant, burning tobacco as an offering and asking its manitou for permission to take others. These attitudes toward the natural world, born in the exchanges between men and women, suggest a relaxed pattern of resource use, in contrast to the attitudes of Americans.[7]

Like nearly all woodland tribes, however, the Kickapoo quickly became enmeshed in the fur trade—an international market created by the European demand for furs, hides, and other forest products, and supplied by the production of thousands of Indians and traders in the North American interior. The Kickapoo first entered the market in the mid-seventeenth century at the French post on Green Bay, exchanging furs for imports: steel or iron traps, knives, kettles, adzes, and axes, as well as glass beads, guns, powder, and liquor.

Just as their traditional culture was constructed on the base of an economy of hunting and horticulture, so too the economy of the fur trade altered the lives of the Kickapoo in important ways. Guns and traps transformed their means of production and created a dependence upon the products of European or American industry. Hunting parties ranged farther and stayed longer in the woods, inviting conflict with other tribes, similarly pressed. While the Kickapoo were still in southern Wisconsin in 1680, the fur trade invasions of the Iroquois and the Sioux violently disrupted their settlements and forced the people to flee for protection to the French post at Green Bay. The Jesuit missionary Jean Allouez reported visiting a Kickapoo village during these troubled times; the Indians greeted him with offerings of tobacco, fat and meal soup, and pleas of "Manitou, take pity on us, guard our land!"[8]

But, unlike the Illinois, the Kickapoo rejected the role of trading-post Indian and in the mid-1680s struck back at the invaders—Iroquois, Sioux, and French alike—with incredible fury. The Illinois, with their strategy of assimilation, provided a cogent example of the degradation that accompanied the wholesale abandonment of traditional beliefs. By contrast, the Kickapoo set themselves up as defenders of the Algonquian Manitou, as keepers of the faith. Religious conservatism provided a spiritual fuel that fired the Kickapoo war machine. Until their withdrawl west of the Mississippi in the 1820s, they furnished the most violent and effective resistance to European settlement of the Illinois Country, consistently opposing the strongest and most threatening imperial presence in the region, fighting with the French, then the British, finally the Americans, and frequently contracting with one force as mercenaries to fight the other. During the 1760s, Kickapoo war chiefs were leaders in the widespread Algonquian resistance that Europeans called "Pontiac's Conspiracy." Pontiac's murder at the hands of an Illinois Indian in 1769 confirmed both the Kickapoo hatred of assimilationists and their belief in the efficacy of violent resistance. Settler John Reynolds believed that "this nation was the most bitter enemy the whites ever had."[9]

The nearly constant war-footing of the Kickapoo strategy added to forces of change within the tribe. Small bands of Kickapoo scattered their villages over a considerable territory, close enough to provide mutual protection yet far apart enough to prevent mass destruction in case of attack. Gradually, over the eighteenth century, these bands formed into two loose contingents, one including several villages in the

Wabash drainage, the other the Illinois and Sangamon river towns. General tribal authority gave way to the power of these smaller units, and the authority of war chiefs rose at the expense of peace chiefs. Among whites and Indians alike, the Kickapoo acquired a reputation as the banditti of the Illinois prairies.

Kickapoo resistance demanded internal social and cultural change and was obviously unsuccessful in stopping American settlement. But the strategy did succeed in preserving Kickapoo traditional culture. Two anthropologists who conducted fieldwork at the Kickapoo colony at Nacimiento Kickapoo, Mexico, in the 1950s, declared that, by contrast with other tribes, the band had retained their central Algonquian traditions to "an almost unbelievable degree." To one who walks into the village, they wrote, "the general effect is one of entering a Wisconsin woodland village of two hundred years ago." Not only did Kickapoo material culture remain notably conservative, but the tribe had been able to preserve many of its customs and beliefs, resisting missionary efforts, including those of the peyote-cult Native American Church. The Kickapoo Nation, its headquarters in Oklahoma, includes the highest percentage of full-bloods of any tribe in the United States. The reciprocal structure of social relations remains strong. In short, the Kickapoo transported a woodlands culture to the Southwest "with its core intact." The strength of the Kickapoo conviction about resisting assimilation was suggested by one old matron who confided to another team of anthropologists in the 1960s that "this world will come to an end when the Kickapoos no longer keep their old ways."[10]

The "old ways," however, included a strong connection with European culture through trade. From the mid-eighteenth century until after the War of 1812, the Kickapoo possessed the bottomlands, hunting grounds, and groves of maple along the waterways of central Illinois, and they exchanged the products of their forest industries with independent French, British, or American traders, some of whom exported Indian commodities south along a trail that connected the Illinois and Sangamon Indian towns with the French and American settlements at American Bottom. This "Old Indian Trail" ran from the villages at Peoria south to Kickapoo Town, forded the Sangamon River at the mouth of Sugar Creek, followed the east bank of the creek past the sugar grove and onto the prairie, until it entered the woods at Cahokia Creek and Wood River, sixty miles south. Traders of John Jacob Astor's Southwest Company used this trail in 1816 to import over eighteen thousand dollars' worth of trade goods into central Illinois, and to export to St. Louis Indian commodities worth almost twenty-four thousand dollars, including 10,000 deer hides, 35,000 muskrat pelts, 300 bearskins, hundreds of packs of beaver, otter, mink, cat, and fox furs, as well as over 10,000 pounds of maple sugar mococks. The Sangamon Kickapoo must have produce some proportion of this sugar during the late winter of 1816 in the grove along Sugar Creek.[11]

On his trek to Sugar Creek, Robert Pulliam also followed this Old Indian Trail, worn with years of use yet still a single narrow rut across the prairie. When the pioneer reached the creek, he must have found a plainly marked trace heading into the timber, and evidence there of the Indian sugar camps of many years. From that point northward, the trail widened from the wear of the "travois" that dragged the heavy sugar-making equipment back and forth from Kickapoo Town to the sugar grove. These "ribbon roads" of the travois were the trails of peace, trails leading to the joys of the sugar bush or back to village comforts after months of hunting or living in winter camp. But the narrow trace that Pulliam followed from American Bottom to the sugar grove was a trail of violence, a trail where the Kickapoo might at any moment sweep down on unsuspecting pack trains, fur traders, or missionaries, stealing packs and horses, taking scalps, leaving ruin and destruction in their wake. Americans first discovered the maple grove on Sugar Creek on this warpath.[12]

4

A War of
Extirpation

he settlements at American Bottom on the Mississippi and at Vincennes on the Wabash fell during the American Revolution to an American volunteer force commanded by George Rogers Clark in 1778 and 1779. The Kickapoo acted as his scouts and actively fought the British. Afterward, Clark acknowledged their aid, assuring the tribe that Americans had no plans to settle the Illinois Country. "We were so far from having any design on their lands that I looked upon it that we were on their land," he wrote to George Mason in 1779; "we claim no land in their country." Before the tribe he declared that "the first man to take their lands by violence must strike the tomahawk in my head."[1]

Yet Illinois required administration: boundaries had to be defended, trade encouraged, order established and maintained. Both the French governor of Canada, in 1748, and the British colonial secretary of state for North America, in 1770, suggested that the only way imperial authorities might secure effective control over the arrogant Kickapoo and their allies of the Illinois Country would be "to allow a certain degree of colonization," but since that would seriously threaten the chief benefit of the region, its furs, they held back settlement. The Americans, however, were as interested in the potential for farms as the potential for furs. By the 1780s, despite Clark's declaration, the American settlement of the Illinois was no longer a question of whether, but when. A rapidly expanding population south of the Ohio River in Kentucky could hardly be restrained from exploiting the rich, sparsely settled lands of the Old Northwest. Governor William Henry Harrison of Indiana Territory, including the Illinois Country, emphasized the extent to which Americans and Indians contended for the same resources when he noted in 1802 that Kentuckians regularly hunted lands many miles north of the Ohio. "One white hunter," he wrote, "will destroy more game than five of the common Indians—the latter generally contenting himself with a sufficiency for present subsistence—while the other eager after game, hunt for the skin of the animal alone."[2]

After the Revolution, American policymakers thrust American settlers to the front lines of an advancing continental empire by encouraging their de facto colonization of the Northwest. In 1783, General Philip Schuyler of New York argued, in a letter to the Continental Congress, that "as our settlements approach their country," the Indians "must from the scarcity of game, which that approach will induce, retire farther back, and dispose of their lands." "Unless," he added, "they dwindle comparatively to nothing, as all savages have done, who gain their sustenance by the chase, when compelled to live in the vicinity of civilized people, and thus leave us the country without the expense of a purchase, trifling as that will probably be." First Washington, then every succeeding president (until James Monroe adopted a policy of outright Indian removal in 1825) endorsed this cynical approach.[3]

This policy shifted the bulk of the fighting from the army to frontiersmen who had few reservations about taking the lands of Indians they had fought for a generation. "Some of the backwoodsmen have been following the Indians from the frontiers of Virginia, North and South Carolina, and Georgia, through the States of Kentucky, Tennessee, Ohio, Indiana, and Illinois, without being much more settled than the Indians themselves," wrote Englishman John Woods in 1822 after living for two years among them. "These backwoodsmen have a strong dislike to the Indians and having been brought up with sentiments of antipathy towards them from their childhood; many of them declare they should not mind shooting an Indian more than a wild cat or raccoon." Pioneering, in other words, was a paramilitary occupation.[4]

The word *pioneer* itself had military associations. Derived from the French *pionnier*, it entered the English lexicon in the sixteenth century to signify those foot-soldiers who cleared the way for an army. Washington used this meaning when he wrote, during the anti-French campaigns of 1755, of employing "mulattoes and negroes" in his force "as Pioneers of Hatchetmen." During the first decades of the republic, the word came to refer to those men who led the way to settlement, as when Timothy Dwight of Yale wrote, in 1817, that "a considerable part of all those who begin the cultivation of the wilderness may be denominated foresters or pioneers." But the word *pioneer* continued to retain some of its older military meaning as late as 1842, when the *New Orleans Picayune* referred to a quasi-military band of Texans who had set out aggressively for Mexico as "the pioneers."[5]

Americans began to settle in southern Illinois as early as 1778, and land companies quickly formed to promote the benefits of homesteading there. The Kickapoo, allied with the Shawnees and the Miamis, proposed a militant Algonquian resistance to the American settler, "that great land animal," comparing a white settlement to a drop of raccoon's grease fallen on a new blanket: at first scarcely visible, in time the stain grows to cover every inch. Fighting between Kickapoo and Americans began near American Bottom in 1786. In one raid, Indians killed five settlers and took two women prisoner. In another, they killed an emigrant widow and one of her sons, hacking their bodies horribly as a warning to others. John Moredock, a surviving son, witnessed the mutilation and vowed revenge, pursuing it with such a vengeance that he became an American folk hero. The brutal Kickapoo raids outraged American settlers. Along the banks of the Ohio in the 1780s Americans lost some fifteen hundred men, women, and children, and over twenty thousand horses to Algonquian guerrillas.[6]

During 1790 and 1791, while Kickapoo men were away on the hunt, Kentucky militia attacked and burned several villages along the Wabash, notably the Kickapoo town of Kithtippecanoe, destroying large cornfields and taking nearly one hundred women and children prisoner. Although returning Kickapoo warriors participated in defeats of American armies in 1791 and 1792, many of the Wabash Kickapoo fled their devastated villages to the safety of the Sangamon River settlements, whence the destructive guerrilla war continued. Pecan, a war chief from the San-gam-ma, raided American Bottom in 1793, then fled north along the Indian Trail with a stolen herd of horses. A posse of Americans, led by William Whiteside, followed in pursuit and ambushed the warriors on the prairie twenty-five miles south of Sugar Creek, killing Pecan's son. In revenge, Pecan and his braves murdered two Whiteside children near their homestead the following year, and in 1795 Whiteside and his neighbors continued the cycle of violence by massacring a Kickapoo hunting party near American Bottom, leaving their scalped and mutilated bodies to rot and their bones to bleach on the steaming Mississippi mud. A delegation of Indians, including Potawatomi and Kickapoo, arrived in Philadelphia, in 1793, where they demanded that Secretary of State Thomas Jefferson stop this invasion by the Kentuckians and keep the pledge of George Rogers Clark. Little Doe, a Kickapoo from central Illinois, clearly indicated the tribe's sense of its territorial bounds when he told

Jefferson, "I am a Kickapoo, and drink the waters of the Wabash and the Mississippi."[7]

The Americans considered the Kickapoo absolute savages, but the experience of fur trapper William Biggs, captured and held captive by them in 1788, tempers this image. As Biggs and a companion were returning to American Bottom from the north, their ponies loaded down with packs of furs, sixteen unmounted Kickapoo surprised and fired upon them. They shot Biggs's partner as he rode away; he died later of his wounds. The warriors captured Biggs, however, after he nearly outran them. Impressed by the trapper's pluck, the Kickapoo spared his life and walked him over 250 miles to a tribal sugar camp near the Wabash. There a young maiden set to work for him, as she would have for a returning Kickapoo brave. According to Biggs, she prepared a meal of "hominy, beat in a mortar, as white as snow, and handsome as I ever saw and very well cooked. She fried some dried meat, pounded very fine in a mortar, in oil, and sprinkled it with sugar. She prepared a very good bed for me, with bear-skins and blankets." In the morning she brought hot water, soap, and a razor, and when he had finished his toilet she sat and began to comb his hair. "It was then the fashion to wear long hair," Biggs remembered thirty years later; "my hair was very long and very thick and very much matted and tangled. She combed out my hair very tenderly, and then took the fine comb, and combed and looked my head over nearly one hour," culling the lice. "She then went to a trunk and got a ribbon and queued my hair very nicely," queues being the traditional fashion for Kickapoo men both then and now. In the 1820s, old Biggs remembered that the woman was "a very handsome girl, about 18 years of age, a beautiful full figure, and handsomely featured." She was "very white for a squaw," he recalled, "almost as white as dark complexioned women generally are." This caveat was necessary to Biggs, because the Kickapoo had a reputation as the most savage of Indians, and the girl's whiteness perhaps provided him with a partial explanation for the affectionate care he received.[8]

In 1794 American General Anthony Wayne defeated the combined forces of the central Algonquians at the Battle of Fallen Timbers on the Maumee River in northern Ohio. The Treaty of Greenville, signed the next year, did not directly affect the Kickapoo lands and towns along the Sangamon or the Wabash rivers, but an article to the treaty gave the Americans the right of preemption should any Northwest tribes decide to sell. In the meantime, however, the treaty guaranteed the security of the Kickapoo settlements and affirmed "the right of the Indians to hunt," as well as "the privilege of making sugar" upon the land ceded to the United States.[9]

In the aftermath of Wayne's victory, many Kickapoo withdrew to

new settlements on the Missouri in Spanish Louisiana, but most were
back in San-gam-ma Country by 1800. The tribe had to face an American policy that arrogantly ignored the sanctity of Indian territory.
Acting on explicit instructions from President Jefferson, Governor
Harrison pressed each tribe for huge land cessions that would clear the
way for complete American possession of the Old Northwest. In August 1803, the few remaining Illinois Indians ceded the southern section of the territory, and a year later a group of Fox and Sauk were
hoodwinked into turning over northern land along the Mississippi.
Congress then authorized the opening of land offices, including one in
the Illinois Country, for sale of what westerners always called the "congress land" received in these cessions. Although problems in clearing
the complicated French titles at American Bottom delayed the beginning of land sales until 1814, these moves encouraged American settlement, and from 1800 to 1814 over thirteen thousand Americans relocated in Illinois. Over the same period, the Indian population of the
Illinois Country grew from four to six thousand. In the decade before
the War of 1812, then, the numerical majority in Illinois shifted from
Indians to Americans. The Kickapoo villages on the Sangamon River
stood as the most important barrier to further American settlement
north. Jefferson wrote Harrison of the "urgent necessity" of arranging
a Kickapoo cession.[10]

At a conference between the Kickapoo and American authorities,
held in St. Louis in 1805, General James Wilkinson tried to "bullyrag"
the proud Kickapoo with harsh and threatening words. Chief Powatomo, from the Sangamon River villages, began his response by complaining about Wilkinson's language: "You called us your little children," he said, "and at the same time, spoke to us with a degree of
anger, instead of that mild way, always used by a father when speaking
to his children." In pointing to the use of kinship terms, Powatomo
could hardly have been more perceptive about the cultural distance
between the two peoples.

> The Master of the World, when he placed us on this earth, took
> Care to provide us with all the necessaries of life. He gave us
> stones to make our arms. The earth and clay to form our pots,
> wood for our bows and arrows to enable us to hunt our game. . . .
> You came, my Father, you took us under your protection and
> recommended to us hunting, where at the same time you were
> depriving us of the means of taking our lands and suffering
> establishments to be made on the same, and on the very spot
> where we before were accustomed to hunt our game. Never did
> the French, Spaniards, or British suffer such an invasion of our
> rights. . . . We did not come to this council fire to beg anything of

you. We want nothing but our own. We came to see you and listen
to your talks. . . . Excuse, my Father, the boldness of my talk,
should it appear so to you, it is in our nature to speak as we feel.
You threatened us to withdraw your traders from among us; we
do not want them; the Great Spirit has provided for us plen-
tifully. He gave us the earth for a Mother, from whence we derive
our subsistence; the wild animals for our game and the maintenance of our wives and children; we skin them and trade with
them; hence do we derive our clothing and that of our wives and
children. We do not, then, look to you for those articles which we
now procure by hunting; the only thing we ask is that we may not
be deprived of it, by being dispossessed of our lands, and by that
of our game.

The contrast between the American approach and that of the previous
imperial powers in the Illinois Country was palpable. Powatomo's bold
challenge to both the official and the de facto American policies suggested that only a change in the American position, or the force or
arms, would settle the conflict.[11]

The move of American settlers like Pulliam into Wood River that
same year provoked new violence. In the summer of 1805, women
from Kickapoo Town planted corn on Cahokia Creek, as was their
custom. In the fall, while these women were harvesting their crop and
gathering persimmons, American men from the settlement established
a few months before attacked, abused, and insulted them. The Americans also captured and held prisoner the son of chief Powatomo himself, releasing him only after they had beaten him badly and threatened to kill him if they caught the boy in the Wood River area again.
The Kickapoo would not tolerate such a challenge to their territorial
sovereignty, and in December war parties moved down the Indian
Trail, attacking several isolated Wood River settlements on Christmas
Eve. The guerrilla war was on again, and every "Indian summer"
thereafter, when Kickapoo men had finished their horticultural labor,
it flared up again.[12]

By the end of the decade the American strategy of de facto limitations on Indian hunting had reached a critical stage. Governor Harrison reported that, because of the competition for game, "the Indians
of this country are in fact Miserable. The Game which was formerly so
abundant is now so scarce as barely to afford subsistence to the most
active hunter—The greater part of each Tribe are half the year in a
state of starvation." When Kickapoo from the Sangamon River showed
up in Vincennes to receive annuities due them under the Treaty of
Greenville, Harrison noted that they looked emaciated and were "almost literally naked." Meanwhile, spies of Ninian Edwards, appointed

governor of newly established Illinois Territory in 1809, reported that "all the Indians of the Illinois River, Kickapoos and Potawatomies, . . . have not been able to hunt, and are now in a state of starvation." Indian and American alike knew that the final stage of the conflict was rapidly approaching.[13]

In these ominous times the Kickapoo joined the movement of Tecumseh and Tenskwatawa the Prophet, Shawnee-Creek brothers who preached pan-Indian resistance to further American encroachments in the Northwest. The Kickapoo and these charismatic leaders wanted the same things: a return to tribal traditions, the rejection of alcohol and drunkenness, and the affirmation of a principle of the common holding of Indian land, so that no tribe might alienate land without agreement from all others. Harrison's relentless pursuit of land cessions infuriated Tecumseh's nationalist movement, especially when the governor cajoled and threatened renegade delegations of the Shawnee and Kickapoo themselves into signing cession treaties in 1809 and 1810. The Kickapoo were the most fervent of Tecumseh's nationalist supporters and formed his inner circle and bodyguard. The forces of Tecumseh were "principally composed of Kickapoos and Winnebagos," Harrison wrote, and noted that his Kickapoo warriors were "better than those of any other tribe." The growing pan-nationalist forces picked the site of the former Kickapoo village of Kithtippecanoe near the Wabash as the headquarters for their movement.[14]

In the fall of 1811 a large comet appeared in the heavens. "This comet," John Reynolds remembered, "was believed by many to be a true harbinger of war." And, a few weeks later, while Tecumseh was south with his Kickapoo guard appealing for Creek support, Harrison attacked Kithtippecanoe. The Battle of Tippecanoe, fought on November 7, 1811, did not defeat but merely scattered Indian nationalist forces and began the war for American possession of the Northwest in earnest. A few days later the great New Madrid earthquake tore through the Midwest, another inauspicious sign. "Our family all were asleep in a log-cabin," wrote Reynolds, "and my father leaped out of bed crying aloud 'the Indians are on the house.'" In fact, after the Battle of Tippecanoe, the Sangamon River Kickapoo had fled north to safer quarters on Lake Peoria. But from there, and from villages on the Wabash, they were soon raiding American settlements from Wood River to Vincennes, feeding their starving families from the plunder and striking terror into every American homestead. During the prolonged violence that began in late 1811 and lasted until 1815, many Americans fled back to Kentucky, while others huddled in community blockhouses, as a strike force of mobile American Rangers and Kickapoo warriors acted out the violent tragedy. "What other course is there left for us to pursue," Harrison wrote to the secretary of war regarding the Kickapoo, "but to make a war of extirpation upon them?"[15]

The Old Indian Trail from American Bottom figured in the decisive act of the War of 1812 in Illinois. In October 1812, Governor Edwards marched a small army of volunteers north, supplied by the first wagons to roll into central Illinois. Edwards ordered his men to burn the deserted Kickapoo Town on the north side of the Sangamon River, then force-marched his army to Peoria Lake, where they surprised Powatomo's people, plundered and burned the village, and killed twenty-four warriors. Most of the Kickapoo, however, disappeared into a "dismal swamp" behind the village. As the American troops reassembled, one warrior boldly appeared on a bluff overlooking the Americans. When riflemen began taking potshots at him, the man scornfully laughed aloud, deliberately turned his back, and calmly walked away amid the fire. To young John Reynolds, this act of "Indian bravado" proved the most memorable incident of the war, demonstrating Kickapoo arrogance and courage, as well as vividly acting out the Kickapoo withdrawal insult.[16]

Now that their towns and stores were destroyed, the Kickapoo found themselves only able to keep up furtive guerrilla actions. Sangamon River bands stole down the Indian Trail in the spring of 1813, eluding American defenses and killing several settlers, including one who was making maple sugar along the Kaskaskia, a few miles upriver from John Pulliam's ferry. Americans responded by sending another small army north, where they found Kickapoo Town rebuilt and cornfields replanted; they burned summerhouses, huts, and maize. The Kickapoo continued to break the American lines, however, and in 1814 slaughtered members of the Reagan and Moore families near Robert Pulliam's Wood River place. Settlers pursued this band up the Indian Trail to the headwaters of Sugar Creek, where they killed one warrior in the timber and recovered Mrs. Reagan's scalp from his pouch. Late that year the territorial legislature established a bounty of fifty dollars for the scalp of any Indian—man, woman, or child—who entered an American settlement with "murderous intent."[17]

Sporadic violence continued, but Edward's march had broken the Kickapoo defense of their land. After 1812 Americans controlled the Indian Trail, now renamed Edward's Trace in honor of the governor's decisive march, and rangers regularly moved up its increasingly familiar course, often bringing American Bottom cattle in their wake, to graze the rich prairie grasses. On the trail along Sugar Creek, in December 1814, one of the final violent incidents of the war took place. Fifty rangers, camped near the sugar grove with a drove of cattle, caught sight of a small party of Kickapoo in the timber. After a desperate chase across the prairie, William Hewit captured one warrior. Despite the helpless position of the Indian, John Moredock, "the Indian Hater" who since his mother's mutilation had taken revenge on every Indian who crossed his path, leveled his flintlock at point-blank range; in an instant the Kickapoo had grabbed a gun, and, as Moredock's ball crashed fatally into his chest, he fired and killed Hewit. Sugar Creek was branded forever into this dramatic war story told by the frontier rangers of Illinois.[18]

The War of 1812 in the Old Northwest ended the Kickapoo power to retard American settlement. In September 1815, at Portage des Sioux, across the Mississippi from Wood River, the Kickapoo reluctantly accepted defeat and signed a peace treaty ending hostilities but conceding nothing. Many Kickapoo bands chose to withdraw across the Mississippi. Those who remained partially rebuilt the Sangamon River villages and attempted to rouse Potawatomi and Chippewa support for renewed resistance in 1816, but to no avail. The next two years tribal leaders spent west of the Mississippi, planning for the complete emigration of their people. Six months after Illinois was admitted to the Union as the twenty-first state, on July 30, 1819, at the state capital of Edwardsville, the Kickapoo formally exchanged their Illinois lands for tracts on the Osage River in Missouri. Those who had not already left moved out in small, straggling bands, and by the early 1820s most had set up permanent summer villages across the Mississippi.[19]

Frontier settlers like Pulliam were well aware of the drift of events in central Illinois. Pulliam took a risk by moving into Kickapoo territory before the tribe had formally ceded its hunting lands and sugar groves, but when Pulliam arrived at Sugar Creek in fall 1817, most Kickapoo were either in Missouri or preparing to move there. Although the exact details that led Pulliam to Sugar Creek are forever lost, the context suggests a convergence of circumstances. The end of hostilities implied the Kickapoo's pending withdrawal west of the Mississippi. As a participant in the defense of the Wood River community during the war, Pulliam had every opportunity to know of the grazing land and the sugar grove along Sugar Creek. Finally, the beginning of land sales in Wood River forced upon him a decision regarding his family's future. It is likely that all these circumstances combined to recommend a course familiar to the pioneer: selling his "improvements" on the Wood River place, using his small capital to buy a herd of cattle, then moving his stock north over Edwards' Trace in the fall, looking for those grazing lands free for the using, planning to make sugar in the spring, perhaps intending to stake a claim at the grove, a place where he and his family might settle and produce a small income. Surely Pulliam's timing suggests purpose, for his move took place in lock-step with the events that dispossessed the Kickapoo. Pulliam was no hero, no Moses; he was a bold, one-legged man who put himself in the right place at the right time.

The Americans who followed Pulliam to Sugar Creek over the next few years encountered a few remaining Kickapoo. Erastus Wright and young William Herndon frequently caught sight of small bands walking single-file along the Old Indian Trail, and George Brunk told of hunting with Kickapoo parties in 1821. Kickapoo families set up their *wikiups* near the new log cabin of Sarah Pyle Husband, who emigrated from Kentucky with her family in the fall of 1820. She traded her cornbread for game with the hunters at her doorstep. "While encamped on the farm," she remembered, "an Indian child died, and the Indians made a box of bark in which they put the corpse and suspended it from the top of a tall tree, thus keeping it until the tribe was ready to return to the burying grounds." James Baker loved to play with Indian boys and declared to his brothers that he would run away with them; when he reached manhood he and his brother John headed west. In the 1850s, returning Sugar Creek forty-niners reported meeting the Baker boys at a ferry they operated near Fort Bridger, in western Wyoming; dressed in buckskin, wearing their hair long and straight, the boys had become adopted members of the Shoshone tribe. In the early 1820s John England also played with Indian boys without hesitation; "fear of Indians," he later remembered, "was not one of the trials and tribulations" of pioneer life.[20]

For most participants in the wars, however, the fear and hatred died slowly. One Kickapoo band, led by the war chief Mecina, continued to keep summer residence at the old village site near Lake Peoria. From there his warriors looted Americans along the north side of the Sangamon River, shooting cattle and hogs, and declaring, according to the terrorized settlers, that "the land is theirs and that the whites are intruders upon it, and that they will fight before they will leave it." Other Indians showed up at cabin doors, begging for handouts, looking, according to one settler, "as filthy as the barn-yard stock," and "devouring corn-pone and bacon by the pound, clawing their food with their dirty fingers, and bolting it like half-starved hyenas." Settlers commonly compared Indians to animals. "The dweller upon the frontier continues to regard the Indian with a degree of terror and hatred similar to that which he feels towards the rattlesnake or panther," wrote Illinois editor James Hall; these sentiments, he continued, "are handed down from generation to generation, and remain in full force

long after all danger from the savages has ceased, and all intercourse
with them been discontinued."[21]

When feelings run this strong people are sometimes killed. Indians
murdered Edward and John Fowler, Sugar Creek settlers of 1820, as
they were traveling north of the river; their younger brother, Thomas,
left home seeking revenge and spent a haunted life on the frontier.
When Black Hawk's band of Sauk and Fox began a frontier war in 1832
by crossing the Mississippi to plant maize in their ancestral Illinois
fields, Mecina's band and other Kickapoo, perhaps as many as four
hundred warriors, joined the defense of their Fox brothers. On the
American side, scores of enthusiastic Sugar Creek farmers joined the
call to arms during this so-called Black Hawk War and participated
joyously in the slaughter and mutilation of Indian men, women, and
children at Bad Axe River. A continuing glorification of and fascina-
tion with things military was one of the enduring legacies of the pioneer period.[22]

Within a generation other concerns and conflicts outweighed mem-
ories of the Indian wars. Pulliam's children suffered through night-
mares of savage Indians throwing American babies into bubbling
caldrons; his grandchildren would dream of an awful war between
white brothers. Forty years after the Kickapoo ceded their lands at
Edwardsville and ended over a half-century of residence in central
Illinois, commentators like James H. Matheny reduced all that had
come before Pulliam and the pioneer generation to a "howling wilderness."

But it was a wilderness rich in human experience, rich in human
history. "Sugar" provided the creek with its name, and provided the
motive for the first exclusively American economic activity in the San-
gam-ma, thus linking Pulliam and the history that followed in his wake
with the Indian past. For all the differences between the Kickapoo and
American societies, they were both predicated on the utilization of
forest and prairie resources, on the production of Indian corn in the
rich timber and bottomland soil. Pulliam's appropriation of the sugar
grove may serve as a reminder that the operative word in this history is
dispossession. By ignoring the context and setting for Pulliam's adven-
ture, Matheny side-stepped this uncomfortable conclusion.

But from the first plowing of Sugar Creek sod until our own time,
farmers working their fields turned up the artifacts of a once living
people: stone arrowheads, corn grinders, and other tools and trifles by

the hundreds. With the passage of time, as Americans lost what little understanding they had once possessed of the Kickapoo, these objects became mute cyphers. Sanford Cox lived on a farm near the site of a Kickapoo town, where as a boy growing up in the years before the Civil War he found "blades of butcher knives, tomahawks, brass kettles, gun-barrels" as he played amid the ruins of a former civilization. The scores of trade beads he found strewn about the tall grasses set his boyish mind to imagining that they might have "graced the neck of some Queen or maids of honor." But nature had a way of swallowing up even these romantic attempts at historical reconstruction. One day his little sister came running into the house with her hands full, shouting: "Ma! Ain't this a rich country, where even the grass and weeds grow beads?"[23]

PART TWO

The Country of Plenty to Eat

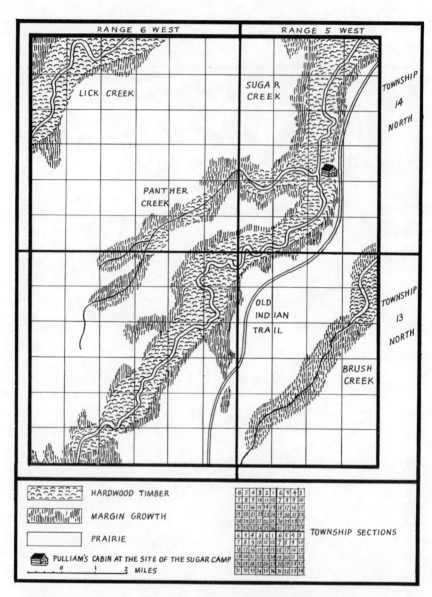

RANGE 6 WEST RANGE 5 WEST

LICK CREEK

SUGAR CREEK

TOWNSHIP 14 NORTH

PANTHER CREEK

OLD INDIAN TRAIL

TOWNSHIP 13 NORTH

BRUSH CREEK

HARDWOOD TIMBER

MARGIN GROWTH

PRAIRIE

PULLIAM'S CABIN AT THE SITE OF THE SUGAR CAMP

0   1   2 MILES

TOWNSHIP SECTIONS

6	5	4	3	2	1	6	5	4	3
7	8	9	10	11	12	7	8	9	10
18	17	16	15	14	13	18	17	16	15
19	20	21	22	23	24	19	20	21	22
30	29	28	27	26	25	30	29	28	27
31	32	33	34	35	36	31	32	33	34
6	5	4	3	2	1	6	5	4	3
7	8	9	10	11	12	7	8	9	10
18	17	16	15	14	13	18	17	16	15
19	20	21	22	23	24	19	20	21	22
30	29	28	27	26	25	30	29	28	27
31	32	33	34	35	36	31	32	33	34

SOURCES: "Township Plats," 17:13–15, 38–40 (mss, ISA); U.S. Department of Agriculture, Soil Conservation Service, in cooperation with the Illinois Agricultural Experiment Station, *Soil Survey of Sangamon County. Soil Report No. 111* (n.p.: n.p., 1980); Zimi A. Enos, "The Old Indian Trail, Sangamon County, Illinois," *JISHS* (1911) 4:218–22.

SUGAR CREEK IN 1817

5

Land-Looker

Deputy surveyor Angus Lewis Langham and his crew began the federal survey of Sugar Creek lands on March 30, 1821. Slowly proceeding from south to north, east to west, the surveyors criss-crossed more than five hundred linear miles of Sugar Creek country in two months, taking all spring and summer to survey the San-gam-ma district. They advanced upon unplowed prairie and virgin timber and left behind blazed trees, numbered posts, and mounds of earth, the template of a new, rational landscape. Extinguish Indian title, survey, and sell: that was national policy, and Langham was the instrument of the second stage in Sugar Creek.

Because of its role in securing clear title to land, surveying was an important frontier occupation, and over the years many western men practiced the craft. At sixteen, George Washington received an appointment as surveyor of Culpepper County, Virginia, and in the 1740s, before beginning his military career, he distinguished himself as a surveyor of wilderness lands. George Rogers Clark surveyed for the Ohio Company along the Kentucky River in the early 1770s, and his younger brother William was not only a surveyor but a competent mapmaker, which made him a valuable coleader with Meriwether Lewis of Jefferson's expedition to the Pacific coast.

Surveyors were usually self-trained. In the early nineteenth century, before this trade became a profession, many aspirants learned their skills from local practitioners like John Messinger, one of the first surveyors in the Illinois Country, "a celebrated artizan," as John Reynolds remarked, who summarized his learning in *A Manual, or Hand Book, Intended for Convenience in Practical Surveying*, published in St. Louis in 1821. Other men taught themselves by studying Messinger's text or other useful little books such as Able Flint's *A System of Geometry and Trigonometry* (1804) or Robert Gibson's *A Treatise on Practical Surveying* (1803). Abraham Lincoln, who laid out several town sites north of the Sangamon River during the 1830s, later remembered that he "procured a compass and chain, studied Flint and Gibson a little and went at it."[1]

Lincoln made it sound easy, but surveying was hard outdoor labor. In all kinds of weather, over all kinds of country, the men moved directly on the compass lines to make their measurements, through shoulder-high prairie grasses, over upland, swampland, and timber. The deputy surveyor, or "land-looker" as people sometimes called him, directed the operation through the sights of his mounted magnetic compass, called a "circumferator." His crew included two chainmen, to stretch the traditional four-rod measuring chain on the line; at least one flagman, to mark the spot determined by the deputy and toward which the chainmen aimed; one or two axmen, to clear the line of vision as well as blaze and mark the corners; and sometimes a hunter and cook. If there was a cook in the party, the men might count on a hot meal after a long day in the field; if not, and this was more common, dinner might consist of some pan-bread, boiled beans, and the inevitable salt pork. For next day's lunch in the field, each man would carve off a hunk of the previous evening's bread, stuff it with more salt pork, and at noon cook the pork before a campfire on his own spit, catching the fat on the bread and washing it all down with water from a nearby stream or spring. With confused syntax, but clear sentiment, the surveyor-general of land north of the Ohio River wrote admiringly about his crews: "None but Men as hard as a Savage who is always at Home in Woods & Swamps, can live upon what they afford (if occasions so require), who can travel for Days up to the knees in mud & mire, can drink any fluid he finds while he is drenched with water also, and has a knowledge of the lands, who are equally patient & perseverant under similar hardships, can make anything by surveying the kind of Country we have to Survey."[2]

Indians presented other difficulties for frontier surveyors. During their last years in Illinois, Mecina's band of Kickapoo sought out surveying crews in the so-called Military Tract between the Illinois and Mississippi rivers, interrupting their work, destroying compasses and chains ("the things that steal the land"), burning field notes. In north Texas during the 1830s, the Kickapoo stalked surveyors who were encroaching on their hunting grounds, and in one ambush on a surveyor's night camp they took sixteen scalps and critically wounded five more Texans. Knowing that settlers would follow in the wake of a completed survey, Indians sometimes delayed surveyors in Michigan, Iowa, and the Dakotas by stealing their supplies and horses. One Northwestern surveyor testified that "the red men in the vicinity, thinking the survey of the land would be likely to interfere with their sugar-making, had for some time manifested displeasure by hindering and obstructing the work." Although Langham and his crew were undoubtedly on their guard, no such attacks stopped their surveys, which were confined to the south side of the Sangamon.[3]

Despite these hardships, men competed intensely for the available deputy surveying jobs. In each survey district the surveyor-general issued instructions of his own to subordinates, and his deputies worked under private contract to him. At the rate of three dollars a surveyed mile, the enterprise could turn a handsome profit, even though the deputy collected his fee only on the successful completion of his contract and had to pay his crew from his own pocket in the meantime. Many men looked on surveying as a way to get an advance look at prime lands before the rush of settlers, and make money doing it.

The contract system created opportunities for abuse. In 1823 President Monroe removed William Rector of St. Louis, the surveyor-general who had issued Langham's contract, when public documents revealed that he had awarded more than one in five of his lucrative contracts to relatives and associates, some of whom sublet the surveying to incompetent men for less than the going rate. Some of Rector's vast territory in Missouri, Arkansas, and Illinois had to be resurveyed. Langham's four contracts netted the deputy surveyor very well by the monetary standards of the time, paying him better than twelve thousand dollars, before expenses, for two seasons' work. But unlike the work of some of Rector's deputies, Langham's surveys of the San-gamma stood the test of time and showed no outstanding irregularities.[4]

The system of marking boundaries used by Langham and other deputy surveyors departed fundamentally from the traditional English surveying employed during the colonial period. In that "metes and bounds" approach, the surveyor described the boundaries of every parcel of land by the direction and length of the successive property lines of adjoining parcels, using the features of land and flora to set them off. This proved adequate on a case-by-case basis and continued in use for real estate transactions, divisions of estate, and road surveys. But when used to open vast new territories for quick settlement, "metes and bounds" could produce enormous boundary problems. The land mess in Kentucky during the 1780s was a salient case in point.

To combat such problems, Congress designed a nationally uniform federal land survey in the Land Ordinance of 1785 (later refined by subsequent legislation and administrative orders). Surveyors oriented each large tract to lines of latitude and longitude: an arbitrarily placed north-south principal meridian and an east-west baseline. The central Illinois surveys, for example, measured from the Third Principal Meridian, running due north from the mouth of the Ohio River on the Mississippi, and a baseline running across southern Illinois and Indiana. Numbered range and township lines, running parallel to the meridian and baselines, respectively, and intersecting each other at six-mile intervals, established a grid of numbered "townships." Langham and his crew laid down this grid, then subdivided each township into thirty-six square-mile "sections" of 640 acres, numbered 1 to 36, that could be further broken into quarter-sections of 160, or even "quarter-quarters" of 40 acres each.

This system was largely the product of the rationalist thinking of Thomas Jefferson, who chaired the congressional committee that drew up the first draft. It laid down an abstract, systematic grid, oriented to the spheres, and systematically numbered and counted each parcel of land, making it very easy to locate any piece of "congress land" within the public domain by reference to its section, township, and range numbers. Most important, Congress hoped that by ordering the land in advance of settlement they could avoid the problems produced by "metes and bounds" determinations, run after settlement had begun, and shape the landscape of settlement. By incorporating the "township" from New England's tradition of compact settlement, the grid system suggested the intention of creating an orderly landscape of small communities. The provision that the federal government retain four sections of each township for future sale and reserve one section for the support of education further suggested a degree of social engineering. As many historians have since commented, the ideal represented an Enlightenment triumph of geometry over geography.[5]

But a persistent traditionalism continued amid the design for this, the most rational land survey yet devised by man. While the principal meridians pointed true north, they began from the mouths of rivers, testimony less to universals than to the specific historical importance of inland waterways in the early American West. The sections within each township were numbered systematically but in oscillating rows, reading from right to left, then left to right, in the manner that "the plow follows the ox." Jefferson argued for a decimal system of measurement, but Congress rejected this feature in favor of English mathematician Edmund Gunter's seventeenth-century system, whose basic unit of measurement, the 66-foot chain, allowed the incorporation of the traditional rod, acre, and statute mile.[6]

Other customary notions were reflected in Langham's field notes and plat map. So that the federal Land Office might assemble systematic information on the quality of its congress land, surveyors general instructed their deputies to note "the kinds of timber and under-growth with which the land may be covered," a task that called for standards of evaluation. Langham employed the traditional rule that a soil's fertility was revealed by the quantity and quality of its flora. The lands along the creek itself he judged "1st rate," for the large and "noble" trees growing there—"oak, hickory, locust, walnut"—were traditional indicators of rich soil. The smaller streams feeding the creek supported only "2d rate Timber"; there the grand woodland species were overrun with "hackberry, coffeenut, elm, spruce, plumb, crab, thorn, briars, etc.," their profusion suggesting poorer soil. On his plat, Langham sketched in the timberline surrounding the creek, label-ing the remainder "prairie"; those lands, supporting nothing but grasses, were a "barrens." In fact, the prairie soils were the richest along Sugar Creek, but Langham's evaluation, shared by the early settlers, greatly affected the pattern of settlement.[7]

Finally, frontiersmen like Pulliam, who deliberately set out to stake their claims in advance of the surveyors, subverted the intention of ordering the land in advance of settlement. By the time the land looker moved through the timber and prairie in 1821, emigrants had already begun the process of transforming Sugar Creek into an American farming community. Langham carefully marked his plat map to indi-cate the presence of forty-three squatter claims from the headwaters of Sugar Creek to the junction with Lick Creek. The remarkable mobility of American backcountry folk considerably outpaced the ability of the state to order the land.[8]

In some areas, American squatters on congress lands tried to delay the survey, as did the Indians, believing that additional time might allow them to marshal the capital required for purchase at the federal land auction. Some deputy surveyors complained that squatters felled blazed trees and ripped up marking posts and mounds. In other places, however, squatters welcomed the surveyors, making their work a little easier by bringing some fellowship to the crew in its evening camp or even offering cabins as places to take meals and sleep. Sur-veyors like to brag of the nubile squatter's daughters seduced during those nocturnal stays. Although Langham did not record his reception by the Sugar Creek squatters, he indicated their presence on his map.[9]

While Langham's section lines determined the sale of Sugar Creek land, for the most part his geometric template lay dormant, to awaken fully only with the stirrings of rural commercial development in the 1840s, when the federal survey directed the making of the now famil-iar "checkerboard" landscape of the Midwest. Meanwhile, for the first quarter-century of their history, the settlers of Sugar Creek con-structed their landscape upon customs that owed less to the Enlighten-ment than to the patterns of traditional agrarian society in America.

6

American Tartars

The American settlement of the San-gam-ma began in earnest in spring of 1818, three years before the surveyor Langham arrived. In meandering lines that at a distance must have looked very similar to the straggling bands of Kickapoo families moving west at the same moment, American families advanced north from Wood River, building cabins and breaking soil along the timbered rivers and creeks. Some carried their "truck and plunder" in wagons, but more used carts; some rode, but most walked. Theirs was a motley parade. One Kentucky woman rode north on a mount to which she had lashed the family featherbed, with her babe in arms and leading another horse loaded unmercifully with household goods and farm implements; her husband walked ahead with their boy astride his shoulders. By 1819 approximately two hundred families had settled above the line of survey in Madison County, some as far north as the Sangamon River.[1]

The first report of settlement along Sugar Creek itself, dated August 1819, was written by a German traveler, Ferdinand Ernst, who came up Edward's Trace to visit the San-gam-ma Country and explore the site of Kickapoo Town. Riding north along the east side of Sugar Creek timber, he found a newly arrived family building a log cabin, and three miles north of there he spent the night at an excellent spring where three other families had built huts and planted crops. The speed with which these pioneers had set about transforming the vista startled Ernst: "they have only broken up the sod with the plow and planted

44

their corn, and now one sees these splendid fields covered almost without exception with corn from ten to 15 feet high." The maple groves of the San-gam-ma, Ernst noted, "gave those people the most promising prospect of a harvest of sugar." The German counted sixty families laying out farms along the timber margin from the source of the creek to its mouth on the Sangamon River and marveled at the number of "venturesome daredevils" who had risked coming north to this "beautiful land" even before the Kickapoo had ceded their proprietorship at Edwardsville. Now that Indian title was extinguished, he wondered, "how many will migrate hither, since everything is quiet and safe here!"[2]

Only two years later, in 1821, the young geologist and ethnologist Henry Rowe Schoolcraft, coasting down the Illinois on a journey of exploration, heard such praise for the San-gam-ma among his boatmen that he pronounced it "a district almost proverbial for its fertility, and fast rising into importance." That same year, when surveyor Langham found forty-three households along upper Sugar Creek, the population of central Illinois was estimated at five thousand, and the state laid off a huge territory, from Sugar Creek on the south to Peoria on the north, as "Sangamo County," establishing a county seat at "Springfield" on Spring Creek, south of the river, in the settlement of the populous Kelly family. During the fall of 1825, according to one report, each month over two hundred and fifty wagons, each carrying an average of five persons, rolled through southern Illinois headed for the Sangamo Country. By decade's end, although the county had been pared to about half its original size, it contained over 2,000 households and thirteen thousand residents, including 113 households filled with nearly nine hundred people along the upper creek. In 1840 the number of Sugar Creek households reached 134, the community's population nearly one thousand.[3]

Three-quarters of the heads of household who immigrated before 1840 came directly from homes in Kentucky, Tennessee, or the upcountry of Virginia and the Carolinas. Fewer than one in ten came from a state north of the Mason-Dixon line. The balance removed from southern Ohio, Indiana, or Illinois, but most of these men had lived north of the Ohio for only a few years. Nine in ten heads of settling families were born in the South—four in Virginia, three in Kentucky, two in the Carolinas. Farm wives were also southerners, the majority born in Kentucky.[4]

Throughout central Illinois the great majority of residents before the Civil War were, in the jargon of the day, "white folks" from the South. "Our neighbors," New Englander Lucy Maynard wrote home from central Illinois, "are principally from Indiana and Kentucky, some from Virginia, all friendly but very different from our people in their manners and language and every other way." "They think," she noted, "that a boiled dish as we boil it is not fit to eat; it is true they boil their food, but each separate. It won't do to boil cabbage or turnips or beets, carrots or parsnips with their meat nor potatoes without pairing and the water that the meat is boiled in must be all boiled down so that there is nothing left but the fat and a very little of the water and that is taken up on the dish with the meat and answers for gravy." But despite the Southern distaste for the boiled dinners that Mrs. Maynard persisted in setting on her table, the goodwife found her neighbors a "very likely people."[5]

"You would be diverted indeed, Julia, if you were to hear some of their uncouth and vulgar expressions," Sarah Aiken, another "Yankee," wrote home to New York about her Southern neighbors. A settler *toted* his *truck and plunder* to *Elanoy* with his *old woman* by his side, where, he *allowed*, they stood a *right smart chance* to break a *scrumptious* farm. He *reckoned* the time of day by the sun: *long before day, good light, about sun-up,* and, after rising, one, two, three hours *by sun,* and so on until *dinnertime,* when after working *tarnation* hard, he sat down to consume *a heap o' vittles.* He counted his afternoon labor four hours by sun, three, two, one, until sundown, followed by *early candlelightin'* an hour or so before *turnin' in.* To this farmer a large sum of money was *filthy lucre,* while the denominations commonly found in his purse consisted of *shillings* and *bits.* Much of this language harkened back to the vernacular speech of seventeenth- and eighteenth-century British colonists. "It really seems to me," Sarah Aiken concluded, "that I must be living the days of our forefathers over again." Commenting on their distinctive speech and customs, visiting Englishman William Oliver wrote that these Southern emigrants were "decent people of simple manners," as unlike Yankees "as if they were of different nations."[6]

What lay behind this massive out-migration from the South? Many emigrants later suggested that opposition to slavery was an important factor in their decision to move north of the Ohio River. Sugar Creek settler James Wallace, born and raised in the backwoods of South Carolina in the era of the American Revolution, left home to seek his fortune as a young man and lived for some years in the Northeast, where he married, had twin sons, and accumulated some savings before he returned, expecting to settle near the family farm. But, according to Wallace family tradition, after "having lived where all men were free," Wallace found himself overcome by the feeling that slavery was "the sum of all villanies," so he and his brother George determined to move their families north. The Wallace clan arrived in Sugar Creek in 1822. Peter Cartwright, a Methodist lay preacher from western Tennessee and later a famous circuit rider in central Illinois, wrote in his autobiography that in part he moved to "carry the Gospel to destitute

HUSBAND JOHN WALLACE (1808–54) AND WIFE EVELINE RIEGER WALLACE (1812–76) in photographs taken during the early 1850s. Both came to Sugar Creek with their parents and siblings in the 1820s, he from South Carolina, where his father, James Wallace, had concluded that he could no longer live with slavery; she, from Tennessee. Married in 1830, they raised ten children, including two sets of twins, on land they farmed west of the creek in section 14, township 13/6. After her husband's death in 1854, Eveline ran the farm until her youngest daughter was married and the real property distributed to the heirs ten years later.

souls that had, by their removal into some new country, been deprived
of the means of grace." But antislavery attitudes also propelled him; in
a free state, he thought, "I would get entirely clear of the evil of slavery," "could raise my children to work where work was not thought a
degradation," and "could better my temporal circumstances and procure lands for my children as they grew up." In 1824, the year Cartwright brought his family, Illinois voters rejected a referendum to
permit slavery in the state by the relatively narrow margin of some
seventeen hundred votes out of twelve thousand cast; Sangamo
County voters like Wallace and Cartwright, however, overwhelmingly
rejected the referendum by nearly five to one.[7]

As Cartwright's comments suggested, emigrant antislavery sentiment had less to do with concern for Afro-Americans than with fears of
the debasing effects of slavery on free white farmers. Simon O'Ferrall,
a British traveler in the West in 1830, wrote that "during our journeys
across Illinois, we passed several large bodies of settlers on their way to
Sangamo and Morgan counties in that state. The mass of those persons
were Georgians, Virginians, and Kentuckians, whose comparative pov-
erty rendered their residence in slave states unpleasant." Despite the
hatred of slavery among his southern Illinois neighbors, however,
John Woods found that they had retained "many of the prejudices
imbibed in infancy, and still hold negroes in the utmost contempt; not
allowing them to be of the same species of themselves, but look on
negers, as they call them, and Indians, as an inferior race of beings, and
treat them as such."[8]

Several emigrant families brought black servants—individuals and
sometimes couples—with them to Sugar Creek, and although the census marshals listed them as "free colored" on the federal census, these
black men and women labored under "contracts of indenture" created
to discourage free black emigration to Illinois and to manage those
who came as slaves in all but name. William Caldwell emigrated from
Kentucky in 1836, repelled by the slave system after two black fugitives
had attacked and killed his daughter-in-law. Captain Caldwell brought
along his personal servant, Josh, a young black man of about twenty.
When the Caldwell clan moved to a nearby township, Moses Wadsworth of Sugar Creek later remembered, "Josh, of course, went too,"
and when Caldwell died, "his son John succeeded to the charge."
Jonathan Jarret owned slaves in Virginia and brought two servants
with the family when they emigrated in 1826; the wife of one of the
men followed the next year, and all, according to family tradition, were
"content to work as they had done in slavery—some of them even
better." One of the men was a tanner, and Jarrett employed his talents
to run a tanyard on his farm through the 1830s. No one in Sugar Creek

seemed to object to the presence of these few blacks as household servants.[9]

The objections were to the *system* of slavery, for, as a system, slavery offered a powerful symbol of the negative effects of economic progress in the South. In the eighteenth century the colonial administrators of Pennsylvania, Virginia, and the Carolinas encouraged the frontier settlement of migrant European peoples—principally English, Scotch-Irish, and Germans. These immigrants served two important colonial purposes, military and economic: wresting the frontier from the Indians and establishing a buffer to protect coastal populations from possible native attacks while at the same time inaugurating agricultural development. Then, as tidewater farmers, planters, and merchants prospered within the protected colonial seaboard, they expanded their operations inland, in many cases transforming the frontier economy from Indian trading and subsistence farming to slave-based, commodity-producing agriculture. In the interior South, one of the best indicators of the development of agriculture was the increasing Afro-American proportion of the population and the increasing proportion of household heads who owned slaves. Through this transition, some farmers prospered and became masters, others were less successful but found a niche as yeomen farmers amid the slave system; but over time the majority of residents chose to move, to extend the frontier, to begin the settlement process again. Farmers who felt constrained by the pressures of economic development, then, had to look no further than the slave for a potent symbol of what was forcing them out.[10]

By the last quarter of the eighteenth century, when the squeeze of economic development began to press on backcountry communities in Virginia and Carolina, trans-Appalachia became a refuge. But as the history of Kentucky and Tennessee demonstrates, pioneers did not necessarily win title there either. By the end of the century, the development of the trans-Appalachian West forced thousands of families, unable to buy their farms, off the lands they had broken. Beginning the process again, these thousands "removed" to the next frontier. After Indian resistance ended in the Mississippi Valley in 1815, from Pennsylvania and Virginia, Kentucky and Tennesse, thousands of families poured into Alabama, Missouri, and Illinois, where, as English immigrant George Flower wrote, there was "good land dog-cheap everywhere, and for nothing, if you will go far enough for it." Contemporaries christened this mass movement "The Great Migration." Baptist preacher and educator John Mason Peck watched the procession of men and women from his southern Illinois porch and fancied that "Kentucky and Tennessee were breaking up and moving to the 'Far West.'"[11]

Over half of the Sugar Creek emigrants before 1840 came directly from the Green River Country, several counties between the Green and Cumberland rivers in the southwestern part of Kentucky. Speculators and commodity farmers in Kentucky had originally considered this area a "barrens," both because of its sandy soil and its distance from market, concentrating their attention on the rich Bluegrass region near Lexington, where a plantation and horse-breeding economy quickly took root, leaving the Green River Country to hundreds of small farmers, particular Revolutionary War veterans who held land bounties entitling them to small plots. But as commodity agriculture expanded its operations, speculators moved into Green River Country, bidding up land prices, and yeoman farmers began to experience a familiar difficulty in securing title. Beginning in the 1790s and extending through the first several decades of the nineteenth century, the Green River Country exported thousands of farming families to Missouri and Illinois.[12]

"Many of our neighbors are true backwoodsmen, always fond of moving," John Woods noted of his fellow southern Illinois farmers in 1820, and now some "wish to sell their land, with its improvements, to go to the Sangamond [sic] river, 150 miles towards the north-west." Among these "extensive travelers," he wrote, "to have resided in three or four states, and several places in each state, is not uncommon." Like Robert Pulliam, a number of Sugar Creek settlers were prodigious movers. Samuel and Isaac Vancil, for instance, were born in the 1760s into a German immigrant family in Lancaster County, Pennsylvania, and after the Revolution moved with their parents from that hearth of pioneers into Virginia, where in the 1790s they both married and began families. By 1800 the brothers and their growing kinship group were living in Kentucky; by 1811 in Ohio near Cincinnati; and, after a few more years, across the state boundary in Warren County, Indiana. When the Vancils came to the Sangamo in 1818, it was the eighth "remove" for them. Before settling in Sugar Creek, eight in ten heads of Sugar Creek households had made at least one interstate move, and 35 percent moved two or more times.[13]

Patterns of family migration greatly affected the development of the Sugar Creek community. While communities in early-nineteenth-century New England were characterized by dicennial persistence rates of 50 to 60 percent of households, communities in the American West experienced rates of 30 percent or less. Sugar Creek was no exception to this western pattern. At least two-thirds of heads of household moved elsewhere during the course of each decade. The presence of surnames not found on the federal enumerations in Sugar Creek poll books, militia rolls, and local lists of roadwork crews, suggests that numerous other families came and departed between the dicennial

census counts. Some of these families may have pushed further west-
ward; others, defeated in the struggle against the wilderness, may have
returned to their communities of origin. Transience was an important
fact of life in Sugar Creek.[14]

Historians of the American frontier generally emphasize the legacy
of the settlers who followed what George Flower called "the old hunter's rule": "when you hear the sound of a neighbor's gun, it is time to
move away." Frederick Jackson Turner, the influential historian of the
American frontier, wrote that patterns of migration offered Americans "a gate of escape from the bondage of the past." "The advance of
the frontier," Turner wrote, "has meant a steady growth of independence on American lines. And to study this advance, the men who grew
up under these conditions and the political, economic and social results
of it, is to study the really American part of our history." In Turner's
judgment, the process of migration and resettlement, and the cultural
attitudes and character they engendered, were peculiarly American,
dramatically contrasting with the conservatism and persistence of traditional European societies.[15]

Most early-nineteenth-century contemporaries, however, did not
celebrate but feared such mobility; transience, they believed, encouraged backsliding into a lower social state. "This line of frontiersmen,"
wrote Englishman William Strickland, "affords the singular spectacle
of a race, seeking and voluntarily sinking into barbarism, out of a state
of civilized life." Yale clergyman Timothy Dwight lamented in 1819
that the pioneers, "impatient of the restraints of law, religion, and
morality," were "too idle, too talkative, too passionate, too prodigal,
and too shiftless to acquire either property or character."[16]

Such fears had a long history. In the 1730s, planter William Byrd
railed against hordes of Scotch-Irish pioneers flooding into southern
Virginia "like the Goths and Vandals of old." Forty years later, British
conservative Edmund Burke argued in Parliament that colonial authorities must encourage settlement in "fixed establishments" with
"the ruling power" near at hand to encourage frontiersmen "to believe
in the mysterious virtue of wax and parchment." Otherwise, he warned, the backwoodsmen "would wander without a possibility of re-
straint" and soon "would become hordes of English Tartars." Forty
years later, according to Timothy Flint, a Yankee transplanted to the
Ohio Valley, Burke's fears had materialized. "Everything shifts under
your eye," he despaired; "the present occupants sell, pack, depart.
Strangers replace them. Before they have gained the confidence of

their neighbors, they hear of a better place, pack up, and follow their precursors. This circumstance adds to the instability of connexions." "The general inclination here," concluded Flint, "is too much like that of the Tartars."[17]

By the time these critics were employing the labels "Vandals" and "Tartars," the words had come to refer not only to the Germanic and Mongol hordes of history but to contemporary vagabonds, thieves, and shiftless persons as well. With its connotations of violence and barbarism, this was a language of condemnation. But for pure evocation their language is preferable to Turner's, for whereas his sought to isolate the pioneer experience as unique and exceptional, theirs linked frontier settlement with the tradition of folk migration. Despite the obvious differences between Tartarian tribes and Americans, most successful folk migrations have been conducted by populations armed and organized to dispossess the native inhabitants. In this regard, the historian William H. MacNeill explicitly compares such otherwise disparate peoples and argues that "the American frontier was merely an extreme case of contact and collision between societies at different levels of skill—a pattern that runs throughout recorded history and constitutes one of the main themes of the human past."[18]

Although during their periods of migration the Vandals and the Tartars—like the Celts, Angles, Saxons, and Normans—could be described as transient peoples, they soon turned to farming and settled in permanent communities. Likewise, though mobility played an important role in shaping the character of American society, and despite the regular "turnover" in the population of the creek, a stable community soon developed amid the timber and the prairie. The history of Sugar Creek is part of the history of folk migrations, the story both of a transient majority, the people called "movers" by contemporaries, and those men and women who persisted in the area and put down roots.[19]

Though persistent families constituted only a minority before the Civil War, it was this "core" of families that provided the continuity and cohesion necessary for communal life. The settlers "are not always in motion," wrote James Hall, a "booster" of Illinois but also a careful and sympathetic observer of the pioneers. "They remain for years in one spot, forming the mass of the settled population, and giving a tone to the institutions of the country; and at each remove, a few are left behind, who cling permanently to the soil, and bequeath their landed possessions to their posterity." As Hall suggested, posterity and landed possessions, family and land, shaped the character of the Sugar Creek community as much as mobility. Frederick Jackson Turner and Timothy Flint, for reasons of their own, focused on those who moved. But the community created by those who stayed behind is also a "really American part of our history."[20]

7

Customs of Association

The settlers that surveyor Angus Langham encountered along Sugar Creek in 1821 were all squatters with no legal right to the public domain. From the beginnings of the federal land system, illegal squatting gave families a way of dealing with the problem of frontier development but posed a serious problem for the integrity of the law. In the Land Act of 1796, Congress set the minimum purchase price of public lands at two dollars an acre for 640 acres, an initial investment far beyond the financial resources of most pioneers. Moreover, the act required settlers to buy the land at auction, where land speculators might bid against them. Legal reforms of 1800 and 1804 lowered the minimum to 160 acres and introduced a complicated credit system to accommodate buyers who lacked sufficient cash, but retained the auction, required nearly a hundred dollars as a down payment from the settler, and provided for federal reposession in the case of missed payments. From its inception, Congress designed the land system principally to raise revenue, not to provide farms for republican farmers, and the law appealed more to speculators than to settlers.[1]

As early as 1776, Jefferson warned his more conservative colleagues that the pioneers "will settle the lands in spite of everybody," and throughout the West that was precisely what they did. In 1789, just four years after passage of the first land law, frontier representatives were pushing Congress for a "preemption" provision that would allow settlers to select or "preempt" the congress land of their choice before it came on the market and would guarantee sale at a fair price to the farmer who "improved" the land. But Congress refused, in several instances federal authorities forcibly evicted squatters north of the Ohio, and the conflict between frontiersmen like Pulliam and the federal government continued. Scores of squatter petitions failed to move the public lands committee of Congress, which declared in 1806 that squatters had "settled without authority," and that "any hardships to which they may be exposed are chargeable only to their own indiscretion."[2]

The extent to which settlers ignored the law of the land was evident in the growth of the Illinois population to over thirteen thousand persons before the beginning of federal land sales in 1814. Confronted with such a massive violation and intent on discouraging a withdrawal of Americans during the War of 1812, Congress reversed itself in 1813, forgiving the Illinois squatters, granting them preemption rights in the territory, and allowing them three years to file and purchase their claims. This Illinois preemption provision was not repeated and did not affect the men and women who settled Sugar Creek after Pulliam's trek in 1817, but it did suggest a congressional shift toward policies encouraging settlement. This tendency was affirmed in the Land Act of 1820, the single most important piece of land legislation since the original 1785 ordinance. With the collapse of the credit system during the financial depression of 1819, Congress lowered the minimum price of land to $1.25 an acre and reduced the minimum purchase to eighty acres, making it possible for a settler to receive clear title to half of a quarter-section of congress land for one hundred dollars in cash. When the Springfield land office opened for business in the fall of 1823, settlers were able to buy title to their claims under the most liberal provisions in the history of the republic.[3]

Thirteen heads of Sugar Creek households purchased land at the land office during the auction in 1823, and over the next seven years a total of fifty-four men and one woman bought plots of Sugar Creek land from the federal government. According to the census returns of 1830, forty-five of these claimants lived along the creek in that year. Of those missing, nine had either died or moved, and only one was clearly a nonresident land speculator. Moreover, by comparison with the sale of public lands in other areas, Sugar Creek sales were fairly evenly distributed. Although a small group of local men accumulated relatively large parcels of real estate, over three-quarters of the claimants from the creek filed for the minimum of eighty acres. But not all settlers could afford to purchase their claims. To buy and fully open a farm, a man did best to bring about five hundred dollars in cash with him, and many settlers simply never had such financial resources. Reflecting this reality, two-thirds of the state's farmers in 1828 were squatters on the public domain, according to the estimates of Illinois officials, and the proportion of squatters among the farming population remained high for the next fifteen years. Along the creek, 46 of the 113 households in 1830, 53 of the 134 households in 1840, were occupied by squatter families.[4]

These squatters found support for their continued occupation of the land in the customs of the country. In early May 1819, for example, Robert Pulliam returned to Sugar Creek with his wife, Mary, and their three daughters and two sons ranging in age from thirteen years to twenty-four months, planning to house them all in the one-room, sixteen square-foot sugarhouse he had erected in 1817. When they arrived at the sugar grove, however, they found the cabin occupied by Zachariah and Nancy Peter, who, with their five young children, had arrived the previous September and, finding the cabin empty, had put up there for the winter. But by right of "improvement"—namely, the cabin he had built in the grove—Pulliam had a customary claim to what, after 1821, would be "the west half of Section 21, Township 14, Range 5 West of the Third Principal Meridian." The Peters vacated and Zachariah built his family another dwelling three miles north, in unclaimed timber along the creek. Pulliam crammed his family into the little cabin, which protected them from the exceptionally harsh winter of 1819–20.[5]

Not only did settlers mutually acknowledge the rights of squatters to their improvements, but they acted together to defend these customary rights against legal encroachments. According to Pascal P. Enos, registrar at the Springfield office in the 1820s, there were no instances "of any person biding more than the Govt. prices, or any persons biding against a person that held by possession." Speculators were probably intimidated in Springfield, as they were elsewhere, by associations of squatters showing up en masse to protect their claims. In Wisconsin in 1835, according to one contemporary report, "if a speculator should bid on a settler's farm, he was knocked down and dragged out of the land office, and if the striker was prosecuted and fined, the settlers paid the expense by common consent among themselves." "A kind of common-law was established by common consent and common necessity," John Reynolds wrote, "that the improvements on congress land shall not be purchased by any person except he who made the improvement."[6]

Custom protected the right of any settler to squat, improve, and farm his land for a term, but there came a day when he either had to buy his claim or sell his improvements. Of the fifty-five owners along Sugar Creek in 1830, better than seven in ten were still present in 1840, but of the forty-six squatters, fewer than three in ten persisted through the decade. The distinction between those families who purchased land and remained in the community and those who moved on was, of course, largely determined by available funds. But the extent to which settlers came to Sugar Creek in association with their relations, and established family and kin connections there, also played an important part in providing people with the wherewithal to remain. Among persistent heads of household, eight in ten came to Sugar Creek as members of large kith and kin associations, and each census enumeration found eight in ten persistent heads of household living near kinfolk in other households. By contrast, only one in three settlers who appeared on just one enumeration had kin connections in the Sangamo. The Sugar Creek community, in other words, was built by families in association.[7]

In the fall of 1817, after the corn was in the crib, the families of William and Mary Drennan, Billy's younger brother and sister-in-law, Joseph and Rebecca Drennan, and his daughter and son-in-law, Mattie and Joseph Dodds, with the family of their neighbor George Cox— some thirty-five persons in all—loaded their belongings onto farm wagons, left their homes in the Green River Country, crossed the Ohio at the Shawneetown ferry, and rode north to winter camp near Wood River, Illinois. Next March, accompanied by their six oldest boys and guided by a ranger of the late war, the four fathers led their ox-teams onto Edward's Trace and headed for the San-gam-ma; the mothers and two half-grown daughters kept camp on Wood River, tending the sixteen children.[8]

After a day or two scouting Sugar Creek, the men picked what they considered an excellent site for their farmsteads near a clear spring on the west side of the creek, about two miles southwest of the sugar grove. Here the timber along Sugar Creek and its branch, Panther Creek, formed a three-sided enclosure around a square-mile cul-de-sac of high grass that for the next half-century would be known as "Drennan's Prairie" in deference to Billy Drennan, patriarch of the kin association that was to form the core of this neighborhood. During the spring of 1818, the forest rang with the sound of broad ax against hardwood, as the men cleared timberland, built log huts and fences, and raised summer crops of Indian corn and pumpkins. The four families of the Drennan party, like the Pilgrim settlers of Plymouth two hundred years before, agreed to work in common, with the understanding that by the end of the second year each household would have an equal-sized plot of cleared land for its own use. Some men cleared, plowed, and planted; others hunted and cooked.

In the history of Southern pioneering, men typically went ahead to plant crops and build cabins, while the womenfolk remained at a base camp with children and farm stock. William Faux, a British traveler in Illinois, encountered an advance male party of "semi-barbarians" in 1819. They would return to their wives, he wrote "when the job is done, or their shirts are rotting off their backs. They rarely shave, but clip off the beard, and their flesh is never washed; they look pale, wan, yellow, and smoke-dried." The men of the Drennan party brought north only the most necessary provisions, supporting themselves largely on game, wild honey, and the milk of their cows. When the party ran short of bread, they dried wild turkey breast over a slow fire and used the jerky as a substitute. Whether for clean shirts or meal, several times that summer the older boys retraced their tracks to Wood River for resupply. When the corn was "laid by" in August (after which it needed no further cultivation) the fathers and younger boys returned to complete the final move of the families, while the older boys remained at Sugar Creek to guard the claims and to hunt. By the fall of 1818, when the women and children joined their husbands and fathers, accompanied by several more families, including those of the highly mobile Vancil brothers, corn was already in the shock on the newly broken ground.[9]

Some kinship groups migrated sequentially but no less cohesively than those who came together. A year after the Drennan party arrived, fifty-year-old Thomas Black and his forty-year-old wife, Edith Pyle, who had raised seven children together in Christian County, Kentucky, immigrated to Sugar Creek with their offspring, including their married daughter, Sarah, her husband, and their two children. Thomas Black staked a claim to timber and prairie land on the east side of the creek about a mile south of Drennan's Prairie. The following year Edith's niece Sarah Pyle Husband joined the Blacks, bringing with her a large assortment of kin: husband Harmon and the children; brother-in-law Flower Husband with his family; sister-in-law Polly Husband Patton, with her husband, James Patton, and three young children; and the aged parents of the Husband siblings. All settled on land contiguous with Black's. Five years later, Nicholas and Ann Pyle came with their two grown sons and settled near Thomas Black; Nicholas was Edith Black's brother, Ann Thomas's sister—marriage of brother and sister to another brother and sister was very common. Two years later, in 1827, Matthew Patton Kenny, nephew of James Patton, moved to the creek, located on land west of his uncle, married a local girl, and raised a family. These interrelated farm families formed a compact neighborhood that shared work, tools, and the products of their labor. The neighborhood gradually took the name "The Patton Settlement," as James Patton emerged as the most powerful landowner there.[10]

In other instances a single nuclear family first emigrated alone. In November 1819, Job and Mary Fletcher, a newly married couple with a three-month daughter, Permelia, arrived in Sugar Creek and built a three-faced camp in which to spend the winter on land facing north onto Drennan's Prairie. After the death of his parents, Fletcher had been raised by Elizabeth McElvain Fletcher, the wife of his older brother John, in Christian County, Kentucky. Job proved himself a bright boy in school and was soon teaching his fellow students. His "hand" was so clear and neat that folks from all over his neighborhood sought him out to write their letters and legal papers. On the evening of his arrival in Sugar Creek, the wife of George Cox, who lay dying in his cabin, called on Job to write out the first will to be executed in the Sangamo. Fletcher's reputation had accompanied him to Sugar Creek.

Job Fletcher had been in the Northwest before. In 1811, at eighteen, he joined a Kentucky militia company on its way to fight with William Henry Harrison, and the young man was at the battle of Tippecanoe; he missed the fighting, but was assigned the grisly task of helping to bury the dead. In 1820, a year after his arrival, Fletcher was appointed the first justice of the peace in the Sangamo and organized the creation of the first precinct for the elections of 1820. Within a very few years, "Squire" Fletcher had acquired a large local following as a teacher, a churchman, and a spokesman for the "American System" of Henry Clay.

Like most young families who came to Sugar Creek and persisted, the Fletchers were soon joined by relations. Inspired by brother Job's success in the new country, the Christian County Fletcher clan emigrated between 1828 and 1830; first, brother James, with his family of ten children, accompanied by the family of Samuel McElvain, brother of James's wife, Jane; the next year Jeremiah and Hannah Abell, parents of McElvain's wife, Penelope, with several of their children's families, as well as John Fletcher and Elizabeth McElvain Fletcher (sister of Samuel and Jane, sister-in-law and surrogate mother of Job) with her mother Margaret, her eight children, including their eldest, Job Fletcher, Jr. (known as "Captain Fletcher" in deference to a militia commission awarded in Kentucky, and to distinguish him from his uncle), his wife, Frances, and their two babies. A few years later more Abells, with connected in-law families, joined this growing kin association.

Like the Black-Husband-Patton clan, these families settled adjoining lands. John and Elizabeth, Job and Frances, and their children, first moved into a cabin that Squire Job had built, then bought land of their own several miles south where others had built their cabins. Both James and John Fletcher died soon after arriving in Sugar Creek, and their widows, the McElvain sisters, ran their farms for the next twenty years in association with brother and neighbor, Samuel, nearby several households of Vancils and Wallaces, in the neighborhood referred to in the earliest county records as "the sources of Sugar Creek."[11]

Another young family, Willis and Nancy Cartmell Cassity and their two children, similarly settled on Sugar Creek in 1829. Two of Willis's sisters and one of his brothers had married Lockridges in Bath County, Kentucky, and in 1835 these Lockridge-Cassity families, with many associated in-laws, including the four Bridges brothers, three of whom had married Lockridge girls, as well as several Fosters, Morgans, and Ducks, came to Sugar Creek in a huge overland party of over twenty-five adults and fifty children, led by seventy-seven-year-old Revolutionary War veteran John Lockridge. Nearly all of them settled lands on the northern side of Drennan's Prairie, where some were forced to build their cabins on the grassland, because by the late thirties most timberland had been taken.[12]

Micajah and Susannah Donner Organ and their five children came to Sangamo County with Susannah's three wanderlustful Donner brothers and their associated in-law families in 1828. The clan settled in the northeast portion of the county; but the next year Micajah moved his family to the Sugar Creek neighborhood at "the sources," encouraged by Donner nephew Greenberry Walter's report of fertile lands and open country there. When Lydia Donner Walters lost her husband in Indiana in 1838, she decided to relocate her brood near her younger sister, Susannah. She led her seven unmarried children, her son Noble with his wife and family, as well as sister Elizabeth's boy, Greenberry, his wife and four children, to Sugar Creek in 1839. Meanwhile, in the mid-1840s, brother George Donner, who had prospered on his Sangamo lands yet had tired of Illinois, decided to recruit family and kin for a grand migration to California. But the Donner sisters, now comfortably settled neighbors on Sugar Creek, declined to make the trip. In April 1846, Lydia and Susannah bid sad farewell to their brothers, sisters-in-law, nephews, and nieces,—all bound for California on the ill-fated journey of the Donner Party.[13]

Although the majority of persistent Sugar Creek families were members of kin associations, some came without kin yet managed to persist. Zachariah and Nancy Peter, for example, who occupied the Pulliam cabin during the winter of 1818–19 and continued to reside in the neighborhood of "Sugar Camp," apparently had no relations in the area but successfully farmed and raised a brood of children who married into local families. Zachariah became a respected county commissioner, probate judge, and justice of the peace. It is likely, however, that many, if not most, of the single men and families who came with-

out associates passed through the community. A lack of kin, as well as a
lack of funds, seems to have accounted for their lack of permanence.
The private histories of the mobile majority are largely lost to us. The
recoverable histories of those who persisted, on the other hand, tell us
much about the importance of traditional family and kinship patterns
on the moving frontier.[14]

8

With Milk
and Honey Flow

The lines that surveyor Angus Langham drew across the land helped families to locate their claims precisely, but otherwise they had little impact on the shape of settlement during the first quarter-century of the American period. The look of the landscape was determined, not by an abstract grid, but by cultural traditions of kinship and resource use in association with natural patterns of woodland and prairie.

The prairies with their tall grasses were the most outstanding physical feature of the Sangamo. Most travelers found them stunningly beautiful. William Cullen Bryant, who toured in the 1830s, was moved to verse:

These are the gardens of the desert, these
The unshorn fields, boundless and beautiful,
For which the speech of England has no name—
The Prairies. I behold them for the first,
And my heart swells, while the dilated sight
Takes in the encircling vastness.

Emigrants, too, could appreciate their beauty. Riding north across the prairies with a party of emigrants on his way to the Sangamo in 1828, John Stuart stretched tall in his saddle, gazed about, and exclaimed to himself, "How grand, how beautiful the view!" Moses Wadsworth of Sugar Creek wrote that "the first comers were enraptured with the beautiful country spread out before them."[1]

But, unlike touring poets, settlers also had to contend with the realities of prairie living. In the winter, winds unhindered by forest cover
swept down upon the grasslands, punishing stock unmercifully, and
unless penned they soon "took to the timber," just as sensible men did
in the same storms. In the summer, according to Captain Job Fletcher,
thousands of green-headed flies swarmed over the prairies east and
west of Sugar Creek, their bites so painful that horses bolted uncon-
trollably and threw their riders. "A journey across the big prairies was,
in the summer time, undertaken only at night," Dewitt Smith remembered, "because on a hot summer day horses would be literally stung
and worried to death."[2]

In the fall, devastating prairie fires, driven by high winds, frequently swept over the grasslands, raising an ominous roar, creating
huge banks of dark smoke, and lighting the midnight sky with the glare
of midday. In the fall of 1819, when the eight-foot prairie grass was as
dry as powder, the Vancil family assembled around the deathbed of
Samuel's daughter Elizabeth, only to be startled from their grief by the
roar of an approaching fire propelled by a strong westerly wind. All
rushed out, soaked the house with buckets of water filled from the
creek, beat wet blankets against the approaching flames, and succeeded in saving the cabin where Elizabeth lay; but they lost the winter
supply of prairie hay curing in stacks on the grassland. The exhausted
fire fighters returned to find that the girl had died during the excitement.[3]

The early emigrants, then, found the prairies an unfamiliar and
hostile environment. Trained by experience for a life in the woods,
pioneers repeated stories and tall tales of the dangers that accompanied travel across the shadeless expanses, where, it was said, great
hunters succumbed to the prostrating heat and mounted men emerged from the sea of grass to find their boots barnacled with rattlesnakes
hanging by their fangs. Prairies also disappointed common expecta-
tions of what an agricultural landscape ought to look like. On the
grasslands, wrote Caleb Atwater in 1818, "no pleasant variety of hill
and dale, no rapidly running brook delights the eye, and no sound of
woodland music strikes the ear." The locational patterns of many settlers may be accounted for that simply.[4]

But emigrants rejected laying their farmsteads upon the prairie
because of the difficulties of farming there. Most Americans held to
the popular theory espoused by Langham in his evaluation of the
land—soil reveals its fertility by the vegetation it supports—so the
absence of timber signaled to them the prairies' agricultural worth-
lessness. In 1786, as Jefferson labored on his draft of the Land Ordinance, James Madison wrote to him that the "miserably poor" Illinois
Country "consists of extensive plains wh[ich] have not, from ap-

pearances & will not have a single bush on them, for ages. The districts, therefore, within wh[ich] these fall will never contain a sufficient number of Inhabitants to entitle them to membership in the confederacy." Twenty years later, a group of farmers from fertile American Bottom wrote, in a petition to Congress, that the "unfertile" prairies "cannot in the common course of things, for centuries yet to come, be supported with the least benefit." Actually, prairie soils, with their rich legacy of generations of grasses, were higher in organic content and natural fertility, and less prone to water and wind erosion, than adjacent timber soils. But in an age before scientific soil analysis, even brilliant men could not fathom the mysteries of the sea of grass.[5]

Nor, more importantly, could they break the ground's surface with their plows; for, theories notwithstanding, many settlers tried to farm the grasslands. When she emigrated with her husband and children in 1826, Sarah Burtle brought seeds from Kentucky. To the wild prairie flowers she intended to add marigolds, larkspur, damask roses, hollyhocks, and bachelor's buttons for drying, stringing, and hanging about the cabin for ornament. After selecting a garden spot in front of the cabin, on the verge of the prairie, she began to chop at the sod, only to have her garden hoe rebound as if she had struck solid rock. The sod was impervious to horticultural tools, as the Indians had long known. The knot of prairie roots, some as thick as a man's finger, extended several feet underground in a maze that could be cut only with a heavy iron plow, and then only with the greatest exertion. But even the best-prepared Southern emigrants had brought only their shovel plows, designed to "jump" over large roots, stirring up the rest of the soil, and these were useless on the prairie.[6]

The Drennan and Dodds men later remembered looking longingly at the adjacent prairie in the spring of 1818, for how much easier it would have been simply to farm the grassland without the added difficulty of removing the trees; but they could not succeed in getting their plow to break the prairie sod. They uncoupled one of their wagons, hitched four horses to the front wheels, and fastened the plow to the axle, but still could not force the plow to enter. Finally, they tried shaving the grass with sharpened hoes, digging in their corn and pumpkin seed with chopping axes, and in this way raised a good crop on the fertile silt loam, but at a heavy cost in labor. In similar ways, men cleared small patches of prairie during the first two decades of settlement, but most grassland remained in its pristine condition, at least until the development of the heavy prairie plow in the late 1830s. Driven by five to ten yoke of oxen, this massive instrument could cut two or three feet into the sod, but the expense of hiring the thing was too great for most farm families. Not until the use of John Deere's steel plow became common in the 1840s and 1850s was much prairie land

broken for farming. The draining of swampy prairie land had to await
tile drainage systems of the late nineteenth century.[7]

There were, on the other hand, important advantages to locating
farmsteads in or near the timber. Beneath the leaf cover farmers found
a moderately fertile soil that drained well and plowed so easily that, as
they worked the ground, the Drennan men sank into it up to their
ankles. Fruit trees, corn and squash, legumes and clover all did well on
these upland timber soils, although because of the neglect of proper
manuring, and ignorance of contour plowing, erosion and the leeching
of soil nutrients soon created problems for families on these "crick-
farms."[8]

Using chopping axes, farmers removed underbrush and small trees,
then "girdled" the giants with a deep gash around the circumference
of the trunk (a trick learned from the Indians), killing the tree and
preventing it from shading the corn crop, which was planted amid
roots, stumps, and arboreal skeletons. Clearing was dangerous work:
crushed hands and limbs were common, slipped axes mangled men for
life, and falling trees, knocking into standing ones, could catapult backward and crush a woodsman like a bug. Girdled trees, too, were dangerous things—"widow-makers" people called them—whose dead
branches and limbs might fall and snuff out a life at any moment; so
mothers tried to keep children out of girdled fields, and careful farmers fired the dead trees after the first crop. Noah Mason, of Sugar
Creek, recalled several close scrapes he had amid the timber. When he
was a boy swimming in the creek as his father felled trees on the bank,
he started at a noise above, looked up, and saw a massive trunk falling
toward him. He dove and came up amid the branches, unharmed. A
few years later, when he was helping his father in a lot of girdled
timber, a large limb suddenly broke and fell, but he threw himself
down next to a large log and was saved again. Later in life, now a
farmer with a timber lot of his own, Mason had loaded his wagon with
rails and begun to ford the creek when the wagon suddenly lurched
and the load slipped forward, throwing him into the water and nearly
pinning him under the surface. Many had their horror stories to tell,
but pioneers well understood these forest dangers.[9]

Moreover, in this "age of wood" farmers were helpless without the
forest crop of materials for tools, homes, furniture, fences, and fuel,
and no far-sighted man wished to be left without a large "woodlot"
nearby. The timber could also produce salable commodities. William
Riley McLaren, from north of the Sangamon River, recalled that "our
chief source of revenue was the dense gigantic growth of virgin timber.
When the bark would peal in May and June, the yellow, black, and pin-
oaks yielded us their harvest of tan-bark. The white oak, bur-oak, and
walnut their wealth of staves, saw-timber, & rails. And the hoop-pole

crop was a game at which the boys could play. What sport to cut, trim, pile, and tie in bundles those long & slim hickory withes for use in cooper shops." It was, then, with a deep appreciation for the uses of wood that men staked their first claims to timberland. The pioneers "made it a point," recalled Robert Wilson, "to secure choice lots of timber land," and Moses Wadsworth remembered that "believing the demand for wood for fuel, and for rails for fences, must constantly increase," the first generation "held on to their forest acres with an iron grasp."[10]

A location in the creek's timber also provided relatively easy access to water. In the nineteenth century, before Sugar Creek became muddied by systematic damming or polluted by the chemical effluents of modern farming, it ran crystal-clear. In the first years few farmers dug wells; rainwater was collected in barrels and troughs from cabin runoff, but when this ran short, as it often did, farm women hauled water from the creek. "All of us had small sleds with a barrel securely fastened on," wrote one woman, "to which was an old gentle horse hitched." Other wives and daughters carried water with the aid of the shoulder yoke. In the winter, the creek froze over, providing ice for summer storage.[11]

The timber also provided farmers with an excellent place to run their hogs. Farmers paid little or no attention to breeding, and their swine did not fatten as well as improved stock, reaching a maximum weight of only some two hundred pounds; but the most important consideration was the ability of these fiesty "razorbacks" to survive on forest provender, with a little occasional corn in the farmyard to keep them somewhat connected to their owners. A typical farm required a dozen swine to support the carnivorous appetites of the family, although some farmers built up herds of fifty or more. "Pigs were frequently seen running about the forest," wrote Patrick Shirreff after a visit to a farm near Springfield; "the acorn season had arrived, and I was amused at the pigs scrambling for this fruit. They ran grunting from tree to tree, and the noise of a falling acorn was the prelude to a race and fight." These "elm-peelers," "stump-suckers," or "landsharks," as westerners variously called their swine, produced a lean, pleasant-tasting flesh in years of abundant mast. Many farmers rounded them up and corn-fed them before hog-killing time in November or December, but usually they found the boars too wild to handle. More farmers were injured by boar tusks than by all the wild animals of the country, so men hunted them just like other game.[12]

For all these reasons, most emigrants first located their homesites in the timber, usually in the margin near the edge of the prairie, for this area of thinly spaced trees was easiest to clear, and farmsteads in the margin offered the use of adjacent prairies as a grazing ground for the cattle. "If he places his house at the edge of one of these prairies," one emigrant guidebook suggested, "it furnishes him food for any number of cattle he may choose to keep." Timothy Flint noted that on the prairies "the summer range for cattle is inexhaustible." In winter, farmers did not generally shelter their cattle but let them seek the timber cover, where they fed on prairie hay. The dominant prairie grasses—bluestem, Indian grass, and switchgrass—made good winter hay but also provided excellent grazing at other seasons, as the rangers had discovered during the war. The farm families of the 1830s, most of whom raised from five to fifteen head of cattle, including a milk cow or two, allowed their stock to graze freely on the prairie associated with their homesites in the timber's edge.[13]

Settlers placed themselves at this junction of environments, exploiting each to advantage. From the margin, farmers found it easy to hunt either in the timber or on the prairie, and in the fall, after the crops were in, hunting became the main business of every farmer, not only for meat and tallow, but furs and peltries as well. Throughout the first quarter-century American men hunted wild turkey, goose, duck, and prairie chicken with abandon; in the timber of what quickly became known as Panther Creek, they frequently encountered and killed those large American felines. Farmers kept up a nearly continual slaughter, so it was inevitable that some wildlife species quickly disappeared. The aquatic mammals, with their rich furs, were the first to go, followed by the large and occasionally dangerous brown bear, panther, and gray wolf. Certain wildlife populations, however, actually increased as their natural predators declined, and cornfields replaced the original provender of the margin. Rabbits and squirrels, feeding in the fields, damaged young corn shoots but in exchange offered their savory meat to the Illinois "burgoo," or stew, that simmered in nearly every cabin. The corn attracted deer, too, especially at night, when men might lie in wait, a case of the game coming to the hunter. Until well into the 1840s, large herds of deer ran free on the prairies east and west of Sugar Creek. "Deer are more abundant than at the first settlement of the country," Abner Jones wrote in the 1830s, and "they increase, to a certain extent, with the population."[14]

The seven hundred county households estimated by Illinois officials to have located in Sangamon County by 1821 were clustered in the timber margin along the creeks and waterways or at the edge of prairies. At the Kelly family settlement on the south side of Spring Creek, enterprising merchants platted the town of Springfield in 1821; it became the permanent county seat in 1825 and the state capital in 1837. North and east of this central site lay the smaller communities of Fancy Creek, Wolf Creek, German Prairie, and Round Prairie; west was Island Grove; and south, Lick Creek, Horse Creek, and Sugar Creek, where surveyor Langham found that squatter families had confined themselves to the timber margin, avoiding the prairies altogether. "At the present the settler builds his cabin in the edges of the timbered land," wrote Benjamin Harding after a tour through Illinois in 1819, and he predicted that "the great distance between the timbered land . . . will leave it thinly settled in places for some time." Two decades later, in 1840, county population had grown to over fourteen thousand, but the households along upper Sugar Creek remained confined to the timber margin. Robert Wilson, zigzagging across the country county from one Whig rally to another during the political campaigns of the late thirties, found the prairies "entirely unoccupied," and at about the same time, Patrick Shirreff noted that the farmers of the Sangamo were "chiefly settled on the skirts of the forest, the middle of prairies being altogether unoccupied."[15]

So although the land of Sugar Creek was three-quarters prairie, timberlands accounted for over 65 percent of settlers' purchases before 1840. Emigrants, many bound together by ties of kinship, chose and improved their lands in compact fashion, remaining within the timber margin and only gradually moving out east and west from the creek onto the prairies. Natural features of watercourse, timber, and grassland combined with the clustering tendencies of kinship to produce several distinct neighborhoods by the early 1820s. On the east side of the creek were the neighborhoods of "Sugar Camp" and "Patton Settlement," on the west side, "Drennan's Prairie" and "The Sources."[16]

Included within the bounds of these neighborhoods were emigrants who added smithies, carpentry works, or tanneries to their farms. James Patton of Patton Settlement, for example, had apprenticed in the tanner's trade with his father, who ran a leather and saddlery business in Baltimore during the Revolution and, according to family tradition, had outfitted one of Washington's regiments. Upon his father's death, Patton inherited the tools of the trade and the capital of the family business, and soon after his arrival at Sugar Creek he set up a tannery, the first of its kind in the Sangamo, and supplied leather goods to the neighborhood.[17]

Millers fulfilled a particularly important function, converting wheat and corn into flour and meal for local consumption, and soon enterprising farmers established horse- or ox-powered grist mills in every neighborhood. In 1820, near his sugar grove, Robert Pulliam built a horse mill that could, at peak capacity, grind eight bushels of corn in a day. Sugar Camp residents frequented Pulliam's mill, often waiting a day or more for their turn, in the meantime lounging at the pioneer's licensed tavern. Further south, in Patton Settlement, Thomas Black set up a horse mill and distillery, and near Drennan's Prairie Methodist class-leader James Sims operated another.[18]

It was not long before the demand for building materials stimulated the construction of water mills. Along the creek, at the southern end of Drennan's Prairie, Robert Crow purchased congress land near his brother-in-law Squire Job Fletcher in 1824. The next year, after Crow obtained permission from the county commissioners to build a dam and a lumber mill, he sent word of his plans through the neighborhood, and on the appointed day the neighborhood assembled and raised a six-foot dam. At Crow's millpond, on early mornings, boys fished for bluegills, carp, pike, and bottom-loving catfish, and on sunny summer afternoons nude riders charged their horses into the deep, cool waters, drawing applause from multitudes of men on the bank. Larger crowds assembled after Thomas Black completed a bridge over the creek in 1827, linking Drennan's Prairie with Patton Settlement to the southeast. That same year, several men raised another sawmill seven miles north on the creek, at the head of the prairie east of Sugar Camp, about four miles from Pulliam's, where an attached distillery furnished diversion. By the end of the decade Japhet Ball had constructed a third to the northwest, on Lick Creek.[19]

The subsistence nature of the economy offered little outlet for the lumber produced by water-powered mills. Ball testified that he did little cash business, and that his net income from the mill amounted to "exactly seventy-five cents" during the hard times of 1837. As for grist, the availability of horse mills and the lack of local markets for grain delayed the addition of stone burrs for grinding at local mills until the 1840s. "Fact is," Moses Wadsworth wrote, mills "never did pay, and were built principally to accommodate the community."[20]

Families settled more slowly at The Sources than elsewhere along upper Sugar Creek, in large part because throughout the 1820s no miller operated there. Organ, Vancil, or McElvain boys, sacks of grain thrown across their ponies, had to travel five miles north and ford the creek to get to Black's horse mill. The attraction of this neighborhood improved dramatically, however, when several interrelated families, among them miller Jacob Rauch with his wife Pauline Poley and two toddling sons, settled there in 1830. Rauch came from Muhlenburg County, Kentucky, but the miller's heavy German accent suggested that he had seen a bit of the world. Originally from Stuttgart, where he was born in 1796, Rauch sailed to Philadelphia in 1818, and there on the docks, unable to speak a word of English, he was cheated of his passage by an unscrupulous captain who bound the young German into debt servitude with a Southern merchant. Rauch spent his first three years in America at hard labor on the Tennessee River in north-

(*Top*) CROW'S MILL, established by Robert Crow in 1825 and rebuilt by his sons in the 1840s, in a photograph taken during the 1850s. "Crow's mill pond was a favorite resort by crowds of men and boys on Saturday afternoons for swimming exercises," one resident remembered. "The swimmers frequently rode their horses into the pond, and the steeds, swimming with their nude riders, drew out great applause from the multitude on the banks." (*Bottom*) RAUCH'S CUSTOM MILLS, founded by the German immigrant Jacob Rauch in 1830, showing the bridge over Sugar Creek, during the late 1860s, After Rauch's death in 1843, his wife, Pauline Poley Rauch, whose brother Joseph Poley lived down the road, operated the mill for several years. Her sons, Charles and Andrew, took over operations in the 1850s.

ern Alabama before fleeing north in desperation. In Kentucky the young fugitive located other German-speaking folk, settled, married, and in 1824 used skills he had acquired on the river to open and operate a sawmill. Rauch soon established himself as a successful miller, but the specter of his involuntary servitude continued to haunt him. During his last years, still bitter over his humiliating "welcome" to the United States, Rauch scrawled these words in German on the margin of the contract that had legalized his slavery: "Jacob Rauch says this indenture was not good!" In the late twenties he resolved to move across the Ohio to Illinois, leaving slavery forever behind him.

Accompanied by his brother-in-law, Joseph Poley, Rauch reconnoitered land along Sugar Creek and in 1828 filed a claim to a site near the headwaters, where fourteen years before rangers had killed a fleeing Kickapoo and recovered the scalp of an American woman. A twist in the creek and a sudden fall in elevation there created an opportunity to exploit water power. In 1830, as the Rauch, Poley, Gates, and Shutt families (all of German background) carved farms out of the timber margin at The Sources, Jacob petitioned the county commissioners for permission to erect a dam, and after "twelve Good & lawful men" of the neighborhood had met, viewed the site, and determined that "the Erection of a mill at Said place would be of great neighborhood convenience," Rauch constructed the first water-powered grist mill along the creek. There, through the next three decades, weary northbound emigrants rested as they crossed the line into Sangamon County. Rauch's Mill, the first Sangamon landmark on the road from American Bottom to Springfield, became widely known for the hospitality of its German-born proprietor, who recounted to all who would listen the story of his Alabama trials and Illinois successes. Rauch's became a center for settlers from both banks of the southernmost reaches of Sugar Creek, and stamped the eastern bank of this southernmost neighborhood with the German's name. Up and down the creek, water mills served as community centers, the most visible landmarks of neighborhoods.[21]

Water mills were, as well, visible evidence of what settlers called the "improvement" taking place on the map—their word for landscape. Improvements began at the level of the farmstead. Settlers defended the tradition of farming unclaimed land for family subsistence, but squatters held proprietary rights to these claims only if they "improved" them. Newcomers might buy the lands that squatters occupied, but only after agreeing to pay a fair price for those improvements. In the early 1830s, John and Rebecca Burlend, who farmed fifty miles west of Sugar Creek in Pike County, paid "a good cow, a heifer, and seventy bushels of wheat" for the "pre-emption rights" to their neighbor's improved farm.[22]

An improved farm was one that had several acres cleared, plowed,

"OLD HOMESTEAD, LATE RESIDENCE OF R. H. CONSTANT." A typical Sangamon log cabin, with added kitchen ell, and enclosed by a split-rail Virginia or "worm" fence.

and enclosed by the trunks of fallen trees, or better, by split rails in the zigzag formation known as a Virginia or worm fence, to protect crops from the freely grazing stock. In the 1830s the typical Sugar Creek farm included about sixty acres of improved farmland on which farmers annually raised a thousand bushels of corn, one or two hundred bushels of wheat, oats, and other small grain, potatoes, and garden crops. An improved farm might also include a small orchard, such as the apple orchard Robert Pulliam supposedly planted in the spring of 1817, just before returning to Pulliam's Ferry.[23]

Improvements also implied a finished shelter of some sort for the family. Many Sugar Creek settlers, the Dodds and Fletcher families among them, spent their first winter in an open-faced camp: a three-sided structure with poles laid across it for a roof, with the open side facing away from the prevailing winds toward a large log fire that furnished warmth and kept away the forest critters. By the second year most settlers had set to work on a full cabin. Billy Drennan's was typical of those constructed throughout the Sangamo: a one-room enclosure of large logs piled one atop the other to a height of ten feet and joined at the corners by a technique known as half-dovetailing; door and windows hacked out; the spaces between the logs "chinked" with clay, grass, and small chips of wood; roofed with clapboards held in place with a latticework of ridgepoles; a large stone fireplace along one wall; a dirt floor later replaced by log "puncheons" laid over a shallow root cellar. When the family outgrew this one-room cabin another might be built by its side and the two joined by a covered passage called a "dog-trot," or a rear extension, called an "ell," added as a kitchen, store house, or sleeping quarter. Finished cabins were more substantial than the first shelters, but still, according to Moses Wadsworth, were "more or less open huts."[24]

Settlers carried this building tradition, particularly the dogtrot house, into Illinois from the Kentucky-Tennessee frontier. In the eighteenth century, German emigrants first introduced into America the idea of building with logs and demonstrated the technique of corner-timbering that made the whole construction possible. Celtic emigrants fused these ideas with the traditional spatial concepts of the British Isles, where single-room, gabled-end cottages of mud or stone housed most commoners. The typical Sugar Creek cabin was some sixteen feet square, very similar to the traditional English single-bay cottage. American pioneers also retained the English practice of using the walls for storage by attaching pegs and shelves to them, keeping the center of the room free for work. Some farmers, particularly emigrants from the Northeast, began to build in newer frame housing forms as early as the 1830s, but as late as the 1850s the typical farm family in Sugar Creek continued to live in a log cabin, although it may have been enlarged, sided with exterior clapboards and interior plaster, and even painted with newly fashionable lead paint.[25]

A final necessary "improvement" was a cart path linking cabin and farmstead to the "trace," and thus to other farms and the outside world. Cart paths and traces hardly qualified for the designation "road," their condition was so deplorable. Traveling through central Illinois in the mid-thirties, Abner Jones wrote of his route that "*road* it ought not to be called, *track* is a fitter name. Not a tree had been fallen, and every one went hither and thither among the trees, in search of a better path, as his judgment dictated or his horse inclined. Large and deep holes, still filled with water, whose surface was thickly coated with green slime, continually obstructed our way. Into these were we occasionally obliged to plunge, much to our own annoyance, and that of our poor animals, who were ready to sink under the intense heat." His complaints were typical. In the 1870s one early settler remarked that "forty or fifty years ago men traveled by 'taking a point,' for there were no roads; and by thus sighting a direction, made their way." These improvements were not roads so much as routes with many tracks, some on the high ground, some on the low—different tracks for different seasons or different weather conditions. By 1830 several such routes connected Sugar Creek to points north and south, and cart paths linked the farms of settlers to their neighbors, but they meandered according to the elevation of the country, the extent of the timber, or the wetness of the soil. Arrow-straight "section roads," following the lines laid down by the 1821 survey, did not begin to be a feature of the Sugar Creek landscape until the 1850s.[26]

Moses Wadsworth came to the Sangamo from Maine as a boy of fourteen in 1840, and his first remembered view of Sugar Creek provides a summary of the "improved" landscape after over two decades of American settlement. When he arrived, nearly a thousand people were living along the reaches of upper Sugar Creek, 90 percent of them "from the hilly regions of Virginia and Kentucky." These southerners crowded into one hundred and thirty or more "unhewn log cabins" clustered into several "settlements," where kin groups had originally claimed land at resource sites like Drennan's Prairie or Pulliam's Sugar Camp, and where families continued to farm in association. Linking the cabins and settlements together were "occasional, rarely used wagon tracks" and "Indian trails that were still visible."

Most of the cabins were "confined to the timber line," where they were surrounded by small rail-fenced fields of Indian corn and by even smaller garden plots. "Hardly any one had any better shelter for his animals than a rail fence," Wadsworth recalled; the cattle, hogs, and sheep raised by the farm families ran free on a "commons" of virgin forest and high grass prairies, on which "a field of timothy grass or clover was a rare sight." In fact, "the prairies were generally a trackless waste," and "any man who bought and improved land out in mid-prairie, at that day, was laughed at for his folly." The grasslands continued to be home for deer who "bounded in the broad prairies," as well as for "flocks of prairie chickens, vast enough to darken the air as they flew." Wild turkeys and wolves "still abounded in the woods, in their season." Thus did Wadsworth remember, in the 1880s, "the rude and crude accommodations of two score years ago."[27]

The settlers commonly used the word *elegant*—meaning "useful"— to describe their improvements. "An *elegant improvement*," English immigrant Morris Birkbeck wrote disparagingly, "is a cabin of rude logs, and a few acres with the trees cut down to the height of three feet, and surrounded by a worm-fence, or zig-zag railing. You hear of an *elegant* mill, and *elegant* orchard, and *elegant* tanyard, etc., and familiarly of *elegant* roads—meaning such as you may pass with extreme peril." If Englishman Birkbeck was not much impressed with these "improvements" in the 1810s, neither was Frenchman Alexis de Tocqueville, traveling through the Mississippi Valley in the early 1830s. "The trees have been cut but not grubbed up," he wrote. "Their trunks still cover and block the land they used to shade. Round this withered debris, wheat, shoots of oak, plants of all kinds, and weeds of all sorts are scattered pell-mell and grow up together in the untamed and still half-wild ground. It is in the middle of this vigorous and variegated growth of vegetation that the planter's dwelling or, as it is called in this country, his log-house, rises. Just like the field around it, this rustic dwelling shows every sign of new and hurried work." The landscape, Tocqueville believed, suggested "an unequal fight against nature."[28]

Illinois editor and writer James Hall commented on just such unsympathetic views. "The traveler," he wrote, "accustomed to different modes of life, is struck with the crude and uncomfortable appearance of everything about this people—the rudeness of their habitations, the carelessness of their agriculture, the unsightly coarseness of all their implements and furniture, the unambitious homeliness of all their goods and chattels." But, Hall continued, the visitor to Illinois "is mistaken in supposing them to be indolent and improvident, and is little aware how much ingenuity and toil have been exerted in procuring the few comforts which they possess, in a country without arts, mechanics, money, or commercial intercourse." Where Tocqueville saw squalor, the settlers saw the evidence of honest toil and earthly reward.[29]

Certainly the settlers spoke glowingly of the landscape. Men and women, Wadsworth wrote, "sent back enthusiastic accounts of the country to the friends they had left behind. Their attractive representations brought others, and 'the San-gam-ma country' came to be known as the farmers' paradise." In a similar paean to the landscape, John Reynolds wrote that "in the Pottawatomie language, Sangamon means 'the country where there is plenty to eat.' According to our parlance, it would be termed 'the land of milk and honey.'" Thus Reynolds translated the Algonquian into a commonplace biblical phrase familiar to the pioneers. President Washington, for example, had described the Ohio country as a "land of promise, with milk and honey," and most western settlers had grown up with the verses of Samuel Stenett's familiar hymn ringing in their ears:

> O, the transporting, rapturous scene
> That rises to my sight!
> Sweet fields arrayed in living green,
> And rivers of delight.
>
> There generous fruits that never fail
> On trees immortal grow;
> There rock, and hill, and brook, and vale
> With milk and honey flow.[30]

The word *Sangamon*, however, meant nothing like Reynolds's proposed translation. The word—which Americans first pronounced San-gam-ma, then Sangamo, and finally Sangamon—probably derived from the Algonquian *saginawa,* or "river's mouth," and was a cognate of other Algonquian river names like "Saginaw" and "Sagatuck." Indeed, rather than conveying an Indian sense of the landscape, Reynolds's translation unintentionally captured something of the important "improvements" that Americans introduced into central Illinois.[31]

There were, to be sure, similarities between the Americans and their Algonquian predecessors; both peoples supported themselves on Indian corn and the hunt, exploiting the same varieties of maize and game. But "the land of milk and honey," with its cows and bees, was a mixture of a traditional European material culture with a North American environment. Rangers first drove milk-producing cows and oxen onto the Sugar Creek prairies as part of the logistics of a war for possession. Cattle then transformed the manner in which human beings made their living from the rich land of the Sangamo, for the drawing power of oxen made agriculture possible, and agriculture was the most powerful force available for transforming the landscape. To make room for their crops, American settlers attacked the trees and wildlife of the timber margin, and over two decades replaced the gradual transition zone between forest and prairie with cultivated fields at the edge of an abrupt "timberline." Agriculture in the Sangamo planted fixed settlements where they had never before existed and allowed the population along the waterways quickly to surpass the size of the previous Kickapoo communities.

The Sangamo was also a land of sweetness. In addition to sugar maple, the timber contained colonies of bees that produced some of the greatest quantities of honey in the West. American pioneers loved bee-hunting along the creeks, and men bragged of excelling in the art of watching errant drones for the "beeline" to the hive, marking the hive-tree with their initials, and returning to harvest the sweet crop in the fall. On one excursion along the Sangamon River in 1822, Samuel Williams and his father found thirty bee trees, returning home with over fifty gallons of honey and sixty pounds of beeswax. Bee-keeping soon superseded the maple grove as the main producer of local sweetener. But, like cattle, honeybees, too, were European immigrants. Unlike the cattle that came with the pioneers, however, bees, with their swarming and migrating habits, preceded human immigrants by a hundred miles or more. "In the Military bounty lands above the junction of the Illinois with the Mississippi," Gershom Flagg reported in 1819, "the bee has not been seen more than fifteen years." The Kickapoo did not exploit these bees, or celebrate the sweetness of their syrup, but looked upon them as harbingers of the hated settlers, as "white people's flies." The settlers' land of milk and honey was of their own making.[32]

PART THREE

Lords of the Soil,
Tenants of the Hearth

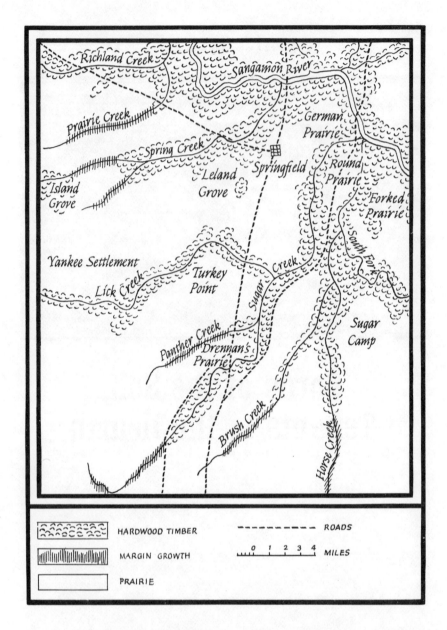

SOURCES: Timber and margin cover based on soil types in U.S. Department of Agriculture, Soil Conservation Service, in cooperation with the Illinois Agricultural Experimental Station, *Soil Survey of Sangamon County. Soil Report No. 111* (n.p.: n.p., 1980).

THE SANGAMO COUNTRY IN 1830

9

Totally and Forever Dissolved

I n late December 1836, in Judge Stephen T. Logan's Circuit Court, held in Springfield, Elizabeth Richardson Drennan of Sugar Creek filed divorce proceedings against her husband, Joseph Drennan, Jr.

Your oratrix Elizabeth Drennan, late Elizabeth Richardson humbly complaining showeth to your Honor That on the 23d day of February A.D. 1833 within the County of Sangamon State of Illinois She was married to one Joseph Drennan Jr. in due form of Law. That at the time of Said Marriage your oratrix did verily believe that said Joseph Drennan was a sober industrious Young man. That since said Marriage said Joseph hath become intemperate in the use of intoxicating Drinks and improvident in regard to a Support for his family—That notwithstanding the earnest entreaties of your oratrix The said Joseph persisted in his course of Intemperance—neglecting to provide a Support for your oratrix & her infant child—and often treating your oratrix with extreme cruelty—That for the space of more than two years last Past The said Joseph hath been a habitual Drunkard in so much that your oratrix cannot in safety live with him—Your oratrix hath no encouragement to labor for the purpose of procuring a Support whilst living with him—either for herself or child because he either wantonly destroys or Spends the same for intoxicating Drink. Your oratrix Therefore prays that said Joseph

Drennan be made defendant to this Bill and that a Summons Issue—

Your oratrix Prays your Honor that she may be divorced from the said Joseph and that the marriage contract between your oratrix and the said Joseph be totally & forever dissolved. That her infant Son, Smith Drennan, aged [three] years may be left in her care & custody. That she is now encient with another child, which she prays may be decreed to her if alive when your Honor shall render a decree in this cause. Your oratrix further prays that a certain Bed and Bedding—the single Remnant of her Patrimonial estate—may be decreed to her for Alimony & that such other & further Relief may be granted your oratrix as to right & Equity shall appertain. And as in duty Bound your oratrix will ever Pray.[1]

Both Elizabeth and Joseph grew up in the Sugar Creek community. At the time of her complaint, the twenty-one-year-old daughter of William and Elizabeth Richardson had resided in the neighborhood of Drennan's Prairie since her parents' move from Kentucky in the mid-1820s. Her bridegroom was a neighbor, the fifth-born child of Joseph and Rebecca Drennan, one of the first American families to settle the creek. Elizabeth's cousins, John and Ruth Smith, for whose family the young mother named her son, also took Drennans for spouses, marrying Joseph's siblings, Ruth and Andrew. These marriages, like many along Sugar Creek, united two sets of kin.[2]

Weddings, the premier events of the rural social season, celebrated not only the joining of a new couple but their entrance into the body of families that made up the community. On the morning of the wedding day, the groom and his cronies assembled at the house of his parents and from there caroused through the neighborhood, jugs in hand, inviting farmers in their fields to toast the groom and rousing neighborhood families to celebration. By noon the young men, along with the rest of the guests, arrived at the home of the bride, where her parents hosted the ceremony. There, for the neighborhood to inspect, the bride and her friends frequently displayed the dowry. One woman later remembered seeing cabin walls draped with homespun linen, and another recalled laying out piles of coverlets, blankets, sheets, pillow slips, and tablecloths at her sister's wedding. In addition, the "patrimonial estate" might include a bed, kitchen equipment, a few heirloom pieces handed down by the women of the family, and, occasionally, farm property on which the couple could begin to raise a subsistence.[3]

After a local preacher performed a short service, following the orders of a well-thumbed handbook, the guests might join in the singing of an old religious folk song like "Wedlock":

When Adam was created he dwell'd in Eden's shade,
As Moses has related, and soon an Eve was made.

Then Adam he rejoiced to see his loving bride,
A part of his own body, the product of his side.

This woman was not taken from Adam's feet, we see;
So he must not abuse her, the meaning seems to be.

This woman was not taken from Adam's head, we know;
To show she must not rule him, 'tis evidently so.

This woman she was taken from near to Adam's heart,
By which we are directed that they should never part.

This woman she was taken from under Adam's arm,
And she must be protected from injury and harm.

The husband is commanded to love his loving bride,
And live as does a Christian, and for his house provide.[4]

Then the party began. One woman remembered a winter wedding of the 1830s when, "ceremony and congratulations being over, the door was removed from its wooden hangings, and placed across some benches, then covered with homespun linen which served as a table. Upon this was placed the dinner which consisted of turkey, venison, corn, and wheat bread, maple sugar doughnuts, pumpkin pie, and other wholesome edibles which received due attention from all. When all had been satisfied and the cloth removed, the door was again lifted to its place, closed, and the room became warm again." After the meal neighbors danced "reels" or "longway dances," descended from the traditions of English country dance, and "square fours" or "quadrilles," derived from French cotillion dancing. In these social dances, facing rows of men and women or circles of couples danced together, as partners danced in and out of the lines or entered the circle for a "jig" until they "cut out," too tired to continue, and were replaced by another pair who tried to outdo their predecessors. In these "hoedowns" the community welcomed newlyweds into the association of households.[5]

The dancing and merriment continued until mid-evening, when, if the couple were bedding down at the bride's parent's cabin, her bridesmaids would escort her to bed, followed by the groom's party, who would tuck him in beside her, the couple spending their first night together while the noisy celebration continued late into the night. "I have an invitation to a wedding next Thursday," one Sangamon farmer wrote home to his parents in the 1830s, "and expect to have a real succor wedding. It is to be in a log cabin with only one room, we shall probably stay all night as the custom is in this country, and the probability is, the floor will be the common bedstead of us all." If the couple sought privacy in a cabin of their own, revelers were almost certain to shadow them home to "shivaree" them, an American version of the European practice of "charivari" or "rough music." Francis Grierson, who lived in the south Sangamon County area in the 1850s, wrote of people bringing "ole tin pans, kittles, whistles, cow-bells, horns en everything they could make a howlin' noise with, en set up a kinder war-dance 'round the cabin." The merriment went on well into the night, and often into the next day at the "infair," a housewarming for the bride and groom, sometimes held at the groom's parents house, but more often in the cabin of the newlyweds.[6]

Once consummated, most marriages endured until the death of one of the partners. Divorce was an unusual way to terminate a marriage during the first half of the nineteenth century. One Sangamon settler recalled that before the Civil War "boys and girls got married, and remained married. We had no divorces, and considered it far better to fight it out on the old plan than be disgraced by a divorce." His recollection was not strictly true, for both the daily schedule of attorneys and the extant files of the circuit court attest to the fact that divorce cases were tried with some regularly in Sangamon County. Over the first four decades of American settlement, however, out of the hundreds of couples united, only three Sugar Creek unions ended in divorce. This relative infrequency of divorce replicated the national pattern. In the United States until the last quarter of the nineteenth century, divorce terminated about one in every thousand marriages. In 1980, by contrast, the rate had risen to one in every fifty.[7]

After their weddings, Elizabeth's cousins settled into a lifetime of typical marital routine, but the troubles between Elizabeth and Joseph surfaced quickly, led to irresolvable conflict, and ended up in court. There, in March 1837, Joseph offered no defense against his wife's charges. Attorney Thomas Moffitt corroborated the complaint by calling to the witness stand the fathers of both husband and wife, Elizabeth's brother, Daniel, her cousin, John Smith, her brother-in-law, Andrew Drennan, and several other neighbors and relatives. Judge Logan issued his decree the same day, granting the young woman's plea and ordering "that said Elizabeth Drennan have the care & custody of her infant son Smith Drennan and Also the child when born of which she said Elizabeth is now Pregnant. And that she have as her own Separate property one Bed & Bedding remaining in her Custody a part of her patrimony as her Alimony."

Elizabeth Drennan then slips from the historical record. She did not remarry in the county. The record does preserve, however, her son's service with other neighborhood youths in Company B of the 10th Illinois Cavalry during the Civil War, as well as his marriage soon afterward and the birth of his children on a farm in Sugar Creek; so it seems likely that after her divorce Elizabeth moved her patrimonial bed to the household of kin and continued to live as a single woman in the community with her children. Her divorced spouse, however, remarried in 1839 and moved twenty miles south to a farm in Macoupin County, where he and his new wife raised ten children; when this wife died in the 1860s, Drennan married for a third time and had six more children. Joseph's later marriages better represent the course of marriage in Sugar Creek than does his divorce. All his thirty-odd brother, sister, and cousin Drennans married; their unions lasted an average of thirty years; they each had an average of eight children. Before the Civil War no other Drennans obtained divorces.

The second of the three Sugar Creek divorce petitions was filed sixteen years later, in April 1853. Elijah A. West, whose parents lived near Rauch's Mill at The Sources, came before Circuit Court Judge David Davis in Springfield, in complaint against his wife. West represented himself, and the clerk of the court provided a summary of his plea.

Your orator Elijah A. West humbly complaining sheweth unto your honor that your orator on or about the [left blank] day of February A.D. 1850 was married to Elizabeth Marx, now Elizabeth West, then a widow. That after said marriage your orator and his said wife Elizabeth lived together about six weeks when your orator discovered for the first time that said Elizabeth was then pregnant. Your orator would show also that he was lubbey-led into said marriage by the artifice of one Russel who took advantage of your orator when intoxicated to induce your orator to consent to said marriage. Your orator would further show that said Elizabeth has taken up with one [left blank] pretending to have been lawfully married to him and as your orator supposes is now living with him in a state of adultery. Your orator would further show that at the time of said marriage the said Elizabeth was pregnant as above stated in a manner proving her not to have been a virtuous female and to be unfit for the life of a respectable man, and that at the time of said marriage this was wholly unknown to your orator.

In tender consideration of all which your orator would pray your honor to dissolve the bonds of matrimony between your orator and the said Elizabeth and such other and further relief as the case may resign.

In August the court issued a summons for Mrs. West to appear before it, but after two months the county sheriff returned it unserved, with the notation scrawled on the back that "the within named Elizabeth West not in my Bailiwick." Judge Davis granted West's divorce at the November term of the court, apparently convinced of Elizabeth's adultery by the fact of her disappearance.[8]

Several months later, in June 1854, Elliot Herndon, brother of Lincoln's law partner, William Herndon, filed another bill of divorce for a client from the creek.

> Humbly complaining your oratrix, Mary Ann Pulliam, would show unto your honor that on the [17th] day of January A.D. 1851 she was lawfully united in marriage with Thomas J. Pulliam and that your oratrix and the said Thomas J. her husband lived together as man and wife in a state that was no cause of regret to either your oratrix or her said husband But then without any cause known to your oratrix and really without any cause justifying a separation of your oratrix from the said Thomas J., the said Thomas J. deserted your oratrix his lawful wife leaving your oratrix entirely destitute of the means of support and hopeless of the comforts and happiness of a wedded state. Your oratrix would show that the said Thomas J. has during all the time of his said desertion entirely neglected to provide a home or support for your oratrix his lawful wife and that without the assistance of a kind father would have been entirely destitute of both food and shelter. Your oratrix would further show the desertion of her said husband has been continual and uninterrupted for the space of at least two years and that the same was willful and without cause.
>
> In tender consideration of all which your oratrix would humbly pray that the said Thomas J. Pulliam be made defendant to this bill of complaint and he answer thereunto, that process be issued commanding [unclear]. And that your honor would decree that the bonds of matrimony between your oratrix and the said Thomas J. be forever severed and such other and further relief as to your honor would seem meet.

Twenty-one-year-old Mary Ann was the firstborn of John and Eliza Levi, a farm family from Kentucky. Thomas J. was twenty-five, grandson of Robert Pulliam, the second child born to Martin G. Pulliam and his wife, Lucy Knotts. The two young people grew up in the Sugar Camp neighborhood.

Judge Davis (later appointed to the United States Supreme Court by President Lincoln) issued his decree at the same June session:

It appearing to the satisfaction of the Court that the said Defendant has been duly and legally served with process herein more than ten days before the first day of the present term of this Court and he being three times solemnly called came not but made default. It is therefore ordered, adjudged and decreed by the Court that complainant Bill and the allegations there be taken as confessed against the said Defendant. And now this cause coming on to be heard upon the Bill and oral testimony in open Court, and the court being satisfied from the proof that the allegations of Complainants Bill are true; that the said Thomas J. Pulliam the Defendant has willfully deserted the said Complainant for more than two years previous hereto and that he has failed neglected and refused to contribute to her support. It is therefore ordered adjudged and decreed by the Court that the bonds of matrimony heretofore and now existing between the said Thomas J. Pulliam and Mary J. [sic] Pulliam be and the same are hereby dissolved annulled and set aside, and henceforth for naught existence and that the said Mary Ann Pulliam be and she is hereby entitled to all the rights and privileges of a *femme sole*. It is further ordered and decreed by the Court that the said Thomas J. Pulliam pay the costs of this proceeding and that Execution issue thereof.

Six months later Mary Ann remarried John E. Hartsock, of another Sugar Creek family. Thomas waited several years before he married Elizabeth McLaughlin and removed south to Macoupin County.[9]

These records offer a glimpse into popular attitudes about the nature of marriage. The settlers of Sugar Creek were common folk who rarely committed their thoughts to paper even if they could write, and rarely saved the paper if they did. Legal documents, preserved in the files of the circuit or county commissioners' court, provide a way to recover their thoughts and concerns, if not their voices. Elijah West was illiterate—he signed his plea with his "mark"—but the court record preserves both his argument that he had been led to the altar like a "lubby" or "lubber"—a clumsy, impotent man, in the rural vernacular—as well as his conviction that he had been tricked by a scheming, worldly-wise widow. In their petitions, Elizabeth Drennan and Mary Ann Pulliam emphasized the extent to which they felt at risk in their marriages, as victims of husbands who were "improvident" and practiced "extreme cruelty." With references to "kind fathers" and "Patrimonial estates," both young women contrasted their present misery with former states of security in their families of origin. The divorce records document disappointment but also a commitment to an ideal of family, an institution in which "virtuous females" and "respectable men" combined to "provide a home and a support" and secure the "comforts and happiness of a wedded state."

These were important values, for family and household were the building blocks of Sugar Creek society. From 1830 to 1860, families from newlywed couples to widows with dependent children comprised ninety-two of every hundred Sugar Creek households. But this was the fabled West, the region to which thousands of young American men came seeking their fortunes, so there were also numbers of single men in the community, a fact reflected in a sex ratio of approximately eleven adult men to every ten adult women during the 1820s and 1830s. However, nearly all these men resided with families as boarders or hired hands. From 1830 to 1860 unmarried men headed fewer than two out of every hundred Sugar Creek households.[10]

The importance of the household constituted a deep and slowly changing current of social life that united Sugar Creek with European rural societies of the distant past. The family, which had been "at the centre of a whole network of links" in the villages of medieval Europe, remained at the center in Sugar Creek. Men and women lived out their lives within the walls of their cabins and the bounds of their fields; there they loved and hated, bore and raised their children, performed society's necessary labor, learned and ordered the relations of their world. In this society of families what were the "comforts and happiness of the wedded state?" What did it mean to "provide a support?" How might the relationship between men and women in Sugar Creek be characterized?[11]

10

_____

In Sickness
and in Health

I have one objection to marrying in this state," Matthew S. Marsh wrote home from the Sangamo in the 1830s to a brother in New Hampshire, "& that is, the women have such an everlasting number of children—twelve is the least number that can be counted on." Marsh exaggerated, but not by much. Early marriage, regular pregnancy, and late last birth meant that Sugar Creek women born before 1810 and surviving past age forty-five raised an average of better than eight children. Children were the most obvious consequence of the wedded state, and the large number of children that women bore was the first of a triad of traditional features of Sugar Creek family life.[1]

In an age before accessible contraception practices, or a culture that supported their use, the years of a woman's fertility largely determined the number of children she bore. Marriage initiated the active period of child-bearing. A pattern of early marriage and large numbers of children previlaed in western Europe before the sixteenth century, but thereafter late marriage became the norm, men and women marrying in their mid- to late twenties. Historians do not agree on the exact causes of this trend toward later marriage, but it seemed to characterize societies with increasing commercial life. In the North American colonies, however, which had an economy considered primitive by European standards, English-speaking women continued to marry before their twenty-second birthdays through the eighteenth century; but with both commercial and urban development, the age at marriage

87

for American women increased, and by 1800 much of coastal North American society had fallen in line with the European pattern. In the backcountry, however, an area that included a large proportion of the population, the pattern of early marriage and large families continued. Women who immigrated to Sugar Creek followed in the traditions of their mothers and grandmothers, marrying at an early average age of nineteen; their daughters married at an average age of twenty-one.[2]

The young brides of the 1820s bore their first child within a year of their marriage, when they were in their early twenties; their last, in their early forties, for a total fertility period of better than twenty years. Within that span, women regularly gave birth at intervals of twenty-six to thirty months, intervals consistent with the common practice of nursing babies until about their second birthday, and suggesting little systematic attempt on the part of couples to limit conception. In 1830 the ratio of children under ten to women between the ages of sixteen and forty-five was almost twenty-five hundred per thousand, a rate about average for northern or southern backcountry regions and significantly higher than rural or urban areas of the Northeast.[3]

Only one in ten first-generation Sugar Creek wives had fewer than five children, six in ten had between six and nine, and three in ten raised ten or more. Sarah Pyle Husband, the farm wife who traded cornbread at her cabin door with the Kickapoo in 1820, married in Kentucky in 1811 at age twenty and bore her first child fifteen months later. When the family arrived in Sugar Creek she was caring for five children, the youngest just nine months' old. Over the next fourteen years, Sarah delivered seven more babies, including twins in 1831. Sarah's neighbor from across the creek, Mattie Drennan Dodds, married in Kentucky in the spring of 1810, at only sixteen. Her firstborn arrived in the late summer of 1811, and babies followed about every two years thereafter. Mattie bore her fourth, a son, in the camp along Wood River as her male kin broke land at the edge of Drennan's Prairie, and she nursed her baby during the first Sugar Creek winter spent in an "open-faced camp." She had seven more children before she reached forty-two.[4]

The forces of life waged an open struggle with the forces of death in the Illinois Country. Work made hard demands on rural men and women, and accidents occurred frequently. In the first forty years of American settlement in Sugar Creek, people froze to death in harsh winter blizzards, drowned in millponds or in the swollen creek, were struck by lightning as they plowed open fields, were crushed by falling timber, gored by enraged bulls, or dragged to death by runaway teams of horses. But in the western interior, just as on the Atlantic coast, childhood diseases, intestinal disorders, pneumonia, and tuberculosis (or consumption) were the main instruments of the grim reaper. Periodic epidemics of typhoid or "brain fever" struck in late summer or fall, when the deadly bacilli, spread by omnipresent stock and houseflies, flourished in the stagnant pools, rotting offal, or open sewage that abounded on farms.

Death rides on every passing breeze
And lurks in every flower,
Each season has its own disease
Its peril every hour.

One Sangamon settler recalled huge numbers of deaths during the unusually wet summers of the mid-1830s, when the sick frequently outnumbered the well and the dead accumulated so quickly that people had to bury them in blankets, two to a grave.[5]

In 1832 Asiatic cholera made its first appearance in North America, and by late summer the horrible pandemic arrived in Sugar Creek, imported by infected federal troops who landed in Chicago to quell the Black Hawk Indian uprising. The disease, with its frighteningly violent and usually fatal symptoms, continued into 1833 and 1834 before subsiding. Another outbreak began in 1849–50, when 5 percent of Sangamon County deaths were attributed directly to cholera, 10 percent to typhoid, 11 percent to "lung fever" or pneumonia, and another 11 percent to "consumption." By 1860 cholera had practically disappeared, but the incidence of fatal typhoid had nearly doubled, consumption and lung fever continued to claim their steady share of victims, and scarlet fever swept away the lives of fifty-five county children.[6]

These diseases were common throughout the country. The Mississippi Valley, however, had a particularly bad reputation for unhealthiness among contemporaries. English visitor Frances Trollope reported that in the West "long, disabling, and expensive fits of sickness are incontestably more frequent," and an old settler, John Reynolds, acknowledged that "the idea prevailed that Illinois was a 'graveyard.'" One of the worst health dangers in the West was malaria, an infectious disease caused by parasitic protozoa spread by the bites of the anopheles mosquito, which was indigenous to the Mississippi Valley. No reports of the fever in the West exist before the 1760s, but by 1800, after the influx of large numbers of settlers, traders, and troops into Illinois, several malarial epidemics had decimated whole communities, and "fever and ague" became a danger endemic to the country. In short, human carriers brought malaria to the West and infected the local mosquitoes, or "gallinippers," as westerners called them.[7]

Pioneer cabins, because of their darkness, humidity, and warmth, as well as their gaping windows and doors, made ideal environments for mosquitoes, and settlers had no choice but to share their space with the stinging insects. One Illinois visitor of the thirties observed a mother and her half-dozen children through the open window of one of these cabins, their hands and arms flailing the air as they went about their tasks. At first he thought he was witnessing the ceremony of an eccentric western religious sect, "but on entering, I saw they were all busy in warring with the mosquitoes." Medical authorities did not recognize the insects as carriers of malaria until the end of the century. In the meantime, the prevailing theory held that malaria "was derived from impure water and air, which was always developed in the opening up of a new country of rank soil like that of Sangamon county," as one Sangamon resident continued to claim in the 1880s. Many authorities predicted that because of its environment the American heartland might never be healthy; "it is to be suspected that no changes and no cultivation will ever bring it into a state of salubrity," one medical doctor pronounced in 1829.[8]

The development of the malarial parasite in the human bloodstream induced a cyclical pattern of severe chills, followed by high fever, then chills again—repeating daily, every other day, or every three days. The victim jaundiced, turned sallow, and was overwhelmed by general listlessness. Pioneers came to think of this as part of the settlement process, a necessary "seasoning" for newcomers, and did not consider the "pioneer shakes" a disease at all. Generally, malaria itself did not threaten life, although census enumerators of 1850 and 1860 listed it as the cause of 10 percent of the deaths, mostly of children. In the bloodstream the parasite destroyed iron-rich hemoglobin, producing chronic anemia and incapacitating men and women during late summer and fall, precisely the time when the harvest demanded strenuous labor; so malaria lowered the community's overall productivity. As one man wrote from the Sangamo in 1821, "life is at least fifty percent below par in the months of August and September." The disease also lowered the body's resistance, leaving settlers at risk of contracting more serious maladies such as typhoid, consumption, or pneumonia, which in turn increased the general death rate.[9]

In the fight against malaria medical practice had little of positive value to offer. The licensing of physicians did not begin in Illinois until the 1870s, and few doctors had any formal training; most "regulars," as they called themselves, learned their trade through apprenticeship. Regular doctors held to the medieval theory that imbalances of the body's humors, or fluids, caused disease, and for nearly every ailment they prescribed bleeding and the administration of powerful cathartic or emetic drugs to reestablish the balance. Few anemic malaria sufferers benefited from the standard treatment: bleeding with the lancet until the patient fainted, inducing vomiting with ipecac, clearing out the bowels with calomel, then administering opium to calm the inevitable internal irritation. Settlers often carried the scars of frequent bleedings, as well as toothless gums and uncontrolled drool, symptoms of the mercury poisoning that occurred as a result of regular doses of calomel or mercurous chloride.[10]

Despite all this, most settlers welcomed a doctor's presence in the community. Several physicians practiced in the Sugar Creek area from the 1830s to the 1850s, including Charles Kerr and W. C. Johnson, competitors who belittled each other's treatments and admonished their patients to take the other's medicine only at risk of death. In the cholera year of 1833, several Sugar Creek residents recommended another local doctor to readers of the *Sangamo Journal*.

We the undersigned, wishing to express our gratitude to Dr. J. M. S. SMITH for his unwearied attention to the sick of our Creek this past season—and particularly to those of our own families, do certify, that no physician has been more successful, as far as our knowledge extends, having had, we believe, about 60 cases of the common fever of this country, together with about thirty cases of various kinds, and we believe has not lost a single patient, with the exception of one of cholera: and that we have the fullest confidence in his capacity and acquirements as a physician, and can with pleasure recommend him to our friends.

James Patton   John McLaughlin
Silas Harlan   Job Fletcher, p.m.
Robert Crow   Job Fletcher [Jr.]

Smith practiced in Sugar Creek through the mid-1830s, then moved to Edwardsville, where he died of cholera during the pandemic of 1849. His practice was taken over by Dr. Alexander Shields, who moved to Illinois from Pennsylvania and settled in the neighborhood of Sugar Camp.[11]

Many ordinary folk, however, expressed skepticism toward "regulars" and held instead to the tenets of folk medicine. Much of the latter was superstition. Children's diseases, "brain fever," and rickets, people ascribed to the malevolent influence of witches. Strange and unknown maladies like cholera they attributed to spells. A great meteor shower in the early winter of 1833, during the first pandemic of cholera, caused widespread terror. But folk medicine was also partly lore; much of it was drawn from the herbal pharmacopoeia of both Indians and Europeans and was generally practiced by the women of the family. American mothers and daughters knew almost as well as Indian women did where to look in the timber and prairie for curative plants, sure in the belief that "every disease has a herb that cures it." They used black snakeroot as a general cure-all for snakebite, rheumatism, dropsy, hysteria, and a variety of nervous disorders; culver's root and lobelia for their powerful emetic and cathartic effects; tall ironweed and horseweed to treat stomach and intestinal ailments; Maryland figwort to calm anxiety and induce sleep.

Women also grew their own medicinal plants. Elizabeth McDowell Hill remembered that when her family moved to Illinois "they loaded one wagon with grains, garden seeds, and different kinds of herbs and roots. Grandmother neglected not one of her healing herbs, alcumpane, rhue, tansey, and other healing balms." Among cultivated varieties, ground ivy made an effective physic to relieve backaches or lung troubles; heart-of-the-earth, a good gargle to soothe sore throats or, in a poultice, to heal wounds; peppermint tea to allay nausea and relieve sudden cramps; and catnip to comfort the tummys of children who had indulged in eating too many green apples.[12]

Some of these remedies had genuine therapeutic effects, and their successes inspired new botanic medical traditions that prospered in the face of people's understandable fears of "regular" treatment. "Your faith doctor is one who practices without a diploma," wrote James Hall, "and vanquishes diseases without drug or lancet; who neither nauseates the palate nor mars the fair proportions of the patient." But although malaria treatment of snakeroot, yellow birch tea, or cobweb pills surely caused less harm than "regular" therapy, it was equally ineffective. The best treatment for malaria is to strengthen the patient by controlling the symptoms, something best achieved by large, prolonged doses of quinine, a compound lethal to the malarial parasite. But despite the availability of quinine in the West by the 1830s and the scientific demonstration of its curative powers, "regulars" and "herbalists" alike accepted its benefits very slowly. Eastern writer Caroline Kirkland, who lived in a Michigan backwoods community for several years in the 1830s and 1840s, wrote that the practitioners of folk medicine universally railed against "Queen Ann," as they called quinine, or any other "doctor's physic," "while lobelia, and other poisonous plants, which happen to grow wild in the woods, are used with the most reckless rashness. The opinion that each region produces the medicines which its own diseases require, prevails extensively,—a notion which, though perhaps theoretically correct to a certain extent, is a most dangerous one for the ignorant to practice upon."[13]

Kirkland appreciated the success of herbal medicine without sentimentalizing it. Folk medicine depended on prescientific notions of correspondence, on continuing folk belief in magical cures, charms, faith doctors, seventh sons, and the powers of the moon. Round-lobed hepatica could cure bilious ailments because its leaf supposedly resembled the human liver; the fits brought on by sneezeweed might rid the body of "evil spirits"; bittersweet nightshade might be used to counteract the effects of witchcraft. "If a petticoated professor of the healing art—a female physician so called—should prescribe the most deadly drugs," Kirkland wrote, "or if she should pronounce oracularly that a dose of centipedes procured from beneath a fallen tree whose head should lie toward the east would cure 'the spinevantosey that comes in the breast,'—she will find supporters who would not employ an educated physician on any account." Many herbal cures especially designated for women's use carried the potential for danger: motherwort for menstrual disorders, partridgeberry or ergot as aids in childbirth, fringed polygala to increase the milk of nursing mothers, or common tansey to induce abortions, sometimes with fatal consequences.[14]

Although herbal concoctions for women could sometimes do harm, the midwives or "granny women" of the rural community generally took a noninterventionist approach to delivery, checking dilation, instructing first-time mothers, "turning" the fetus in complicated cases, perhaps "quilling" the mother by blowing a little dry snuff into her nostrils through a goose quill to bring on convulsive sneezing and the resulting final "push." Often neighboring women simply offered corn whiskey and a steady hand. Although folk practitioners did not effectively confront the problem of disease, with their understanding of the medical and emotional needs of women, "grannys" helped more than "regulars" in the most recurrent medical emergency in the countryside, the delivery bed.[15]

Sugar Creek mothers achieved their high total fertility despite a heavy toll in maternal, fetal, and infant mortality. Illinois kept no systematic statistics on mortality before the late nineteenth century, but available contemporary statistics suggest that for every thousand live births, five to ten mothers perished, a rate compatible with the incidence of death among women of childbearing age in Sugar Creek. These early female deaths were part of a general pattern of relatively high mortality. Women born before 1800, who bore most of their children in Kentucky or Tennessee before coming to Sugar Creek, died at an average age of sixty-seven. But younger emigrant mothers, those born between 1800 and 1840 who spent their childbearing years in Sugar Creek, died at a considerably lower average age of fifty. Male life expectancy fell also, from sixty-one years for men born before 1800, to forty-five for those born thereafter.[16]

HUSBAND GEORGE W. WALLACE (1832–?), WIFE CHARLOTTE DILNER WALLACE
(1837–62), AND DAUGHTER MAY E. WALLACE (1862–63). In the summer of 1862,
several weeks after this photograph was taken, Charlotte died, followed by
baby May six months later. "None but those who have lost companions, parents
or children, can appreciate these most valuable keepsakes," read the advertisement of a Springfield daguerrotypist in the *Daily State Register*. *"When we are in
life let us prepare for death."* George moved to Missouri, where he remarried.

Since genealogists ignored terminated pregnancies and even infant deaths in their family charts, there is no precise way of measuring infant and fetal mortality. But contemporary patterns suggest that at least 50 miscarriages and stillbirths and from 150 to 250 infant deaths occurred for every thousand live births. At the prevailing fertility rates, this would have meant that, on average, each Sugar Creek mother stood the risk of miscarrying once and losing one or two of the children she successfully delivered. In 1850 and 1860, when the Sangamon County census enumerators collected data on mortality, the death of children less than one year old accounted for nearly 20 percent of all deaths, and the death of children under five, for 45 to 50 percent. In the state of Massachusetts in 1865, by contrast, the death of children under five accounted for about one-third of the state's mortality. A doctor of Carlinville, Illinois, twenty-five miles south of Sugar Creek, estimated that in his district "nearly one half the children born die before reaching 5 years of age, and nearly one half of those deaths are from bowel troubles." One Sangamon mother expressed the losses of many:

Sleep, little baby sleep,
Not in thy mother's arms or cradle bed,
But in the grave forever with the dead.[17]

Yet despite these probable rates of infant mortality, less than 15 percent of first-generation Sugar Creek mothers raised fewer than five children. Perhaps the mortality was unevenly distributed, perhaps some women experienced systematic difficulties with pregnancy, or certain families lost large numbers of children in sweeping epidemics. But finally, these numbers suggest that, in the struggle between the forces of fertility and mortality, it was the impressive fecundity of Sugar Creek women that prevailed. In 1830, when 53 percent of the population of the creek was under the age of fifteen, the ratio of children to adult men and women (ages fifteen to fifty-nine) was 117 to 100, compared to a national ratio of just 89. Travelers frequently commented on the abundance of children in the backcountry. Traveling through central Illinois in the 1830s, Washington Irving scribbled in his journal: "Illinois—famous for children and dogs—in house with nineteen children and thirty-seven dogs." In Sugar Creek somewhat fewer people crowded into the average single-room dwellings: 7.1 in 1830, 6.8 in 1840. Apparently no one bothered to take a census of canines.[18]

11

Raising Hogs and Children

he whole stock of the first settlers generally consisted in their two hands," English immigrant and agricultural reformer Morris Birkbeck observed of his Illinois neighbors in 1817; "there is, properly speaking, no *capital* employed in agriculture." Thirteen years later Illinois editor James Hall admitted that "our husbandry is yet in a rude state." Most farmers farmed with simple, home-manufactured tools. "My father knew of every crooked root, and every stick of timber which could be fashioned into some tool or implement of use," William Riley McLaren remembered, "for everything from an ox-yoke to a hay or grain rake was made of wood and by hand." Well into the 1840s, according to Moses Wadsworth, Sugar Creek farmers continued to break timber soil with wooden plows, harrow fields with tree limbs, and thresh wheat by driving their horses over grain strewn on the barn's threshing floor. Inventories of farm property, included in the probate files of Sugar Creek farmers, show that before the 1850s, tools remained essentially unchanged from those of colonial times. Along with poor roads and resulting high farm-to-market costs, primitive hand tools restrained the commercial development of agriculture.[1]

But most agricultural reformers blamed the state of western agriculture on what they considered the backward attitudes of farmers. After a trip through central Illinois in the 1830s, Timothy Flint concluded that "agriculture improvement comes at a slow pace. The people are not given to experiments, they continue to farm in the beaten way." The Sangamo, wrote one northeastern emigrant to the creek, was "destitute of any energy or enterprise among the people, their labors and attention being chiefly confined to the hunting of game." Another Yankee complained that when the snow began to fall in December of 1830, inaugurating what was forever after remembered as the "Winter of the Deep Snow," "it found most of the corn standing on the stalks. The fall had been so warm and wet that the farmers had a better reason than common to indulge the careless habit of leaving their corn in the field, to be gathered in winter when they wanted it." One farmer, born in the 1820s near Drennan's Prairie, later condemned the "slovenly" practice of his neighbors, who left their cornstalks standing all winter, then fired their fields to clear them for plowing in the spring. Unbeknownst to this critic, or even to the farmers he criticized for that matter, this practice, long used by the Indians, helped to return essential nutrients to the overworked and undermanured soil. But lack of "enterprise," "slovenly" and "careless habits," and "the beaten way" seemed to account for the backwardness of western farming.[2]

Undoubtedly, many of these "common" farmers did think differently about the nature of their work than progressive "agriculturalists" did. "Moon farming," for example, was commonplace in the backcountry. Potatoes, radishes, turnips—all root crops, in fact—ought to be planted in "the dark of the moon," otherwise they would go to seed; it was believed that corn should be planted as the moon waxed full, for the "light of the moon" would spur the plant to greater growth. Girdling of trees was best accomplished during the new moon of August, as was the correct setting of fence posts. "The moon is a wonderful worker of miracles," wrote James Hall; "philosophers assign to her the regulation of tides, and rustics endow her with absolute supremacy over the land. No saint in the calendar was ever consulted so often, or with such entire faith. . . . By her changes all farming operations are regulated; seed is sown, fences are made, and children weaned, when the moon is propitious; and, by the same rule, I presume that a maiden who should be courted when the *sign was in the heart* would melt sooner than at any other period." Carl Sandburg, reflecting on his youth in rural Illinois, thought he understood the compelling power of such superstitions: "the worker on the land, who puts in crops and bets on the weather and gambles in seed corn and hazards his toil against so many whimsical, fateful conditions, has a pull on his heart to believe he can read luck signs, and tell good luck or bad luck to come, in dreams of his sleep at night, in changes of the moon, in the manners of chickens and dogs, in little seeming accidents that reveal the intentions and operations of forces beyond sight and smell."[3]

Reports that some farmers determined how much corn to plant

after estimating the quantity of the coming nut crop clashed with the value of accumulation in a capitalist culture. New Englander Christiana Tillson overheard one central Illinois farmer bragging about his "craps." "He was 'getting on right smart'; it had been a good mast year—an abundance of nuts—and his hogs had come out of the woods fat enough to kill. He thought by another winter he should be able to sit by the fire most of the time." "Poor child of nature," this Yankee lady mused, "your wants, how few." Local-color writer Francis Grierson, in a series of sketches of rural life in Macoupin County, just south of Sugar Creek, had old farmer Zach Caverly expound on this point:

> My old daddy larnt me to go through this sorrowin' vale like the varmints do—easy en nat'ral like, never gallopin' when ye kin lope, en never lopin' when ye kin lay down. It's a heap easier. Thar ain't a hog but knows he kin root fer a livin' if ye give him a fair show; thar ain't a squirrel but knows how te stow away 'nough te nibble on when he wakes up en finds his blood's kinder coolin' down en things is p'intin' te zero.
>
> Ez fer me, I kin shoot en trap all I kin eat, jes' plantin' 'nough corn fer hoe-cakes en a lettle fodder, en some taters en turnips en pum'kins; en I hev a sight more smoked venison en b'ar meat in winter than I kin eat ez a single man with on'y one stommick; en I 'low I kin give a traveller hoe-cakes en fried chicken all he wants to fill up on.

Dennis Hanks, a cousin of Lincoln's, told William Herndon that early Illinois farmers placed other priorities before the production and sale of farm commodities. "Every spare time we had," he wrote, "we picked up our rifle and brought in a fine deer or turkey." "I tell you, Billy," Hanks brooded, reflecting on the changes he had witnessed in the Illinois of the fifties and sixties, "I enjoyed myself better then, than I have ever since."[4]

Within the limits established by prevailing attitudes and available technology, a family—a farmer, his wife, and their half-grown children—on a modal eighty-acre Sugar Creek farm could achieve a subsistence living. In 1840 the livestock of an average Sangamon farmer included several score of hogs, a dozen head of cattle, oxen, and milch cows, a small flock of sheep, and assorted poultry. Families raised vegetables and root crops in their gardens, flax or cotton in the "patch," perhaps apples or peaches in a small orchard. Farmers "made a crop" on fifty or sixty enclosed acres, producing averages of 1,100 bushels of Indian corn, 150 bushels of oats, and 50 bushels of wheat—enough, as Hanks put it, "for a cake on Sunday morning." The existing state of the means of production limited capitalist agriculture but allowed most families to achieve a minimum of modest sufficiency, so farmers directed their energies to production for domestic use, placing the security of their families first.[5]

That commitment of energy took its toll. Men's hands hardened from gripping plow handles, their legs bowed from tramping over the clods turned up by the plowshare; women's hands cracked, bled, and developed corns from the hard water of the family wash, their knees grew knobby from years of kneeling to grit corn or scrub puncheon floors. "We had to work very hard clearing ground for to keep soul and body to-gether," remembered Hanks. Yet an English immigrant living south of Sugar Creek wrote his brother in 1841 that "an industrious family," through such labor, could provide nearly all its own food and fodder, and he praised the settlers' ability to "manufacture most of their own clothing, soap, candles, and sometimes sugar."[6]

This labor nearly all came from within the family. Since land was available and free for the using, few men were willing to work as wage laborers. Only a small number of families could afford the cost of a hired hand anyway. "Labour is scarce and highly remunerated," wrote Patrick Shirreff, an English traveler through the Sangamo in 1835; "in a country where Nature is so bountiful and land so abundant and cheap, the wages of labour must necessarily be high." So farming required families. Seven in ten of the young county men who married in 1829 appeared as independent heads of household on the federal census of the next year; eight in ten of the young men who would marry in 1831, on the other hand, were still listed as dependents in their parents' homes on the census roll of 1830. In June 1853, an eighteen-year-old Sugar Creek lad left home on his own, and a few days later his father published a notice in the Springfield papers: "RUNAWAY, my son, Micajah Shutt. I hereby notify all persons against harboring or trusting him on my account as I will not be responsible for any debts of his contracting." Most men lived in the households of their parents until they married, because until they married most men could not muster the labor necessary to begin farms of their own.[7]

Lucinda Casteen emigrated to central Illinois with her husband and children in 1831, accompanied by her unmarried brother, Isham, who farmed an adjoining claim. In letters home to her mother, Lucinda regularly worried about Isham: she rarely saw him, he worked too hard, was too single-mindedly ambitious, and drank too much. But it was his unmarried state that most troubled his sister. How could he manage, Lucinda wondered, without a wife? Isham had "come so well provided in cloths" that he was not yet wanting for weaving; Lucinda herself had somehow found the time amid her busy rounds to make him a suit of jane, and did all his sewing and mending. Isham hired a woman from the neighborhood to do his washing for two bits a month, and "he expects his neighbor's wife to milk for him." "He gets it all tolerably well done," she wrote, yet it was troubling, her brother living alone like that. Isham needed a wife, and when he married in 1838, Lucinda rejoiced in spite of her jealousy over her new sister-in-law's monopoly of her brother's time.[8]

As Timothy Flint wrote in the mid-twenties, "a vigorous and active young man needs but two years of personal labour to have a farm ready for the support of a small family." "It will be to your interest to come or go where you can have a home of your own," Lucinda Casteen counseled her younger sister, still in Kentucky; "but never give your hand or heart to a lasy [sic] man." Marriage created new farm households, and each new household created a new workplace. If high levels of fertility constituted the first traditional feature of family life in Sugar Creek, the intimate and direct connection between the reproductive and productive lives of farm families constituted the second. The times yoked childbearing and work together.[9]

The demand for farm labor helps to account for fertility patterns, for large families were a distinct advantage in the struggle to win a living from the land. Since there was no certain supply of labor outside the family, wrote one midwesterner, "the rule was, that whoever had the strength to work, took hold and helped." Children were an economic necessity, and choices about fertility could not be divorced from the requirements of production. "In this fine country, which literally flows with milk and honey," a traveler commented, "man is the only growth that's wanted"; settlers were taking care of that problem, for "every log Cabin is swarming with half-naked children. Boys of 18 build huts, marry, and raise hogs and children at about the same expense."[10]

Children contributed their full share to this domestic economy. "The first day of March found every able-bodied boy back on the farm whether school was out or not," one settler recalled. "School was a mere incident of minor importance, while 'the call of the wild' or 'back to the farm' was imperative. There were rails to make, fences to build, grubbing to do, lands to clear, and the thousand and one other things to do, to prepare the land for a crop." Boys mucked out barns, made hay, cleared and gleaned fields, hoed, husked, and plowed, so that by the ages of ten or twelve they had assumed most of the working responsibilities of full-grown men. Daughters learned the many small tasks connected with the preparation of yarn and cloth, as well as the finer arts of the needle and, by following mothers through their endless round of chores, quickly learned women's work. Lucinda Casteen wrote her mother that "our [s]chool at home"—the chores and housework that her girls had to perform to keep the place running—absorbed all her daughters' time and kept them from "ABC school." "I fear we can't go on regular," she despaired, "but I think of sparing them 4 hours a day if possible."[11]

The work of children was important, but it was the work of farm wives that made the difference between the success or failure of productive strategies. Besides bearing and caring for a large family of children, besides preparing at least three large meals every day, besides cleaning, washing, ironing, and mending, women produced an abundance of goods without which a family found it hard to survive. In gardens they raised sweet corn, pumpkins, beans, and potatoes, as well as a wide variety of green vegetables, medicinal herbs, flax, and even cotton. Through long evenings they carded, worked at omnipresent spinning wheels, wove cloth, and tailored garments for the family. In henhouse or farmyard they tended flocks of chickens and geese, collected eggs, set hens, plucked down, and strangled roosters for the pot. In the dairy they fed and milked cows, and later, on porch or in pantry, they churned butter and sometimes made cheese. Farm wives produced towels, blankets, and quilts, as well as pickles, cider, dried fruit, soap, candles, and nearly every other thing that made the difference between a hovel and a home.

Wives frequently assisted men in the fields as well. "The farmer himself and one or two big boys made up the laboring strength of the farm," wrote one midwesterner; but he readily acknowledged that under the press of weather or season "the wife or older daughter would be called on to help, and sometimes they would assist in planting and hoeing the corn, raking the grain or hay in harvest." In a typical case of cooperation, Mary and David McCoy, young Sugar Creek emigrants of the 1820s, plowed their fields together—he pushing the plow, she driving the oxen, as their firstborn slept in a box strapped to the plow beam. When illness or accident disabled farmers, farm women picked up the burden of field work that could not wait. Nor did convention restrict a girl's work to the household and barnyard. "In the planting of corn, which was always done by hand," wrote a local resident, "the girls always took a part, usually dropping the corn, but many of them covering with the hand-hoe." In the springtime, on many farms, "the father would take his post at the plow, and the daughter possession of the reins." Folk beliefs that certain crops benefited from cooperative planting by men and women suggest the importance of joint farm work. Certain superstitious farmers sowed flax seed by throwing it against the backsides of wives who walked ahead with their skirts jacked up, and folklorists of the Ozarks have reported a similar custom of the flax patch, in which husband and wife worked the field together stark naked while chanting the line "Up to my ass, an' higher too!"[12]

But farmers could not exist entirely outside the market. Every farm family needed salt, gunpowder, and iron, and desired rope, harness, crockery, coffee, and other manufactured commodities; the proprietors of small country stores set up to meet this demand. In 1819, a young Massachusetts emigrant took over a cabin near the junction of Lick and Sugar creeks and began supplying families along the creek with farm essentials, patent medicines, and locally produced whiskey, a large stock of which he regarded as "indispensable" to conducting a good business. Traveling peddlers from New England, their wagons loaded with notions, began to cover central Illinois almost as soon as the settlers arrived. In 1833, for example, Ezra Barnes left Hartford, Connecticut, headed for the Illinois country with a wagonload of clocks and other manufactured goods, and by November was selling his wares to farm wives along Sugar Creek. After two years of making friends in the Sangamon, he bought land, married a local girl, and began farming along the creek; but other peddlers took his place.[13]

Sugar Creek families before the late 1840s were able to produce a reasonable level of subsistence, but they had a harder time generating the income needed to pay for manufactured commodities. There was a steady, if small, "newcomer's market," for few emigrants brought all they needed from home. Corn for the first winter, livestock, and hay might all be sold to new settlers, although given the scarcity of hard currency, these goods were more often bartered than sold for cash.

Markets outside the local community promised more, but before the 1840s the promise was greater than the reality. The county seat of Springfield, better than fifteen muddy miles north over tracks that could only euphemistically be called roads, included fewer than a thousand persons in 1830. By 1840, the town's population had grown to over twenty-five hundred, partly as a result of the decision of the Illinois legislature to relocate the state capital there, a move completed in 1839. This growth had considerable effects on Springfield's surrounding countryside, and farmers along the nearby creeks shifted their production to marketable garden vegetables, dairy products, and meat to feed the hungry politicians and bureaucrats. The neighborhoods of Sugar Creek, however, were too far removed to participate very much in this local market. Although some town merchants collected "country produce" and shipped it to Beardstown on the Illinois River in the summer, or Alton on the Mississippi in winter, Springfield's lack of access to navigable waters offered few opportunities for export before the coming of the railroad in the 1850s.[14]

The stories told by settlers of their attempts to market their small "surplus" in Springfield were intended to illustrate their failure. Because of its bulk, corn was never a market crop. When prices reached a peak in 1836, one local farmer hired a wagon to haul twenty bushels to the Springfield market; but the best price he could get, five cents per bushel, did not even cover the cost of hauling. Another man, anxious to raise cash to finance a move north, found it impossible to sell his corn crop at any price so bartered it for a barrel of whiskey, swapped the whiskey for a steer, and finally sold the steer for ten dollars. Barter remained the preferred way of doing business in Springfield before the late-1840s.[15]

Corn usually found its way to market as whiskey or pork. Farmers sometimes loaded a Sangamon flatboat with barreled pork and floated down to St. Louis or even New Orleans, but although such trips frequently produced high times in these wide-open market cities, they generated little profit. Men occasionally drove hogs to market. When the weather turned cold enough to make pork-packing safe from rot and disease, a dozen or so farmers might combine their energies, each slitting the ears of his animals in a distinctive fashion so he could identify them, then setting out together down "the trace" to Alton. But there were risks in hog drives. In December 1836, an enterprising local miller bought up more than a thousand hogs from Sugar Creek farms and drove them down the road to American Bottom. Twenty miles south of the Creek a sudden drastic drop in temperature caught him and his men, threatening them with killing cold. As they raced in panic for the shelter of a nearby cabin, their hogs began desperately to pile up on each other for warmth. Those on the inside smothered, those on the outside froze, creating a monumental pyramid of ham, frozen on the hoof. The marketing experiment was a dead loss and the miller financially destroyed.[16]

Not all commercial failures were so dramatic. Captain Job Fletcher and his neighbor Eddin Lewis arranged to have several wagonloads of smoked hams and shoulders transported to St. Louis, but their agent found barreled pork rotting on the Mississippi wharves, and the sale brought only $1.80 a hundred. After paying freight charges, their net differed little from the price paid in nearby Springfield, where a merchant took William Lockridge's pork at $1.25 in 1836 but forced the farmer to accept half his return in store goods at premium retail prices. Wheat was "the only thing," one contemporary observer reported, "that can be relied upon by the farmer to procure the necessary cash." But locally it brought the poor price of twenty to thirty cents per bushel, so farmers sometimes drove their wagons the three-week round trip to American Bottom, selling directly to grain dealers at twenty-five to forty cents. Unless they could find goods to freight back in their otherwise empty wagons, however, transport costs could easily eat up that small price advantage. One farmer remembered that during his first summer near Sugar Creek he worked to raise a crop of oats, hauled his bushels to Springfield, and returned with eight yards of calico cloth to show for his annual "surplus."[17]

Farm wives seemed to have less difficulty finding a ready market for their surplus production of butter, eggs, and homespun, although these commodities, too, brought miserably low prices. In 1850, when the federal census for the first time collected precise production statistics, Sugar Creek women produced over twenty-six thousands pounds of butter, an average of nearly 180 pounds per household, a rate of production that was low compared to the "butter belts" around eastern cities but still impressive considering that such a quantity over the course of a year required each farm wife to milk at least five cows twice a day, in addition to making the butter itself. One woman remembered "selling butter at 5 cts per lb., and that churned in a bowl, with a spoon, as a churn was not to be found." Other women used the dasher-churns frequently itemized in estate inventories. Because not every family produced its own butter, a local market existed for the fresh product, and women preserved the surplus in brine, trading it with local merchants, who shipped it to St. Louis, Chicago, or Detroit.[18]

Households consumed most of their homespun, just as they consumed most of their butter. "We raised cotton, picked it out of the burr, then picked the seeds out with our fingers, then card & spin it, then wove it into cloth making gingham dress goods (of which it took about four yds to make a dress), bed spreds, etc.," Sugar Creek settler Ann McCormick remembered. "We raised flax, making table linen, sheeting, toweling, etc. From wool we carded, spun & wove blankets, civerlids & counterpins, flanels, linsey & janes, doing our coulering with barks from trees & roots, making lovely checks & plads." "I made everything that we wore," wrote Charlotte Webb Jacobs; "I even made my towels and table cloths, sheets and everything in the clothing line." A regular-sized family demanded a considerable amount of textile work. In 1834 Lucinda Casteen wrote to her mother that "I have had 57 yard of cloth wove this winter, & spring been making the childrens summer cloths," and Lucy Maynard complained in 1844 that illness had limited her winter production to "20 or 25 yards of tow and linen."[19]

But a vigorous local trade existed in homespun. When she moved to the Sugar Creek area with her husband and four children in1825, Charlotte Jacobs remembered that "I brought with me three cows, and my husband brought five hounds," but they were without pigs. "The first hogs we had," she reported, "I bought twelve shoats, and paid for them with linsey and jeans of my own make." In other reminiscences women reported weaving hundreds of yards of cloth for trade. At the general store in Springfield in the 1820s, women's commodities figured prominently as items of trade; homespun jean, linen, and cotton cloth were the fabrics most commonly accepted for store goods, with beeswax, honey, and butter next in importance. Storekeepers also traded in wild herbs. In the 1820s and 1830s, Mahala and Sarah Earnest dug ginseng in the timber with which to barter; over the years the insatiable demand for "seng," which many considered an aphrodisiac, nearly wiped the plant from the local flora. As farmers concentrated their attention on the hunt, most farm wives handled the family trading for "boughten goods."[20]

There is no precise way to measure the relative contributions of men and women to the surplus production of the family farm. Even from this distance, however, the mutual dependence of the farmer and his helpmate seems clear, for butter, cloth, and other women's goods, as well as field crops, measurably added to the ability of families not only to practice self-sufficiency but to enter the market. Moreover, many families required income to make payments on their land and to invest in seed, livestock, or tools. Industrious farmers sold not only field crops but furs, fence rails, and whiskey; they toiled as day laborers in the fields of well-to-do neighbors and sweated during hard winters in the lead mines of Galena, in northern Illinois, all in an effort to raise the money needed to buy land. The greater the surplus that women could introduce into the market for household and farm necessities, the more men could dedicate their surplus labor to investment.

The labor of some women contributed more directly to the process of accumulation, just as Charlotte Jacob's homespun helped to stock her family farm with hogs. In the 1830s, one wife produced butter that her husband hauled all the way to Chicago, where he purchased farm equipment with the proceeds. Phoebe Russell Twist, from Seneca Falls, New York, used her talents to make cheeses that her husband regularly carted to St. Louis, saving the earnings until they had raised enough to buy their first eighty acres. Since few women from the upland South made cheese, Phoebe may have sold some of her cheddars locally; she must have accumulated some savings, for in 1833 she bought sixty-six acres of timberland in her own name. Accumulation may have taken second place to consumption, but western families placed a high priority on purchasing the land they worked, and success in this pursuit, like success in self-sufficiency, depended upon the contributions of both sexes.[21]

But mutuality, so necessary in production, did not extend to the ownership of farms. Men constituted 93 percent of Sugar Creek owners on the county tax lists of the mid-1830s and nearly 99 percent of the owners identified on the first published county plat map of 1858. From 1823, when Sangamo lands first came on the market, to the

1850s, when the last quarter-sections passed into private ownership, men composed 98 percent of the over twenty-six hundred individuals who filed federal land claims. In Sugar Creek, as elsewhere, men and women jointly worked farms, but it was the men who owned farm property.[22]

Women labored under legal disability, for by the laws of Illinois, in accord with the English common-law doctrine of coverture, a married women lost the rights she enjoyed as a single woman (a *femme sole*) to own or manage chattel or real property, or to enter into contracts without a cosignature. A husband gained the rights to manage estates brought into the marriage by his wife and, upon the birth of a child, to will any such property to *his* heirs as he saw fit (another legal principle known as curtesy). In the words of Sir William Blackstone, whose eighteenth-century *Commentaries on the Laws of England* became the standard guide to the common law for the American bar, "by marriage, the husband and wife are one person in law; that is, the very being or legal existence of the woman is suspended during the marriage, or at least is incorporated and consolidated into that of the husband; under whose wing, protection, and cover, she performs every thing." In 1836, first-term legislator Abraham Lincoln made a back-handed statement of this principle when he declared that "I go for all sharing the privileges of the government who assist in bearing its burdens. Consequently, I go for admitting all whites to the right of suffrage who pay taxes or bear arms (by no means excluding females)." Some have quoted this statement to applaud Lincoln's "advanced views" on the "woman question," but surely he was commenting tongue-in-cheek, for at the time women neither paid taxes *nor* bore arms—their husbands did. Illinois laws for women changed little before the passage of married women's property acts in the 1860s.[23]

Although a woman could legally avoid certain *femme covert* disabilities by arranging a prenuptial contract with her fiancé, spelling out her rights to specific property, practically speaking, only urban, upper-class families exercised this option for their daughters. Provisions that allowed for the management and ownership of property by widows were the only real exceptions to the legal dispossession of Sugar Creek women. In their wills, husbands with minor children generally left their wives in charge of the property of the estate to manage in the best interests of the family. "Be it known," began one will of 1841, "that I Elijah West of Sangamon County, and State of Illinois, being in Ill health, but of Sound mind & Memory, do make and declare this to be my will. . . . My estate, both Real & personal to belong to my wife Elizabeth West for the Term of Ten years, the proceeds of which to be used for the common Education & maintenance of my children." As he lay dying a decade later, Alexander Cassity declared before witnesses:

"I give and bequeath to my beloved wife Elizabeth all the premises on which I now reside for her use and those of the family that may reside with her until the youngest child becomes of age."[24]

Because of the high mortality of adult men and women, the death of a spouse terminated most marriages before the children reached majority. Since men remarried at a rate better than twice that of women, widows headed more households in the community than widowers; in 1830, widows were directing nearly 5 percent of Sugar Creek farms, and that proportion doubled in the 1840s and 1850s, as the mortality of the first generation, and the greater life expectancy of women, created an even larger group.

Most Sugar Creek husbands died intestate; although few left wills, the law protected widows by exempting enough estate property from debt execution to allow the widow to carry on with the management of the household. Every widow had rights to her "dower," a minimum of a one-third interest in the real and personal property of the estate. Moreover, to protect widows with estates so small that even a one-third interest would not be sufficient for the widow's and family's support, the law provided that courts set aside necessary household goods and utensils; beds and bedding for all in the family; cards, spinning wheel, and loom; one horse, two milch cows, and two calves; a year's supply of fuel, food, fiber, and fodder; as well as the residence of the dwelling house and the use of the farm property for the term of the children's minority.[25]

"It has pleased God in his providense to take my kind companion from me again and leave me to widow in this world of trouble with my litel boy, and I feel my loss very sore," Nancy Moore wrote her grown children after the death of her second husband. But widows may have found some solace in utilizing the legal provisions that allowed them to take over the management of the family farm. In 1830, for example, James Fletcher died intestate just several weeks after emigrating; a local justice of the peace appointed his widow, Jane McElvain Fletcher, administrix of the estate, setting aside the traditional goods as her separate allowance. Then, at the estate sale held to settle James's debts of $111, Jane purchased seventy-five-dollars'-worth of farm equipment and livestock, including hogs, sheep, and cattle, plow, chains, harnesses, and a set of tools. Widow Fletcher continued the operation of the farm until her death twenty-three years later. Her experience was common for Sugar Creek widows: they might not own the family property, but during widowhood they might independently manage it. In Sugar Creek, about 10 to 15 percent of women who married outlived their husbands and managed farms under their own names.[26]

Widows' management of estates and farms and the possession of dower shares, however, were only "life interests"; once the children reached majority, they received partitions of the family estate, and even after partition widows could not sell or otherwise alienate the remaining dower property, for upon their deaths it reverted to its legal heirs, the children. In 1847, the circuit court supervised the partition of James Fletcher's estate into equal shares for his adult children, and Jane agreed to take "as my dower" a portion of the property, as well as the house, where she continued to reside and farm with several unmarried offspring. Upon her death six years later, the probate court disbursed her interest in the dwelling-house, the farm she had managed, and her portion of the partitioned property to her children, under the terms of her husband's probated estate.

A small number of widows accumulated property of their own; widows, for example, filed nine out of ten of the federal land claims entered by women. John Burch came to reconnoiter central Illinois in 1828 and, liking what he found, returned to Kentucky to move his family, but fell ill and died. His widow, Elizabeth, led the move of her six children, including two married daughters and their husbands, and in 1830 filed on 640 acres where she lived and farmed, in close association with her children, for the next thirty years. Other women lost their husbands after the family had squatted on a parcel but before they made their formal claim. John and Lucinda Wilcox moved to Sugar Creek with their eleven children, daughters- and sons-in-law, and grandchildren in 1819; but he died in 1823 before land came on the market, so she filed a claim for eighty acres near the farms of her sons in 1825. Other widows filed on land to add to claims that their husbands had made before their deaths. Jane Fletcher purchased eighty acres after the death of her husband in 1830, but only as a surrogate for her deceased spouse.[27]

The relative freedom of action granted to widows was denied to married women. When Sugar Creek fathers left wills, they generally made a distinction between property granted to sons and to daughters. After providing for his wife's dower in his will of 1847, William McElvain, Jane Fletcher's brother, wrote:

> I give or will to my sons William & James each of them a third of my timber lot of land or the sixty-nine acres of land which contains my timber and the remainder of said timbered land to be equally devided between my Sons after their mothers death. I will to my daughter Terrese Maria the horse Bridle that I have given to her, one Bed & bedding & bedstead, one Buerow worth twenty five dollars, one good cow & calf four sheep & one set of winser chairs. I will that the ballance of my personal property that I have not herin disposed of to be equally divided between my children & after the natural death of my dear wife Penelope I will that the

tract of land Upon which my house stands shall be sold & divided equally between my children.

McElvain's concern that his sons gain immediate possession of some of the productive property, and his bequest of personal property to his daughter, typified the provisions of Sugar Creek wills.[28]

For daughters whose fathers died intestate, the law declared that estates be divided equally among all children, regardless of sex. Women's inherited property, however, was immediately transferred to their husband's names, or was upon their marriage; so although numbers of women gained real property in the partition of estates, they almost never appeared in the records as legal owners. Occasionally, a father who disapproved of his son-in-law would subvert this feature of the law, as did Elijah West, who wrote in his will that "at the end of ten years, or the marriage of my wife, I hereby direct my Executors to sell the whole of my then estate and divide it equally between my children, except Mehaly M. Smith, her portion of my estate to be given to her children and not to be given to her husband Davidson Smith under any circumstances." Even here, however, the property went into trust for her children, not to Mahala Smith herself.[29]

Despite their labor in household and field, and despite their contribution to accumulation, law and custom systematically excluded women from ownership. "The advantage is greatly in favour of the back settler in America," wrote traveler Elias Fordham; "his table is profusely furnished, if he choose, with delicacies. He is lord of the soil he cultivates." Those who set the table, however, were neither lords nor ladies, but tenants of the hearth.[30]

12

She Drained Herself
to Give Them Life

F ew Sangamon settlers left us their impressions of the condition of farm women. But it is possible to extrapolate from available sources. In the three divorce cases involving Sugar Creek folk, for example, there are suggestions about the structure of popular belief. Elijah A. West's charges against Elizabeth Marx were creditable because she was a widow, a woman with a certain freedom of action. On the court circuit, away from home for weeks at a time, lawyers and judges such as David Davis had plenty of opportunities to learn about what William Herndon called the "cheerful, rollicking, daring, reckless gals" who broke "all rules of propriety" and helped lonely men to pass the time. Contrasting with this view of woman was the image that emerges from the divorce petitions of the women. Judge Logan had no difficulty in accepting Elizabeth Drennan's claim that her husband threatened her physical safety, or that he so "wantonly" destroyed property, goods, and income through his drinking that she had "no encouragement to labor" for her own support. Nor did Judge Davis doubt Mary Ann Pulliam's claim that she would have been left "entirely destitute of both food and shelter" had it not been for the intervention of "a kind father." In contrast to West's, the women's petitions partake of a common view of women dependent upon the will and whim of men.[1]

The testimonies of visitors to central Illinois in the years before the Civil War offer a more direct and forceful assessment of farm women. The most articulate of these observers was Frances Trollope, a remarkable Englishwoman who lived for several years during the late 1820s and early 1830s in the frontier town of Cincinnati. Western women married "too young," she believed, and early, frequent pregnancy aged them prematurely.

> It is rare to see a woman in this station who has reached the age of thirty, without losing every trace of youth and beauty. You continually see women with infants on their knee, that you feel sure are their grand-children, till some convincing proof of the contrary is displayed. Even the young girls, though often with lovely features, look pale, thin, and haggard. I do not remember to have seen in any single instance among the poor, a specimen of the plump, rosy, laughing physiognomy so common among our cottage girls.

Mrs. Trollope may have exaggerated the health and contentment of English lasses, but James Fenimore Cooper, after several years abroad, where women commonly married in their mid- to late twenties, concurred that "these early marriages, which are the fruits of abundance, have an obvious tendency to impair the powers of the female, and to produce a premature decay."[2]

Trollope's book on American manners sold well in America, although her comments provoked hostile reactions from Americans, who have never taken well to foreign criticism. But, as Mark Twain observed later in the century, on most matters Trollope simply told the truth. She wrote of her shock at the enormity of the workload reported by a backwoods wife: she "spun and wove all the cotton and woolen garments of the family, and knit all the stockings. . . . She manufactured all the soap and candles they used, and prepared her sugar from the sugar-trees on their farm. All she wanted with money, she said, was to buy coffee, tea, and whiskey, and she could 'get enough any day by sending a batch of butter and chicken to market.'" "The life she leads," Trollope concluded of the western woman, "is one of hardship, privation, and labour." Margaret Fuller, touring Illinois in the early 1840s, agreed that women's work was "disporportioned to their strength, if not to their patience." And Sangamon emigrant Charles Clarke wrote home to New England that "a man can get corn and pork enough to last his family a fortnight for a single day's work, while a woman must keep scrubbing from morning till night the same in this country as in any other."[3]

Trollope admired the proud independence of farm women but was disturbed by the "wild and lonely situation" in which they found themselves. She and others condemned the open-country pattern of western settlement that prevented women from visiting friends or neighbors, and she viewed their isolation as a major disability. Harriet

Martineau, another famous English visitor, watched a lone woman paddling a canoe against the swift current of the mighty Mississippi, probably, she wrote tongue-in-cheek, "to visit a neighbour twenty or thirty miles off. The only comfort was that the current would bring her back four times as quickly as she went up." In Sugar Creek, neighbors often lived miles apart; Mary Jane Drennan Hazlett recalled that, "although the people were sparsely settled we would visit ten or fifteen miles distant and call them neighbors." But distance and the responsibilities of work on the farm kept women at home most of the time. Trollope's backwoods farm wife, "in somewhat a mournful accent," told the visitor " 'tis strange to us to see company: I expect the sun may rise and set a hundred times before I shall see another *human* that does not belong to the family," and a central Illinois pioneer woman wrote that "three visits were all that I made out of our own neighborhood for the first four-and-a-half years."[4]

Isolation robbed women of the company and companionship of female peers. Most young women moved directly from their parents' to their husbands' houses, where they assumed heavy responsibilities at a young age. The absence of a period of semi-independence, when young women might build relationships with each other before the pressures of marriage began, contributed to a pattern of female dependency. This was Mrs. Trollope's most telling criticism. "In no rank of life," she wrote, "do you meet with young women in that delightful period of existence between childhood and marriage, wherein, if only tolerably well spent, so much useful information is gained, and the character takes a sufficient degree of firmness to support with dignity the more important parts of wife and mother. The slender, childish thing, without vigour of mind or body, is made to stem a sea of troubles that dims her young eye and makes her cheek grow pale, even before nature has given it the last beautiful finish of the full-grown woman." Harriet Martineau believed that in rural America "every woman is married before she well knows how serious a matter human life is," with the consequence that wives were lacking in strong intellectual and moral character. "It is unquestioned and unquestionable," she concluded, "that if women were not weak, men could not be wicked."[5]

Some wicked men took advantage of the female vulnerability created by the social system. In April 1831, before a Sangamon County justice of the peace, Sally Marshal, a mother of three in her midtwenties, signed a complaint "that Thomas S. Edwards did on the night of the Second instant enter the dwelling of John Marshal and commence a conversation to his wife in Substance this—that he would do as he pleased with her and Edwards did thow [*sic*] his cloak down on the flour [*sic*] and said he would thow her down there and would fuck her (that is would have carnal knowledge of her) and her Husband should stand and see it." Crimes of rape appeared very rarely in the court record, but Mrs. Trollope believed that in western towns it was "unsafe," indeed "impossible," "for any woman to appear in the streets after *sun down* without a protector."[6]

Trollope may have exaggerated, but Christiana Tillson, a New Englander who moved to central Illinois with her husband, where she practiced the arts of housewifery, encountered a good deal of prejudice against women among her neighboring farmers in central Illinois. One told her that he distrusted women who could read because "women had no business to hurtle away their time, case they could allus find something to du, and there had been a heap of trouble in old Kaintuck with some rich men's gals that had learned to write. They was sent to school, and were high larnt, and cud write letters almost as well as a man, and would write to the young fellows, and bless your soul, get a match fixed up before their father or mother knowed a hait about it." "Such was the standard of at least nine-tenths of the inhabitants that were our neighbors," Tillson concluded. John Reynolds, despite his enlightened support of education, believed that books might "sow the seeds of passion in the breast of a tender, kind-hearted, and hitherto honest girl." Tillson also saw husbands getting their way by bullying, blustering, and generally terrorizing their wives. "The poor wife would shrink down when the blast was heaviest, but after he had gone would brighten up again." "If they had slaves," Tillson wrote of these farmers, "the authority was exercised over them; if not, the wife was the willing slave; perhaps not so much from fear as from want of knowing anything to assert." Mrs. Trollope doubted if the American farmer was any better off than an English peasant but was certain that the life "of his wife and daughter is incomparably worse. It is they who are indeed the slaves of the soil"[7]

The contrast between the successive Indian and American communities of the Sangamo offers a revealing cross-cultural perspective on the relationship between farm men and women. Americans often took the important role of Indian women in production as an indication of their exploited status. "The women do all the work," an early French explorer observed of the Kickapoo, while the men's "entire occupation is hunting and dress." Indian women usually rose before the men to gather wood, start the fire, and get breakfast cooking. When not otherwise occupied, men tended to loll about the village, but women always seemed to have work to do. Among the Kickapoo "the females do all the work," John Reynolds echoed a century later, "while their lords take their ease in smoking. The whole Indian race of the males is grave, sedate, and lazy." Thomas Jefferson spoke for the main current of informed American opinion in 1782 when he wrote that Indian women "are submitted to unjust drudgery. This I believe is the case with every barbarous people. With such, force is law. The stronger sex imposes on the weaker. It is civilization alone which replaces the women in the enjoyment of their natural equality."[8]

These criticisms bore a striking similarity to those leveled at the settlers themselves by foreign observers. Mrs. Trollope harshly criticized men who met, drank, and played together, leaving their country women back at the cabins with "the sordid offices of household drudgery." Traveling through Illinois, several Englishmen came upon an isolated cabin in the woods, with garden and livestock well tended, cabin neatly arranged and larder full, a "respectable-looking female spinning under the little piazza at one side," while her husband was off with his hound for several weeks of hunting bear in the woods. She was overcome with the "lone," she said, and begged them to visit awhile.[9]

The criticism leveled against the men of both societies contained some elements of truth. Among the twentieth-century Mexican Kickapoo, where essentially the same division of labor continued from the prairie days, women complained to anthropologists of overwork and of the laziness of their men. American women frequently lamented their condition, too. On their way to Illinois in the 1820s, Sarah Worthington and her husband met a man full of praise for the new country, and Sarah asked him about the availability of schools, the nearness of neighbors—in short, the conditions for women there. "Oh," he replied, the country "is heaven for men and horses, but a very different place for women and oxen." His answer "took too deep a hold ever to be forgotten," she wrote. "I know that man was very glad that *he* was a man; I am not so sure that *I* was glad that I was a woman."[10]

Yet important differences existed between the lives of Indian and American women. In contrast to American frontier mothers, Kickapoo women rarely bore more than four children, holding down their fertility by long periods of sexual abstinence, prolonged nursing, herbal remedies for contraception and abortion, and, occasionally, infanticide, a reminder that the number of children women bear is not a natural but a cultural statistic. It is, moreover, a demonstrable fact that the historic transition from foraging to agricultural society not only involved considerable growth in population but, as a means to such growth, the establishment of social controls over women's sexuality and reproductive decision-making; the suppression of the means of fertility limitation made possible the rapid rise in population associated with agriculture. Indeed, European men frequently viewed high fertility as a key to social success in agricultural society. As one New Englander argued in the seventeenth century, he and his countrymen enjoyed a biological edge over native peoples through their capacity "to beget and bring forth more children than any other nation in the world."[11]

Like farm women, Kickapoo wives played central roles in food production, but, again in contrast, Kickapoo women controlled the conditions and products of their own work and the distribution of food to the lineage. "It is a maxim among the Indians," Illinois Indian trader Thomas Forsyth wrote in the 1820s, "that every thing belongs to the woman or women except the Indian's hunting and war implements, even the game the Indian brings home on his back. As soon as it enters the lodge, the man ceases to have anything to say in its disposal." Moreover, because of the sedentary nature of their work, Kickapoo women, like the women of many horticultural North American Indian societies, built and owned their own houses. In keeping with this tradition, the Kickapoo practiced matrilocality; when a couple first married, they lived in the lodge of the bride's family, and after the birth of the first or second child the new mother built her own house near the compound of the grandmother. The realities of power for women provided fertile soil in which the Kickapoo ideal of sexual reciprocity might flourish.[12]

Americans, on the other hand, held a belief about the gender division of labor that was only superficially similar to the reciprocal ideal of the Kickapoo: in marriage, men and women practiced an exchange in which wives worked as the "helpmates" of their husbands. The Anglo-American tradition partook of a long-standing belief in marriage as an economic relationship; as Benjamin Wadsworth wrote in New England in the early eighteenth century, husband and wife should "unite their prudent counsels and endeavors, comfortably to maintain themselves and the Family under their joint care." But nonetheless, Wadsworth continued, "the Husband is ever to be esteem'd the Superior, the Head, and to be reverenc'd and obey'd as such." A century and a half later, Elizabeth Ellet wrote that one woman pioneer "had the appearance and used the language of independence, hautiness and authority"; yet, Ellet continued, "it could be said of her without any question that she 'reverenced her husband.'" By law and custom, the patriarchal authority of a husband controlled American woman, and only his good will, or her nearby protective kin, were guarantors of justice.[13]

The Kickapoo practice of gender reciprocity differed precisely in its guarantees to women. An Indian woman with complaints about overwork had recourse to options not open to an American wife. With her economic and residential independence, she could easily divorce a lazy or a mean man; and divorce, in which a man returned to his mother's house, occurred with regularity. Anthropologists who have studied the contemporary Kickapoo report that marriage continues to be a rather brittle institution among them, that consanguine relations are much stronger than affinal ones, and that within the lineage and household, the aged matron is the most revered figure in the society.[14]

At Fourth of July celebrations in the newly founded county seat of Springfield in the early 1820s, the assembled householders raised their cups to the last of a series of political toasts: "To the Fair of Illinois— May housewifery and proper economy ever be their delight. . . . May they adorn their minds with useful knowledge, and their bodies with the fruits of their own industry." Like toasts delivered earlier in the evening addressed to republicanism or to President Adams, these sentiments expressed political convictions. In the countryside, where relations among family members constituted the productive relations of farming as well, the stability of the social order depended upon the orderly regulation of the sexual division of labor. The exclusion of Sugar Creek women from property ownership was no more accidental than were the high levels of fertility.[15]

To be sure, women had a strong place within the social system of the West, a place with power enough to permit them to act as something more than victims. Women's relations with men often took on an assertive quality. The novelist Caroline Kirkland drew this vignette of an exchange between a frontier wife and her husband, after he had entertained cronies in the parlor, where their boots ground farmyard muck into the rag carpet.

> "What time are you going to have dinner, my dear?" says the imperturbable Philo, who is getting ready to go out.
> "Dinner! I'm sure I don't know! There's no time to cook dinner in this house! Nothing but slave, slave, slave, from morning till night, cleaning up after a set of nasty, dirty," &c., &c.
> "Phew!" says Mr. Doubleday, looking at his fuming helpmate with a calm smile, "it'll all rub out when it's dry, if you'll only let it alone."
> "Yes, yes; and it would be plenty clean enough for you if there had been forty horses in here."

Francis Grierson told a story of Jack Haywood, a widower who successfully courted a neighborhood widow, winning her with the metaphor that "his home wus like a hive without a queen bee." Several months after the wedding, as Jack walked into the cabin, his wife suddenly burst out:

> "Looky here, Jack Haywood, I 'low yer hive's all right, en it set close te a clover patch; but whar's the honey? I ain't never see ye bring home nothin' but what sticks te yer feet, en that ain't no mistake 'bout it, thar's plenty comb—fer it's comb, comb, all day long, tryin' te get the hay-seeds out o' yer six sassy tow-heads. Now I tell ye what it is," she says, turnin' from her dough en p'intin' the rollin'-pin straight at him, "you've got the hive en you've got a bee te boss it, but what hex *she* got? Why, she's got six young drones, not includin' two yaller dogs en yerself, en if I had wings, ez I hed orter hev, I'd take a bee-line fer a hive that's got some vittles in it."

When friends asked him how things were with his "queen bee," Jack replied, "she's workin' the comb all right, but she stings with her tongue wus'n any hornet I ever bumped agin'." Farmer John Drury called upon this common image of the assertive wife when he wrote in his diary for August 2, 1830: "Went to Beardstown to shooting match for beef. Polly got home and raised hell again by scolding."[16]

But however cathartic, scolding has never been known to change the order of things. Most wives chose a different course. A cousin of Lincoln's, for example, memorialized Abraham's mother as "neat in her person and habits, industrious, of a kind disposition, very affectionate in her family, never opposed her husband in any thing, was satisfied with what suited him." This portrait of Nancy Hanks Lincoln was clearly intended to mark a standard. The isolation of women from public life at the same time as their central importance to production and reproduction, as Simone de Beauvoir suggests, combined to prescribe accommodation as women's only resort in traditional society: "women were too well integrated in the family, to feel any definite solidarity as a sex," she wrote. "The majority of women resign themselves to their lot without attempting to take any action." Personal, hierarchical relations within the family, not the polarization of opposing groups or classes, mediated the conflicts between men and women. "A tradition of timidity and of submissiveness weighed on them."[17]

On his journey through America in the early 1830s, Alexis de Tocqueville ventured into the backcountry to inspect the conditions of this new man, the American pioneer. But "in speaking of the pioneer," he realized, "one cannot forget the companion of his trials and dangers." Tocqueville provided a complex portrait of the woman of the frontier:

> To devote herself to austere duties, to submit to privations once unknown to her, to embrace an existence for which she was not

made—such has been the work of the best years of her life, such for her have been the delights of conjugal union. Want, suffering, and boredom have changed her fragile frame but not broken down her courage. Amid the deep sadness engraved on her delicate features it is easy to see something of religious resignation, a profound peace, and I cannot say what natural firmness and tranquility that faces all the trials of life without fear or boast.

Half-naked children bursting with health, thoughtless of the morrow, true sons of the wilds, press around this woman. Their mother looks from time to time at them half in sadness half in joy. To see their strength and her weakness, one would say that she had drained herself to give them life and does not regret what they have cost her.[18]

Society achieved the regulation of women's labor through a male-dominated family structure linked to a public world organized to exclude women. Farmers found themselves better able than their wives to break free from the responsibilities of farm work to participate in the larger social world—participation that could take place because their women labored at home with children, cows, and chickens. Men could pursue the work of the public world precisely because the inequitable division of labor at home made them beneficiaries of women's and children's labor. The farming household exploited women as wives, and this constituted a central dynamic of the social system. High fertility, the important place of the family and women in the labor process, and the rule of the father in the household and men in the world, these three features defined an archaic social system known as patriarchy.

PART FOUR

The Sugar Creek Community

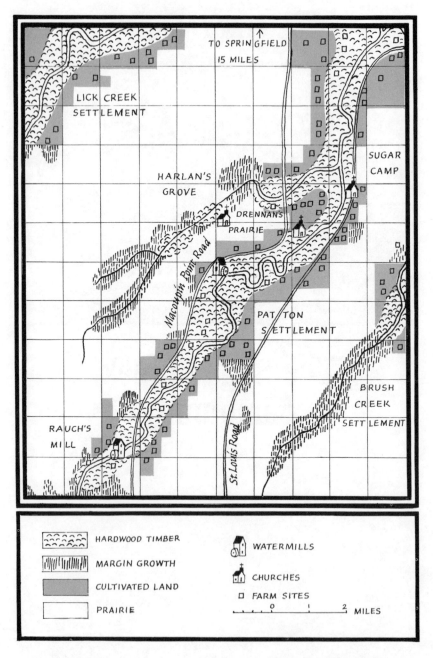

TO SPRINGFIELD
15 MILES

LICK CREEK
SETTLEMENT

HARLAN'S
GROVE

DRENNAN'S
PRAIRIE

SUGAR
CAMP

Macoupin Point Road

PATTON
SETTLEMENT

St. Louis Road

BRUSH
CREEK
SETTLEMENT

RAUCH'S
MILL

HARDWOOD TIMBER

MARGIN GROWTH

CULTIVATED LAND

PRAIRIE

WATERMILLS

CHURCHES

FARM SITES

0   1   2
MILES

SOURCES: "Taxable Lists for Sangamon County, 1832–1838" (mss, ISA); H. C. Whitley and S. B. Wheelock, *Plat Map of Sangamon County, 1858* (St. Louis: Whitley and Wheelock, 1858).

SUGAR CREEK IN 1835

13

A Scene to Rouse Their Passions

During the late winter of 1838 a controversy raged among the households of Sugar Creek and found its way into the Springfield press. "PUBLIC MEETING," read an announcement on the third page of the *Sangamo Journal* for March 10. "Pursuant to previous notice, a portion of the citizens of Sugar Creek convened at the Sugar Creek meeting and school House on Tuesday 1st of March" where the Reverend John McCutchen Berry gave a speech "shewing [*sic*] forth the principles on which our government is founded, and the evil consequences that will follow from a violation of those laws that are intended to bestow blessings on our free and happy country." The assembled men then passed a resolution:

> Resolved. That with a firm reliance on divine Providence for protection, we mutually pledge to each other, our honor, our property, and our lives (if necessary,) in support of our lawful rights, as free citizens, and in the protection of each other, against all violence offered to us or any of us by unlawful assemblages of men.

Thirty-three Sugar Creek heads of household, including early settlers William Drennan, Joseph Dodds, Job Fletcher, and men from the Lockridge, Cassity, and Nuckolls families, signed this resolution, but its context and purpose went unexplained.[1]

Then, on April 7, the *Journal* published a response written by George Wallace, and signed by James Patton and Samuel Williams,

121

representing "a large and respectable portion of the citizens residing on Sugar Creek." "We must solemnly protest," Williams wrote of the March resolution, "against this unfair and unmanly mode of proceeding."

No information is given to the public why it was deemed necessary to hold such a meeting—not a syllable is said of the circumstances that rendered it expedient. The 1st of March is not the anniversary of any important event connected with the rights of men. Consequently the reader of the Journal would be left to unfavorable conjecture relative to the state of our society; or if he should make enquiry [sic] on this head [sic] your committee are informed that there are those who do not hesitate to misrepresent the conduct of some of our most worthy citizens. To such an extent has misrepresentation been practiced that one unacquainted with our population would regard us as an organized and lawless banditti instead of a peaceable and laborious people. In order then to disabuse the public mind your committee conceive it their privilege as well as their duty to make a fair and impartial statement of the circumstances that caused the meeting complained of.

During the last week of February, Williams explained, Sugar Creek schoolmaster Cornelius Lyman, who frequently employed the rod in his classroom, beat one of his students so severely that several angry men urged justice of the peace Zachariah Peter to issue a warrant for the teacher's arrest. At the schoolhouse that night, in the presence of Lyman and an agitated group of Sugar Creek fathers, squire Peter examined the boy. "Rumor with her many tongues had not told the half," wrote Wallace. The boy's "back, sides, and hips exhibited incontrovertible proof that he had been placed under the tuition of one who knew how to torture as well as teach." At that point several angry men tried to seize Lyman from the protection of the school trustees and a brief scuffle ensued. Here was the violent incident, the "unlawful assemblage of men" that the signers of the original resolution condemned.

But Wallace argued that in fact "no violence was committed" by the assembled group of men, although he implied that violence was fully warranted.

It may be proper to state that the child thus oppressed—thus harassed with more than Spanish cruelty or Eastern barbarity, is an orphan—his mother sleeps beneath the silent sod, his father is a wanderer in a distant state, and he himself but nine years old. When these circumstances in his juvenile history were recollected, and his appearance demonstrating that his rights had been shamefully violated observed, shall it not rather be recorded to the honor than to the dishonor of the independent yeomanry of Sugar Creek, that deep excitement was manifest? Who but a heartless wretch would misrepresent the conduct of men when witnessing a scene so well calculated to rouse their passions, should only make one attempt to take the offender from the custody of the trustees of the school without effecting it, when it was so entirely in their power to do so. Nevertheless, there are those near us so lost to all sense of propriety as to use their utmost efforts to destroy the good name and fame of all who had breasts to feel as men should feel on that very interesting occasion.

The Lyman controversy quickly came to a conclusion. Justice Peter indicted the schoolmaster after his examination of the boy that evening, and just a week later, before Squire Joseph Poley, another Sugar Creek justice of the peace, a jury of twelve heads of household heard the evidence against the schoolmaster, as well as his defense, conducted by the Reverend Gilbert Dodds of the Cumberland Presbyterian Church. The jurors found Lyman guilty and fined him ninety-nine dollars, the maximum penalty of a local justice court. The debate in the local press, however, provides an opportunity to examine some of the structures of community life that were brought into the open by the affair. Although later reminiscence usually emphasized harmony, conflict as well as concord were staples of community life.[2]

Cornelius Lyman, the object of this controversy, was a Yankee. Although nine out of ten Sugar Creek settlers before 1840 were from the South, the minority of men and women from the Northeast were influential in the development of local education. Lyman came to Sugar Creek in the winter of 1833 with a colony of fifty Vermont and New York Presbyterians. Most of them settled on Prairie Creek, in the northwest corner of the county, where they founded the village of Farmingdale; but about a third of them, including the families of the Ransom brothers and several households of Lyman kin, settled on grassland two miles north of Drennan's Prairie, where they formed the first concentration of Yankees along the creek. There, in 1835, Luther Ransom purchased two thousand acres of prairie, built a New England frame house, platted the paper "village" of Chatham around it, and helped organize a regular Presbyterian church, whose first pastor, the Reverend Josiah Porter, began his ministry in 1836. As Presbyterians and "Yankees," the men and women of this clan had received common-school educations, and both Cornelius Lyman and his sister-in-law Roxana quickly found work teaching in local subscription schools. Rosana's class met in a little brick smokehouse behind Ransom's dwelling, and Cornelius's scholars assembled in the "Sugar Creek meeting and school House," in the settlement of Drennan's Prairie.[3]

Job Fletcher had taught the first school along Sugar Creek in 1820, but other duties called to this aspiring young politician, so the following year his classes were taken over by Charles Wright, who came to the Sangamo from Vermont with his brother, Erastus, and contracted with Fletcher, Billy Drennan, Robert Pulliam, and several others to teach their children. The schoolmaster "boarded 'round" the neighborhood, part of a teacher's traditional support, and while staying in the Pulliam household he met twenty-year-old Samuel Williams, whom Pulliam employed splitting rails, paying the young man, as usual, "in trade." At their first meeting young Williams, also from New England, lamented his lack of a proper Yankee education, and Wright invited him to attend classes. That winter Williams squeezed out twenty-one school days before the press of farm work concluded the term early the next spring.

The teaching method Wright used, Williams learned, and nearly all common-school teachers in the United States practiced, emphasized memorization and recitation; students learned their lessons by rote, then repeated them aloud to older classmates called "monitors," making it possible for one schoolmaster to handle scores of students of widely different levels and abilities. After his evening chores, Williams worked on his writing and his arithmetic, copied examples on his slate, and brought them in the next day for his schoolmaster to check. He became Wright's prize student.[4]

Wright taught in the Sugar Creek area for several years before giving up teaching in the mid-twenties for a position as a federal deputy surveyor. Some years later, surveying in Arkansas Territory, he was stricken by malarial fever and died. But before he left the Sangamo, Wright had awakened Samuel Williams's considerable intellectual talents, and the farmhand gave up splitting rails to teach children in Forked Prairie, ten miles north of the neighborhoods of upper Sugar Creek. Gradually, Williams developed a reputation as "a good schoolmaster," and in the winter of 1823 he received a call to visit Sugar Creek farmer Thomas Black. When Williams arrived in Patton Settlement, he found Black "in a corn-field, busily engaged with some of his boys, gathering corn." Offering the young man $12 per month "in trade" and a place to board, Black proposed that Williams begin a school on the east bank of the creek. That winter the young schoolmaster commenced teaching "the ABC's" to thirty or more scholars on land of Black's relative, James Patton. The neighborhood soon erected a log structure there that became known as "Patton schoolhouse."[5]

Samuel Williams's one-room schoolhouse included boys and girls as young as five or six, as well as "almost full grown, rough, uncouth young men." Nearly all teachers had persistent problems with the discipline of such a motley group. The big boys of the classroom, for example, practiced the custom of "turning-out" the teacher at Christmas, locking him out of the schoolhouse and forcing him to stand coatless and shivering in the brisk December air "until he treated all around to whiskey and sugar." "The teacher usually yielded," one settler remembered, "and often the boys became unsteady on their feet." In the face of demands like these from students who might well outsize the schoolmaster, "the rod, and a great deal of it, was an indispensable reliance as an educator," as Sugar Creek resident Moses Wadsworth put it. One man recalled that his boyhood schoolmaster had few qualifications as a teacher "except large size and bodily strength to thrash any boy or youth that came to his school." "As for those boys and girls that mind not their books," wrote master-pedagogue Noah Webster in his *Spelling Book,* out of which Samuel Williams and hundreds of other students copied their lessons, "they will come to some bad end, and must be whipt till they mend their ways."[6]

Williams thought of himself as a strict master, and criticized another Sangamon teacher who was "so easy and indulgent with children in regard to his discipline that his school was considered by some as very defective." Yet Cornelius Lyman's regime apparently overstepped acceptable bounds, at least in the view of one segment of the community, a segment that included Williams himself, who signed his name to the second letter to the *Sangamo Journal.*[7]

After the controversy, Lyman was replaced at the Sugar Creek schoolhouse by Tamsen Eustace Dozier, a Yankee woman who achieved a glowing reputation precisely for her ability to muster effective classroom control without resort to violence. She had attended school in Massachusetts, taught in a North Carolina academy during the 1820s, then, following the death of her husband and children in an epidemic of fever, had come to Sangamon County to care for the motherless children of her brother William, who farmed near The Sources. One of her students, who had toiled under Lyman's regime, recalled that when she first entered the classroom, "I looked at her quiet face and diminutive form, and thought how easy it would be for me to pick up two or three such little bodies as she and set them outside the door!" But through her ability to provoke her students' interests, Mrs. Dozier overcame the legacy of violence.

> Her pluck had won our admiration and her quiet dignity held our respect, and we boys ceased to wonder at the ease with which she overturned our plans and made us eager to adopt hers; for no teacher ever taught on Sugar Creek who won the affections and

ruled pupils more easily and happily than she. She expected us to come right up to the mark; but if we got into trouble she was always ready to help us out, and she could do it in the quietest way imaginable. Frequently she would wander through field and meadow with her class in surveying and her class in botany. She sought by creek and over plain for specimens with which to illustrate their lessons.

On one of these field trips, where boys practiced the science of "land-looking" and girls the art of "botanizing," Mrs. Dozier met widower George Donner, in Sugar Creek visiting his sisters, Lydia Donner Walters and Susannah Donner Organ. After a courtship befitting mature and widowed lovers, Tamsen and George married and settled on his farm fifteen miles north on the creek. In 1846, the couple left Sangamon County for California and perished in the Sierra snows along with many others in the "Donner Party."[8]

The Sangamon County school commissioner may have had teaching methods like Dozier's in mind when he wrote, in his report for 1855, that "from long and thorough experience, females are found to be the most suitable, as well as the most economical, for common school instructors." But *economical* was probably the operative word here, because in Illinois the state did not fund education, and the employment of female teachers, who earned 40 to 50 percent less than men, saved limited school funds. Before the establishment of a state system of tax-supported common schools in 1855, the most reliable support for education came from parent subscriptions, often paid in butter or eggs. A prospective teacher circulated among the households in the area with a "subscription paper," and parents put down the number of scholars they wished to send, at a set fee for the three-month term: "The undersigned proposes to teach school for the term of three months commensing [*sic*] Nov. the 18th, 1844. She proposes to teach spelling, reading, writing, and Arithmetic for the sum of $2.25 per scholar, and to keep good order, also to pay strict attention to the improvement of her scholars."[9]

There were certain provisions for the public funding of education, however. In the Land Ordinance of 1787, Congress declared that the proceeds from the sale of section sixteen of every township be used for the support of schools. The Illinois constitution of 1818 empowered citizens to form their own school trustee committees and, under the authority of the county commissioners, to lease these school lands, using the income from the investment of the proceeds to support local public education. Job Fletcher, William Drennan, and Ephraim Darling, all from Drennan's Prairie, formed a school committee for township 14/5 in 1824, as did groups of men in other parts of the county, leasing the school lands to local farmers on shares and selling the trustees' share of the crop to supplement the subscription funds collected by teachers. Cash paid out of these local education funds supplemented subscription fees.[10]

But these provisions worked inequitably. Sugar Creek flowed directly through section sixteen of township 14/5, contributing the wealth of timber and woodland soils that settlers sought. When the Illinois legislature voted to allow the sale of school lands in 1831, the trustees of 14/5 quickly moved their's onto the market; and by 1837, while congress land continued to sell for only $1.25 per acre, their school lands had passed into private hands at an average price of nearly $7.00. Advancing credit at upwards of 10 percent, the trustees used their earnings to subsidize the school on Drennan's Prairie. But south, in township 13/6, section sixteen lay in the midst of the undrained prairie, land for which there was so little demand that trustees David Eastman, James Patton, and Samuel Williams had no choice but to keep their endowment off the market. Even when demand rose in the 1840s, and their school lands sold, the trustees earned little more than $2.50 per acre. As early as 1832, householders of Patton Settlement met at Thomas Black's, where they resolved that "the law authorizing the sale of the school lands has a very unequal bearing on the people of the different townships," and vowed to support candidates for local and state office who would enact more equitable provisions.[11]

Theoretically, any Sugar Creek family might share the good fortune of the neighbors of township 14/5. Children from at least three townships attended the school there; their parents had only to pay the subscription fee that supplemented the trustee payments to schoolmasters. But in addition to discriminating against settlers too poor to pay the teacher, even "in trade," this system forced some children to walk great distances, ford dangerous creeks, or brave dark stands of timber to attend school. Two Sugar Creek sisters remembered walking to school for miles "through high grass and woods, and the stars were often shining when we got home, and there were wolves and panthers plenty. They were frequently seen, and you can well imagine how we felt when the stars began to shine. The oldest ones would form a front and rear guard, and put the smallest in the middle, and hurry them along, all scared nearly to death." Although surviving records suggest that the trustees of 14/5 dispersed some funds to teachers at schools in other neighborhoods, such as Patton Schoolhouse, over 80 percent of the earnings of township 14/5 supported the school in Drennan's Prairie.[12]

So the Sugar Creek meeting and schoolhouse, as it came to be known, was more prosperous and enjoyed a more regular schedule than either the Patton schoolhouse southeast of the creek or other occasional classes taught in settler homes. In 1835 the trustees of 14/5 replaced the original schoolhouse on the edge of Drennan's Prairie with a larger log structure, still rude, but with better heat from a larger fireplace and better light from four real windows. The meeting and schoolhouse became a center of neighborhood activity, drawing not only children to class, but adults to political meetings, to occasional sessions of the justice of the peace court, and to religious services of the Cumberland Presbyterians, who regularly met in the building, organized a Sunday school where Job Fletcher taught in the mid-twenties, and, in 1846, built a frame church building nearby. Cumberland families took to burying their dead in the adjacent timber, and the site became a burial ground that was used for a century and a half. In such ways did an abstract feature of a federal law, the accidental lay of the federal survey, and the activity of local citizens combine to make this location a center for the whole Sugar Creek community.[13]

This institutional history further illuminates the 1838 controversy, for at issue were not only differing teaching styles but the divergent interests of leadership groups from the two townships. The principal authors of the second *Sangamo Journal* notice defending Lyman's attackers included two of the trustees of township 13/6—James Patton, who donated the land for the school south of the creek, and Samuel Williams, the master of the first classes there—both of whom had long-standing reasons to resent the more affluent trustees of the Sugar Creek meeting and schoolhouse. The men who attached their names to this notice all lived south of township 14/5, in Patton Settlement, near Patton schoolhouse and constituted a group of intermarrying and residentially associated families.

The group that signed the original *Journal* notice criticizing "unlawful assemblages of men" even more clearly demonstrated a pattern of association and collective action. Two of the three school trustees of 14/5, Billy Drennan and Job Fletcher, signed the resolution. Moreover, better than seven in ten of the signers lived in Drennan's Prairie within two miles of the schoolhouse, and were members of the Sugar Creek Cumberland Presbyterian Church. The leaders of that church, and the signers of this public notice, including Fletcher, Drennan, his son-in-law, Joseph Dodds, Dodds's brother Gilbert (a Cumberland lay-preacher), the Cassitys, Lockridges, and others formed a neighborhood association of kith and kin.

As it appeared in the *Journal*, the original resolution of this Drennan Prairie clique partook of the political rhetoric of the day. In October 1837, a hostile mob confronted minister Josiah Porter, leader of Lyman's Chatham Presbyterian Church, when he tried to give an antislavery speech in Springfield. Porter, born in South Carolina and raised in Kentucky, had been converted to the cause of antislavery during his theological training at Lane Theological Seminary in Cincinnati. In the aftermath of this incident, a public meeting in Spring-field condemned abolitionism as "at variance with Christianity" and warned that it would "breed contention, broils, and mobs." A month later just such a mob in Alton, Illinois, murdered abolitionist editor Elijah Lovejoy. Local Democrats, for their part, blamed abolitionists ("designing, ambitious men, and dangerous members of society") for inciting such events. Whigs, while careful not to endorse abolitionism, condemned the lawless violence. In January 1838, in an address before the Young Men's Lyceum of Springfield, reprinted in the *Journal*, young Whig state assemblyman Abraham Lincoln spoke out against "the increasing disregard for law which pervades the country—the growing disposition to substitute the wild and furious passions in lieu of the sober judgements of courts and the worse than savage mobs for the executive ministers of justice." The Cumberland Presbyterians in Sugar Creek were solidly Whiggish, advocates of temperance, oppo-nents of slavery, and readers of the *Journal*. In the heated political debates of the late 1830s, they learned a language and discourse that they employed here for local purposes.[14]

The two groups who came to blows in the Cornelius Lyman affair were composed almost entirely of men from the South. The only Yankee among the group from Patton Settlement was Samuel Williams; among the Cumberlands from Drennan's Prairie, only Cornelius Lyman. Yankee-Southern conflict, so important to the contours of political and social conflict in other Illinois communities, was not particularly important here. The political debate over economic progress and social improvement that began in the late 1830s, as well as entirely local debates such as this one, took place among southern emigrants.

The Drennan's Prairie clique demonstrated its power in local affairs after Tamsen Dozier's marriage to George Donner took her from the Sugar Creek meeting and schoolhouse in 1839. In that year, the trust-ees of 14/5 rehired Cornelius Lyman, despite the clear opposition of other Sugar Creek residents. But few men or women taught for long in Sugar Creek, and by 1842 Lyman had left the meeting and school-house for good. With his fellow Yankee Luther Ransom, and a few other Presbyterians, Lyman and his family joined a socialist Fourier "phalanx" in Ohio. Whether because of this, or for some other un-known reason, that same year the Chatham Presbyterian Church ex-communicated the former teacher. Cornelius Lyman's impress on Sugar Creek's history, however, illustrates more than the course of an eccentric schoolmaster. The local controversy he provoked brings to light the multiple structures—of association and collective action, of neighborhood and kinship, of belief and ritual—that had, twenty years after Robert Pulliam's pioneering venture, transformed a collection of emigrant families into a community, with all its attendant harmony and strife.[15]

14

Good Neighborship

he rugged, individualistic fron-
tiersman is an *idée fixe* of American popular culture, which may suggest
why historians have paid relatively little attention to community life in
the American West. Over the past seventy-five years, free-market conservatives from Herbert Hoover to Ronald Reagan have praised the
individualistic "spirit of the frontier," taking their cues from historian
Frederick Jackson Turner, who argued that "the frontier is productive
of individualism" and that the "immemorial custom of tribe or village
community" fell victim to the American pioneer experience. "Complex
society," Turner wrote in 1893, "is precipitated by the wilderness into a
kind of primitive organization based on the family. The tendency is
anti-social." For "these slashers of the forest, these self-sufficing pioneers, raising the corn and live stock for their own need, living scattered and apart," Turner wrote, "individualism was more pronounced
than community life."[1]

Many nineteenth-century observers of the "Old West" saw more
evidence of community than did Turner. In the 1830s, Illinois editor
James Hall, for example, emphasized the communal behavior of
settlers.

> Exposed to common dangers and toils, they become united by the
> closest ties of social intercourse. Accustomed to arm in each
> other's defense, to aid in each other's labour, to assist in the
> affectionate duty of nursing the sick, and the mournful office of

130

burying the dead, the best affections of the heart are kept in
constant exercise; and there is, perhaps, no class of men in our
country, who obey the calls of friendship, or the claims of benev-
olence, with such cheerful promptness, or with so liberal a sacri-
fice of personal convenience.

With Hall's views others found themselves in agreement, although
dissenting, perhaps, from the rosy glow of his affect. After living in a
raw Michigan backcountry community for several years in the 1830s,
New Yorker Caroline Kirkland grudgingly admired the "homely fellowship" among her neighbors, although she often felt oppressed by
prying eyes and wagging tongues. "Any appearance of a desire to
avoid this rather trying fraternization is invariably met by a fierce and
indignant resistance," she complained; "the spirit in which was conceived the motto of the French revolution, 'la fraternité ou la mort,'
exists in full force among us." English immigrant George Flower observed that among his Illinois neighbors any man who tried to live in
isolation from others, like the stereotypical frontier individualist, was
considered to be committing a serious offense against civility. "You
may sin and be wicked in many ways, and in the tolerant circle of
American society receive a full and generous pardon," Flower explained to his English readers, "but this one sin can never be par-
doned." "In no part of the world," concluded Scotsman John Bradbury, after a tour of America, "is *good neighbourship* found in greater
perfection than in the western territory."[2]
  In Turner's defense, he built his argument on certain truths. As a
group, American farmers were uncommonly free of the obligations
that tied many of their European and Latin American counterparts to
village society. And, after all, farming men and women did spend most
of their time pursuing solitary tasks within the limiting circle of the
family. Nevertheless, communal sinew bound together the backcountry society of Sugar Creek. By no means was the dominant tendency
"anti-social," as Turner imagined. With a remarkable degree of gre-
gariousness, farm families reached out from their log cabins to their
neighbors for work and play, politics and prayer.[3]
  The foundation of American agriculture was the private ownership
of the means of agrarian production by men, householders who headed a family labor system. Some of these had families with children too
young to lend a hand and thus were able to convert less land to productive use, or had families without the labor benefits of nearby kin. Families who came with savings, on the other hand, could afford to hire
labor to break land, split rails, or herd cattle. Families pursued but
could only imperfectly achieve the goal of self-sufficiency with surplus.
A stratification of wealth was inevitable but modest: in 1838, two dec-

ades after the settlement of Sugar Creek had begun, the wealthiest 10 percent of owners held a quarter of the privately owned acreage.[4]

But when embedded in a culture that practiced traditions of common use, family proprietorship could provide a foundation for family security. Sugar Creek farmers, like their ancestors and counterparts throughout the nation, utilized important rural productive resources in common with their neighbors. Custom allowed farmers, for example, to hunt game for their own use though they might be in woodlands owned by someone else. Hogs running wild in the timber and surviving on the mast paid no heed to property lines. And despite an 1831 prohibition against "stealing" timber from unclaimed congress land, settlers acted as if the resources of these acres belonged to the neighborhood in common and helped themselves, "hooking" whatever timber they needed. William Oliver, an English observer of Illinois pioneer life, reported that settlers often ransacked unclaimed lands for wood, "never cutting a stick of their own for any purpose so long as there is any suitable that can be stolen from Uncle Sam, as they facetiously term the United States government."[5]

The prairies, according to Moses Wadsworth of Sugar Creek, were considered "a range, open and free" by the community. Before the 1850s, few farmers fenced their pastures but instead enclosed their fields to keep out grazing stock. "A great many cattle are reared on the prairies, which are occupied in common by the inhabitants," Patrick Shirreff noted in 1835, and Englishwoman Rebecca Burlend observed that "all unenclosed lands, whether purchased of government or otherwise are considered common pasturage." "Commons on the prairie" allowed any family to graze cattle, though they might afford only a forty-acre timber parcel, or might not have the wherewithal to file on congress land at all, so squatted. Prairie cattle grew hardy but bred randomly, so cows bore out of season, gave relatively little milk, and their calves suffered a high death rate.[6]

Other priorities, however, outranked the confinement and control of mating necessary for systematic stock improvement. In the late 1820s, the Illinois legislature passed an act prohibiting the running of bulls on the open prairies, a measure designed to improve livestock by regulating breeding. "No one dreamed," recalled the politician Thomas Ford, "that a hurricane of popular indignation was about to be raised, but so it was: the people took sides with the little bulls. The law was denounced as being aristocratic, and intended to favor the rich, who, by their money, had become possessed of large bulls, and were to make a profit by the destruction of the small ones." Farmers opposed stock improvement because they believed it struck at the communal resource pool that supported the independence of small proprietors. Thus was common use linked to the practice of "democracy." Illinois governor John M. Palmer, who had farmed Macoupin County land south of Sugar Creek during the 1830s, admitted to an assembly of old settlers near Drennan's Prairie, in 1871, that he had been "strongly democratic in his opinions in regard to the rights of the people cutting timber where they wished and taking up hogs running at large. The people in early days considered this legitimate."[7]

Common use extended to productive chattel property as well as land. One Sugar Creek settler, Daniel Parkinson, wrote that once an emigrant family had selected a site for their farmstead, the neighbors invariably dropped by to introduce themselves, to express "the warmest sentiments of friendship and good-will," and to assure the head of household "that every thing they possessed, in the way of tools, teams, wagons, provisions, and their own personal services, were entirely at his command." By the end of this first visit, the newcomer family found themselves "well acquainted, and upon the best terms of friendship, with the whole neighborhood." When his family first occupied their cabin, wrote John Regan, an English immigrant to central Illinois, "all the goodwives of the neighborhood" came calling, bringing milk, eggs, and needlework to worry over as they shared community gossip with his wife, and bringing him the news that if their husbands "could aid me in any way, I had only to say so and they would do all they could 'to help me get along.'" "Milk, cream, butter, and all articles for table use, as well as kitchen furniture, maintain a brisk circulation through the community; vegetables and fruits are regarded as common property," Elizabeth Ellet wrote during a tour through central Illinois in the early 1850s. "The borrowing system," she concluded, "is in full operation in these parts."[8]

The "borrowing system" allowed scarce tools, labor, and products to circulate to the benefit of all and responded to the ongoing neighborhood need for exchange and mutual assistance. People utilized this neighborly network for most of the transactions necessary to the practice of farming. To have productive implements "and not be willing to share them in some sort with the whole community is an unpardonable crime," Caroline Kirkland warned prospective emigrants. "Your wheel-barrows, your shovels, your utensils of all sorts, belong, not to yourself, but to the public, who do not think it necessary even to *ask* a loan, but take it for granted." Outsiders, unversed in these customs, frequently misunderstood the social conventions of communal sharing. When Kirkland sent over a side of beef to a needy neighbor she anticipated grateful thanks, but received instead a merely perfunctory "Oh! your pa wants to '*change,* does he? Well, you may put it down." Similarly, Frances Trollope complained that when she loaned household implements, her neighbors responded matter-of-factly, "well, I expect I shall have to do a turn of work for this; you may send for me when you want me." Trollope malevolently concluded that westerners would do almost anything "to avoid uttering that most un-American phrase, 'I thank you.'" She may have been right. But Kirkland and Trollope did not seem to understand that gifts given "unconditionally" required no "thanks" but were part of a system of exchange ("'change") that created an obligation to provide reciprocal aid in the future. Western traveler Charles Latrobe nicely summed up the "borrowing system": "a life in the woods teaches many lessons, and this among the rest, that you must both give assistance to your neighbors, and receive it in return, without either gruding or pouting."[9]

"It was a fixed fact," wrote Sugar Creek farmer James Megredy, "that when one or more of the community would be sick with chills or jaundice, or something else, his neighbors would meet and take care of his harvest, get up wood, or repair his cabin, or plant his corn, or whatever was necessary to be done for the comfort of his family or himself." Household emergencies, however, were not the only occasion for exchanges of labor. Before wage labor became fundamental to the rural economy, 'changing labor was a regular part of day-to-day operations. In their account books, literate farmers carefully "put down" each exchange with their neighbors: "to six days work planting corn [$]3.00"; to 1/2 stack of hay .75": these entries recorded work performed or products traded. "By 3/4 day harvesting .75"; "by one day butchering hogs .50": these recorded work received in exchange. At the beginning of the farm year, in March 1849, Eddin Lewis recorded in his farm book an "old account against James Wilson" for $5.00. During that year, Lewis received from this neighbor nearly 250 pounds of bacon, valued at $4.75 per hundred-weight, in exchange for which he put in twenty days on Wilson's place hauling timber, hewing logs, and gathering corn—labor valued at fifty cents per day. At year's end, Lewis carried over to the next season a continuing credit of $2.89 to Wilson. Such ledgers often ran for years, the debt being settled only upon the death of one of the parties.[10]

The surviving account book of a Sugar Creek blacksmith, John Smith, shows how this reciprocal system accomplished a social division of labor. From July to March of 1837–38, widow Sarah Smith ran up a bill of $10.99 at Smith's shop for shoeing, sharpening tools, and purchasing nails, hinges, and door latches. Over the next nine months she brought into his shop produce from her farm, including 15 pounds of veal, 110 pounds of beef, and over 250 pounds of flour. When he balanced the account, the blacksmith carried over a credit to Mrs. Smith of $2.84. The Sugar Creek community included not only a smith, but a wheelwright, a carpenter, a potter, and several millers, tanners, and physicians, and each conducted his operations in a similar manner. At the mills "they would not take any money," Lemira Gillet recalled, "everything was done on the halves," millers taking "toll-wheat," a share of the milled product, as their fee. In the public interest the county commissioners set rates at mills, as well as those at taverns and ferries; a miller could retain a maximum of an eighth-weight of milled wheat, a seventh-weight of corn, oats, or buckwheat.[11]

The use of monetary values in these accounts, however, suggests that local exchanges within the borrowing system were affected by forces larger than the local community. In other regions of the United States, for example, the values in farmer's account books accurately reflected prices in market centers, so the exchange value of commodities—whether tools, produce, or labor—was clearly a material fact in the relationships between farmers. The effects of the Atlantic economy had long been felt in the valleys of central Illinois, and farmers were no more immune to them than hunters. But though the borrowing system was influenced by market forces, it remained distinct from the market itself. As the medium of marketplace exchange, specie had to be turned to use, invested. Farmers and local craftsmen who frequently extended credit, by contrast, never charged interest, for money in their exchanges functioned simply as a measure of account. "Money is so scarce and hard to be got, we must live without buying much," Lucy Maynard wrote to her sister in Ohio; "but most people get along on what they produce or trade with others for." The borrowing system and the market were separate in the eyes of the settlers. The market provided the opportunity to sell a "surplus" in order to raise the money necessary, for instance, for land purchases. The borrowing system provided access to goods, tools, and community labor that made a sufficiency possible, even for small producers.[12]

It was not the market but the social exchange network, the borrowing system, that could bring out the whole neighborhood for collective labor at "bees," a metaphorical allusion to the social and productive character of those immigrant insects. In the backcountry of Illinois these events were more frequently called "frolics," emphasizing the prominently featured drinking and competitive sport that accompanied them. Men joined in logrolling frolics, wolf- and snake-hunting frolics, husking and reaping frolics, while women assembled for picking, sewing, and quilting frolics. Both sexes took part in these frolics in a spirit of intense competition. "It was the custom" at log rollings, former schoolmaster Samuel Williams later reminisced, "to select two captains, and they to choose their men; then the ground was carefully divided into two parts. There was generally considerable ambition as to who was to get done first." Male frolics celebrated physical prowess, and wrestling or racing often took up as much time as working. "Trials of strength were very common among the pioneers," according to R. B. Rutledge; "lifting weights, as heavy timbers piled one upon another, was a favorite pastime." Wives were not merely in the background, preparing the "edibles" for the hungry workers, but were just as likely engaged in productive frolics of their own, with their own kinds of competition. Elizabeth McDowell Hill told of a spinning frolic where two young ladies "spun a race" to determine who could lay claim to a certain eligible farmer. "They began at six in the morning and spun until six in the evening. Two old ladies carded for them, one for each. At six o'clock Nancy was thirty rounds ahead. Forever afterward the fair Sarah had to look elsewhere for her swain."[13]

Of all the frolics, settlers most frequently recalled the cabin "raising." By custom, the settler family made all the preparations: the farmer and his boys cut the ash, oak, or walnut; logged off eighty or so appropriate lengths and hewed them to proper thickness; prepared oak or chestnut clapboards, shingles, joists, and spans—work that took many days. Once the building materials had been hauled to the chosen spot, the householder could circulate "round among his neighbours, to request their assistance, which will be cheerfully rendered without any remuneration, except good cheer, and it may be, future assistance of a similar kind." "Men an' neighbours," John Regan overheard one farmer toast his comrades at a house-raising, "w're boun' to help every feller who's honest, to make him a home." On the appointed day, men from the surrounding country arrived early, leveling the home site and laying the first logs on the ground at the direction of a local "raising master," whose only blueprints were stored in memory. As men rolled one log after another up supporting poles and into place, axmen at each corner notched intersecting ends to "nest" one within the next in the "half-dovetail" tradition of Upland South construction. The "hands" raised the basic structure in one day. It then fell to the family to chop out doors, windows, and fireplace openings, to fit frames and doors, to lay the roof, and "chink" the gaps between the logs.[14]

Freeholds in Sugar Creek were linked through a reciprocal network. The cabin raising inducted newcomers into the neighborhood system by creating a web of common obligations, thus demonstrating the mixture of private and communal that characterized the backcountry economy.

Sugar Creek first acquired formal governmental institutions when the Illinois legislature included it in the new county of Sangamon in 1821. The county constituted the basic unit of government from which the institutions of civil society took their authority. County voters chose a three-man county commissioner's court, including Sugar Creek settlers William Drennan and Zachariah Peter, to administer county affairs.[15]

County government operated, however, within a narrow administrative range. Except for salaried county clerk Charles Matheny, fees for services furnished the only remuneration for county officials, so most practiced their offices part-time and continued in their former occupations—farmer, merchant, or lawyer—during their terms. The county simply lacked the tax base necessary to fund a bureaucracy of its own. The small tax on personal and real property amounted to a dollar or two a year for the average farmer, and state law allowed men the choice of "working out" their minimal assessments instead of paying them. The commissioners directed the actions of the county sheriff and set prices at local mills, ferries, and taverns, but they delegated most civil concerns—including education, transportation, welfare, defense, law enforcement, and summary justice—directly to local citizens. The networks and patterns of reciprocity worked to provide the structure of civil society as well. The local community breathed collective life into county institutions.[16]

Township school committees, which managed education lands and organized local schools, constituted just one important aspect of this local self-management. Citizens also governed themselves, for example, as members of "road districts." At their first meeting in June 1821, the Sangamon commissioners accepted a petition from "sundry citizens" arguing for the improvement of the Old Indian Trail, or Edward's Trace, which ran through the Sugar Creek community from south to north, and directed three men, including Robert Pulliam, "to vue Said road and make report to the next term of this court." In September the commissioners officially declared this artery a public road and ordered that "all the hands above or south of a road Leading out of Drennan's Prairie crossing Sugar Creek at the ford above R. Pulliams Sugar Camp be assigned to work on said road." State law required householders to work on local public roads for three to five days each year under the direction of a local "supervisor" appointed by the commissioners. In 1822 Congress declared the trace a "post road" with regular mail service, and in everyday conversation the route from American Bottom to Sugar Creek soon acquired its third name in recorded history—the St. Louis Road.[17]

Most neighborhood men participated in the communal days of labor on the roads. One record, kept by supervisor Micajah Organ in the mid-1840s, listed forty-two men from the west side of the creek who labored in common on the public roads one summer—better than eight in ten of the heads of households from that neighborhood enumerated on the 1840 census, and including not only local farmers, but a miller, several craftsmen, two aspiring entrepreneurs, and the local physician as well. Men almost always performed their roadwork between planting and harvesttime, during the "dog days" of July or August, and it took on the character of another "frolic." The notoriously poor state of the roads demonstrated that roadwork rarely got in the way of fun and fellowship.[18]

Local citizens also administered what little provision the state made for the poor. In 1824 Governor Edward Coles boasted that "Illinois has no poor," but Sugar Creek always had a small number of indigents—widows, orphans, and retarded persons without families to support them—who lived in the households of more prosperous farmers, lending what help they could to the household while the patriarch collected a small quarterly allotment from the county commissioners for their upkeep. In December 1839, for example, David Drennan wrote to the commissioners that, as he had passed the impoverished hut of Samuel Johnson one cold November day, the old man hobbled out to tell him "he had nothing to live on but Potatoes, no bead [sic] to sleap on, nothing but A few old quilts, and he Prays your Notice." Over the next ten years Drennan and Charles Nuckolls kept Johnson in their households and, until his death, collected several dollars for his upkeep from the county each year. During the 1850s, Elizabeth Hartsock, "an aged blind woman" of ninety, "entirely helpless and unable to earn a living," with "no relatives who are able to support her," lived in the household of another widow, Sarah Bemington, who collected $60 a year for her support.[19]

From the beginnings of settlement, farmers required farmhands, and the labor of "paupers" offered one alternative in a labor-poor market. At one time or another, nearly every substantial Sugar Creek farmer took in paupers who labored in their fields or kitchen. In 1842 Jacob A. Parker indentured his "idiot" daughter Serepta to the childless couple Peter and Christiana Gates as a servant "until the said Serepta shall have attained the age of eighteen."

> During all which term the said Serepta shall well and faithfully serve and obey the said Peter Gates as a good and faithful servant in all such lawful business as the said Serepta shall be put unto by the command of the said Peter Gates, and honestly and obediently in all things shall behave herself towards the said Peter Gates, and honestly and orderly towards the rest of his family. And the said Peter Gates convenants and agrees to and with the said Serepta that he will teach and instruct her, or cause her to be taught and instructed in the employments and business in which female servants are usually occupied and engaged, and that he will find and allow to her meat, drink, washing, lodging, suitable apparel, and all other necessaries fit and convenient for the said

Serepta during the term aforesaid, to be taught to read and write and at the end of said term shall give to her a new Bible.

Christiana died in 1848, and Peter remarried the same year to Sarah Wood who, within a year, bore the first of eleven children. For reasons at which one may only guess, Gates convinced the commissioners to abrogate Serepta's indenture in 1849, and for the next ten years the young woman shuffled from house to house in Sugar Creek. "I would like to know what I am to do with this Idiot," Justice George Parkinson wrote to the commissioners in 1851, "as every one refuses to take her. They now ask $25 per Quarter. Is there no way to dispose of her case?" In fact, after 1850, the commissioners disposed of most cases by sending the indigent to the county poor farm, opened in 1849, where the *Springfield Register* found conditions so "filthy and uncomfortable" that it cynically suggested that "some gentle means be taken to murder sick paupers before they are taken out to undergo the county's slow torture."[20]

The local community also provided for the common defense. Federal and state law required all adult men to serve in militia companies, but this *possee comitatus* possessed little military might. One observer, present for a county regimental muster, saw

several hundred men formed in what is called a *line*, in every variety of posture and position—some sitting, some lying, some standing on one foot, some on both, and well-spread at that; equipped, too, or non-equipped, with every variety of coat and shirt sleeves, and every variety of weapon, among the latter, however, the corn-stalk, the umbrella, and riding whip predominating almost to uniformity; every man grumbling and thinking the time wholly thrown away; some impatient for the grog-shop, and some for the horse race, and some to attend to their business— certainly there is very little of the military in this display!

Sangamon proved no exception to the rule of a notoriously undisciplined and unreliable nineteenth-century American militia. Samuel Williams described the military performance at a local muster in 1822 "awkward and in some respects comical." County companies "took water," that is, they performed woefully, in the Black Hawk War of 1831, and during the Mexican War of 1846 local volunteer companies supplanted the ineffective local militia. When the state issued a call for regiments during the secession crisis of 1861, it found the local militia system militarily moribund.[21]

But local companies were, as one Sangamon farmer put it, "interwoven with the social life of the community." Musters provided the somewhat scattered farm men with an important opportunity for fellowship, and militia companies helped to arrange elections, to conduct censuses, and, most importantly, to provide the context in which the authority of local male leadership could be tested. In one of their first acts, the Sangamon commissioners divided the county into two "battalions," each with two districts, and called for the organization of companies and the election of officers. One district, they decreed in 1821, "shall include from Mathew Eades including Sugar Creek to source and Lick fork to source and that an election shall be held in said district on the Twenty third Instant at the House of John Taylor on Sugar Creek and Thomas Black, John Darneil, and Job Fletcher be appointed to superintendent [sic] said election." Taylor, the newly appointed county sheriff, lived on a farm in the center of this large district, and each of the "superintendents" came from a different neighborhood. On June 23, 1821, forty-seven Sugar Creek heads of household assembled on Taylor's farm for the first of many quarterly militia "musters." By lining up behind the candidates of their choice, they elected Harmon Husband captain, and David Black, son of Thomas Black and cousin of Harmon, his lieutenant.[22]

With the exception of these militia elections, during the early 1820s Sugar Creek men were forced to travel fifteen to twenty miles to the county courthouse in Springfield in order to cast their ballots. As the area along the creek filled with settlers, however, Sugar Creek farmers petitioned for a separate "precink," and in 1827 the county commissioners obliged, holding the election at the cabin of Samuel Wycoff, on Lick Creek north of Drennan's Prairie. In 1830 the commissioners created separate districts for Lick and Sugar creeks. Where the public road passed his farm, on the north side of Drennan's Prairie, John L. Drennan had established a "stage stand" for the weekly mail stage that came north from Vandalia, the state capital. Federal authorities authorized a Sugar Creek post office at the same site in 1827, and Drennan donated a prairie plot for a communal muster ground. Here was the logical site for the community's polling place, and for the next two decades male social life in Sugar Creek centered at Drennan's.[23]

Each year, after a season of canvassing and campaigning, Sugar Creek electors gathered on the morning of local, state, or national election day at Drennan's "polling place." "They came by dozens from all parts, and on every road, riding on their ponies, which they hitched up or tied to the fences, trees, and bushes," Thomas Ford recalled. "The candidates came also, and addressed the people from wagons, benches, old logs, or stumps newly cut. . . . The stump speeches being over, then commenced the drinking of liquor, and long before night a large portion of the voters would be drunk and staggering about, cursing, swearing, hallooing, yelling, huzzaing for their favorite candidates, throwing their arms up and around, threatening to fight, and fighting."[24]

From the founding of Sangamon County until 1829, voting was by the casting of ballots. But with the arrival of Jacksonian party spirit, the Illinois legislature returned to the more traditional system of viva voce voting, castigating the ballot system as "inconsistent with the spirit of a representative republican government." Individual votes would be cast in an "audible voice" so that the assembled electors could hear a man's political choices. After several hours of stump speaking and political contest at the polling place, voters lined up and announced their choice to the clerks and judges of the election, who recorded the votes in a poll book. Viva voce voting, one early settler recalled, "gave the friends of local candidates an advantage, since they could keep track of the election and call in laggard voters for their candidate or party. Independent or whimsical voting was difficult." Under these procedures, men of local importance and stature might "overawe" and shape the political decisions of their lesser neighbors or kin. Oral voting continued until the ballot again became part of Illinois procedure under the reformed constitution of 1848. Communal discourse and challenge, not individual conscience, mattered most in politics.[25]

In 1827 the legislature, following the lead of Ohio and Indiana, established popular district election of local justices of the peace, as well as constables who enforced the justices' rulings. Previously, justices had been nominated by the county commissioners and approved by the state senate, as Job Fletcher had been in 1820. Justices of the peace furnished summary justice at the local level, having jurisdiction over civil suits (not exceeding $100) and minor criminal offenses, and the power to bind over suspects of more serious crimes. In their first precinct election, Sugar Creek voters elected Zachariah Peter local justice and returned him each time he stood for reelection during the 1830s.[26]

Illinois did not require that local justices have legal training; Peter, for one, had none. "The justice o' the peace knew as much of the law as a sheep knows o' the ways o' panthers an' wolves," according to Francis Grierson. When people spoke of "going to law," they generally meant circuit court, which convened each June and December in Springfield; there folks went for serious civil suits and criminal cases, for divorces, or de novo appeal from the justice of the peace.

L-A-W, Law;
L-A-W, Law!
If you're fond of pure vexation,
And long procrastination,
And a deal of botheration,
I'd advise you go to Law.

Justices of the peace, on the other hand, based their practices partly on English "common law" and partly on local, communal conceptions of fairness. More akin to community arbitrators than representatives of the state, the people paid a justice their highest compliment when they praised his ability to reconcile disputing parties without bringing the case to trial. According to his family, the advice of Joseph Poley, many years a justice of Sugar Creek, "always led to the settlement of difficulties without litigation, and in a peaceful and friendly manner"; and another justice was said to have "used his office to settle difficulties without law, although by that way of doing business he generally deprived himself of fees." These comments reflect less the actual business of the local justice courts than the communal standards by which folk judged them, for most justices of the peace, Zachariah Peter among them, tried many cases and charged many fees, although they were paid as often in kind as in cash. Justices of the peace came from the local community, worked in the interest of community harmony, and were held to honorific standards.[27]

For the men and women of Sugar Creek, the accusation and trial of Cornelius Lyman for child abuse before Zachariah Peter and Joseph Poley, held extempore in the Sugar Creek meeting and schoolhouse in late February 1838, presented an extraordinary scene—a scene "well calculated to rouse their passions," as George Wallace wrote to the *Sangamo Journal.* But more ordinary scenes of political controversy, of locally administered justice, of the local management of local affairs, of community action and collective purpose, were everyday sights along Sugar Creek.

15

Open-Country Connexions

Practically all American settlers after the mid-eighteenth century built their dwellings directly on their arable lands, dispersing themselves across relatively large rural districts. John Reynolds noted the contrast of this tradition with that of the French at American Bottom, who would "not reside on farms, each family to itself, like the Americans. They always live in villages where they may enjoy their social pleasure." Historians and sociologists have frequently interpreted the American preference for "open-country settlement" as a sign of weak communal bonds among the settlers. Historian Kenneth Lockridge, for example, declares that traditional communalism atrophied when eighteenth-century New England townsmen surrendered to "the incoherence of individual opportunism" fostered by the abundance of American land and "abandoned the web of relationships created by residence in the villages" for life in the open country.[1]

Despite the low density of their settlements, however, neighboring families in Sugar Creek demonstrated an impressive ability to act together. They utilized unclaimed prairie and timber in common, shared productive resources through the "borrowing system," and governed themselves. The families of these little neighborhoods, one Sangamon farmer later wrote, "were as sociable and familiar as persons are, who find themselves thus isolated from the great world outside." Sociable yet isolated, the settlers of Sugar Creek lived in a localistic world.[2]

But was this a community? Communities operate through direct, face-to-face connections between people and consequently depend on a degree of population stability. The population of colonial Dedham, Massachusetts, for example, "turned over" so little that Lockridge could describe the community as "closed." But only three in ten Sugar Creek heads of household enumerated on the 1830 census remained to be counted in 1840; and in 1850 and 1860 the percentage of household heads remaining after only ten years fell to two in ten. Sugar Creek represents the riddle of community in the American West: the forms of economy and polity practiced by local folk suggest strong communal ties; but what kind of community could this be with so many men and women moving in and moving out, with people constantly passing through, with neighborhood faces changing so frequently?

First, communities are composed not so much of individuals as of households and families, and there was considerably more social continuity among families than is indicated by the persistence statistics. Of the approximately 175 families who settled before 1840, 44 laid down roots deep enough to persist in Sugar Creek beyond 1860. From the vantage point of these "original settler families" the local population must have appeared more stable. Three-quarters of their children and grandchildren began households and raised children of their own along Sugar Creek. Original settler fathers and sons headed six in ten households in 1840, and although their numerical strength in the community declined during the next two decades, in 1860 family descendants continued to head one-third of the households. Kinship ties, in fact, became increasingly important to the structure of community relations as Sugar Creek matured. In 1830 about one in five heads of household shared his surname with the heads of at least two other households; thirty years later that proportion had doubled.[3]

Moreover, these original settler families strengthened their influence within the community by marrying locally and building family alliances. Seven in ten children and better than half the grandchildren of these original settler families found spouses among Sugar Creek families who had lived in the community for ten years or more. Four of ten children and three of ten grandchildren, in fact, married within the small circle of forty-four original families. In part, of course, this was circumstantial: the opportunities to find marriage partners in such a small, isolated community must have been severely restricted. But the extensive local practice of what some have called "sibling-exchange marriage" suggests that real choice was at work here. Among original settler families, a significant minority of marriages took place among sibling sets: Ann Black married Nicholas

Pyle, and five years later her brother Thomas married Pyle's sister, Edith; Jane and Elizabeth McElvain married James and John Fletcher; Alexander, Martha, and Lavinia Cassity wed Elizabeth, Joseph, and Elijah Lockridge, and three other Cassity girls married the Bridges brothers. During the first half-century of Sugar Creek's history, sibling exchange accounted for nearly one in five of the marriages within the group of original settler families, a pattern that continued unabated into the 1850s, when two of Jacob Rauch's sons married Cassity women. As strange as this pattern may seem today, it merely elaborated the general endogamous custom of the country.[4]

Endogamous marriage strengthened family ties through marriage in one generation, blood relationship in the next. Moreover, within a legal system of partible inheritance, sibling exchange facilitated the concentration of real property that might otherwise be either divided into small parcels or altogether liquidated during probate in order to endow heirs with their appropriate shares. Although the original holdings of many families dissipated through such multiple divisions over the years, families practicing intermarriage and sibling exchange stood a better chance of retaining their original grants by combining their resources with other original settler families. In 1838 members of these forty-four families held nearly 90 percent of the arable timber and margin lands along Sugar Creek. In 1858, although their numerical strength in the community had declined, members of these families continued to hold over three-quarters of timber and margin lands, and better than a third of the newly opened prairie, for a total of over half of the one hundred square miles of land drained by upper Sugar Creek. Intermarriage facilitated the retention and concentration of family property.[5]

The riddle of backcountry community can be resolved by acknowledging the fact that two groups coexisted in Sugar Creek: a majority with high levels of mobility, who farmed for a time before pushing on, and a significantly more permanent landed minority who rooted themselves in the community during the first two decades of settlement, first established the neighborhoods, then lived and worked together in them for many years, intermarrying and passing their improved farms on to their children. The continuity required for community institutions was supplied by these core families, who formed a web of overlapping kin groups and came to control a large portion of the real property along the creek. Within Sugar Creek a community of families with considerable persistence existed alongside a group with considerable mobility.[6]

Between these two groups there existed a potential for political tension, but it was slow to appear. For the first ten or fifteen years of settlement, of course, when all families were relative newcomers,

these distinctions had not yet matured. Equally important, before
1828 republican tradition proscribed class or group use of the political process. Political authority was relegated to men of the "better
sort," to whom the rank and file deferred. Daniel Pope Cook was
elected to Congress in 1819 and returned for three more terms; in
Springfield precinct, which included the voters of Sugar Creek, he
received an average of nine of every ten votes in those four elections.
Men with authority and respect in the local community stood for
office and were generally supported by large majorities. In 1820,
when Zachariah Peter offered himself as a candidate for the state
assembly, he lost but gathered votes from nearly every elector in his
locale. The next year, he and William Drennan were elected Sangamon County commissioners without opposition, and in 1824 Peter
was reelected with nearly universal support. In 1827 Peter began a
long tenure as Sugar Creek justice of the peace. In his first try for
state office, in 1822, Job Fletcher ran third in a field of three but
nevertheless won the support of most of his neighbors; in 1826, he
won election to the Illinois assembly with votes from nine out of ten of
the constituents in his precinct. Fletcher was reelected in 1828.[7]

   These deferential political traditions were challenged during the
first term of President Andrew Jackson. In their zeal for victory in
1828, Jackson men in Sangamon, as elsewhere, mobilized the rural
electorate. Once in power, the administration made it clear that it
expected political loyalty from its appointees. In the bitter presidential contest of 1824, Congressman Cook was vilified by Jackson men
for casting Illinois's lone vote for John Quincy Adams when the dead-
locked electoral college sent the decision to the House of Representatives, and Jackson men made sure of Cook's defeat at the next election. After Jackson ascended to the presidency, his supporters used
the patronage to punish opponents and reward supporters; in 1829,
Dr. John Todd, a Clay supporter of 1824, was unceremoniously removed from his position as receiver of the Springfield Land Office
and replaced by a Jackson man, William L. May. During his first term
President Jackson's war on the Bank of the United States and his
opposition to the use of federal funds for "internal improvements"
alienated many of the aspiring commercial farmers of the Sangamo.
The president's supporters began to speak of their movement as
"The Democracy"—that is, the force of the common people, as distinguished from political movements of the political and economic
elite. The "Era of Good Feelings" was giving way to an era of factional
and class-based party politics.[8]

   But an organized opposition in Sugar Creek did not take form
until 1832. That April a group of local farmers met at Thomas Black's
cabin in Patton Settlement to discuss their options for the upcoming

JOB FLETCHER (1793–1872) in 1836, the year he was reelected as a Whig candidate to the Illinois state senate. Fletcher came to Sugar Creek from Kentucky in 1819 with his wife, Mary Kerchner Fletcher, and their baby, Permelia, and was soon followed by numerous other members of the Fletcher clan. Something of an intellectual, Fletcher taught school, acted as community lawyer and as the county's first justice of the peace, and won election to the state legislature in 1826 and the senate in 1835. During the legislative session of 1836–37, the Sangamon delegation, all Whigs, including Abraham Lincoln, became known as "The Long Nine," because each man stood at least six feet tall. Farmer and active churchman, Fletcher became the leader of the Sugar Creek Whigs.

elections. Their agenda included a number of issues, including the inadequate state funding of public education, but their preeminent concern was the subversion of traditional republicanism under the Jackson aegis. "The present mode of electioneering," they wrote to the *Sangamo Journal,* "prevents in a great degree our ablest citizens from suffering their names to be entered on the list of competitors for office." Jackson men, they complained, won their political battles by "visiting almost every elector within the county or district and treating them with ardent spirits for the purpose of influencing their votes"; this and other such unscrupulous practices were "frought with corruption and dangerous to our liberties, degrading to the candidate and insulting to the elector." The political world of these farmers was inhabited by "able citizens" who stood for office out of civic duty, and by a mass of "electors" liable to be swayed by democratic passions. After meeting periodically through the summer, a committee headed by the local leaders Job Fletcher and Zachariah Peter announced themselves to be in support of Henry Clay's "American System"— federal support for road and canal construction, a national bank, protective tariffs, the gradual emancipation of slaves, and the colonization of freed blacks to Africa. This was the program of a "country party" of conservative landowners.[9]

While he remained in office, President Jackson's immense personal popularity overwhelmed these fledgling efforts at opposition politics. In 1832 Jackson took 56 percent of the Sugar Creek vote, and Joseph Duncan, Jackson candidate for Congress, was reelected, defeating his Clay opponent with 71 percent. Two years later Jackson partisan William May won a congressional seat with the support of 64 percent of the Sugar Creek electors. Jackson's pending retirement, however, opened up new possibilities. Led by Stephen A. Douglas, Illinois Jackson men held their first state convention in 1835, selecting a slate of candidates headed by Martin Van Buren for president and drafting a platform that all "Democrats" (a label just then coming into use) were honor-bound to support. Men were forced to align with either the Democrats or their opponents, who now began to call themselves "Whigs." In a special election that year, held to fill several vacant senate seats, Sugar Creek electors gave 87 percent of their votes to favorite son Job Fletcher and 67 percent to Springfield hosteler Archer Herndon, both anti–Van Buren men. Genuine two-party rivalry had finally come to Sugar Creek.[10]

Over the next few years both Democrats and Whigs strengthened their local party organizations and contested each national, state, and local election. Sugar Creek precinct results reflected an even split between them. Anticipating the congressional and state contests to be decided in August, candidates from both parties attended a forum held at Gideon Vancil's farm on July 18, 1836, where, according to the *Journal,* state representative Abraham Lincoln took the lead in "espousing the Whig side of all questions," and showed great "skill and tack" in handling the often hostile questions from Democratic partisans. In the elections, the Whig congressional candidate again lost the district to William May but gathered 53 percent of the Sugar Creek vote. That November, Van Buren carried the state, but William Henry Harrison, the old governor of the Northwest Territory, won the support of 57 percent of the Sugar Creek electors. Two years later, however, Sugar Creek precinct gave majorities to the Democrats for all state contests, and although Stephen Douglas lost his congressional bid to Whig John Stuart, in Sugar Creek he defeated his opponent. Attesting to the wavering allegiance of the district was the fact that while Sangamon County sent solidly Whig delegations to the state legislature, in successive elections voters from Sugar Creek spread their support between both Whigs and Democrats and even failed to provide Job Fletcher with a local majority in 1836, although Fletcher won the election and spent the next six years in the Illinois senate.[11]

The rise of party politics broke the older pattern of uniform support for candidates of the "better sort" and introduced patterns of group voting into Sugar Creek. The elections of the late 1830s were close contests; but what must have been clear to the men who assembled, argued, drank, and fought over politics at John Drennan's polling place was the fact that the representatives from established families, on the one hand, and representatives from transient and squatting familes, on the other, often supported candidates from the opposing parties. In the congressional races of 1836 and 1838, for example, electors from original settler families gave the Whig candidate approximately six in ten of their votes, while men from families relatively new to the creek voted in almost the same proportion for the Democrat. Because the persistent were usually owners, the transient largely squatters, this political division followed lines of economic cleavage. Electors without real property cast seven in ten of their votes for Stephen Douglas in 1838, but only three in ten voters enumerated on that year's tax list supported the "Little Giant."[12]

Moreover, party identification was a family affair. Two-thirds of the time, voters with the same surname made exactly the same electoral choices. Families developed reputations as being either Whig or Democrat supporters. There were Democrats among the most persistent: the Pulliams, Drennans, Balls, Rauchs, and Lockridges, for example, were prominent supporters of the Democracy. But during the 1830s the majority of men from persistent Sugar Creek families cast their lot with the Whigs. The Whig party in Sugar Creek reflected the developing commercial aspirations of propertied farmers; but

Whig political identity was also part of a growing self-consciousness on the part of the persistent kin groups in the community.

In his reminiscence of Sugar Creek life, Moses Wadsworth incidentally demonstrated how kinship bound the neighbors of this open-country community together. In October 1841, after an unusually productive wheat harvest, fifteen-year-old Moses accompanied several householders who filled their wagons and set out on the week-long round trip to the grain market of St. Louis. This party—Silas Harlan, his brother Elijah with sons Jehu and John, brothers Noah and Thomas Mason, Ezra Barnes, George Eastman, William Crow, and John Dill—all lived in or near Drennan's Prairie, and most counted kin among the group. The parents of the Mason brothers, Noah Sr. and Lucinda, arrived in 1824, some of the few early emigrants from New England. From Sugar Creek, Lucinda began a correspondence with female relations back home and struck the spark for their husbands to emigrate. First in the mid-thirties came the Eastmans, then in 1840 the Wadsworths. Daniel Wadsworth, Moses' father, and George Eastman, his uncle, had married half-sisters, kin of Lucinda Mason; later, when Eastman died, his widow moved in with the Wadsworths. In 1841 Jehu Harlan and Moses' sister Emily were "sparkin'," and they married within the year. Jehu's aunt, Elizabeth Messick Harlan, wife of Silas, had a young sister, Julia, living in her household who saw a good deal of young William Crow; they married in 1843. Ezra Barnes, the New England peddler who settled on Sugar Creek, married Elizabeth Mason, sister to Noah Jr. and Thomas. In short, kinship linked together the lives and fortunes of these traveling companions.[13]

Six years after this trip, in 1847, Moses married Elizabeth Harlan Wheeler, niece of Jehu Harlan, who had married Moses' sister Emily. Into her marriage with Moses, Elizabeth brought a productive patrimony of a hundred-acre farm on the edge of "Spanish Needle Prairie," ten miles south of the Wadsworth family home but near households of Wheelers and Harlans. Over the next ten years Elizabeth bore and raised five children, as Moses struggled to "make a crop" on what proved to be "seepy" or swampy land. Their survival depended upon the aid of Elizabeth's nearby kin, "not one of whom," Moses later wrote, "would accept a cent for the labor of himself." In 1857 Elizabeth died of "childbed fever," and kin again came to the rescue. Catherine Harlan Willson, Elizabeth's sister, took in baby Frank Wadsworth, only a month old, nursed him along with her own babe, and raised the boy; Emily Wadsworth Harlan, Moses' sister, took charge of the youngest daughter, Susan; and Moses returned to his parents' household, where his mother cared for her son's three oldest. Without "the connexions," as Moses called his kin in a letter to a cousin back East, life would have been hard indeed.[14]

Kinship, writes sociologist George Hicks, is the "central organizing principle of social life" in twentieth-century Appalachia. Likewise, in early-nineteenth-century Sugar Creek kinship provided an organizing force which brought farmers together. As in Wadsworth's case, women often played prominent roles in the "association of households" that bound together persistent families in the local community. The bonds of association among the party of male relations on that marketing trip to St. Louis, for example, came more from links among mothers, wives, and sisters than connections among the men themselves. Moreover, second-generation couples took up residence near the wife's kin, who offered aid and support, as often as near kin of the husband. The support that helped Wadsworth during his marriage came largely from his wife's family, and in the crisis brought on by Elizabeth's death, Moses was utterly dependent upon female relations. Because of the high mortality of adult men and women, near kith and kin frequently raised Sugar Creek children, as in the case of the orphan boy abused by schoolmaster Cornelius Lyman, or the sons and daughters of Moses Wadsworth. This shifting around of children, which took place largely within networks of women bound together by kinship, reinforced the mutual dependency of extended families.[15]

Kinship contributed to community by mobilizing groups for public association and participation. Yet despite woman's role in shaping the form of the community through family connections, her place remained domestic, largely "invisible" to the world at large. Public life was dominated by men and their rituals. The public culture that kinship helped bring to life was, in the words of another historian of the Sangamo, "ultra-virle."[16]

Consider drinking and drunkenness. Farm women consumed their share of alcohol, but it was the men who regularly engaged in public boozing. One early settler remembered that at the Sangamon general election of August 1822 tavern-keepers lined up their wares on benches outside the log-cabin Springfield courthouse. Present were "white men," as well as "Indians and darkies, they of course not being allowed the right of suffrage," but all got equally drunk. "The white men sang songs, the Indians and darkies danced, and a general frolic occurred. Every candidate had to fill his portmanteau with whiskey, and go around and see and treat every voter with the poisonous stuff, or stand a chance of being defeated." Whiskey was ever present in

Sangamon society, Lincoln noted in an 1842 temperance address: "government provided it for its soldiers and sailors, and to have a rolling or raising, a hunking or hoe-down, anywhere without it, was *positively insufferable*." It was, as one settler wrote, a "universal custom" to serve corn whiskey—plenty of it—at all public gatherings, customary for the captain of the local militia to treat the company after the drill, customary for candidates to campaign, as the Sugar Creek Whigs complained, with liberal donations of "ardent spirits." The "little brown jug" supplied the "good cheer" that men demanded as their only remuneration at frolics, where, according to Samuel Williams, "three or four gallons of whisky were furnished by the proprietors of the premises, as was said, to make the men better able to endure the toil of the day." More than one Sangamo pioneer told of postponing his cabin raising until he could afford to supply the thirsty neighborhood. William McLaren recalled raisings where fifty or sixty men consumed "firey red whisky" until their faces were "swollen up like bitten with a hundred wasps." Indeed, accidents caused by drunkenness presented the greatest danger at raisings. To supply this demand many farmers added distilleries to their farms. Despite his Whiggish complaints about the boozing of Jackson partisans, Thomas Black operated a copper still and public house on his farm, where he dispensed half-pints of peach brandy for two bits, sour mash for one. Robert Pulliam, a man of "the Democracy," operated a "house of entertainment" at his dwelling, where each day a few men gathered to take their drams, others loitered over sour mash while they waited for their corn to be ground, and on Saturday's farmers took a few hours off to carouse over rounds.

> Hail Columbia, happy land,
> If you ain't drunk, I'll be damned.[17]

Drunk or sober, public fighting was another common occurrence. Moses Wadsworth wrote that on election and muster day "nearly every boy in the precinct, old enough to ride a horse, accompanied the fathers and brothers, and all spent the day. Liquor was usually available, and drunken men and fights were often witnessed." "You needn't be tryin' to bullyrag and scrouge me unless you're spilin' for a fight," one citizen shouted to another, "and if you are, I reckon you'll find me an owdacious scrouger that'll jist bodiacerously split you right open down the middle." "You onery low-down dog," his opponent shot back: "ye needn't try to get shet of me with all yer tomfool brag. I'll knock you into a cocked hat soon'r'n ye kin say Jack Robinson." Samuel Williams remembered that at a muster "some of the men became very boisterous, and several of them stripped to the pants for a fistic fight." In electoral contests between partisans, verbal jousting frequently broke into violence. In the 1838 congressional contest, John Stuart got Stephen Douglas in a headlock and the "Little Giant" bit his opponent's thumb so hard that he left a scar. Through the 1840s, gangs of neighborhood toughs frequently fought out their political differences with their fists as well as their votes. At the polls in 1840, Sugar Creek Democrat Dr. Alexander Shields challenged a leading county Whig to fisticuffs, no holds barred. "His fist was soft; my head was hard, and by the time he raised some five or six knots, his fist was useless. I caught him and drew him down upon me, and then reached to get him by the throat; and my thumb landed in his eye," but before he could pop his victim's eyeball from its socket, Whigs pulled the fighters apart, and the dispute ended with the opponents paying fines for disorderly conduct to the local justice. Men also loved cock-fighting, bull-baiting, and other blood sports. One of the farmers' favorite amusements at log rollings, William McLaren recalled with delight, "was to round up a chip-munk, a rabbit, or a snake, and make him take refuge in a burning log-heap, and watch him squirm and fry," or, at communal hunts, "to skin a wolf alive and watch its 'antics.'"[18]

Not all men drank themselves into oblivion or fought like dogs, of course, but male culture generally accepted such conduct as a regular occurrence of public life. Westerners argued that this spirit of robust competition produced an egalitarian community within which no man was better than another. Caroline Kirkland overheard an Englishman loudly complaining of the lack of respect westerners showed traveling gentlemen. "Respect!" retorted the tavern-keeper, "why should I show more respect to any man than he does to me? Because he wears a finer coat? His coat don't do me any good. Does he pay his taxes any better than I do? Is he kinder to his family? Does he act more honestly by his neighbors? Will he have a higher place in heaven than I shall?"[19]

Western men did demonstrate an undeniable familiarity. It was common, for example, for a man "take a seat on the knee of a friend, and with one arm thrown familiarly around his friend's neck, have a friendly talk, or a legal or political consultation." Men also thought nothing of rolling up together around campfires to keep each other warm, or sharing the few available beds of frontier hotels. One Sangamon lawyer told of two colleagues, Campbell and Benedict, who shared a bed on the circuit until one, feeling greatly put upon by the other's bed behavior, finally objected. "Confound you," exclaimed Campbell, "I have lain with you, but I never did *sleep* with you." Nevertheless, that night Benedict returned from an evening at the tavern, "got undressed, even to the taking off of his drawers," then "jumped into bed and began to fondle" his mate. Campbell had "armed his heel" with one of his spurs for just such a contingency, however, and jabbed it into Benedict's flanks. "Jesus!" Benedict cried as he flew out of bed and across the room, "the fellow has taken me for his blamed old horse." Such familiarity, one settler wrote, "would have shocked our English cousins, and disgusted our Boston brothers," but in the West men found it perfectly acceptable.[20]

Notwithstanding this rustic competition and familiarity, however, the men of Sugar Creek acted deferentially toward community "fathers." Before the era of party politics, and well into it, local leaders almost invariably came from the ranks of men from families whose roots went back to the first ten or fifteen years of settlement, families that practiced intermarriage and succeeded at conserving or extending their property. It is likely that the practice of voting viva voce, of announcing political choices in the presence of the assembled householders of the community, reinforced the influence of the fathers. Squire Job Fletcher or Billy Drennan of Drennan's Prairie, James Patton or Harmon Husband of Patton Settlement, Joseph Poley or George Wallace from The Sources: these were the men who held positions of local leadership during their mature years, serving as supervisors of road districts, as clerks of election, and, ultimately, as justices of the peace, which conferred on them the honorific title of "squire." When fights broke out, Samuel Williams remembered, these patriarchs frequently intervened; their "wiser counsel" prevailing, "all went home peaceably," for in this localistic world, public deference to the "fathers" worked as an important mechanism by which the authority of kinship was carried over into public life. Gatherings of men offered occasions to work out a local hierarchy of loyalty and authority based on persistence, family, kinship, and the patronage of community fathers.[21]

"Women of that day attended none of the rough and exerting sports of men," wrote settler James Haines; they "cultivated the joys and pleasures of the hearth and home." Traveling through northern Illinois in the early 1840s, essayist and feminist Margaret Fuller expressed a somewhat different sensibility concerning this contrast between the vigorous male public life and the mundane household existence of women. Farm women "found themselves confined to a comfortless and laborious life," she wrote, "while their husbands and brothers enjoyed the country in hunting or fishing." A quarter-century later an aging western farmer fondly recalled the cabin raisings, log rollings, and other occasions for "swapping work," the public politics, militia musters, and road duty, the freedom to "roam and fish, or hunt as we pleased, amid the freshness and beauties of nature—in short, the "virile" public life of the antebellum era. "There was excitement in all this— a verve and scope, a freedom, and independence and abandon, suited to our rougher nature and coarser tastes." "But," he pondered, "how was it with our wives: From all these bright, and to us fascinating scenes and pastimes, they were excluded. They were shut up with the children in log cabins."[22]

The language of politics reflected this sexual separation. When, during the congressional campaign in 1834, an anonymous press critic accused Democratic candidate William May of adulterous behavior, he chose not to deny the charge but rather to cast doubt on his critic's manhood, labeling him "some spindle-shanked, toad-eating, man-granny, . . . some *puling* sentimental, *he*-old maid whose cold liver and pulseless heart, never felt a desire which could be tempted!" Similarly, in his 1838 letter to the *Journal,* George Wallace attacked Cornelius Lyman's supporters as "unmanly" and defended the schoolmaster's accusers as men "who had breasts to feel as men should feel."[23]

"Community," then, consists of different kinds of relationships. The ideal, of course, is "membership"; but communities also have their "subjects." Despite the importance of women's roles in the families and kin networks that structured and supported the local community, Sugar Creek was, finally, a community of men, led by fathers, to whom women as a group were "subject." Sugar Creek was, as George Wallace wrote, a community of "independent yeomanry."[24]

As much as any man, Moses Wadsworth benefited from the supports of kinship, and by no means did he lack an appreciation of his "connexions." But when, in the 1880s, he composed a memoir of life along Sugar Creek, it was not the aids and comforts of kinships over which he waxed sentimental but the time spent among men in the public culture of the Sangamo. During that 1841 marketing trip to St. Louis, he wrote, he watched in boyish wonder as "the jolly company surrounded the fire, seated on Nature's footstool, devoured supper with superhuman appetites, and, [with] the ruddy blaze illuminating the landscape for many rods around, related the most marvelous tales of pioneer times—of hunting, fighting, wrestling, encounters with Indians, jokes on each other, etc., until a late hour." To Moses, forty years later, it was the masculine relations of kinship and community on that Indian summer trip that provided "the brightest links in memory's chain."[25]

16

The Community
of Feeling

During the mid-1820s, a group of Catholic families emigrated from Kentucky and settled in Sugar Creek. Joseph Logsdon, with his wife and children, first squatted on the western edge of the prairie in the Sugar Camp neighborhood in 1824, and over the next five years the timber margin north and south of the Logsdon claim filled with other Catholic households, all members of a clan that had been established through intermarriage in Maryland (a colonial refuge for British Catholics), then had moved together to central Kentucky in the 1780s. With them came Logsdon's sister, Elizabeth, her husband, Joseph Durbin, and their four married children with their families; Logsdon's brothers-in-law, James and Richard Simpson, their wives, a score of children, and associated in-laws; William Burtle and his wife, Sarah Ogden, with their nine children, including their married son, John, and his wife, Matilda Simpson; Sarah Burtle's brother, Zachariah Ogdon, his wife and six children; and the widow Ruth Gatton with her five children, including her grown sons, John, Thomas, and their families.[1]

These first Anglo-American Catholic families in central Illinois appealed to the bishop of St. Louis for a priest, and in late 1829 a Jesuit missionary came up the St. Louis Road from American Bottom to celebrate mass. Once or twice each year for the next fifteen years itinerant priests gathered these Catholic families at the William Burtle farm to perform the rituals of faith. When widow Ruth Gatton died in 1832, the Catholics buried her alongside two Burtle children, victims of fever, on a gentle knoll adjacent to the Burtle farm, looking out onto the prairie. They converted family land to consecrated, communal ground.[2]

Sugar Creek Catholics intermarried according to the custom of the country, a pattern encouraged by missionaries, who scarcely disguised their displeasure when a Catholic married outside the church. Josephus Gatton and Mary Burtle wed in 1834, and she bore five children before dying nine years later. After a year as a widower, Gatton married Eveline Husband, daughter of Harmon Husband, who farmed several miles south in Patton Settlement. When Father Philip Conlan, a Jesuit missionary from St. Louis, arrived in Sugar Creek in February 1848, Josephus and Eveline presented to him two new children for baptism. "John Newton and Elizabeth Gatton received private Baptisms, both being sick," Conlan wrote; they are "children to Josephus Gatton a Catholic and Evoline [sic] Husband a vile apposer [sic] to Baptism—in which she does not believe, as having no form of belief." Priests never failed to label non-Catholic spouses as "unpractical Catholics" or "protestants," but only a minority of Sugar Creek Catholics chose spouses outside the clan. The core of the nine most populous Catholic families intermarried at an exceptionally high rate: seven of ten children and grandchildren found mates within the group, and nearly half these marriages were sibling exchanges.[3]

Intermarriage among the Catholics, as among other groups in Sugar Creek, facilitated the retention of family property. Joseph, James, and Mary, children of William and Sarah Burtle, married Maria, Elizabeth, and Josephus Gatton in the 1830s, and the three couples established adjacent households north of Pulliam's sugar grove, where Joseph and James jointly purchased 120 acres of land and raised corn and cattle in common. In 1851, when James Burtle died intestate, the probate court appointed brother Joseph guardian of the five minor children as well as executor of the estate, and the widow's brother, Josephus, stood as his security. Settlement of the estate created complicated problems, for Elizabeth Gatton Burtle was entitled to her dower, the minor children to their partible shares, and Joseph to his half of the farm. Joseph petitioned the circuit court for partition, and the judge appointed three neighbors to "fairly and impartially" determine the division "by metes and bounds." These "commissioners" reported back to the next term of the court, however, "that said lands are not susceptible of division without great injury to the owners or consistently with the interest of said estate."

The lands consist of three forty acre tracts lying adjoining on the East & West. The timber, houses, orchard, and stock water are all upon the West forty, and all these are upon a part of said forty

acres not exceeding ten acres. And if the land is divided the land
is so situated that the houses, orchard, and stock water must be
assigned to one part, and the other parts would have no stock
water. That the remainder of the land, if divided among the five
heirs, would be comparatively valueless, being divided into such
small portions, and destitute of water and other improvements,
except fencing. That the East side of said land is flat wet prairie.
That the lands cannot be divided into two equal parts without
injury to the owners. . . . They believe from their knowledge of
the land and for the above reasons that the land would sell at
higher price in one body, than when divided into two or more
parts.

The court ruled that the estate be sold at auction, and on November
2, 1852, Joseph Burtle successfully bid ten dollars per acre, financing
his purchase of the entire 120-acre parcel with a low-interest loan,
again secured by his brother-in-law, Josephus. The court divided the
proceeds among the widow and the heirs, with the children's portions
held in trust by their guardian, Uncle Joseph. Meanwhile the cooperation of the households continued. When the census taker came by in
1860, he found Joseph, who had also been widowed in the forties,
living with his widowed sister-in-law, Elizabeth, and her children; next
door, in Joseph's former residence, lived his nephew, John Thomas,
James's oldest son, who in 1856 married Eliza Simpson. Kin cooperation kept the lands together, and farm operations continued through
the inheritance crisis.[4]
The concentration of faithful attracted other Catholic families, who
purchased or squatted on lands near the cemetery. A wandering German immigrant and potter, Valentine Boll, for example, found Sugar
Creek to his liking, and in 1836 made the round trip back to Germany
in order to bring his bride, Elizabeth Heller, along with a large collection of Catholic relations, all of whom added considerably to the neighborhood. The proximity of Burtles, Gattons, Simpsons, Ogdons, Bolls,
and other Catholic households on each federal census documents the
concentration of the community and suggests their mutual support in
the "borrowing system." By the mid-1840s, when Catholic families
constructed a small church next to the graveyard—named St. Bernard's for the saint of the wilderness—the parish had grown to include
twenty households.[5]
Through these founding years of the Sugar Creek Catholic community, anti-Catholic sentiment in central Illinois grew "popular and ram-
pant," according to William Herndon. In 1835, Lyman Beecher, president of Lane Theological Seminary in Cincinnati, father of Catharine,
Harriet, and Henry Ward Beecher, published his popular and influen-

HUSBAND JOHN THOMAS BURTLE (1833–90), WIFE ELIZA SIMPSON BURTLE (1841–75), AND SON JAMES ROBERT BURTLE (1861–1949). Third-generation Catholic settlers, the couple married in 1856 and Eliza bore nine children before dying at the age of thirty-four. John was photographed during the Civil War at the county fair in Springfield wearing his everyday clothes.

tial anti-Catholic tract *Plea for the West,* in which he worried over an imaginary but ominous popish plot to take over the American frontier for Rome. Anti-Catholicism played right into local politics; it was an issue, for example, in the presidential contest of 1840, when Whigs accused Democrats of manipulating Irish Catholics in order to carry the state for Van Buren. In the presidential election of 1856, the anti-Catholic and anti-immigrant American or "Know-Nothing" party captured a third of the Sangamon county vote, including a like proportion of Sugar Creek ballots. In response, perhaps, to the anti-Catholicism in local culture, the Catholics were the most endogamous and self-contained of all Sugar Creek groups.[6]

But the Catholics were distinguished only by the degree of their exclusivity, for local Protestant congregations followed similar patterns of in-group association. A group of interrelated families constituted the core of each of the Sugar Creek churches. Several Methodist families established a "class" in the early 1820s; another group of kin founded the revivalist Cumberland Presbyterian congregation in 1824, and other Presbyterians began a "regular" Old School church in 1830; the Baptists held meetings in settler cabins during the twenties, then split into two separate meetings. The "borrowing system" and local self-governance offered both the requirement and the opportunity for cooperation; neighborhood landscapes and kinship loyalties wove dispersed households into a common fabric. But in the churches these social relationships came together in a single system of communal association.[7]

Protestant expansion in the American West relied on two vital institution, those of the preacher-organizer and the "camp meeting," both developed during the "Great Revival," an explosion of trans-Appalachian religious enthusiasm that broke out in Kentucky and Tennessee in the late 1790s and continued for a half-dozen years. The preachers were perhaps most important. Methodist circuit riders and "class leaders," and itinerant Baptist and Presbyterian evangelists, were ministers of a new breed—organizers who understood and sympathized with the indigenous culture of the frontier. Established eastern denominations, declared Peter Cartwright, famous circuit rider of the Sangamo, "had no adaptation to the country or people" of the West. He ridiculed preachers who "had regularly studied theology in some of the Eastern States, where they manufacture young preachers like they do lettuce in hot-houses," preachers who carried around bundles of "old manuscript" sermons but who had little ability to capture the imaginations of the people. "The great mass of our Western people wanted a preacher who could mount a stump, a block, or old log, or stand in the bed of a wagon," he remembered, "and without note or manuscript, quote, expound, and apply the word of God to the hearts and consciences of the people."[8]

The most effective preachers, wrote former Illinois Governor Thomas Ford, "sprung up from the body of the people at home," and religious organizers along Sugar Creek either were "circuit-riders," like Cartwright, who arose from the laity and perhaps studied John Wesley's *Notes on the New Testament* but were otherwise unschooled, or "farmer-preachers," men who received "the call" to preach and got themselves licensed by a revivalist sect but supported themselves by farming or a trade. Rural opinion in the Sangamo was opposed to the establishment of a professional, salaried clergy, favoring instead a "secularized ministry." As one local Baptist preacher put it, "the Gospel cannot be carried on silver wheels." The people insisted on a ministry linked directly to folk culture, separated neither by formal training nor professionalism.[9]

Gilbert Dodds, who served for a quarter of a century as minister to the Cumberland Presbyterian congregation at the Sugar Creek meeting and schoolhouse, exemplified the preacher-organizer. Born in South Carolina, the brother of Joseph Dodds, one of the earliest settlers along the creek, Gilbert came to the Sangamo in 1824 to join his kin and organize for the Cumberlands, a revivalist sect that had been expelled from the Presbyterian General Assembly in 1809 for licensing uneducated exhorters like Dodds. Although he lacked formal schooling, as a Kentucky boy Dodds had fallen in love with reading. His hunger for texts led him to Thomas Paine's deist tract *The Age of Reason*, a book, he later remarked, "that came very near to ruining my soul." But a Presbyterian evangelist pulled Dodds back from the precipice in the nick of time, and thereafter the young man dedicated himself to Christian education, preaching the gospel among his frontier neighbors. The year of his arrival in Sugar Creek, he organized five or six families, including his Dodds and Drennan kin, into the first Cumberland congregation in central Illinois. Never one to flinch from a fight, Dodds made the support of public education, advocacy of temperance, and opposition to Southern slavery hallmarks of his ministry.[10]

Running against the current of popular opinion, Billy Drennan, father-in-law of Gilbert's brother, Joseph, convinced the brothers and sisters of the church to retain Dodds, his talented if imperious kinsman, as their "regular pastor" in 1827. Dodds was to "spend one-half of his time in the discharge of his duties" and the other half in farming; the "Sugar Creek society," for its part, was "to liberally contribute for the support of said Dodds." But less than two years later, in 1829, the Cumberland Sangamon Synod approved the dissolution of the contract, "the church failing on their part" to provide the preacher's salary on schedule. As late as the 1850s not one Cumberland preacher in Illinois received financial support from his congregation; all continued, like Dodds, to be "farmer-preachers."[11]

The second organizational tool of the Protestants, the "camp meeting," came to Sugar Creek with the very first settlers. During the "Great Revival" at Cane Ridge in central Kentucky in 1801, a crowd of country folk estimated at an astounding ten to twenty-five thousand, led by a score of Presbyterian, Baptist, and Methodist preachers, shouted, sang, and prayed in the open air for a week, and over three thousand people experienced conversion. Although western camp meetings never again achieved such monumental proportions, Cane Ridge suggested the prototype for thousands of smaller meetings. Throughout the first half of the nineteenth century, preachers of different denominations combined forces and organized revivals in homes or shady groves.[12]

Camp meetings, usually held during the late summer between "laying-by" and harvest, took on the tone of other western gatherings; hundreds of farm families came from a radius of forty or fifty miles to worship, but also to enjoy robust fellowship, male gaming and drinking, female socializing and gossiping. "A camp-meeting *out there* is the most mammoth picnic possible," wrote an eastern observer; "as at a barbecue, the very heart and soul of hospitality and kindness is wide open and poured freely forth." But camp meetings offered something more than mere socializing, something special and awe-inspiring. For one thing, outdoor revivals partook of an ancient and persistent Anglo-Saxon folk belief in the spiritual nature of "sacred groves," a belief summed up in the first line of William Cullen Bryant's popular poem "A Forest Hymn," written in 1825: "The groves were God's first temples." Moritz Busch, a perceptive German romantic traveling through the West, noted the camp meeting's evocation of this heritage. In the grove, he wrote, "the solitude, the shadows, the magical effects, the rustling and humming of the trees, acted upon the imagination."

> The fear of God trembled in them like a mysterious shudder, the spirit of the Pentecost burned in them like a subterranean fire. Or was it the great Pan who was revived in this forest solitude? Or the 'Manito of the Dreams'—the spirit of primeval vegetation, the shadow of the wilderness, the melancholy voice of the lake? It really doesn't matter what the source of this magic was: its influence was almighty.

After attending a grove revival on her tour through Illinois in 1843, Margaret Fuller wrote that she "was never in a better place for vespers."[13]

A proper camp-meeting grove offered nearby pasture, water, and the chance for worshipers to "lay-over" for several days, "securing time for the mind to disentangle itself of worldly care, and rise to an undistracted contemplation of spiritual realities," in the words of a manual for camp-meeting organizers. The anxious, milling crowds, the unusual mingling of both sexes in public space, the campfires casting their eerie light through the forest at evening—all these effects heightened the sense of the extraordinary that suffused the successful camp meeting. Preacher-organizers carefully guided the meeting through distinct phases, spread out over several days, in which exhorters accused the participants of unspeakable guilt, flailed them with the probability of their fall into the bottomless pit, and, after wearing down all resistance, offered sinners the redemptive power of salvation.

> Come, O' thou traveller unknown,
> Whom still I hold but cannot see,
> My company before is gone,
> And I am left alone with thee.
> With thee all night I mean to stay,
> And wrestle till the break of day.[14]

Participants often responded to the preachers' harangues with uncontrolled, highly physical exhibitions of emotional release: singing, running, jerking, barking. Rebecca Burlend, an English immigrant to central Illinois, described an occasion during which "a circle or ring was immediately formed, by the whole assembly taking hold of hands, and capering about surprisingly. Their gesture could not be called dancing, and yet no term that I can employ describes it better." A man then jumped, and shrieking "I feel it!" writhed and trembled until he fell to the ground, exhausted. Christiana Tillson, recently from New England, testified to another meeting where the preacher "got happy" and "frothed at the mouth," while the men and women cried "amen!" and "glory, glory, glory to God!"—all the time dancing, spinning, and falling out one-by-one in exhaustion. One woman on her way home from "meeting" shouted as she walked along the road. Asked the meaning of her outbursts, she cried, "Oh, that blessed word the preacher said, 'meet-a-physic'! Glory! religion's meat and physic both!" "Why do they make so much noise?" John Regan inquired of his neighbor at a large Illinois camp meeting in the 1840s. "Oh! I wouldn't give a straw for a Camp Meeting if they didn't make noise," his guide replied. "If you only once got into the spirit of the thing, you would enjoy the noise as much as I do."[15]

Outsiders like Regan found these emotional displays disturbing, even disgusting, and tried to explain them away as a manifestation of the "simple nature" of the "children of the forest." Modern interpreters, with a psychological perspective, have viewed camp-meeting emotionalism as an outlet for "anxieties generated by status deprivation, guilt, and illness," or as a way of satisfying needs met in our own times by "organized sports, jazz, and movies." These perspectives, however, neglect the religious purposes of the camp meeting and fail to consider westerners' own views of these events. "The pioneer was no hypocrite," one old settler wrote; "if he believed in horse-racing, whisky-drinking, card-playing, or anything of like character, he practiced them openly and above board. If he was of a religious turn of mind he was not ashamed to own it. He could truthfully sing 'I'm not ashamed to own my Lord / Or blush to speak his name.'"

Westerners, in other words, held an ingenuous belief in the miraculous nature of the camp proceedings. Violent physical outbursts expressed the suffering and "penitential conflict" necessary to receive God's grace. These physical "signs" offered powerful evidence that God yet walked the land, speaking to His people as He had to the children of Israel. Moreover, the conversion of the individual took place in a dramatic communal context; it was God's means of founding new congregations or adding new and revitalized members to existing ones. The camp meeting, in short, was a sacred organizing process which transferred the fervor and commitment of revival Protestantism into communal institutions. At the camp meeting not only individuals and churches, but whole communities got organized and were provided with a mystical, sanctified genesis.[16]

In October 1819, as the few remaining Kickapoo families were building the last of their traditional winter *wikiups* south of the sugar grove and the first American squatters harvesting corn from the newly broken soil, Methodist organizers pulled together over a hundred settlers from the Sugar Creek district for a revival in the timber on the east side of sugar camp prairie. This was the first organized social gathering of Americans in the Sangamo, and it provided a kind of symbolic ribbon-cutting for the Sugar Creek community. Out of this revival emerged several Methodist classes, including one led by grist miller James Sims of Drennan's Prairie. In the mid-twenties, this class moved to the cabin of John French, located in "Cherry Grove," a prominent stand of timber on Panther Creek renamed "Harlan's Grove" after Methodist farmer Silas Harlan filed a claim there in 1827. Over the next quarter-century, Methodists and others held annual revivals at the "Sugar Creek Camp Ground" in Harlan's Grove, amid what one participant later called "forty acres of the most magnificent timber, perfectly cleared from undergrowth and brush, and presenting a deep, unbroken shade, with a carpet under your feet of the deepest green." Harlan's Grove became one of the most important religious and social sites along Sugar Creek.[17]

The Methodists were not alone. Gilbert Dodds first brought the Cumberland Presbyterians together at revivals, using these "protracted meetings" to build the membership of his church. Baptists, too, held camp meetings in the mid-twenties. Both groups soon found permanent locations for their churches and built congregations that sustained the communal bonds among associating households. Along with the presence of kin, membership in a church dramatically increased the chances of heads of household persisting in the community. Nearly nine out of ten original settler families were affiliates of Sugar Creek churches.

The unlettered farmer-preachers of Sugar Creek and their equally unliterate congregants left few documents of their inner spiritual lives. But other texts exist. During the early nineteenth century, scores of American publishers issued regional compilations of the songs of country folk, books designed for use by the masters of "singing schools," evening classes held in cabins, churches, and schools, in which farm families could learn the "rudiments of music" and master choral singing in three- or four-part harmony. Regardless of their denominational proclivities, Moses Wadsworth remembered, residents attended singing schools simply because they loved to sing. James Magredy of Sugar Creek remembered that "with a *Missouri Harmony* under your arm as a passport," a young man could call at the cabin of a young woman with assurance that her parents would let them attend "singin' school" together, and the couple would spend the evening "sparkin'" to song while eagerly anticipating the slow ride home together through the dark timber.[18]

These cardboard-bound songbooks were one of the first commodities of American popular culture, and since the publisher's goal was to sell them, the books included the most traditional and accessible music of the country, drawing on a repertoire that included love ballads, work songs, and dance jigs, but they most prominently featured spiritual songs. When William Herndon asked one of his many correspondents to write down the words of the songs folks used to sing, the man, knowing of Herndon's interest in the profane, replied in apology, "I have forgotten all but the pious songs." In this light it is perhaps not surprising that most of the lyrics in the most popular and widely available Illinois songbook, *The Missouri Harmony* (first published in 1819), were strictly religious. These songbooks, then, provide a source for understanding something of the religious sentiment of rural communities such as Sugar Creek.[19]

Psalm-songs, practically unchanged from versions in the English psalters of the sixteenth century, constituted the core of the *Missouri Harmony* collection. In singing schools and churches the leader "lined-out" these metered verses, and the people sang them to familiar modal melodies, like "Old Hundreth:"

> Before Jehovah's awful throne,
> Ye nations bow with sacred joy;
> Know that the Lord is God alone,
> He can create, and He destroy.

Versified by eighteenth-century English hymnist Isaac Watts, as were many of the most treasured lyrics, these lines emphasized God's almighty power. Even newer lyrics, dating from the years of the Great Revival, proclaimed God's omnipresence, although often with a more typical nineteenth-century emphasis on His revelation through nature:

> Thru all the world below,
> God is seen all around,
> Search hills and valleys through,
> There He's found.
> The growing of the corn,
> The lily and the thorn,
> The pleasant and forlorn,
> All declare, God is there,
> In meadows drest in green,
> There He's seen.

Country folk sang these lines to the popular five-tone folk melody "Captain Kidd," a tune to which British and American folk had set both sacred and profane lyrics for at least three centuries.[20]

The frailty of man, the catechismal corollary to God's sovereignty, supplied the most prominent theme in *The Missouri Harmony*. Folks sang this popular verse of Watts to another doleful, folkish melody:

> Hark! from the tombs a doleful sound,
> Mine ears attend the cry:
> "Ye living men come view the ground
> Where you must shortly lie."

So persistently did songs dwell on the themes of death, decay, and depravity, that musicologist Alan Lomax's conclusion that "the people were in love with death, the great leveler" seems fully warranted. Although this notion contradicts the idea that western American Protestantism was a "democratic" and "happy" version of Christianity, the lyrics in *The Missouri Harmony* seem fully in accord with the bare facts of life and death in Sugar Creek.

Why should we start, and fear to die?
What tim'rous worms we mortals are!
Death is the gate to endless joy,
And yet we dred to enter there.

The pains, the groans, the dying-strife,
Fright our approaching souls away;
Still shrink we back again to life,
Fond of our prison and our clay.

Although these settlers placed a greater emphasis than had their seventeenth-century forebears on the necessity of human preparation for, and acceptance of, God's saving grace, modifying somewhat the "awful doctrine of predestination," by no means should this suggest that they held an optimistic view of the human prospect. The cardinal points of the traditional Reformed faith remained prominent in the common songs of the singing schools as well as the churches.[21]

Human frailty, however, did not suggest passivity. "I am Sory that your father and mother is sic," John Ross wrote his cousin. "I hope that they all better by this time. We are all Sojourners as all our fathers weare. We Should be up and doing while it is day be four the night of death comes." The Methodists, Baptists, and Cumberland Presbyterians of Sugar Creek all committed themselves intensely to "be up and doing" the work of the world, to reform the most worldly of the cultural habits of the settlers. A good deal of the moral power and authority of the churches accrued from the war they waged against sin.[22]

Church fathers acted not only as guiding lights and political leaders but as disciplinarians for farm families. In many churches male leaders sat as a moral court, judging congregational and individual conduct. In August 1828, for example, following a walloping party after the notoriously rowdy local elections held the first Tuesday of the month, the Cumberland elders hauled several affiliated men before the congregation and accused them of moral offenses ranging from "Drunkenness and Frolicing," to "Dancing and Profane Cursing and Swearing." The elders restored to good graces one man who demonstrated a "change of heart," but suspended the other "from the communion of the church," for though they "made confession," they "would not profess sorrow and showed no signs of repentance" for their sin of "cavortin'." The Methodists similarly brought two men before the church and accused them of engaging in an unbrotherly fight: "Barger acknowledged the truth of the specified charges that on his own premises, Easley got very abusive, threatened to shoot him, then set on him and hit him, called him a damned hog. He is very sorry that this happened on the Sabboth [sic] or that there was occasion for it." The church

reprimanded both men. Church courts supplemented local justice-of-
the-peace courts, handling offenses against Christian communal
conduct.[23]

Churches, as forces of order, reinforced the basic cultural assumptions. Women played active roles in their congregations, and, perhaps
because men usually denied them the public stage, participated prominently in the emotional outpourings associated with camp meetings
and revivals. "Under the influence of high religious excitement," wrote
one Cumberland evangelist, young women at camp meetings broke
into a babble that sounded like "the mere incoherent ravings of an
unbridled imagination" but took its inspiration from God; the "mothers in Isreal threw themselves earnestly and decidedly into the work of
the times." Yet women's church work did not challenge but rather
affirmed patriarchy. The churches of the Sangamo had separate en-
trances for the sexes, and men and women sat on benches on opposite
sides of the meetinghouse, just as at camp meetings preachers tried to
keep men and women in separate groups, and at public celebrations
the sexes kept themselves separated. Women never led services or
spoke from the pulpit. The leadership in the church—the preachers,
deacons, and elders—echoed the male leadership of the community.[24]

Leaders of the Sugar Creek Cumberland church commonly called
up women accused of "Immoral Conduct" before the congregation to
chastise them publicly. In May 1840, for example, twenty-year-old
Jane Nuckolls stood before the church and acknowledged her crime of
fornication; later that year, before the same congregants, she married
John Lockridge. "In a little village or in a new and sparsely settled
country," William Herndon wisely observed, "everybody knows everybody, and any man's business is the business of the whole community.
Such people love to tattle and to lie about one another. They have
nothing to do but to tattle and to lie in small things. In cities no man's
business is his neighbor's, and so each man and woman tends to his or
her business and goes on unnoticed and uncriticized, but woe to the
woman in a little village if she makes a false step." Churches, in short,
offered a communal mainstay of the traditional family order.[25]

Finally, the churches were a bulwark of support for the national
imperial enterprise that brought Americans to Sugar Creek. On his
way to the Illinois Country with his family, in 1800, John Reynolds
came to the banks of the Ohio. "The pleasures we enjoyed at the sight
of this beautiful stream soon vanished," he remembered, "when we
cast our eyes across it to the dreary waste of wilderness . . . filled with
savages and wild beasts, and extending on the north to the pole itself,
and on the west to China." Their Judeo-Christian faith in their role as a
"chosen people" in a "promised land" reserved exclusively for them by
God calmed the fears of settlers struggling in the wilderness.

Thus saith the mercy of the Lord,
"I'll be a God to thee;
I'll bless thy numerous race, and they
Shall be a seed for me."

The ideology of a heavenly mission to tame the wilderness provided settlers with a way to justify their labors and sacrifices.

Where nothing dwelt but beasts of prey,
Or men as fierce and wild as they,
He bids th' oppressed and poor repair,
And builds them towns and cities there.

They sow the fields, and trees they plant,
Whose yearly fruit supplies their want:
Their race grows up from fruitful stocks,
Their wealth increases with their flocks.[26]

The steamy atmosphere of revivalism produced a good deal of strident sectarian competition among the Protestant denominations. One Sangamo Presbyterian minister was kept busy defending himself against Methodist charges that he preached the "fierce" Calvinist doctrine that "hell is paved with infants' skulls," as well as charges from "Old School" Calvinists within his own denomination that he was "leading the people to the gulf of Arminianism," the belief in free will. Meanwhile, a group of young free-thinkers in Springfield, including Abraham Lincoln, William Herndon, and others, found themselves so alienated by the sectarian animosity that they came to question the value of denominational Protestantism altogether. But despite these rivalries, Protestant churches in Sugar Creek shared in common a message that amounted to a cultural consensus for most country folk. Each denomination held to the traditional points of the creed forged during the seventeenth-century English Reformation and accepted the worldly responsibility of the church to regulate the moral behavior of the community. These values identify the communicants of Sugar Creek, and the West in general, as moral descendants of the Puritans, pioneers on another North American frontier two centuries before.[27]

The poet Edgar Lee Masters, reflecting on his boyhood in the Sangamo during the 1870s, wrote that "if there was a culture, a spiritual flowering and growth in the Sangamon River country it was among the Cumberland Presbyterians, these humble, generous souls. . . . They read the Psalms and the poetry of the Bible, and they sang the hymns of

Watts and the Wesleys. Like primitive Christians they stood for moral virtue, good will, as the means of accomplishing what they regarded as the supreme object of life, the eternal salvation of the soul." The Cumberlands were the most populous denomination in Sugar Creek, with affiliates among a quarter of all households and, more importantly, among a majority of the families in the neighborhood of Drennan's Prairie. The Sugar Creek meeting and schoolhouse, just south of John Drennan's stage stop, muster ground, and polling place, was a center of neighborhood life. At the meeting house of the Cumberland society, under the leadership of Gilbert Dodds, the strands of neighborhood, self-governance, and kinship came together in a communal whole as real as it had been for the colonial Puritans.[28]

The "primitive" characteristics of which Masters wrote did not exist among Cumberlands alone, however, but among Baptists and Methodists as well. The word *community* carries amid its many meanings a vision of men and women living in "communion," sharing something more than the rather prosaic bonds of neighboring, borrowing, collectively working, and intermarrying. Sugar Creek churches offered a communion of cultural values that, as Masters wrote, added a "culture" to these cohesive social bonds. The extent of the shared sentiment among his Illinois neighbors struck the English immigrant George Flower; "in all men and women's affairs and motives," he wrote, "there is a sort of community of feeling."[29]

By 1840, as a result of the campaign against sin, waged with native organizational genius, half the Sugar Creek heads of household had found spiritual homes among five local Protestant congregations, while another 10 percent of the households worshiped with the Catholics. The settlers had transported a traditional social and cultural order to a new environment and transformed the landscape in ways compatible with their own priorities. The churches sustained the association of households and helped to provide a communal consensus. The settlers of Sugar Creek were united by the "community of feeling."[30]

PART FIVE

All Is Changed

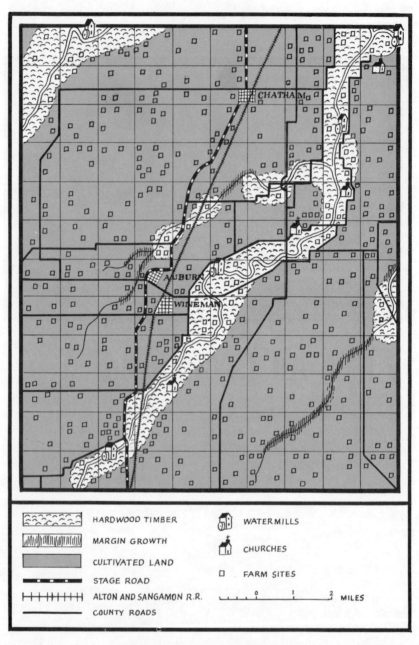

SOURCE: H. C. Whitley and S. B. Wheelock, *Plat Map of Sangamon County, 1858* (St. Louis: Whitley and Wheelock, 1858).

SUGAR CREEK IN 1860

17

It Answers Well for a Village

In the spring of 1840, Daniel Wadsworth, a forty-year-old carpenter from Hallowell, Maine, rode the St. Louis Road to Sugar Creek. During the winter a carpenter could find little work in Maine, so, in keeping with his annual custom, Wadsworth had signed on as ship's carpenter on a Kennebec River schooner the previous fall and plied his trade in the Gulf Coast port of Mobile. Rather than returning by his usual coastal route, however, this year instead he bought a ticket on a northbound Mississippi steamboat so he could "see the elephant"—the American "Far West"—for himself. Wadsworth's old friend David Eastman, and his brother-in-law, George Eastman, had moved from Maine to Sangamon County with their wives and children, parents and siblings several years before, and the carpenter planned to visit with them for a few weeks before he returned east. Disembarking in Alton, Illinois, he caught the northbound Springfield stage and two days later rattled into Sugar Creek, where he found the Eastmans living along the stage road in a newly laid out village called "Auburn," five or six dwellings clustered about a rough-cut public square of bluestem grass, on a slight knoll at the entrance to Drennan's Prairie.[1]

The Eastmans convinced Wadsworth that Auburn needed a skilled carpenter and offered to sell him good, cheap land. Almost on impulse he paid David Eastman sixty dollars out of his winter earnings for ten acres on the south side of the square and began to build a frame house of his own on the road near the Eastman dwellings. In late summer he

173

left to fetch his family, and by mid-November, after three weeks of travel by ferry, railroad, canal boat, Ohio River stern-wheeler, and farm wagon, he returned with his wife, Margaret, daughter Emily, and son Moses. Margaret never knew what convinced her husband to migrate, although she told her daughter that his prolonged winter absences made it easier for him to leave the lifetime haunts and relations of Maine. His children remembered Daniel as a loving but unexpressive father; as granddaughter Mary Wadsworth Jones later wrote, although he rarely lost his temper or fell into bad humor, Daniel "always seemed a serious person," and "none of his children ever remembered seeing him laugh, though at times he engaged in a chuckle." Margaret told granddaughter Mary how her "heart failed her many times" during the first years in Illinois, "particularly when she saw her children suffering from chills and fever, as did all the settlers for years until the land was drained and cultivated," and often openly lamented "the beauty and security of the older community which she had left so far behind."

Auburn, Illinois, certainly was not Hallowell, Maine, but by comparison with life in the open countryside it seemed a bit of transplanted New England, and there in the house Daniel built on the stage road the Wadsworths spent the next half-century. Before the railroads introduced factory-milled pine lumber into central Illinois, Daniel made his living by building houses from hand-hewn oak and walnut cut from the creek's timber, and by selling cuttings from the russet, northern spy, early harvest, and other varieties of northeastern apples he raised in a small nursery on his place. Her children remembered Margaret making apple butter or soap in a large kettle over an open fire in the backyard, like any other farm wife, but always with one eye on the traffic along the road. In 1841 Daniel became postmaster of the third-class office in Auburn, a position he held for better than a decade. The counter and post boxes filled an entire wing of the family dwelling, turning it topsy-turvy with the comings and goings of Sugar Creek society, but both husband and wife preferred this busy round to the slower and lonelier life of the farm.

Auburn represented western land speculation as much as it did the traditions of village living. When Wadsworth's friends came to Illinois from Maine in 1830, David Eastman's aging father, Thomas, had capital to invest, and with sons Asa and George he bought into a milling business in Morgan County, west of Sangamon. In mid-decade his boys began to accumulate land along Sugar Creek, buying nearly eight hundred acres between them and concentrating their purchases in the prairie lands of township 13/6. On this land, in 1835, Asa and George surveyed and laid out a village, which their sister Hannah named for Auburn, Maine, a county seat near the Eastman family home. Next to the Sugar Creek tanyard David Eastman opened in 1836, Asa and George built a steam-powered flour mill, planning to export the produce of the rich Illinois soil.[2]

The Eastmans were participating in the unprecedented boom in western land sales that peaked in 1836 and 1837, when over thirty-eight million public acres of American congress land passed into private hands. Since most Sugar Creek land claims filed before 1835 were to timber or timber margin acreage, enormous tracts of prairie, used by the community for common grazing, remained on the market, and during the boom, land speculators staged what historian Paul Gates calls "a mass attack" upon these common lands. In these years the Springfield office did the biggest business in the state, issuing patents to over seven million acres. After 1835, prairie land accounted for 84 percent of Sugar Creek land claims.[3]

Several speculators tried to develop and sell town lots on these prairie plots. "As the settlers all want to get wood on their farms, they settle all around the borders of the prairie," one Illinois investor wrote, "& leave the center—which may be taken at government prices—& answers well for a village." In the 1830s western investors platted hundreds of these "paper villages," hoping to sell lots in towns yet unborn to tradesmen and merchants willing to take a risk. In Sangamon County alone, speculators laid out at least twelve villages from 1835 to 1838. Auburn was one.[4]

As capitalist ventures, however, these prairie villages proved disappointing. After several years of promotion, Auburn contained but a handful of residents. The Eastmans sold a number of lots, including several to William Swaney, who ran a roadside tavern and rented space to John Smith for his blacksmith shop on the ground level. Swaney frequently left his large family in Auburn when he traveled to Illinois River towns in his fancy two-horse carriage. Local gossips rumored that he was a professional gambler, and the neighborhood fairly buzzed with speculation when Swaney failed to return from a trip in 1843. In this case, rumor was close to truth, for after several weeks Mrs. Swaney learned that a disgruntled loser at the gaming tables had murdered her husband. At the estate auction held to dispose of Swaney's nearly $1,800 in accumulated debts, Smith bought the shop and tavern and Thomas Black a parcel of outlying timberland, but in the absence of any great demand, the Eastmans had to reclaim Swaney's other Auburn properties. That same year Daniel Wadsworth's friend David Eastman died, and for lack of outside interest, Asa Eastman had to buy up his brother's town lots at the estate sale.[5]

From a developer's point of view, then, the Eastman project in Auburn failed. Unable to drum up sufficient business among subsistence-oriented Sugar Creek farmers, Asa and George closed their steam mill in 1841 and moved the machinery to Springfield, where their families soon joined them. In Springfield the Eastmans did a much better business, and by the 1860s Asa had acquired a reputation as the "grain and flour king" of central Illinois. But the Eastman removal left the village an even smaller place, with only six households headed by a carpenter, a joiner, a blacksmith, and three farmers. Although mobility changed several village faces over the next few years, the population in 1850 remained unchanged from ten years before.[6]

If the failure of Auburn to fulfill the speculative hopes of its founders was commonplace, however, the village's survival into the forties was not. Most Sangamon County "paper villages" faded quickly into obscurity. The village of "Mazeppa," for example, platted in the prairie, east of Sugar Camp, boasted a militia ground and a "grocery" that dispensed its own brand of corn whiskey; but by 1840 the village, in Edgar Lee Masters' phrase, "as a poplar tree, had thrived / And aged too soon, and died." "Mazeppa never had a post office," a later chronicler wrote, "and of course could not flourish, for what place without mail privileges could ever exist?" There could be no mail without a mail stage, no mail stage without a post road. In short, Auburn struggled along because it had succeeded John Drennan's Stage Stop as the Sugar Creek embarcation on the stage line from St. Louis to Springfield.[7]

A stage company had begun fortnightly "wagon" service from St. Louis to Springfield in 1822, and in 1834 it upgraded the line with twice-weekly Concord coaches. These four-horse stages carried the mail to Springfield where settlers could pick it up, a great inconvenience to people living in Sugar Creek, fifteen to twenty miles of poor roads south. In 1827 another line opened the "Macoupin Point Road," which forded Sugar Creek a few miles north of its headwaters, forging a trace through the margin of the westside timber, past Crow's Mill, the meeting and schoolhouse, and up the east side of Drennan's Prairie to Drennan's stage stand, where drivers changed teams and dropped the Sugar Creek mail. The Macoupin Point Road reinforced factors of geography, community, and kinship, placing Drennan Prairie at the center of Sugar Creek life.[8]

Families at The Sources, however, remained eight to ten miles from their mail, and as an inducement to a revised stage route, Jacob Rauch, Micajah Organ, Samuel McElvain, and others of the southernmost neighborhood built a fifty-foot oak span across the creek at Rauch's mill in 1838. From this bridge north in the spring of 1839, the stage line blazed a new road directly across the prairies, cutting at least six miles off the old route to Springfield and replacing Drennan's stage stand with Auburn as the location of the Sugar Creek post office. Auburn was small, a capitalistic failure, but the new Alton-to-Springfield road kept the town busy serving the needs of the surrounding countryside. By 1840, William Caldwell, supervisor of the road district, reported to the county commissioners that "the mail stage crosses the Bridge every day in the year except Sundays," and in 1848 postmaster Wadsworth complained to his congressman, Abraham Lincoln, that since he and Margaret had to "get up twice every night or *fourteen times a week*" to receive the mail, the government ought to increase his salary.[9]

More and more, as one incident from Auburn's early history suggests, the concerns of the Sugar Creek community focused on this road. One winter evening in 1842, as the stage driver was delivering the Sugar Creek mail to postmaster Wadsworth, a passenger discovered that his trunk, filled with clothing, money, and fine cigars, had been stolen from the rear baggage compartment of the coach. Rumors about this first "road crime" in Sugar Creek flew across the countryside, but there were no clues as to the identity of the thief. Then, as Moses Wadsworth remembered it, "John Kennedy, a young man of about eighteen, living with his parents on the Harlan place, was very liberal with a lot of fragrant Havanas at the Cumberland Church the next Sunday, dividing them around among the irreverent boys who made a practice of going punctually to meeting and remaining out of doors to discuss horseflesh during service." When Daniel caught Moses with a cigar, the boy told where he had gotten it, and the postmaster suddenly recalled that the Kennedy boy had been hanging around the post office the afternoon of the robbery, asking questions about the stage's arrival. Confronted with this circumstantial evidence, Kennedy finally confessed to cutting the trunk from the rest of the baggage as the stage slowly forded Panther Creek, near his father's cabin, and he then led a posse of men to a corn shock where he had cached his booty. Constable James Easley took the culprit into custody, but Kennedy somehow managed to escape, stole a horse, and fled south down the road to St. Louis and out of Sugar Creek history. All this created "great excitement throughout the country," Moses wrote. The road and its stories had become the biggest thing along Sugar Creek.[10]

In the competition for transportation links, the success of one site often marked the demise of another. When the stage company abandoned the Macoupin Point line and dropped Drennan's as a stage stop in 1839, for example, men from Drennan's Prairie and farms down the western margin of Sugar Creek timber petitioned the county to declare the old stage route a "county road" so that they might maintain it with their roadwork. The commissioners quickly agreed. This petition was the first of many efforts on the part of citizens over the next twenty years to alter and improve not only the arterial roadways but also the lanes and cartpaths that linked the farms of the community together. Increasingly, during the 1840s and 1850s, farm owners oriented their

work to the production of agricultural commodities, and Sangamo
men appeared to be more and more convinced that transportation
development offered the best way to break into the market economy.
The agitation for better transportation soon turned to the prospect for
railroads.[11]

Early promoters of transportation development believed, as one
booster wrote in 1823, that the Sangamon River could, "at a trifling
expense, be made navigable for nearly 200 miles," but these hopes
expired after the steamboat *Talisman* nearly foundered on the river's
sandbars and shallows in 1832. In the early 1840s, driven by a passion
for "internal improvements," the state invested nearly a million dollars
in a rail line from Springfield to the Illinois River, but poor engineering, shoddy construction, and a lack of demand from farmers still
committed to self-sufficiency doomed the line. By the mid-forties the
state had auctioned it for scrap. But the success of railroads elsewhere
demanded that they be introduced into Illinois, and in 1847 the state
chartered the "Alton and Sangamon Rail Road Company" to build a
line from American Bottom to Springfield, following the same general
route that Pulliam had taken in 1817.[12]

Everyone knew that the route selected would greatly affect the future of Sugar Creek, just as the course of the stage road had. No
topological barriers prevented the line from passing through Auburn,
and most residents expected that it would bring great things to the
fledgling village. In early 1851 the Alton and Sangamon Company
made the long-awaited announcement of its route: they would build on
the west side of the creek, paralleling the stage road south to Macoupin
County, but would bypass Auburn to the east by a mile. Disappointed
but not yet defeated, village men began "a vigorous and persistent
effort" to convince the company to locate a water tank and station on
the line due east of the village, expecting that Auburn could eventually
incorporate the intervening territory. It soon became clear, however,
that the Alton and Sangamon had cut a deal with local landowner
Phillip Wineman, who had purchased nearly two hundred acres a mile
south of Auburn and had offered the railroad donations of land in the
midst of a new paper village he platted there and named after himself.

A "long and fierce" struggle ensued between community factions
aligned with either Wineman and his new town or with the Eastmans
and Auburn. "It seemed a pity," Moses Wadsworth later wrote, "that so
pretty a site as that of the old town should be abandoned for so un-
promising a one as the north-east quarter of section 10 then appeared—much of it a mere swamp—but railroad corporations possess
no bowels of compassion, the practical more than the beautiful being
their object." The first cars rumbling into Wineman station on September 10, 1852, delivered a death sentence for the village of Auburn.

The cars on the Chicago and Alton Railroad, as the company had renamed its line, averaged better than thirty miles per hour, cutting the trip between the Mississippi and Springfield from over two days to under twelve hours, and the accompanying telegraph line that ran along the railroad right of way suddenly brought Sugar Creek into almost instant communication with the eastern United States. Within a year the stage line closed its operations and the federal government relocated the post office in Wineman. Daniel Wadsworth lost his position, Auburn lost its purpose. The next year Asa Eastman bought up the lots of all those who wished to sell and sold the town site to farmer Madison Curvey, who plowed up blocks, public square, and all, and planted corn in their place. Although the Wadsworths stubbornly remained in their house, most residents yielded to the inevitable and relocated south, many dragging the buildings Wadsworth had built with them on ox-drawn sledges, setting them up on lots purchased from Wineman. The stage road had made the village of Auburn. The railroad unmade it.[13]

The railroad changed other things along Sugar Creek. The Springfield papers regularly reported stock mangled by engines, derailed cars along the line, and sometimes the deaths of engineers and firemen; in July 1855, the five-year-old daughter of a prairie farmer was run down and killed as she was crossing the tracks south of Chatham. The average engine on the line hauled twenty cars, with space for fifty to one hundred passengers, bringing new and unfamiliar faces into town. Even more important, the construction and maintenance of the road introduced groups of Irish workmen into the community. In April 1851, as they worked on the grade north of old Auburn, the laborers went out on strike for better wages. James Irwin, an eighteen-year-old Irish immigrant, took work on the Harlan place during the strike and stayed on as a tenant farmer. Three years later he married Silas Harlan's fourteen-year-old daughter. After Rachel Harlan Irwin came into her inheritance, Harlan's Grove gradually became "Irwin's Grove" in deference to the owner, who continued to allow its use as a place for community assembly, opening it "for any national, religious, or social gathering."[14]

During the 1850s the attention of the Sugar Creek countryside focused on the entrepôt of Wineman where, by 1860, nearly two hundred and fifty people lived in over forty households, transacting business in more than twenty establishments, including five grocery and general stores, two farm implement establishments, a furniture store, two hotels, and two saloons. Increased traffic on the road during the Civil War added more residents and businesses, and by 1866 the town's population had grown to three hundred and fifty. Families from the surrounding countryside made regular trips to the town, or to the nearby railroad villages of Chatham or Lowder five miles north and five miles southwest, respectively. By the early 1870s, no Sugar Creek farmer was farther than five miles from a freight depot.[15]

By offering an outlet for farm products, by importing commodities from Michigan pine lumber to Long Island oysters, and by linking farmers to the outside world by iron rails and electrified steel wires, the railroad ushered in a new reality with profound implications for Sugar Creek. In 1865 the Illinois legislature incorporated Wineman's substantial town on the railroad. But in a departing gesture to the failed village on the stage road, the legislators rejected the name Wineman and christened the new town Auburn—much to Phil Wineman's chagrin and Daniel Wadsworth's delight. After the Civil War, no one spoke any longer of the "Sugar Creek" community, but only of "Auburn," the railroad town, and its surrounding countryside.[16]

18

Landlords and
Tenants

Squatters made up over half of the one hundred and thirteen farm households along Sugar Creek in 1830. Poor farm families could build their cabins and plant their corn on unclaimed acres, graze their stock on prairie commons, and hook their timber from congress land. Old settlers later looked back on these times as a "golden age," but Sugar Creek was no Arcadia. Squatter families might subsist for much of the year on boiled pumpkins and the watery milk of a couple of mangy cows, while their better-off neighbors feasted on fried pork, corn pone, and butter. Nevertheless, the communal customs of the borrowing system provided a self-sufficing place for the poor as well as the well-to-do, and the rhetoric of this democratic age promised the conversion of squatting farmers into owner-operators.

Twenty years later, squatting had indeed disappeared from Sugar Creek life, replaced, however, not by universal republican ownership, but by tenantry and the rural proletarianization of the poor. Of the forty-six heads of squatter families of 1830, only nine succeeded in buying Sangamon County land over the next decade, and most left the county, leaving little behind to document the causes of their failure to become landowners. The experience of Robert Pulliam, the pioneer of Sugar Creek, however, illustrates some of the difficulties that settlers could experience in buying and holding land.[1]

In November 1823, Robert Pulliam purchased 480 acres, including the sugar grove, from the federal government, paying six hundred

181

dollars, five hundred of which he borrowed from Springfield mer-
chant-speculators at an annual rate of 12.5 percent, putting up his
property as security. During the 1820s, the one-legged pioneer and his
family not only farmed and raised stock, but each year produced a
thousand pounds or more of maple sugar, ground the corn of neighbors at the horse mill, and dispensed corn whiskey at the public
house—income-producing activities that helped to meet the annual
interest payments of over sixty dollars. The Pulliam children married
into neighborhood families, two daughters eventually moving to Iowa
with their husbands and children. The youngest son, George, a retarded invalid, lived at home.[2]

The five-hundred-dollar note came due in the early 1830s, and
circumstances suggest that the pioneer desperately sought ways to increase his income in order to pay off the looming principal. Pulliam
borrowed some $1,150 from fifteen different lenders at usurious rates
of up to 50 percent and paid off the original note; with a scheme of
damming the creek and establishing a new water mill near the sugar
grove, he purchased an adjacent eighty acres across the creek in 1831
and filed a request for an ad quod damnum with the county commissioners. But the projected dam did not materialize, and Pulliam soon
had difficulty meeting the payments on the new series of loans. In
August of 1832, two of his creditors obtained default judgments
against him in local justice courts; and when Pulliam failed to pay, they
placed a notice in the *Sangamo Journal* that "Pulliam had deserted from
this state," and that his property would be attached and auctioned—in
effect, a call for all Pulliam's creditors to join en masse in the assault on
his property. Over the next few weeks, while Pulliam laid low, several
justices of the peace issued judgments against the pioneer for over five
hundred and fifty dollars in back debts.[3]

Had Pulliam established a better record with the local justices of the
peace, things might have gone better for him, but the feisty frontiersman had appeared before them many times during the 1820s for
the default of small debts and offenses "against the peace and dignity
of the people." In the most grave of these infractions, Pulliam's neighbor Henry Clark swore before Zachariah Peter in June 1830 that
Pulliam "did by force and arms in a violent manner accost him the said
Henry while imploid with James Clark in driving several *yoak* of cattle
from said Pulliams. The said Pulliam did then and there take or drive
away from out of the possession of the said Henry & James one pare of
stears in yoke by presenting at the said Henry a cocked Pestal and
threatning to shoot said Henry & James & thereby taking off said
stears." A Jury of "twelve good & lawful men not of kin to said Pulliam
nor Henry Clark" found the pioneer guilty and assessed $30.50 in
damages and $7.815 in court costs against him. Just four months later,

John Wallace accused Pulliam of "taking away and converting to his own use one hog," and Robert was saddled with another $10 in damages as well as $16.50 in court costs. The pioneer could not expect much good will from the justices when his creditors dragged him into court.[4]

Despite the judgments against him, Pulliam was still unable to pay his debts, and his creditors presented their cases before the judge of the circuit court in Springfield, who issued a warrant for Pulliam's arrest when he failed to appear. Several weeks later the pioneer surrendered, offering an ingenious explanation for his absence:

> The Asiatic or Spasmodic Cholera was then prevailing in Springfield. Such was the panic occasioned thereby that he could not procure any person to go with him to Springfield to become his security so that he was unable to give any security until the time for appeal had elapsed. Indeed there was an almost total suspension of business in and about Springfield occasioned by the alarm, but for which circumstance your petitioner would undoubtedly have taken an appeal in the regular mode.

But appeals were fruitless. Creditors even tried, unsuccessfully, to attach the property of Pulliam's sons. In July 1833, the mortgage on the sugar grove was foreclosed, and it was sold to the agent of a Natchez land speculator. The sheriff auctioned off the adjacent land partially to repay the other creditors.[5]

But other bill collectors continued to plague the Pulliams like the cholera itself, so Robert and Mary packed their personal belongings and fled the county, taking up an exiled residence in Macoupin County. Pulliam had never been a religious man, but, according to his sons, during these bitter years he came to regret his wild and wooly ways, and both he and Mary joined a revivalist congregation. A few years later, in July 1838, during a visit to his sons in Sugar Creek, sixty-two-year-old Pulliam fell sick, was carried to the house of a neighbor, Dr. Alexander Shields, but expired. Robert Pulliam died as landless as his father before him.[6]

At least Pulliam had held the title to land against which he could secure loans; but because squatters had no property to mortgage, most of them could obtain no credit at all. Democratic politicians, President Andrew Jackson prominent among them, constantly talked of increasing the farmer's ability to purchase and hold the land he farmed, but very little was actually done for the squatters. Indeed, when Jackson refused to recharter the Bank of the United States, instead depositing federal funds in state banks in 1834, he inadvertently provided capital for loans to land speculators, fueling with state-issued paper currency the greatest land boom yet seen in the United States. In 1837, belatedly awakened to these effects of his emotional war on the bank, Jackson declared his intention to "save the new States from a nonresident proprietorship," issuing his famous "Specie Circular," an executive order declaring gold or silver the only legal tender for the purchase of public land. The president's action indeed burst the speculative bubble, bringing on financial panic, deflation, and a decade of agricultural depression. During the ensuing hard times, almost no congress land sold in the West. Then, in the wake of the general business expansion that accompanied the California Gold Rush in 1849, speculators gobbled up the last available Sugar Creek sections.[7]

During the first period of Sugar Creek land sales, from 1823 to 1833, most purchasers were resident settlers; non resident speculators bought only about two thousand acres, less than 15 percent of the total. But in the land boom of 1834–37, then again during 1849–51, speculators—several well-to-do Sugar Creek farmers among them—gained control of nearly seventy-five square miles of prairie land, 70 percent of all Sugar Creek lands sold. Joseph Poley and his brother-in-law, Jacob Rauch, for example, participated in both land booms, accumulating several sections of prairie holdings at The Sources of the creek; James Patton and his boys bought the equivalent of two sections of prairie southeast of their neighborhood; and Philip Wineman accumulated over twelve hundred acres of prairie south of Auburn village.[8]

Despite these prairie sales, however, into the 1840s Sugar Creek farmers continued to use the grasslands for common grazing, and a number of families continued to reside on otherwise unused land, though it was now privately owned. During the 1830s and early 1840s, when this opportunity to squat continued to exist, the number of owner-operator farms along the creek increased only slightly. But with the upturn of the national economy in the late forties, the new owners of the prairies began to warn off squatters, mark off prairie farms, and sell them at three to five dollars an acre, using newly available steel plows to break the formidable sod. The number of owner-operators, which had held steady through the decades of the twenties and thirties, jumped from 66 in 1840 to 128 in 1850, and to 189 by 1860. But only a quarter of the 53 squatter households of 1840 succeeded in buying parcels and persisting through the decade, and most of those who did were descendants of original settler families with nearby kin to assist them. The best that most squatter families could manage was the sale of their "improvements" to emigrants known as "strong-handed farmers"—men who arrived with capital enough to buy them out. After 1840, as the opportunities for squatting disappeared, and as conditions for the poor grew harsher, ten-year rates of persistence fell to just one household head in five.[9]

By the 1850s, Sugar Creek had become a society with considerable distinctions of wealth. But differences in residents' access to productive property emerged not because control of the land passed from "cultivators" to "nonresident speculators," as Democrats feared, but as a result of dynamics internal to the Sugar Creek community. Elsewhere in central Illinois, nonresident speculators did create magnificent estates for large-scale farming, stock-raising, or tenant farming, but in Sugar Creek by the late 1850s, nonresident speculators had sold off their holdings in the form of rather modest-sized farms. Although Pulliam's sugar-grove farm had been bought by a nonresident land speculator, for example, it was sold in the mid-forties to Kentucky emigrant James Scott. By 1858 outsiders held only 16 percent of the land along the creek, and fewer than ten nonresident landlords owned estates in excess of two hundred acres. Well-to-do Sugar Creek farmers who participated in the land booms, on the other hand, tended to hold on to the acres they accumulated. After nonresident speculators had come and gone, these owner-operators with large estates remained. The transfer of large portions of the prairie commons from the federal government to a small group of resident farmers accomplished the single most important economic change along Sugar Creek since Americans had dispossessed the Kickapoo.[10]

In 1838, the wealthiest tenth of Sugar Creek heads of household held 25 percent of the privately owned acreage; twenty years later, their proportion had risen to 35 percent. At the other end of the ownership scale, the poorest fifth owned 10 percent of the acreage in 1838 but only 5 percent in 1858. The rapid disappearance of the public domain compounded the effects of this increasing concentration of wealth. By the 1850s, the 35 to 40 percent of households without title to land had found ways other than squatting to subsist. The coexistence of a small group of families with large landed resources, on the one hand, and a large group of landless farmers, on the other, created the conditions for a new set of rural social relationships.[11]

Between 1840 and 1860, tenant farming replaced squatting as the most common alternative for landless families. In 1850 at least 10 percent of farm households rented the land they cultivated from resident or absentee landlords, paying for the use of the land with shares of their crops. In the standard arrangement, the tenant family that provided tools, stock, and seed, and built their own cabin, gave over one-third of their crop; the tenant family that borrowed everything from the landlord, including the cabin, gave over two-thirds or, without the cabin, one-half:

An agreement entered into between Willis F. Berry of one part
and William Ward of the other part—the sd Berry having rented
to sd Ward sixteen acres of ground more or less in his field it
being the ground South of where sd Berry has sowed oats—the
sd Berry agrees to furnish teem to work the ground & his plows &
how [hoe] and horse free—and sd Ward agrees to work the
ground in good farming order in corn, and to deliver one half of
the corn in sd Berrys crib for the above consideration, and to
gether sd crop against the first day of January next, and sd Berry
reserves the pasture of the field and privelige of sowing wheat on
the ground.

Illinois farmers tilled fields on shares as early as the 1820s, but the
practice was relatively rare until the 1840s, when the alienation of
common land forced increasing numbers of landless families into a
landlord-tenant relationship. According to agricultural essayist James
Caird, tenancy had become "very common in Illinois" by the mid-
fifties. It became increasingly important in Sugar Creek as well, for by
1860, eighty-seven tenant families, a quarter of all Sugar Creek households, farmed land on shares, their ranks four times greater than a
decade before.[12]
    By that year Joseph Poley owned over seventeen hundred acres in
the southeastern prairie sections of township 13/6, although his household of eight farmed only the quarter section upon which they had
built their dwelling in 1828. His grown son Elisha Poley and family,
and daughter Nancy, with her husband, Thomas Parks, and their
children, lived on nearby land donated by their father. North of the
Poleys lived James Patton, on what had grown into a twelve-hundred-
acre estate. By 1860, Patton, now a widower approaching his three
score and ten, lived with his youngest son, David, and daughter-in-law,
Susan Organ. Nearby were the households of his oldest son's widow,
his son Matthew and family, his daughter Rebecca and son-in-law,
Elihu Stout, surrounding old man Patton with fourteen grandchildren. In addition to the forty-eight members of their extended
families, however, associated with Poley and Patton on the run of the
1860 census were another sixteen tenant households. Each tenant family raised corn on an average of fifty acres and ran stock, presumably
on Poley and Patton's unbroken prairie meadows; together, their operations supported ninety-eight persons. No records of the transactions
between these landlords and tenants survive, but the transfer of produce that took place must have added measurably to the accumulating
wealth of the Patton and the Poley estates.[13]
    The 1860 census enumeration reveals a number of tenant house-
holds associated with each of the largest landowners in Sugar Creek. At

the western end of Drennan's Prairie, near Harlan's Grove, for example, the Masons and Lockridges owned over half of the arable land and
rented to thirteen tenant and laborer families. The Kennedys, whose
boy robbed the stage in 1842, were early tenants in this area. North of
the sugar grove, Jonathan Peddicord owned an entire section where he
farmed and rented land to five other households. Of the ten largest
property owners along the creek, only Philip Wineman, second to
Poley in the size of his real estate, seemed to have no tenants; instead,
Wineman used his prairie acres to lay out the new railroad village
named for himself.[14]

An alternate subsistence strategy for the poor took landless men and
boys to work as farm laborers. During the 1850s the number of male
farm laborers in the community tripled; most were young single men
who lived with their employers. Prosperous farmers had always hired
help, particularly during the busy harvest season, but by the 1850s the
practice of hiring wage labor became widespread and commonplace.
The changing sex ratio for the segment of the community in its twenties and thirties suggests the magnitude of the change; the 1830 ratio of
107 men to every 100 women had grown to 159:100 by 1860. In that
year, over half the owner-operator households of Sugar Creek included live-in hands. Nine hired men and one woman lived in the
households of the Patton brothers; Noah Mason's household included
two young neighborhood boys and an Irish couple; Jon Peddicord
employed three Irish laborers and a young Tennessee girl who helped
his wife, Minerva, in the kitchen; and Phil Wineman employed three
single men and a young couple to work in his fields, stockyard, orchard, garden, and kitchen. As wealthy farmers, these men could afford this many hands; the average owner-operator hired two.[15]

A new relationship thus characterized the Sugar Creek economy of
the 1850s. The ten richest Sugar Creek heads of household in 1860,
seven of whom were members of original settler families, owned an
average of nearly $26,000 in real property; but only two-thirds of this
capital was invested in their own farms. These men were now landlords
as well as farmers, renting their excess acres to tenant families, collecting rents in the form of crop shares, and employing several hired
hands. For well-off Sugar Creek farmers like these, production had
advanced well beyond mere subsistence needs, presenting them with
both the opportunity and the necessity to market agricultural surpluses. The increased capitalist orientation of Sangamon farmers in
the 1840s and 1850s, in other words, was not simply the result of a
growing inclination to participate in the marketplace, but the result of
a changing rural social structure.

Changes in the communal landscape also mirrored these new social
relationships. Road improvement was perhaps the most important.

During the early 1820s, Sugar Creek householders circulated and presented to the commissioners eight separate petitions for the declaration or relocation of county roads through their neighborhoods, all of
them arteries like the St. Louis Road that linked Sugar Creek with
other communities to the north and south. When this basic structure
was in place, the number of Sugar Creek road petitions declined; from
1828 to 1845 only four were laid before the commissioners. In the
mid-1840s, however, the changing economic relationships of the country side made good roads more of a necessity. Improved transportation
from farm to market, many believed, offered the best chance of marketing the increasing surplus of agricultural commodities at fair prices.
From 1846 to 1860 Sugar Creek men filed sixty-one petitions for the
relocation and improvement of old roads and for the laying out of new
ones.[16]

Reform of the transportation system utilized the traditions of citizen
participation and local autonomy. Since the county levied road duty as
a "poll-tax" on all males over eighteen, "all hands" in the neighborhoods improved or "threw up" roads together; and since there was
no county planning authority, the initiative for location or improvement depended upon groups of local men deciding what they needed,
soliciting the support of their neighbors, and petitioning the commissioners for approval. The enthusiasm for reform, however, came predominantly from the landed sector of the community. Before 1845
owners made up only half of the signers of petitions for relocation or
declaration; but on petitions filed between 1846 and 1860, by contrast,
the proportion of owners rose to four signators out of five, despite the
relatively constant proportion of landed men in the Sugar Creek community. By and large, road improvement was the project of Sugar
Creek owner-operators and landlords.[17]

Owner-operator petitions brought about several changes in the
landscape. Eight new east-west county roads in the Sugar Creek community linked newly created prairie farms with the main north-south
highways. These new roads channeled traffic from both prairie and
timber toward the village of Auburn. In 1846 a large group from the
west side of the creek, "feeling the great necessity of a permanent
county road" to the village, petitioned the commissioners to authorize a
route on "the nearest and best route to Auburn, having due regard to
private property & the right of way." The village, small as it was,
nevertheless attracted open-country farmers to its tavern, shops, post
office, and fellowship. A decade later, the same west-bank group wrote
of the "high importance" of improving the road from Chatham to
Auburn for "the convenience of the neighbourhood and the publick
generally" and "begged" for an appropriation "for the purpose of
building a Bridge over Panther Creek," which "would render the road

more useful to the Public." When the railroad made it clear that Wine-man, not old Auburn, would become the dominant central place, these citizens "prayed" the court "to grant a revew [*sic*] of the Road leading from Chatham . . . so as to run due South to the Town of Wyne-man."[18]

These petitions paid increasing attention to property lines. Citizens laid out their new roads precisely along the section lines, so as not to infringe on the land of adjacent owners. Owners similarly petitioned to change the routes of older north-south roadways. In the early 1850s, for example, a group of owners appealed to the commissioners to

> change so much of the Alton and Springfield state road as lies between Micajah Organs and the north-east corner of section sixteen . . . beginning at or near the aforesaid Organs Lane and running to the south-east corner of the north-east quarter of section twenty-one, making the road on the west side of said line until said road strikes the south-east corner of section sixteen, running on the east line of sixteen, and from thence to the north-east corner of said sixteenth section, and from thence to the original road, which will be about two hundred yards, we the under assigned petitioners being satisfied that the said change of road will add verry little to the distance of the aforesaid road as it will run over better ground by the aforesaid change.

Like all the original north-south highways, this stage road had struck a course across the prairie in a beeline from the bridge at Rauch's mill to the village. The galloping stage teams required these sweeping curves. But the railroad outmoded the stage and allowed farmers to modify the course of highways.[19]

By the end of the 1850s, after a long series of petitions from owner-operators, most highways had been realigned to conform to section lines, or, where the original road had angled radically across the sec-tions, to jog in ninety-degree twists and turns to protect the property lines and corners of owners. This reform made the roads impossible for the old stage to navigate without slowing almost to a stop, but it presented no problem for lumbering farmers' wagons carrying crops to village markets, or for the light buggies that came into fashion in the 1850s. The highways would no longer, in the words of another peti-tion, "run angling across lands," cutting through fields and meadows now increasingly valuable for commodity production. The vestiges of old highways that clung to contours of land or timber might still be found in a few "angling" roads, or in those odd, perpendicular turns. But by 1860 a general reform of the landscape was well under way, bringing it into greater conformity with the rectilinear precision of the federal surveyor's original plat.[20]

Accompanying the new arrow-straight section roads came other changes in the look of things. As the improvement of stock became more important with the new commercial outlook, farmers used pine lumber imported by the railroad to enclose their stockyards with post and board fencing. Farm implement dealers in Chatham and Auburn sold steel plows, and men broke the prairies to plant corn where big bluestem had flourished, breaking up as well the old rail fences that had once protected the crops from marauding stock thus eliminating the shelter provided for prairie critters by the interstices of the rails, overgrown with grass and vines. In the decades of the 1850s and 1860s, the most prosperous owner-operators built new dwellings, replacing log cabins with substantial two-story frame houses, usually simple "I" houses in the popular Greek Revival style—houses that were the very symbol of agrarian stability. Successful owners also first constructed small but solid barns in the 1840s.[21]

Thus did a "common" landscape give way to a landscape of class. Most Sugar Creek residents, certainly the tenants and poor laboring heads of household, continued to live in log cabins until late in the century, giving architectural testimony to the difference between landlord and tenant. Stock, timber, and hunting laws, passed in the late 1850s, restricted tenants, laborers, and poor farmers from grazing their herds on prairie meadows or helping themselves to the fruits of the countryside. Farm owners initiated the creation of a new landscape, one that we now consider typical of the rural American Midwest; but that now familiar landscape was part of a profound social change that marked the departure of an old era.[22]

During the 1840s, as tenantry replaced squatting, the rural poor needed a political organization to articulate their needs. Appealing to the Illinois Assembly in 1846 for a 160-acre limitation on land holding, one group of rural residents argued that "under the existing laws, the lands are passing out of the hands of cultivators and into those of speculators." Two years later John Wentworth, Democratic congressman from Chicago, argued that unless soon checked, speculation would lead to the creation of "separate classes in society." The Illinois Democrats, presenting themselves as the party of the people, including the poor, proclaimed the Whig party a "Money Dynasty," attacked the American System "because that system robs the mechanics, the farmer, and the laborer, and benefits the drones of society," and championed "squatter's rights" and free homesteads for operators in the trans-Mississippi West. Yet, beginning in 1840, both Sugar Creek precinct

"WASHINGTON HALL'S HOMESTEAD PLACE," west of Sugar Creek, after the Civil War, showing the tenant cabin located a mile south of the farm.

and Sangamon County turned from wavering support for both parties to consistent support of Whig candidates in local, state, and national elections, and locally the Democrats became an embattled party.[23]

In the 1840 presidential contest, the Whigs threw any former reticence about partisan politics to the winds as they campaigned for William Henry Harrison, once again their candidate. A Whig state central committee, operating out of Springfield, assisted in the organization of precinct-level Harrison committees that were to make "perfect lists" of all electors, to encourage Whigs to "keep in line," and to seek out and convert wavering Democrats. The Sugar Creek committee, declaring "no confidence in the wisdom or the political virtue of the present Executive of the U.S., Martin Van Buren," organized the precinct as it had never been organized before. The Whigs made every attempt to appeal to the common folk. "We all know that Patriotism resides among our yeomanry," declared the *Journal*, "the watchfires of Liberty are guarded and fed by the dwellers of Log Cabins. We are proud therefore, of the opportunity of supporting a Log-Cabin candidate for President." Years later, Dr. Alexander Shields, a Democratic party activist and member of the county Democratic central committee in the 1840s and 1850s who lived in the western timber of Sugar Camp, remained bitter when he remembered what he called "the leading Whig principles" of 1840: "coon-skins, log cabins with the string of the latch never pulled in, hard cider, two dollars a day, and roast beef." Local Whig campaign verses struck the same theme.

> Van Buren may drink his champaign,
> And have himself toasted from Georgia to Maine.
> But we in log cabins, with hearts warm and true,
> Drink a gourd of hard cider t' ol' Tippecanoe.

Castigating the president as an aristocrat and running as "populists," the Whigs stole a page from the Democrats, who had consistently employed such appeals throughout the thirties.[24]

For most voters, patterns of party loyalty were determined in the formative struggles of the 1830s; for example, 80 percent of the Sugar Creek electors who voted in each of seven elections from 1836 to 1848 for which poll books survive held to their party allegiance through each contest. Moreover, through the 1840s, economic distinctions played an important role in determining the choices of Sugar Creek electors. In 1840, 61 percent of propertied men, but only 46 percent of the land-less, cast their votes for Harrison. Eight years later, in the presidential contest between Democrat Lewis Cass and Whig Zachary Taylor, voting in Sugar Creek was again highly stratified by wealth: the richest tenth of property owners gave Taylor 78 percent of their votes, all owners 54 percent; but tenants split their vote evenly between the two parties, and 65 percent of nonowners voted Democratic. The foundation of Whig support in the community, in other words, remained the "better sort," owner-operators who often rented land to tenants, farm-ers who formed, as the *Journal* put it, "the bustling, speculating class whose wealth and fortunes enable them to court pleasure of enjoyment or repose." Social cleavage along class lines helps to explain why local political battles were often bitterly fought.[25]

Nevertheless, Whig candidate Harrison captured a total of 54 per-cent of Sugar Creek's vote in the election of 1840. Whig support among owner-operators, strong in the 1830s, remained essentially unchanged over the next fifteen years; but there was significant erosion of Demo-cratic support among the landless. Nearly one Democrat in five turned to Harrison, and half of these apostate Jacksonians continued to sup-port Whig candidates over the next few years. John French, a tenant farmer in whose Harlan's Grove cabin local Methodists held their class-es, for example, first cast his ballot for the Whigs in 1840, then voted for Whig candidates through the rest of the decade. This increased Whig strength among the poor and landless requires explanation.[26]

There were, first, important differences between the approach of local Democrats and local Whigs to economic development, the most pressing local issue. The Democratic party took what one might call a "quantitative" approach, emphasizing the extension of opportunity through the conquest of new lands for agricultural settlement. "The white race must go west," the editor of the Democratic *Register* declared; "all the black races will disappear from the face of the earth, as the savages of North America have faded away at the approach of civilization." The United States would soon "rule safely to ourselves the whole of North America," he predicted, "and ultimately the entire southern territory 'to Cape Horn'—islands and all." Throughout the 1840s and 1850s, the *Register* argued the case for acquiring land in Oregon and even Canada, and drooled over the possibilities of American armed expansion at the expense of the "black race" nations of Mexico, Cuba, and Nicaragua. Even so, Illinois, according to the *Register,* still contained considerable possibilities for the settlement of the poor. If workers from the overcrowded cities of the East would only come to the Sangamo, "they would find plenty of employment, at high prices, and in a short time become proprietors of farms, which in a few years would make them independent and influential. The plea that they have no capital to begin with affords no excuse, for it is a fact that nine out of ten of the wealthy farmers of this state commenced the world without a dollar." The rather obvious fact that the economic situation in central Illinois had changed significantly since the first settlers had emigrated in the 1820s did not impress the *Register,* which completely ignored the growing problem of tenantry of the countryside in its coverage of local events.[27]

In fact, the county Democratic leadership identified more closely with the problems and prospects of bustling Springfield than with those of the surrounding countryside. Through the 1840s and 1850s, the Illinois Democratic party controlled the state government located in Springfield, and perhaps this fact helped to confine the attention of the local party leadership to within the city limits. To the *Register,* "the people," that Democratic godhead, inhabited the growing wards of the city. The rural precincts, by contrast, were settled by "country folk" who came to town once or twice a season to "lay in their family stores"; of these farm families the Democratic press understood little and wrote even less. The county Democratic party maintained the strength of its rural organization only with great difficulty: "we have heard of no appointments for any of their meetings," the *Register* complained of the rural districts in 1852, "but we have no doubt the precinct committees are attending to the matter." In fact, organizers were not attentive, and the party was again badly mauled in the local elections of that year.[28]

Whigs in Sugar Creek, meanwhile, declared themselves "friends of the American System, or the policy of protecting and encouraging our arts, agriculture, commerce, and manufacture." So while the Democrats took a quantitative approach, the Whigs emphasized "qualitative" improvement. To men and women actively engaged in building new farms, homes, and villages—people preoccupied with the problems of economic development and the prospects for putting down roots—the notion of improvement had strong appeal, and John L. Drennan, William Lockridge, and J. A. Ball—Democrat organizers from the creek—were kept busy arguing against the Whig version of it.

They scored some success on the Whig support for protective tariffs. Democrat Dr. Shields told of one Jacksonian miller who prepared a "toll-dish" twice the regulated size and announced to his Whiggishly inclined patrons that they would have to pay him with the larger measure since, he facetiously explained, "Whig logic" suggested that "the bigger the toll, the less you pay for grinding, and the more meal you get." In 1844 Lincoln spoke at a political debate held in the Sugar Creek meeting and schoolhouse, where, according to the correspondent for the *Register,* "he attempted to make the farmer believe that the high pressure tariff made everything they bought cheaper"; when local Democrats dared him to show how that could be, Lincoln admitted that "he could not tell the reason, but only that it was so." "The poor, ignorant people were enlightened," the correspondent drolly concluded. But despite the unpopularity of their tariff policies, Whigs persisted in their talk of "improvement," arguing that their program would benefit rich and poor alike; and they seem to have captured the field on this issue, for support among the landless continued to be high enough to sustain winning Whig margins. Indeed, the *Journal's* coverage of rural affairs was consistently better than the *Register's,* demonstrating a clearer understanding of rural needs—of owner-operators, if not of tenants. Local Democrats were reduced to suggesting that farmers had been fooled into voting against their own self-interest; "the ease with which the people were cajoled, duped, misled, presents a mortifying but solemn admonition to the patriot," lamented the *Register* after one particularly bad showing. This would not have been the first time voters were duped, but Democratic failure to represent the interests of the rural poor was probably more important in accounting for Whig successes than was Whig sophistry.[29]

The strength of Whig precinct organization, when compared to Democratic weakness, was also decisive. The party forged an alliance with the leadership of local churches. Whigs and churchmen alike preached "improvement" not only through their economic program but also through the notion of individual reform. An important part of this Whig–church compact in Sugar Creek was the movement to reform popular drinking behavior. In the early forties, Whigs and county churchmen together began to proselytize on the temperance

issue, and in 1845 they organized a Sangamon County Temperance
Union with chapters in nearly every settlement, including Sugar Creek
precinct. On Sunday afternoons in the Cumberland church meeting
house, Gilbert Dodds employed camp-meeting techniques to move
men to sign their names to the temperance pledge. Over the next two
years more than a hundred converts took the pledge in Sugar Creek.[30]

There was a direct connection between this kind of evangelical reform and Whig politics. At a county convention of the Temperance
Union held in May 1847 at the Cumberland meetinghouse, Dodds
urged the membership to political action: "While we sympathize with
the inebriate and his unfortunate family, we should not forget to keep
before the people those abominable establishments (the fountainhead
of all this evil) in their true character, that manufacture and retail
alcoholic drinks, and the laws that authorize their existence." Later that
year a county grand jury, including Sugar Creek Whigs Eddin Lewis,
William Chambers, and Zachariah Peter, urged the outlawry of the
"grog-shop or drunkery" in order to put an end to "loafing, drunkenness, reveling, whoring, gambling," to "bruised heads, bloated visages,
red or black eyes." Since the early thirties temperance had been a part
of the Whig agenda, part of the attack on the abuses of democracy. The
Temperance Union dedicated its energies to the passage of a "Maine
Law," a state prohibition on the sale of alcohol.[31]

This was only one of the close connections between religion and
politics. Dodds ran for state assembly on the Whig line in the forties; he
was unsuccessful, but the cochair of the local chapter of the Temperance Union, Job Fletcher, was Sugar Creek's leading Whig. Both
were also leaders of the Cumberland church, and their meetinghouse
was the scene of frequent Whig meetings and forums. At times it must
have been difficult to distinguish between the various religious, reform, or political meetings held at the meetinghouse in Drennan's
Prairie, for all were conducted in the same ritualistic manner. In 1848,
for example, the Sangamon synod of the Cumberland Presbyterians
held periodic conferences at the meetinghouse on Saturdays, preachers and elders meeting through the morning, then assembling outside
in the timber margin for a meal prepared by the "goodwives" of the
church. One September Saturday in 1848, Sugar Creek Whigs held a
"Taylor bar-b-q," where speech-making and singing was followed by a
procession led by Job Fletcher that stretched a half-mile through the
timber to tables set with "substantials, excellent breads, and well-
cooked meats." Six months later, at the annual convention of the Temperance Union, three hundred representatives from around the
county met at the church where, after morning business was concluded, "the wives of the citizens of Sugar Creek made a bountious
provision for all the persons present" and all "marched in procession

from the meeting to the place outdoors where a dinner was set." Delegates to this convention included not only Dodds, Fletcher, his nephew, Job Fletcher, Jr., and James Easley representing the Cumberland church, but Methodist John French, Baptist John Clayton, and Catholics William Burtle and Owen Maynard, representing their congregations as well.[32]

The attempt of temperance men to enact a prohibition on the sale of alcohol proved unsuccessful; in 1855, for example, county residents helped to defeat soundly a prohibition referendum on the state ballot. The measure of the Temperance Union's success, however, was not in legislative but in cultural reform. The temperance campaign did change local attitudes about drink. "Drinking in primitive times was fashionable and polite," John Reynolds wrote, "and liquor was considered an element in the conviviality of all circles." "But now," he lamented in 1855, society "severely condemns it." New attitudes about drinking fit neatly with other aspects of Whig political culture. The contextual and ritual connection between religion and politics was a powerful cultural combination that could not help but attract a portion of the evangelical poor. By all appearances, during the 1840s the Whigs in Sugar Creek were most successful on the cultural front.[33]

The Cumberland church was one of the most important organizations of persistent families in Sugar Creek, a force for moral and civil "improvement." The church's organizing efforts were largely in the interests of landed families who supported the Whig cause. But as a controversy in the Drennan's Prairie settlement in 1847 demonstrated, things are never quite so neat and clear. In April of that year, forty-one neighborhood residents petitioned the commissioners to open and declare a new road. Writing for the group, William Lockridge, Democrat, and Captain Job Fletcher, Jr., Whig nephew of Squire Job, pointed out that "our farming land and timber are disconnected by more than the distance of a mile," and that "by the uniting of the pasture fence of John L. Drennan to the fence of Mr. Gilbert Dodds we are almost entirely cut off from any at all reasonable pass way to or from our timber, also shutting us out from the county road leading south from Springfield." This proposed east-west road was to pass on the section line between Drennan's meadow on the south and grazing land of Eddin Lewis and Gilbert Dodds on the north. Lewis, married to Fletcher's cousin, quickly granted his kinsman a right of way. But although the petitioners offered to submit the dispute to "two or more disinterested men, and abide by their decision," Dodds insisted that he could not spare a single rod of his valuable grazing land, leaving the petitioners, in their own words, "no other alternative then to make our earnest and candid appeal to the Court." The language of this, as compared to other petitions, suggested an understandable hesitation to bring the issue to law, since Dodds was Fletcher's pastor. The petition also hinted at this issue when Lockridge and Fletcher argued that the road would not only "open a passway into the newly laid out road leading south from Springfield," but would also allow them "to get to the newly erected Presbyterian Church on Sugar Creek, or otherwise we must remain almost excluded from that most desirable of all other privileges."[34]

Despite the appeals to Dodds's sympathy, however, the preacher garnered the signatures of thirty-eight of his neighbors and parishioners on a "remonstrance" against the petition. Confronted with two influential opposing sides, the commissioners, at their May meeting, appointed Japhet Ball and William Chambers, one a Democrat, the other a Whig, to attempt a compromise between the factions. Nothing productive came of their good offices. Growing impatient, forty-three west-bank residents again wrote the commissioners, pointing out that Drennan and Dodds had violated a prevailing norm of community passage through lands that had once been used in common: "we view with regret the existing difficulties that seriously effect our neighbourhood from the too common practice of neighbours uniting their fences, and closing passways of great utility to other neighbours and the public generally." They urged the court not to be deterred by the sentiments of a minority, but to get on with declaring the road.[35]

Meanwhile Dodds began proceedings of his own in the Cumberland church, to which all parties to this dispute belonged. On July 3 he called a special meeting of representatives of the Sangamon Presbytery to consider a two-charge indictment: "I now charge Job Fletcher Junr. of telling a falsehood, in saying I shut him up, and of injustice for trying to get a road through my land by the civil law where I thought it ought not to go." On August 11, the preachers from three Sangamon Cumberland congregations assembled in the Cumberland meetinghouse to preside over the church trial of Captain Job Fletcher on charges of "falsehood" and "injustice."[36]

In the church proceeding, both Fletcher and Dodds fought for their immediate interests: Fletcher for the right of access to the increasingly important road system, Dodds for the right to enclose his pasture. But they chose to base their respective cases on traditional values: Fletcher invoking the tradition of common passage; Dodds, the traditional authority of the church and its pastor. The Sugar Creek Cumberland session retired to consider the evidence, and soon returned to announce that "We, the session after hearing the testimony and what facts were made known to us: In reference to the first charge, we believe it was sustained but in view of all circumstances we believe that Brother Job Fletcher should not be suspended from Church Privileges, but do honestly and conscientiously believe that he deserves reproof and admonition. With regard to the second specification in the charge, we believe it was not sustained." This was a hollow victory for Dodds: Fletcher was reprimanded for publicly speaking ill of his pastor, but the church elders implicitly endorsed his resort to civil law over Dodds's head. At their September term, the commissioners approved the new road and, while the season still allowed for roadwork, a group of west-bank men, including Fletcher, Daniel Wadsworth, Jehu Harlan, and Eddin Lewis, laid it out. The next winter Dodds sold his Sugar Creek farm and retired with his wife and children north to Menard County, leaving behind, in the wake of his rejection, a quarter-century of work.[37]

19

Conservative Change

The economic recovery that be-
gan in the mid-1840s inaugurated a period of unprecedented prosperity and change for American farmers, including the farmers of
Sugar Creek. By 1850, the northeastern United States could truly be
called a manufacturing region, and industry profoundly affected agriculture. After years of struggle with poor roads, the railroad offered
efficient access to a market rapidly expanding with the demand created by an industrial work force and a burgeoning export industry.
Other new "sharp contraptions" permeated the countryside—horse-
driven corn-planters, mowers, reapers, and machine-threshers—to increase agricultural productivity. Yet, startling as these transformations
were, they did not suddenly overthrow the weight of tradition but
altered everyday rural life within the context of traditional values and
practices. Perhaps that is the way with all revolutions.

Conservative change is apparent in the lives of some of Sugar
Creek's most innovative men. Eddin Lewis, a prosperous farmer of
Drennan's Prairie, offers a case in point. In January 1850, after confinement to his bed for five days, Lewis died of what was then described
as "lung fever"—pneumonia. James B. Easley and Job Fletcher, Jr.,
the brother and cousin of Lewis's first and second wives, respectively,
served as executors of his estate and left a trove of documents that
illustrate the activities of a well-to-do farmer during the first stirrings
of the new commercial era.[1]

In 1830, Eddin and Winnifred Easley Lewis, a young couple with

199

two small children, left Kentucky with Winnifred's parents, Daniel and Margaret Ritchie Easley, bound for Sugar Creek, where Margaret's brothers, Alexander and John Ritchie, had made farms on the rich soil of Drennan's Prairie and found wives among women of the Drennan-Dodds clan. Upon his arrival, Eddin filed on 120 acres of land along Panther Creek, just north of John L. Drennan's farm, on the stage road to Springfield. Over the next twelve years Winnie bore six more children before dying of childbirth complications in 1843. The next year Lewis married Permelia Fletcher, the twenty-four-year-old daughter of his neighbor, Squire Job Fletcher, and they soon added two more children to the already large household.

Lewis farmed in association with his neighboring father-in-law, Daniel Easley. They were joined during the 1830s and 1840s by Lewis's four siblings and their families, as well as by other of Easley's grown children. By the mid-forties the clan had grown to include nine households, forming a residentially based kinship association with complicated connections to Drennans, Dodds, and Fletchers, and strengthened by membership in the Cumberland Presbyterian Church. The Easley-Lewis households did not farm in common, but they 'changed labor so regularly that any given day might find one or another of the men laboring in the fields or hog yards of a brother, brother-in-law, or cousin. When, after harvest and before hog-killing time in 1848, Eddin built a new frame dwelling-house to replace his settler's cabin on the picturesque south bank of Panther Creek, he was assisted by the men of the clan. For the foundation and chimney they hauled golden-hued limestone from the same quarries along Sugar Creek that supplied the stone for the new state house, built in Springfield in 1837, and for the Illinois block destined for the Washington Monument, then under construction. For the beams and clapboards they felled hardwood trees from along the creek and had them sawed into board at Crow's nearby mill. Then, at the end of October, they raised the house. Eddin ran up a considerable labor debt among his kin, which they collected during 1849 by taking bacon, hams, and fresh pork from his ample supply, as well as by setting him to work in their fields and stockyard like any common farmer.

But in the Sugar Creek world of 1848 Eddin Lewis was not just any common farmer. He was a community leader. In 1842 the Cumberland elders chose him as their clerk, a position he held until his death. Lewis helped found the Temperance Union and participated in its annual conventions. In 1842, local Whigs elected him vice-president, then in 1844 president of the Sugar Creek Clay Club, and through the decade sent him as delegate every two years to the Whig county conventions, where Eddin became a friend of Lincoln's, who frequently supped at the Lewis home after meetings at the Cumberland meeting house. He married the firstborn daughter of Squire Job Fletcher, who was again representing his district in the Illinois Assembly. These positions of responsibility reflected the community's respect for Eddin's ability, as well as its deferential regard for one of the wealthiest farmers along the creek. Lewis's fine new dwelling-house symbolized his prosperity and position.[2]

From his first year in Illinois, while neighbors concentrated on self-sufficiency, Lewis concentrated on the commercial production of hogs. During the winter of the "Deep Snow," in 1831–32, for example, fearful of losing the brood sow he had carried from Kentucky, Eddin wrestled her through the one-room family cabin and pitched her down into the root cellar with her suckling pigs. His young son, James, was terrified by the desperate squealing that came from beneath the puncheon floor all winter, but the action demonstrated the enterprising spirit that propelled Eddin's business. Lewis was one of the first Sugar Creek farmers to drive herds of swine down the road to St. Louis markets, and when that proved less than efficient, he became one of the first local men to butcher and barrel his own pork for export. By the mid-1840s, Lewis had established regular connections to meat wholesalers in St. Louis, who trusted the quality of his produce, and had become the largest hog exporter along the creek. His accounts for 1847 and 1848 show that in November he butchered 255 hogs, averaging 270 pounds apiece, and shipped 6,000 pounds of barreled pork and lard south to the Mississippi River market early the next year. From this, as well as from the sale of live hogs, several sides of butchered beef, and 350 bushels of corn, Eddin recorded a cash income of over $350 for 1848.

What did this successful man do with his profits? Judging from his account book, the family continued to practice self-sufficiency, raising their own food and fiber, paying for hired labor in pork, corn, or the use of a field to raise a crop. There were, of course, certain cash expenses. The stone, lumber, nails, and paint for the new house in 1848 cost him nearly $150. The annual tax on his real estate came to $35, and his annual accounts with merchants ran to around $100. In his ledger for spring 1849, for example, Lewis recorded paying $11 to Phil Wineman for sugar and salt hauled from St. Louis, buying new shoes for the family and the hands, and advancing a dollar to Albert Stacey, a young hired man who lived with Eddin's father-in-law, so he could pay the admission price to a "show" in Springfield; but these added up to rather minor outlays of cash. Lewis indulged himself in two fancy trotters to draw the family buggy, but by contemporary standards of middle-class culture, the family lived simply; except for a mahogany bureau, a mantle clock, a large dining table, and a set of blue-edged queensware on the upper shelf of the corner cupboard, Permelia furnished their new dwelling with little adornment.

Increased farm income allowed prosperous farmers to expand their investment in tools and equipment. The essence of the "agricultural revolution" was the intensification of production, the wringing of ever more products from a steady supply of land and labor; and new farm machinery could greatly increase productivity. Throughout the fifties the newspapers kept readers fully abreast of new developments in mechanization. In 1856, Christian Wrightsman, a convert to the new ways from Patton Settlement, wrote to inform the readers of the *Journal* that with his new "Manny" reaper he had harvested over two hundred acres of wheat and hay with incredible efficiency and without problems. No problems with the machinery, perhaps, but many people experienced tragedy when their hands and limbs were mangled in the grinding teeth of the unfamiliar engines; in 1860 one of Robert Pulliam's grandchildren was impaled on the gears of a sugar mill and lost his arm below the elbow. By that year the average farmer from among the wealthiest 40 percent owned farm equipment worth $250, an increase of 60 percent over the estimated value of ten years before; yet mechanized farm equipment still remained something of an experiment, and most investments went to improved versions of traditional hand tools. The inventory of Eddin Lewis's estate, compiled in 1851, for example, listed no mechanized implements. Several years later, when James Easley, one of Lewis's executors, died, his inventory included a half-share in a "Manny"; but, like his brother-in-law Lewis, Easley invested in metal pitchforks and harrows to replace the homemade wooden implements common on poorer farms, and in elaborate sets of collars, harnesses, bridles, trees, and gears for his double-team wagon and the new family carriage.[3]

In 1847, Abraham Lincoln appealed to progressive men of Sangamon County to invest in stock of the Alton and Sangamon Rail Road, and Lewis bought several shares. But over the years he invested most of his profits in land. By the time of his death, the original 120-acre homestead had grown to 800 acres of improved farmland and 100 acres of timber. In this pattern of investment, Lewis was representative of other well-off Sugar Creek farmers. Over the twenty years from 1838 to 1858, the wealthiest 40 percent of owner-operators increased the size of their farms from an average of 225 to 350 acres and expanded their share of Sugar Creek landholding from 64 to 74 percent. Moreover, they invested substantial money and energy in the improvement of their acres through clearing, draining, fencing, and manuring. During the 1850s alone, the ratio of improved to unimproved land for this group percent rose from 1.2 to 3.4; and the cash value of their estates climbed by 225 percent.

The wealthiest 40 percent of farmers constituted about a quarter of the farming households in 1860. On their farms, eight to fifteen horses and mules provided the power to cultivate over two hundred acres devoted to corn, wheat, oats, and hay. Crops of this size produced a surplus. Deducting for seed, and for the annual food requirements of a family, for example, the wheat crops of 1859 alone should have produced cash incomes of two to five hundred dollars per household. On their extensive grassland meadows, many farmers chose to run large herds of sheep or several dozen head of cattle, and most supported five to ten milk cows. Surpluses of corn fattened the cattle and the herds of fifty to eighty hogs. Dairy products, wool, beef, and pork all were potential income producers. Moreover, farmers with land rented out had tenant crop chares to collect, adding measurably to their surplus. Eddin Lewis, for example, rented a substantial portion of this farm-land to his brothers-in-law, William and Ambrose Easley, and his brothers, James, John, and Larkin Lewis.[4]

Before her husband's personal property was sold at a "crying sale" to settle the numerous small claims against the estate, Permelia Fletcher Lewis took, as her dower, household and farm goods valued at approximately one-third of the estimated $2,500 value. The widow continued to reside on the farm, a mile north of her father, supporting herself and the family from a portion of the tenant rent; but in their capacity as executors of the estate, her neighboring male kin, Captain Job Fletcher and James Easley, took over the management of the estate and collected most of the rents in trust for the nine children. During the next few years, as the offspring of Eddin's first marriage reached majority, married, and left Permelia's household, the executors sold off the property in order to award them their portions. Then, in 1857, the widow took a second husband—Larkin Lewis, Eddin's younger brother, a forty-three-year-old farmer whose three sons were already on their own. Since he had emigrated to Sugar Creek in the early 1840s after the death of his wife in Kentucky, Larkin had farmed his broth-er's land on shares. The marriage to Permelia did nothing to change his economic position in the community, for while she was entitled to keep the bedsteads, bureaus, looking glass and other household goods that made up her dower, she brought no real property of her own into the marriage. In 1860, when the census marshal took his tally of their tenant farm, Larkin and Permelia were renting forty acres of land from Eddin's estate.

Only one in ten tenants of 1860 was a member of an original settler family, so Larkin was unusual in that regard, but in other ways he typified poor farmers just as his late brother had typified the well-to-do. The characteristic tenant family rented forty acres of improved land, planting twenty-five acres to corn, another five to ten acres to wheat and oats, the rest to grass for hay and grazing. They kept two or three draft animals (sometimes oxen, but increasingly horses or mules), two or three milk cows, and a dozen hogs. Owner-operators of the poorest 40 percent were a little better off; their small tracts of forty to eighty acres produced correspondingly bigger crops of corn, grain, and hay, and allowed them to run a few head of beef cattle besides. The typical tenant or poor landed family produced from seven hundred to a thousand bushels of corn, one to two hundred bushels of wheat and oats, and ten to fifteen tons of hay. Over the decade of the 1850s there was no appreciable rise in the size of the operations of the poor. In fact, while the better-off owner-operators of the community added considerably to the value of their estates through this first dawning of the agricultural revolution, the value of tools and equipment on tenant and poor owner-operator farms actually fell by 15 percent, suggesting that they found it difficult not only to purchase new tools but even to replace old ones. The requirements for seed, animal feed, and family food suggest that the levels of their production could support little more than basic subsistence, especially considering that tenants gave from a third to two-thirds of their crops as rent. Together, these families made up 60 percent of the farming households of Sugar Creek in 1860.

These examples of the progress of the antebellum agricultural revolution in Sugar Creek suggest two salient points. First, that progress was characterized by what economists call "uneven development," by the improvement of one segment of the community and the stagnation or decline of another. Between tenants and landlords there was a significant transfer of wealth that helped to finance the improvement of more prosperous farms. Second, prosperous farmers continued to hold to the traditional logic that a man could never own too much land. When profits came their way, they were more likely to bargain with a hard-pressed neighbor for the adjoining "forty," or invest labor and capital in improving their holdings, than to buy the new mower on display at the farm implement dealer's place in Wineman or Chatham. Renting land on shares was a more prudent choice than increasing production through mechanization. During the first years of the new era, men with capital like Eddin Lewis might be better described as conservatives than innovators, improving the well-worn paths of the past rather than breaking new highways to the future.

So change came, but often in conservative form. The same was true of change in women's lives. In outline, for example, the marriage patterns of second-generation Sugar Creek women—women born from 1810 to 1849—appeared to differ little from those of their mothers. Although they married at the slightly later age of twenty-one (compared to a marriage age of nineteen for their mothers), women continued to bear their first child within a year of their weddings and to deliver the rest of their children at about two-year intervals thereafter. Systematic birth control through some form of contraception remained a thing of the distant future. But nevertheless, compared to their mothers, second-generation women lowered their total completed fertility by 20 percent—from 8.2 for the first generation to 5.9 for the second. Four in ten second-generation mothers had five or fewer children, and only one in five raised more than ten. These lower rates of completed fertility were almost entirely due to an earlier termination of childbearing. Women of the first generation continued to bear children well into their forties, but typical second-generation women quit having children some five years earlier, before they reached the age of thirty-nine. This evidence fits with more general studies that have suggested that, as the available land of rural communities disappeared, families restricted their childbearing for fear of the declining opportunities for the next generation.[5]

This change was experienced by women from families at all economic levels, and it had an effect on the demographic shape of the community. In 1860 there were roughly nineteen hundred children under ten years of age for every thousand women from ages sixteen to forty-five, a decline of better than 20 percent from 1830 levels. Mean household size for the Sugar Creek community as a whole also fell during the same period, from a modal size of seven to five persons. The dependency ratio—the number of children (aged fifteen and under) supported by each economically active man or woman (between fifteen and fifty-nine)—fell from 1.2 in 1830 to .8 in 1860. These were subtle shifts, more in the nature of structural reforms than the transformations that were more commonly noted and commented upon.[6]

But while these changes may not seem dramatic, they were important. First, because fewer dependents lowered the amount of food and fiber necessary for minimum levels of household subsistence; second, and perhaps more important, because they suggest that women, in small ways perhaps, were taking hold of their lives, doing what they could to change them. Beginning in the 1840s, many Sugar Creek mothers in their thirties apparently decided that five or six children were enough. Family limitation might then be accomplished, with the active cooperation of their husbands, by practicing coitus interruptus or withdrawal, by abstinence from sexual intercourse, or by abortion.

MARY JANE WALLACE (1835–1924), daughter of John and Eveline Rieger Wallace, a formal portrait taken on the eve of her marriage to neighboring farmer Thomas Black, Jr., in 1855. Mary bore the last of her three children in 1871 at the age of thirty-six.

During the 1850s, advertisements for abortifacients began to appear in the Springfield press under the notation "IMPORTANT TO FEMALES." "Dr. Cheeseman's Pills," for example, were recommended as a pregnancy preventative for "ladies whose health will not permit an increase of their family"; users were advised not to take the pills during pregnancy, "as they would be sure to cause a miscarriage." Similarly, pregnant women were "warned" against taking "Dr. Duponco's Golden Periodical Pills for Females," although they were assured that the medication's "mildness would prevent any injury to health." The ineffectiveness of these dubious concoctions is not the point; clearly a market for family limitation aids had emerged.[7]

While general household size fell from 1830 to 1860, the households of farm owners proved an exception, holding steady at seven persons. But landed families tended to be in a later stage of their history than landless ones, the wives further along in their childbearing. In 1830, when the social and economic distinctions between owners and squatters were not yet as important as the distinction between owners and tenants was to become, the average head of household, squatter or owner, was a man in his mid-forties, his wife, a woman in her late thirties. By 1860, however, the age of the average tenant farmer had fallen to thirty-three, and the age of the tenant farm wife to twenty-nine; both were ten years younger than the average owner-operator couple. The more expensive speculator land could be purchased only by mature families who moved to Sugar Creek with savings; younger families, who had fewer resources, were forced to rent or hire themselves out as farm laborers. The census of owner-operator households included many of these hired hands, who lived with their employers. Owner-operator households were not larger because their women bore a greater number of children; age and prosperity made the difference.

The changing composition of owner-operator households also affected the division of productive labor within the family. Dairy work, for example, traditionally had been women's responsibility in the culture of the upland South. A male Kentuckian was mortified if caught milking, wrote Daniel Drake, and according to Moses Wadsworth, Sugar Creek settlers in the 1830s "entertained a supreme contempt for a man who attended to the milking. The women here did all the milking. No matter if there *were* two or three men about the house, and but one hard-worked woman, the former couldn't degrade themselves." Hired hands did not at first take any easier to the task; but Wadsworth recalled that although they balked at milking, hired men could be encouraged to take it on if "several dollars were added to the price."[8]

As more prosperous owner-operators shifted into commodity production, however, and employed men and boys to supplement the family labor pool, the importance of dairy work to the family economy declined. From 1849 to 1859, the manufacture of butter among the top three-fifths of owners declined by nearly 10 percent, while productivity (butter production per dairy cow) remained constant. Among tenants and poor farmers, however, butter production rose by 25 percent over the decade, while productivity increased by over 60 percent. A hired man could almost always find something more useful to do than churn, but tenant families sweated their own labor, especially in areas of production such as the dairy, where they did not have to share the product with their landlords. In the most well-to-do families, women's income-producing labor tended to be replaced or outmoded, while in poorer households, women continued to contribute to the family economy in the same old way. This same process occurred in other areas of the family economy. While the wealthiest farmers, for example, redirected their efforts into growing wheat during the 1850s, cutting back on their hog production by a third, tenants maintained their small herds of swine, for these represented an irreducible subsistence minimum.

Another indication of the changing nature of women's work in the family economy was the drastic decline in the production of what the census labeled "home manufactures." In 1839 Sangamon households produced an average of $27 in textiles; by 1849 that had fallen to $23 but continued to be quite high by national standards, suggesting that the home production of cloth remained an important subsistence activity. In 1859, however, after six years of railroad imports, the average Sugar Creek household produced only $3-worth of home manufactures. Cheap cottons and woolens from eastern factories replaced homespun, and the market for homemade cloth collapsed.

Averages, however, hide some interesting differences among households. Three-quarters of all the farms along Sugar Creek reported home manufactures in 1849; in 1859, only one in ten. For those who did produce, however, the value of their product did not fall. And most continuing household production was found in neither especially wealthy nor especially poor households but those in the middle. In the 1870s, Robert Patterson wrote that after the Civil War he found Illinois wheelwrights still making spinning wheels, "not to sell as curiosities, but to supply an actual demand from families that yet *preferred* to manufacture their own clothing as in former times." Elizabeth McDowell Hill later remembered that when her father first successfully began to market his agricultural surpluses, during the 1850s, he announced: "wife and daughters, store away your loom, wheels, warping bars, spool rack, winding blades, all your utensils for weaving cloth up in the loft. The boys and I can make enough by increasing our herds."

"There appeared to be a spirit of progressiveness all over the country," wrote Hill, but "the old ladies could not give up holding up their end of the 'single tree' as yet, so they continued with the spinning." The "single tree," a crosspiece for connecting a double-team of horses to a plow or wagon, symbolized the cooperative and reciprocal labor of men and women in the self-sufficient family. Tenant and poor families could not afford to maintain this economically inefficient production, but among families of the middling sort, there was some persistence of older patterns.[9]

The importance of women's work continued; it merely shifted from income-producing to strictly "reproductive" labor. As late as the 1920s, Illinois farm women regularly produced dairy products for home consumption, tended to the chickens, laid out, weeded, and gathered from the garden, canned vegetables and prepared meat for cooking, cut and sewed nearly all the family's clothing, and even continued to make soap in large outdoor cauldrons. For other, wealthier farmers, however, there was an important shift in work and sensibility. Elizabeth Hill remembered neighbor girls being excited by their new freedom from production. "They clapped their hands with delight and said 'we can now piece quilts,' for at this time it had become the fad to piece quilts and see who could bleach their hands and keep them the whitest. The girls were wild to get to work on the Star of Bethlehem and the Rose of Sharon." Hill thought of patchwork quilts, today the very symbol of all that was traditional in the lives of rural women, as an expression of "modern" Victorian domesticity. Even the change to a new fashion in femininity expressed itself through conservative and traditional stitchery.[10]

In 1860, Sugar Creek farmer Philemon Stout, Jr., began a diary that he continued for the next half-century. In those pages Stout recorded the mixture of tradition and innovation that characterized the mid-century in Sugar Creek history. Stout was the ninth-born child and the youngest son of Penelope Anderson and Philemon Stout, Sr., a couple who emigrated to Sugar Creek from Kentucky, settling with their children in the northern section of the Sugar Camp neighborhood in 1836. Because his older brothers were married with households of their own, it fell to Philemon Jr. to work with his father to improve the farm, breaking the sod with a wooden plow, hoeing corn, hauling loads of grain, and driving herds of cattle down the St. Louis road. When his father died in 1846, Philemon, still unmarried at twenty-four, took over the management of the 350-acre estate. He soon demonstrated a sagacious nature, buying his siblings' portions of the family homestead, investing his available capital in real estate, and building several tenant houses in order to rent out his excess acres. He first married a twenty-year-old neighborhood girl, Melissa Shoup; she died delivering her fourth child in 1855. Stout soon remarried, and he and his new wife raised three more children. By 1860, Philemon Stout was among the wealthiest farmers along Sugar Creek, raising corn, oats, and wheat, horses, hogs, and cattle on over four hundred acres of prime farmland, and renting the equivalent of another quarter-section to tenants on shares.[11]

In January 1860, corn from the previous season still stood in symmetrical shocks in Philemon's fields. Through the fall and well into the spring, he and his hands pulled and husked ears from the shocks, then turned cattle and hogs into fields littered with fodder. When the stock finished their gleaning, the men broke, raked, then burned the stripped stalks to ready the fields for the spring plowing that began in late March. Fields were "laid off" in cross furrows and, in mid-April, planted in "fine order," several kernels being dropped by hand at each corner. By June, one of the hired men was hoeing and thinning the young plants, while Philemon and his ten-year-old son, Sammy, ran the "double shovel" cultivator through the rows. "Finished plowing corn the 3d time and begun plowing it the 4th & last," he wrote on June 16th; "corn looks very fine." By the 20th he had "laid by" his maize. In November, with his harvest in the shock, Stout estimated his yield at over 2,000 bushels, a rate of about 50 bushels per acre. With his staple crop, Stout fed his stock, traded with his neighbors, and periodically "shelled a sack of corn & went to mill" for his own meal. Corn was not a cash crop. Although Stout used better equipment, his routine remained little changed from that of his father. Work in the cornfields would continue to be a hand operation until the twentieth century.

Mechanization was more evident in Philemon's small grain production. He bought and used a Manny reaper for harvesting his oats and wheat and mowing his hay. But there was still a great deal of hand labor on Stout's farm. He sowed oats broadcast in March, wheat amid the skeletal cornstalks in October, then harrowed the seed in. During the winter, his hands "tramped" oats on the threshing floor in the barn. In September, neighbor Jonathan Peddicord brought his new threshing machine to Stout's for the first time and began threshing his wheat and oats. Philemon was well pleased with the savings in labor and time that the reaper and Peddicord's machine introduced, but it was years before hand-threshing ceased to be a part of Stout's annual round.

The biggest discontinuity from his father's day was not mechanization but Stout's extensive relationship to hired laborers and tenants. William and James, sons of neighbor George Saunders, "set in to work" at the planting season in March for $12 per month. The labor of these young men supplemented that of several live-in hands: Bob Maher, an Irish immigrant in his early twenties, Virgil and Charles Downey, boys in their teens, as well as Cynthia Lard, in her early thirties, who worked in the kitchen. "Made a bargain with Bob for another year at $186," Philemon wrote in January, and in December noted settling with Cynthia for the year by paying her $84. The Downeys, children of impoverished friends of the family, worked for their keep. Philemon took a paternal attitude toward his help. He spent several days in Springfield unsuccessfully trying to find an apprenticeship for Virgil, and in November sponsored Bob when the young immigrant applied for naturalization. Cynthia almost always accompanied the family on trips to the county seat, as in May, when Philemon "went to Springfield & took the children & Cynthia to the Animal show & Circus." Cynthia and Bob married in the mid-sixties, and they named their first child Louisa P., after Mrs. Stout.

In April, Philemon visited James and Hannah Lupton, a young tenant couple on an eighty-acre farm Stout owned along Horse Creek, three miles east of his homestead, and he happily recorded that he "found a very good pen of corn for my part." After his own corn was laid by, he and son Sammy took five days to haul "last year's rent" from the Horse Creek farm. Stout delighted in his profits, although he lamented that his tenants seemed so "very poor." In November he returned to survey the season's progress. "Mr Lupton has a very good crop of corn," he wrote; "I think I will get eight hundred bushel." The corn from his fields and the fields of his tenants filled Stout's cribs to overflowing. During the last months of the year, he purchased cattle in small lots from various neighboring farmers and had his hands stall-feed them on the corn. He resold the steers to other farmers, including Ezra Barnes of Drennan's Prairie, who bought forty head. At the end of 1860, he calculated his profits from his cattle trading at $1,248.

Like other Sugar Creek farmers, Stout invested his profits in land. In 1860 Philemon had a regular relationship with J. E. Hocker, a real-estate agent in Springfield, who purchased land warrants for him and selected a section of Kansas land at seventy-five cents an acre. By 1874, Hocker's local investments had more than doubled Stout's 1860 holdings of six hundred Sugar Creek acres, and in 1881, when Philemon decided to deed two-thirds of his real estate to his children, he owned over twenty-three hundred acres. Late in his life, Stout was described as having "won splendid success in business," and Philemon himself believed that he had been "greatly blessed." Historian Paul Gates reminds us that the success of farmers like Stout, however, "was accomplished not alone by the head of the family and his children, but with the aid of hired men." In Stout's case, and in the cases of the most

successful of Sugar Creek farmers, the labor of tenants like the Lup-
tons was equally important.[12]

Relations with hired men and tenants were something of a departure from former patterns, but in other important ways Stout's social
life connected directly with the past. The family belonged to the Primitive Baptist Church, and each Saturday and Sunday found them at
"meeting," attentive to the preaching of one or more itinerant Baptist
ministers. Philemon donated an acre near his dwelling-house and
there erected a meetinghouse in the 1850s, where the local Baptist
community buried their own. A brother and several sister Stouts and
their families lived nearby and also were Baptists, as were most of the
neighbors clustered at the north of sugar camp prairie. With kith and
extended kin, Philemon regularly exchanged labor and participated in
neighborhood frolics and raisings. In March 1861, he and his family
attended the annual "sugaring off" at the old Pulliam grove. The
complex of church, kin, and residential connections kept the Stouts
very much a part of the traditional rural community.

Philemon was also actively involved in civic affairs. During 1860 he
served as a commissioner to partition the estate and set aside the dower
for his first wife's sister, the widow, Maria Shoup Brunk. In his capacity
as one of the trustees of the school district, he regularly visited the local
schoolhouse, contracted for its improvement, and boarded the neighborhood schoolmaster. In 1861, local justice of the peace William Burtle swore him in as road commissioner for township 14/5. He participated regularly in the musters of his militia company, activated when
President Lincoln called for troops in 1861.

These were years of intense political excitement, and in his diary
Philemon paid careful attention. He was a Democrat, as were most of
his neighbors, and he took part in the state convention that ratified the
nomination of Stephen A. Douglas for president; but he also attended
Republican meetings out of interest. On November 6, 1860, he "went
to Chatham to the election." "So far as voting was concerned all was
peaceable," he wrote, although the local boys "had some liquor—&
hard fighting." Political fist-fights continued to be part of the local
scene. That fall a political argument on the Springfield square between
Stout's neighbors Samuel Shoup, his intensely Republican kinsman,
Dr. Alexander Shields, the Democratic organizer, and Joseph Ledlie,
the acerbic county surveyor and Democratic candidate for state representative, erupted into violence when Shoup called Shields a liar, then
Ledlie jumped into the fray and "pronounced Mr. Shoup a d——d
liar," a red flag that never failed to incite the bullish nature of men. The
Springfield justice fined Shoup for his temper and Ledlie for his
tongue.[13]

National political affairs could create important local events along the creek; that had been a fact in 1840, and it was even truer in the watershed election year of 1860. But, nevertheless, the most important event of the year for residents of Stout's neighborhood was eminently local. At the end of 1859 Philemon's neighbor Albion Knotts hosted a Christmas party for the Sugar Camp neighborhood; the young men engaged in some heavy drinking and some typical tussling that was broken up by Knott's son-in-law George Pulliam, a grandson of Robert, the pioneer of Sugar Creek. A little later, in the flush of a Virginia reel, a young neighbor called out to Richard Whited, who had been in the thick of the fight: "Dick, ain't the ball going on nice?" "It'll be better," Dick grumbled, "once I get a chance at that man there," pointing to Pulliam. Later that evening, Whited showed young Rachel Hammond, a hired girl who worked in the household of his brother-in-law Joseph Newlund, a small leather shot bag with which, he declared, he could "knock a man cold." "Somebody would soon get his fist," he threatened as he doubled the "slung shot," something like a blackjack, in his fist while motioning at Pulliam.[14]

Three weeks later, at another winter dancing party held in Joe Newlund's two-room cabin on the west side of the creek near Chatham, Whited settled his grudge. As couples danced in the front room, a dozen men crowded into the back ell to drink and gamble. There another fight began, and Pulliam again intervened. Now on his own kin's turf, Whited, a heavy six-footer, rushed at the peacemaker: "Stand back, Pulliam, I've taken a great deal off'n you, but I'm takin' nothing more." The insuing exchange, as later reported by witnesses, was painfully familiar: "Shut up, Dick, you've got nothing to do with this"—"Damn you, I'll say what I please, and you, Pulliam, are the cause of this fuss"—"You're a damned liar!" There it was, the inevitable verbal signal for violence. Amid the confusion, all the yelling and pushing, men saw Whited suddenly bring his powerful clenched fist down on Pulliam, saw Pulliam stagger back, then, in the dimly lit room, saw the gleam of light on the blade as Pulliam whipped out his bowie knife, slashed Dick's face, then mortally drove it into the big man's chest. The slung shot was later found underneath Whited's body.

The Stouts attended Pulliam's "trial for his life" in Springfield in May 1860. The courtroom was "crowded during the day with anxious spectators," the kin, friends, and neighbors of Pulliam and Whited from Sugar Camp and Chatham. At the end of two days of testimony, defense attorney James Matheny urged the jury to remember that Pulliam had acted out of fear for his own life, while state's attorney J. B. White argued that the defendant, who had come to the party armed, had committed first-degree murder. The spectators waited while the jury deliberated for two hours, then brought in a verdict of man-slaughter. Philemon and Louisa Stout watched as Pulliam was sentenced to seven years of hard labor at the state penitentiary at Joilet.

From the very first Sangamon County murder trial and execution in 1826, women had attended those fascinating and horrifying proceedings with their menfolk. By the late 1850s, however, Louisa accompanied Philemon on nearly all his social and civic rounds: on visits to family and neighbors, to Baptist meeting in the family carriage, north on the railroad cars for an excursion, to Springfield in the fall to attend the county fair where she had her "likeness" taken, even to political rallies. In September the Stouts attended a Republican barbecue held in the pasture of neighboring kinsman Samuel Shoup; then, in October, "Louisa the children and me went to Springfield to hear Douglas speak." There had been a time, not long before, when women were not welcome at such occasions, but things now were different, and women were expressly invited in the newspaper announcements of political rallies. In most ways, the Stout's social life affirmed traditional values, but the character of the relationship between Philemon and Louisa, as it can be gleaned from his diary, was certainly one of the new things in Sugar Creek.[15]

On each of his trips to town, it was Stout's custom to take with him some farm products to sell. He took particular pride in coming back not only with the "artikles" he bought—shoes, nails, sweet potato plants, and lady's magazines for Louisa—but with a little change jangling in his deep farmer's pockets. "Went to Springfield with turkeys, eggs & butter," he wrote in December, and "sold them for $12.77." But Louisa had nothing to do with the manufacture of these traditional women's products. "Virgil worked at the milk house," Philemon wrote in April, and recorded throughout the year how the hands made butter, collected eggs, tended poultry. Louisa was the daughter of substantial Menard County farmer James Brasfield, had attended the Female Academy in Jacksonville before her marriage, and although she toiled in house and kitchen, even the garden was given over to Virgil and Bob. In short, Louisa was a lady. In 1861 Stout purchased a new cast-iron stove and a sewing machine for her. For the well-to-do in Sugar Creek, this was a new age.

The new age was nowhere more evident than in Louisa's childbearing pattern. From her marriage to Philemon in 1855 until 1862, she successfully delivered three children, including "a black headed boy" born in April 1860 whom they named Joab. But after her thirty-seventh year Louisa conceived no more. In this she was as typical of her generation as Philemon's mother had been of hers. In November 1860, after a long and painful illness, his mother, Penelope Stout, died in the

"FARM RESIDENCE OF PHILEMON STOUT" looking west toward the Sugar Creek timber in the late 1860s. Philemon and Louisa Stout, shown here riding together before their well-laden estate, built this "I" house in 1854, replacing the original log cabin, which here serves as one of several outbuildings. The pine board fencing was an innovation that came with the railroad.

original settler's cabin which she and her husband had built in 1836, and which she refused to vacate when her son built his new frame house next door in 1854. In her day, widow Stout had delivered thirteen children, six of whom had died in infancy.

20

The Remnant of
That Pioneer Band

Change captured public attention during the 1850s. As the railroad connection through Sugar Creek neared completion in 1851, the *Journal* reported that "nearly every acre of vacant land within 10 miles of the line has been purchased." A year after the rail connection to St. Louis had opened, the *Register* found that land near the railroad had increased in value one hundred percent, and in 1856 the *Journal* noted with pleasure increases of as much as nine times in selling prices. "The rumble of the cars and the whistle of the engines" brought the country and the station-stops along the line "alive with progress and improvements." The course of local events, the *Journal* asserted confidently, would now "be onward and upward." But there was a measure of anxiety in all this as well. In the decade before 1860, the population of Springfield nearly doubled, reaching almost ten thousand, and along Sugar Creek, the Eastmans' sleepy stagecoach village gave way to Wineman's bustling railroad town. A considerable number of these new residents were foreigners, mostly Irish railroad workers who lived in bunkhouses and ramshackle "railroad hotels" along the tracks. By 1860, almost a quarter of the population of the two Sugar Creek villages was made up of Irish-born young men. In both village and city, merchants and craftsmen changed their way of doing business. "I HAVE DONE IT!" a Springfield jeweler announced, "ADOPTED THE CASH SYSTEM," and beneath a banner proclaiming "CASH! MONEY!" a merchant cobbler advertised that "from January 1st, 1858, I intend doing a strictly cash business." Thus did generations of tradition fall by the wayside. The pace of change, wrote one correspondent, seemed "more like a sketch from some part of the Arabian Nights than a matter of stern reality."[1]

Uncertainty was also rife in politics. The national crisis over the status of slavery in the territories, which reached fever pitch in Illinois during the Kansas-Nebraska controversy of 1854–55, destroyed the old Democrat-Whig political alignment in Sangamon County. In 1854 an "Anti-Nebraska" coalition of free-soil advocates replaced the Whigs as the opposition party. Two years later, in the 1856 elections for president, county voters were confronted by candidates from three parties: Democrat James Buchanan, Millard Fillmore of the anti-Catholic and nativist American or "Know-Nothing" party, and John C. Frémont of the newly formed Republicans.

Along Sugar Creek this political turmoil had the effect of seriously splintering the opposition to the Democrats. In September 1856 Democrats held a political rally in the timber north of Drennan's Prairie that, according to the *Register,* attracted nearly fifteen hundred "country people," "including a large number of ladies." Before this crowd of kin, friends, and neighbors, the old leader of the Sugar Creek Whigs, Job Fletcher, denounced the new political combinations, and for the first time in his political life endorsed the Democratic ticket. While not mentioning this important defection from the ranks, the *Journal* concurred that this meeting qualified as a "monster rally" but contended that of the five hundred people *it* counted there, "over one-half, we are informed, were Frémont men." A month later the local correspondent for the *Journal* wrote that "the Old Whigs of Sugar Creek were out in full force on last Saturday afternoon at the Frémont meeting in Auburn. Frémont has many warm friends on Sugar Creek and his cause is constantly gaining accessions here."

But old Whig loyalties did not automatically extend to the new Republican party. Sugar Creek voters, organized now into the precincts of Auburn and Chatham, cast little more than 10 percent of their ballots for Frémont in 1856, providing majorities instead for Democratic candidates for governor, Congress, and president. Even after the demise of the American party returned the political system to its traditional two-party structure, Democrats held on to a majority in both Sugar Creek and Sangamon County. "Old Sangamon Redeemed!!" the *Register* rang out after a string of unexpected victories in 1857. And in 1858, at the conclusion of the famous campaign featuring the Lincoln-Douglas debates, when Democrats carried all but three county precincts, the *Register* ran a banner headline declaring the "GLORIOUS TRIUMPH OF DEMOCRACY!!" and noted that "after twenty-five years spent in a minority, the gallant democracy of old Sangamon, the whig citadel, takes its position among the formost democratic counties of the

state. Sangamon repudiates Lincoln and his abolitionism!" Indeed, in
the presidential election of 1860, Douglas defeated Lincoln in Auburn
and Chatham, capturing nearly 57 percent of the vote.[2]

This represented an important shift in Sugar Creek voting patterns.
While many midwestern precincts turned solidly Republican in the late
fifties, the neighborhoods along Sugar Creek transferred a critical
margin of their support from Whigs to Democrats. From 1836 to 1852,
in elections for state and national office, Sugar Creek cast 46 percent of
its vote for Democratic candidates; from 1856 to 1872, however, Democrats took 55 percent. Seeking an explanation for this shift, one observer suggested that "the citizens of Sangamon county, being largely
from the Southern States, did not spontaneously enter into the Republican movement. Many old Whigs drifted into the Democratic party." Former Sugar Creek Whigs like Job Fletcher, William Burtle, and
Josephus Gatton joined forces with the Douglas Democrats in the late
1850s, perhaps swayed by Democratic rhetoric that branded Republicans "nigger worshippers" and "black abolitionists." And while
the addition of Irish electors in Sugar Creek undoubtedly added to
Democratic strength, voting patterns of the 1840s suggest that during
the mid-fifties a critical number of tenants and poor farmers shifted
their support toward the Democrats. However the new majority was
created, the political system was thrown into considerable turmoil by
the events of the decade.[3]

Part of the pervasive uncertainty of the 1850s was the knowledge
that the original generation of settlers was passing away. In an article
on a Fourth of July celebration held at Harlan's Grove in 1856, the
Journal noted that "among the hundreds congregated, but few of the
old settlers with their grey hairs could be seen. They have gone to sleep
with their fathers." A year later, in the course of an obituary for Sugar
Creek settler James Easley, the newspaper commented that "the early
settlers of Sangamon county are fast passing away. They have lived to
see the wild prairies, the haunts of the savage and buffalo, become the
abodes of a prosperous and happy people—with schools, churches,
and all those institutions which make a virtuous and prosperous community—the resoluts [*sic*] of their own labors, which now have ceased."
"Another Pioneer Gone!" mourned the headline to a similar obituary
in the *Register* for 1858. There was, indeed, a demographic reality to
these observations: by the mid-fifties death had claimed over two-
thirds of the first generation of Sangamon's original settlers, and surviving pioneers were well into their seventies.[4]

Spurred perhaps by this generational passing, both Springfield
newspapers began to print columns of history on a regular basis in the
early fifties. Writers such as former Illinois governor John Reynolds
sang the praises of forgotten heroes like surveyor John Messenger,

who led the way into the wilderness with his ax and circumferator, and reminisced about "olden days" in the Sangamo, when neighborhoods came together for "amusement and mirth" at frolics, when families grew their own flax, wool, or cotton, and produced their own cloth on the "old-fashioned wheel."

No! we'll not forget the old wool-wheel,
Nor the hank on the old count-reel;
We'll not forget how we used to eat
The sweet honey-comb with the fat deer meat;
We'll not forget how we used to bake,
That best of bread, old Johnny-cake!

Nostalgia for a simpler past became a popular sensibility in these years. But the fact that such "old-fashioned" conditions were a continuing reality for tenants and poor farmers marked this kind of writing as unabashedly sentimental. The lives of many Sugar Creek and Sangamon farmers, in fact, remained closer to the conditions of pioneer times than the urban editors of either the *Journal* or the *Register* cared to notice.[5]

Late in May 1859, in the columns of both Springfield newspapers, there appeared a petition from sixty-one Sangamon County residents calling for the formation of a local historical society:

Old Settlers' Convention

The undersigned, desirous of preserving the early history of the city of Springfield and Sangamon county, now known in a great degree only to a few "Pioneers," would suggest a meeting at the court house on the 1st of June, of all surviving settlers who became residents of the county previous to the "winter of the deep snow" (1830–1831) for the purpose of organizing a permanent society in furtherance of this object.

The publication in both papers simultaneously was significant, for it signaled the intention of the organizers to insulate this "Old Settlers' Society" from political turmoil. At its first official meeting, in fact, the society ruled "against the admission of partisan politics into its meetings." The Old Settlers' Society offered up nostalgia for "pioneer times" as relief from the dogged partisan contention that characterized public debate about the future. In the words of the *Register,* local history provided a unique opportunity to "have a good time."[6]

Among the signers of this call were a number of genuine old settlers, including several linked to the early history of Sugar Creek: Zachariah Peter, seventy-eight, long-time local justice of the peace; and Sangamon County school commissioner Erastus Wright, eighty, brother of the pioneer Sugar Creek schoolmaster, Charles Wright. But, in fact, fewer than a third of the "old residents" who signed the petition had passed their sixtieth birthday, their average age was only fifty, and a quarter were not yet beyond their thirties. Pascal P. Enos, Jr., forty-three, son of the first Springfield land-office registrar, and Noah Matheny, also forty-three, son of the first county clerk, wrote and circulated the petition. Like Enos and Matheny, most who signed it were not really pioneers at all, but the sons of pioneers—sons of successful farmers, stock-raisers, millers, and merchants. From the Sugar Creek area they included James Darneil, thirty-seven, son of pioneer John Darneil, who broke a farm near Chatham, and William D. Crow, forty-seven, successor to his father Robert's milling business.

Moreover, while the majority of Sangamon's heads of household practiced farming, three-quarters of these petitioners worked at urban occupations; and while seven in ten county residents lived in the countryside, eight in ten petitioners resided in Springfield. Among the signers were William Grimsley, fifty-five, who made a fortune producing flour at his modern "Phoenix Steam Mill" in the capital; Hugh Armstrong, fifty, Springfield woolen manufacturer; John Roll, forty-five, who contracted much of the housing built during the preceding boom decade; and successful lawyers Abraham Lincoln, fifty, his former partner, John T. Stuart, fifty-two, and his present partner, William H. Herndon, forty-one. Based on the values they reported for personal and real property on the census of 1860, the median worth of all the signers was about $15,000, on a par with the richest 20 percent of Sugar Creek farmers. But included among these men were the truly wealthy: the census marshal listed Stuart's worth at $60,000, Grimsley's at $65,000, Roll's at over $100,000. Signer John Williams, Springfield merchant, banker, and railroad builder, who got his start raising hogs on his large Sangamon county farm, by 1849 was producing, according to the *Journal*, "lard enough to fry a heap of doughnuts of the size of Pike's Peak"; by 1859 he had become one of the state's wealthiest citizens. So, by and large, the petitioners were the movers and shakers of a new commercial order, based in Springfield.[7]

Most of these men reached manhood during the late 1830s and early 1840s, the age of "Young America." Stephen Douglas led a partisan Democratic movement by that name which celebrated nationalism, manifest destiny, and economic progress; but the local press more consistently used the phrase to denominate a new generation of men eager to seize national leadership from the formidable grip of the "founders." "Young America is something more than a political doctrine," declared the *Register*. "It is republicanism with hands and feet, shovel and tongs, axes and plows . . . , republicanism getting out of forms into everyday facts and stamping its name on things as well as words." The label applied not only to the new generation of political

leaders like Lincoln and Douglas, but to such local Sugar Creek Democrats as William Lockridge and John L. Drennan, to local Whigs Job
Fletcher, Jr., and Eddin Lewis; it applied not only to urban business
leaders, but to aspiring commercial farmers as well. These were practical men who ardently advanced various public and private schemes
for economic development. Whether Democrat or Whig, they sought
to reshape the inherited world in accord with their own vision of
"modernity."[8]

As they came into their own in the 1850s, however, the mood of
many "Young Americans" changed; their celebration of change
waned. Milton Hay, uncle of John Hay, Lincoln's young presidential
secretary during the Civil War, later tried to explain this interesting
psychological phenomenon. He arrived in Springfield fresh from his
Kentucky birthplace in 1832 at the age of fifteen, read law in Lincoln's
office, won admission to the bar in 1840, and practiced in the capital
for the next forty years. During the forties and fifties, in company with
many other young business and professional men, Hay struggled "step
by step" for "progress in improvements and civilization." Despite this
"earnest desire," he recalled, "we were somewhat unconscious of the
extent of the changes as they occurred." It was the "quickened pulsa-
tions of a more commercial life" brought on by the completion of the
railroad that forced Hay and his colleagues to "open our eyes widely"
to the transforming powers of improvement and to question some of
the benefits of economic progress. The railroad, he wrote, constituted
"a dividing line in point of time between the new and the old."

> Not only our homemade manufactures, but our homemade life
> and habits to a great measure disappeared. The ox and the Carey
> plow, the spinning wheel and the loom, disappeared together.
> We began to build houses of a different style and with different
> materials. We farmed not only with different implements but in a
> different mode. Then we began to inquire what the markets were
> and what product of the farm we could raise and sell to the best
> advantage. The farmer enlarged his farm and no longer con-
> tented himself with the land that himself or his boys could culti-
> vate, but he must have hired hands and hired help to cultivate his
> enlarged possessions. Then it was our families discovered their
> inability to do the housework of the family, and required hired
> assistance. Customs in religious exercises even underwent a
> change. The "forty-minute" sermon began to be preached; the
> minister ceased to line off the hymn for the congregation, and the
> congregation quit singing.

"Then we began sadly to recall the old days and the old times," wrote
Hay. "Then we began to look around for the remnant of that pioneer
band of 'early settlers,' whose experience and memory of a far differ-

ent condition of things would prove interesting to a generation which knew nothing of that by-gone time but from tradition." The old settlers were called forward by Young America to play a final part in the history of the Sangamo, to testify to the meaning of the pioneer experience.[9]

Nostalgia such as Hay's for the past of the founding generation became a national cultural passion in the 1850s, a passion perhaps best typified by the consuming interest in historical commemorations like the construction of the Washington Monument and the preservation of Mount Vernon, or by the popularity of reverential historical oratory from men like Edward Everett. Young America's attempt to overthrow and transform the world of the fathers generated among its cohorts considerable anxiety and uncertainty. The organizers of the Old Settlers' Society acted in accord with national cultural trends. But they also responded to imperatives of their own construction. As men remaking the Sangamo, they sought to claim as their own the legacy and legitimacy of the pioneers, sought to wrap themselves in the homespun mantle of the founding generation.[10]

Membership in the Old Settlers' Society was originally limited to pioneers who had settled before the "Deep Snow." But as the century wore on and the ranks of the pioneers thinned, the date for defining "early" was moved later and later, and in practice the society was always composed not of individuals but of *families,* the descendants of original settler families. Moreover, factors of mobility and attrition built into the process of economic development determined that the members of the society came overwhelmingly from the class of owner-operators within the neighborhoods. In Sugar Creek in 1860, for example, three of four descendants of original settler families were owner-operators, and although descendants represented only 30 percent of community households, they made up nearly half of all farm owners and held nearly 80 percent of the arable land along the creek. The constituency of the Old Settlers' Society, then, was the class of landowners in the local neighborhoods. and its proceedings must be read in that light.

This rather select group of householders first assembled several months after the initial organizing call on a "gloriously fine" Indian summer day in October 1859, in Pulliam's sugar grove, the month and the place having been selected to commemorate the arrival of the pioneer of Sugar Creek forty-two years before. In the mid-morning, after a crowd of some fifteen hundred men, women, and children from all over the county had assembled by the side of the road that ran along the edge of the timber, the "Young America Band" struck up "Three Cheers for the Red, White, and Blue" and led the throng on a meandering procession through the colorful foliage into the center of the sugar bush, where two wagons had been placed over a mound of earth that marked the site of Pulliam's original "sugar house." Nearby, tables were "bountifully spread" with food prepared by the "good dames" of Sugar Creek. As at so many other public gatherings in the Sugar Creek timber, however, dinner came only after the praying, preaching, and speech-making.[11]

Jim Matheny, featured orator of the day, opened his talk by acknowledging the sense that had brought them all together. "All has changed!" he declared. "Ah, yes! a change indeed, a change glorious beyond all conception." But Matheny had not come to celebrate the changes that as lawyer, civil servant, and politician he had so vigorously struggled to achieve. His task was to revivify the past. Man's struggle for a better future served human progress, he asserted, and to this end man had made the present "an age of mind," an age of rationality. But Young America had so let reason dominate "that everything else in life bends to it, the ties of home, kindred and friends are readily torn asunder." Contrasting with this present age was the generation of the pioneers, for theirs "was not an age of mind," but "an age of heart."

Standing amid the sugar grove, Matheny conjured up the man he proposed as the exemplar of that era of sentiment, old Robert Pulliam himself.

> Could that old man now come from his silent grave, with what a wondering awe would he gaze upon the scene that now melts our vision. Let us call him from his lonely bed, let us arouse him from his dreamless sleep. In imagination I can see him coming—in fancy's ear I hear his solemn tread. Slowly he comes, with uncertain tread, as though seeking for the old familiar pathway; now he stands by my side; now he is gazing upon the forms before him.

In imagination Pulliam came, still hobbling on that peg-leg that had never kept him down; and with the ghost of the pioneer in place on the wagon platform, Matheny assembled the imperfections of the age for his phantom inspection.

Yours was an age of community, Matheny reminded the ghost, but community had now dissolved into the "busy whirl of life"; "then the latch string always hung on the outside of the batten door; now it is not only pulled in, but the panel door is bolted on the inside." The borrowing system had gone, replaced by a tendency to see all relations as commercial, to calculate the profit and loss rather than to think in terms of neighborliness. Moral character, too, was superior in your age, he continued, for people then held to the "quaint and curious idea, that honesty was the best policy." Now, Matheny lamented, with honesty replaced by cunning, we "laugh at such crude and unsophisticated notions as these." In political life, the men of your generation "were so foolishly patriotic that they positively loved their country better than they loved themselves." But see how in these times party or section has become all; "one party proposes a measure, the other for that reason only opposes it, and in their mad fury, they threaten that if that measure does or does not become a law, that they will dissolve the Union!" Most important, he continued, you pioneers had faith in God, "an unswerving trust in His Providence," and people came to the old-time services, conducted in the rude meetinghouse or the shady grove, truly to worship God. Matheny bid his ghostly companion consider the contrast presented by the contemporary church service: "look around upon this congregation; scan well their faces and tell me for what purpose they came. You answer promptly and at once, 'To see and be seen.'" The conjured shade had seen enough.

> With a mournful shake of the head he turns away. The old famil-
> iar faces, where are they? Alas! too many have gone away, and
> gone forever, and strange forms now fill their places; and now,
> with wearied, disappointed look he goes back to his dreamless
> bed. Sleep on, old man, sleep quietly. There are many here who
> still remember thee, and it may be that on some other day, these
> strangers whom you pioneered to this godly land, will gather
> about your humble grave, and erect some monument telling to
> coming generations, where you are sleeping the "dreamless
> sleep."

Matheny's address was fatuous history. Perhaps none knew the limits of his conjuring so well as those who still remembered Robert Pulliam, his neighbors assembled in his sugar grove. Before the local justices, many of whom sat listening, the real Robert Pulliam had stood many times, charged with cantankerousness, dishonesty, and un-neighborly dealings. The real Pulliam had been an avid partisan of Jacksonian Democracy, voting for Democratic candidates in every election in which he participated, a political loyalty he passed on to his sons Martin and Irwin. The real Pulliam had kept his distance from the local Protestant sects, at least until the very last years of his life, when he supposedly "changed his course," rejected his lifelong habits of gambling and drinking, and united with a congregation in Macoupin County—a suspiciously moral gloss to an otherwise inglorious end.[12]

But the circumstances of this first "reunion" required Matheny to take his text from the book of Pulliam's life, and it would not do to encumber the sermon with uncomfortable facts. Matheny lamented about the negative effects of "uplift and improvement," but as one of the architects of change in the Sangamon, he preached not an instrumental but a sentimental jeremiad, not intended to bring the pioneers and their children forward to the mourners' bench, burdened with the sins of success, but only to offer an emotional and psychic retreat from the realities of the present. The real Pulliam, in fact, provided one of the best examples of some the failed promises of "improvement," but Matheny was speaking not to the failed but to the persistent and successful. "You, gray-headed fathers, you have done your work. You can see the land won by your good right arm from its wilderness state, and from a savage foe, pass to the hands of your children, and your children's children, literally, 'a land flowing with milk and honey'—a land fairer and brighter and more glorious than any other land beneath the blue arch of Heaven." For the crowd of owner-operators gathered in Pulliam's sugar grove, Matheny's history provided a sentimental refuge in an uncertain time. In order to accomplish this, Matheny had to distort the past to fit the needs of the present. Pulliam had been rehabilitated at last.

Matheny's notion that "all had changed," so central to the nostalgic sensibility, had a strictly limited meaning in Sugar Creek. The commercial era had begun, and if the gathered throng had listened carefully that October day they might have heard the whistle and rumble of the Chicago and Alton engines along the tracks west of the creek. But through the 1850s, traditional agricultural techniques, tools, and seasonal work rounds persisted, and production levels did not greatly increase; decisions about investment continued to conform to old principles; local governance, local churches, and, most of all, endogamous kinship remained the sustaining elements of the rural community. What had changed most were the structure of class relations, the increasing inequities in the distribution of property, the consequences of advancing commercialism—but these important changes had not rent the fabric of everyday life, nor would they be acknowledged at this gathering of landlords.

Even more than the coming of the railroad, the Civil War constructed a wall that separated present from past; after its ravages, all that had come before seemed set off like the world before the Deluge. Fueled by industrial munitions, fed by iron rails, the war consumed men by the thousands in its dark, satanic engines, and Sangamon County counted a mournful share of over five hundred on its "honor roll" of this first American combat of the industrial era.

But although the weight of the experience of the war emphasized the new age, it also demonstrated important continuities in the social and cultural life of the countryside. When, in the spring of 1861, Lincoln called for seventy-five thousand volunteers to put down the rebellion, the assessor of each Illinois township compiled a list of all men, eighteen to forty-five, ostensibly serving in local militia companies. Nearly a thousand names appeared on the upper Sugar Creek lists, but these companies were useless as fighting units, and it would have been folly to "mobilize" them. Instead, local men of standing and importance in the community, men like Augustus Shutt from The Sources and Philemon Stout's cousin Samuel Shoup, formed local companies into which they recruited young men from their neighborhoods. Though Sugar Creek boys signed into virtually all the Illinois regiments, most joined the three or four infantry and cavalry companies recruited locally.[13]

"There is great excitement on the war question," Moses Wadsworth wrote from Auburn in August 1861, "and new regiments are forming continually. A great many trains laden with soldiers have passed down on this railroad. Two long trains have gone through today and 3 last Sunday. Their destination is Missouri." Forty men from Sugar Creek, most grouped under the leadership of Lieutenant Shutt in Company B of the 10th Illinois Cavalry, were among those that rode the Chicago and Alton south to American Bottom. From Missouri they fought their way into Arkansas, then joined the siege of Vicksburg in 1863 and participated in the fighting along the Mississippi River. During these campaigns at least ten Sugar Creek men were lost in battle or from disease, including several neighborhood boys from Drennan's Prairie: William Drennan III, killed in a guerrilla ambush in Missouri; Erastus Harlan Roberts, mortally wounded at the Battle of Little Rock; and Corporal Robert Lockridge, son of Elijah and Lavinia Cassity Lockridge, killed at Marshfield, Missouri. Lockridge's cousin, Levi Cassity, lost his left arm in a cavalry charge at the Battle of Prairie Grove, in Arkansas.[14]

Other Cassitys served with nearly fifty other young men from the creek who joined local companies merged into the 73d and 114th Illinois infantries. They fought together at the battles of Fort Henry and Fort Donelson, at Shiloh, Memphis, and Vicksburg, then farther south into Mississippi or across Georgia with Sherman. The casualties on these fronts were frightening; nearly half the men of the 114th, and two-thirds of the men of the 73d died of influenza or battle wounds. Seven in ten of the Sangamon County dead perished in these bloody campaigns, including twenty boys from the creek. On the battlefield of Tupelo, Joseph Campbell, son-in-law of John Brownell, suffered wounds that took his life, and Sergeant James C. Dodds, son of the Reverend Gilbert Dodds, was killed leading his men in a battle charge. John T. Drennan, grandson of Billy Drennan, lay wounded for five days at Chickamauga before he received any medical attention, and Alexander Cassity was mangled at the Battle of Stone's River; both returned from the war hopeless cripples. Cassity's brother John died in 1864 during Sherman's siege of Atlanta.

The death of young men, often neighbors, in the same campaigns, branded the war into the community's memory. They had completed the final act in the drama of settlement, John Todd Stuart preached to a reunion of old settlers in 1877. Men and women had emigrated from the South "to subdue the wilderness, to found States, to carry forward the banner of civilization." Their descendants were then called back, "to return, at no very distant day, in arms under the gallant Sherman, to save the Union from disruption." Sugar Creek boys returned to fight and die together, just as their parents and grandparents had come, in groups bound by neighborhood and kinship, in "community companies."[15]

As Stuart's comment implied, for many the war had the effect of renewing the faith of the fathers. For many, the war provided the occasion for demonstrating the mighty power of the Lord. Four young Sugar Creek neighbors, James Pulliam (grandson of Robert), Samuel Lewis (son of Eddin), Benjamin Fletcher (son of Captain Job), and Stephen Bell (related to both Shoups and Gattons)—all twenty-two years old—joined Company B of the 114th Infantry together at a recruiting rally in Chatham during the late summer of 1862. By 1863 they had been thrown into the awful siege of Vicksburg. Then, in June 1864, during fierce fighting at Guntown, Mississippi, they were captured and, along with nearly fifty other Sangamon men, sent to the prisoner of war camp at Andersonville, Georgia, where each day some hundred of the thirty thousand internees died of disease and starvation. By early the next year, twenty-three Sangamon prisoners of war had perished in the squalid camp.[16]

As they told the story, these four young men from the creek survived that experience only as the result of divine intervention. The prisoners' water supply came from a creek polluted with the refuse and offal of the Confederate guards upstream. In August of 1864, sick and delirious, Pulliam, Lewis, Fletcher, and Bell, along with hundreds of other prisoners, witnessed the eruption of a spring of pure water in the center of camp during the darkest days of their confinement. The water that saved their lives, they testified, was "a direct interposition of Providence." The miracle of "Providence Spring" strengthened their sense that God yet walked among them and their people.

Back at home, emaciated but alive, the veterans gave testimony in a local revival of religious enthusiasm that included camp meetings again in the grove along Panther Creek and at the Sugar Creek churches. In October 1865, when the synod of the Cumberland Presbyterians met at the Drennan's Prairie meetinghouse to review "how is it with God and the people of his covenant" in this "valley of churches," they pondered the meaning of this revival. God "has been sorely chastening us for some cause or causes," they agreed; "the sword has been all through the land and sad and desolating has been the result." But now that the affliction had been lifted, they could begin to see the wonder of God's ways.

> Not a small degree of a revival spirit is now seen and enjoyed, and all minds seem to recognize the Hand of God now outstretched to lead us into a new field and renew our strength and cause us to mount up as on wings of Eagles, and run and not be weary, and walk and not faint. As God has saved us undivided in civil right He will much more save us to enjoy all the great rights of religion, and religious liberty, and thereby give and secure to us a power that will fill all our hearts with gladness, and the land with revived and enlarged churches. . . . If we are not greatly mistaken in the signs of the times, God expects us, as the offspring of the *great revival of 1800,* to yet do a great and good work in this fair favored and broad land abounding in all the elements of the great and good, that we should be strong in the Lord and in the power of his might.

The Civil War marked the beginning of a new era in the nation's history, but along Sugar Creek it also confirmed the community of feeling.[17]

After a lapse of several years during the war, the Old Settlers' Society reorganized in 1868 and remained active for the next half-century. Their "reunions," in the tradition of camp meetings, political rallies, and barbeques, drew together as many as several thousand people in a rural grove during the "dog days" of August. From the speakers' stand, decorated with evergreen boughs, wildflowers, and yards of starred-and-striped bunting, preachers prayed, singing school choirs performed traditional anthems and fugues, and old men, and occasionally old women, spoke of pioneer times. Reunions in 1871 at Irwin's (formerly Harlan's) Grove, in the neighborhood of Drennan's Prairie, and in 1874 at Crow's Mill, in its new location on Sugar Creek at the north end of the Sugar Camp neighborhood, brought together many of the original settler families from the creek, including the Brownells, Burtles, Cassitys, Crows, Dodds, Drennans, Fletchers, Knotts, Masons, Nuckolls, Pattons, Pulliams, Stouts, and Wadsworths. At those gatherings the membership elected Job Fletcher, Jr., and

William Burtle, Jr., representatives of their respective neighborhoods on the west and east banks of the creek, to serve as presidents of the society.[18]

The society's officers were dedicated to keeping alive the historical tradition; in 1872 they commissioned John Carrol Power, a Springfield writer, to produce a volume of local history. With the assistance of his wife, Power spent four years circulating through the county, interviewing many old settlers, corresponding with others. Appearing during the nation's centennial celebration in 1876, his *History of the Early Settlers of Sangamon County, Illinois* was an immediate local success, winning the compiler the gratitude and applause of the assembled at the annual reunion in 1877, where he rose to recommend, somewhat mercenarily and immodestly, that each Sangamon household ought to include on its shelf the Bible, Webster's American dictionary, and his *Early Settlers*.

Power's collection of antebellum Sangamon reminiscences and genealogy represented an important contribution to local history but was marred by a significant limitation. "In this history," Power wrote to the society's publications committee in 1872, "all the old settlers will be incidentally mentioned, but for those who take sufficient interest in it to subscribe for one or more copies of the book, a concisely written biographical sketch will be given of themselves and families." At ten dollars a copy, this meant that Power's book tended to glorify the county's most successful families. The bias clearly had commercial benefits to recommend it, but the concentration on the families who had laid down roots was also part of the nostalgic impulse to read history as a legitimation of the successful and the persistent. The limitations of *Early Settlers* echoed those of the Old Settlers' Society itself. "It is well for 'Young America' to look back on those early days," one member wrote in 1880, for "it was the life that made men of character." Then, to drive home the point, he added: "Sangamon county to-day has no better men than the immediate descendants of those who built their cabins in the forest, and by patient endurance wrought out of the wilderness the landmarks for a prosperous commonwealth." But Sangamon and Sugar Creek had been wrought by others besides those who had persisted and succeed, although they were cast aside in the official history.[19]

The past recounted by the Old Settlers' Society served those present and accounted for. This was demonstrated with force in the discussion concerning the role of women in the county's settlement. In his old settler's address in 1879, Judge Milton Hay developed a contrast between pioneer women and their granddaughters. "The patient, untiring devotion of the women of that day to all the duties of their situation was without exception," he argued, and "the failings and shortcomings of many a trifling husband" were more than compensated "by a patient and industrious wife and mother." But the traditional decorum that had served both sexes so well had now been tossed aside, the sexual proprieties of a former era had now disappeared. Men and women no longer "divided off on each side of the church," but now mingled indiscriminately in public space. In contrast with the pioneer mothers, so highly skilled in domestic arts, their female descendants had "discovered their inability to do the housework of the family, and required hired assistance." As another commentator wrote, by contrast with "ladies," "the pioneer girl thinks but little of fine dress, knows less of the fashions, has probably heard of the opera but does not understand its meaning, has been told of the piano but has never seen one, wears a dress 'buttoned up behind,' has on 'leather boots,' and 'drives plow' for father."[20]

John M. Palmer, governor of Illinois in the early seventies and a frequent speaker at these reunions, consistently made this same point. The old women had not had an easy time of it, he acknowledged, and he retold again the tired old anecdote of Illinois as a heaven for men and horses but "hell on women and oxen." These hardships, however, only proved women's mettle. "To the old women let me say: No wives ever so well acted their parts as the wives of the pioneers; and passing away they will not be forgotten." But Palmer evoked this sentimental image of the pioneer mother in order to criticize what he saw as the indulgences of the contemporary woman. He freely broadcast his frustrations: "Young ladies can hardly comprehend that the women of other days could be beautiful, wearing only their own hair," he fretted, "and yet those women were as lovely as those of to-day." He asked the crowd to look around at "the young ladies' toggery of to-day—the flounces, the ruffles, and . . . I don't know what you call them!" Palmer's sputtering was palpable. He displayed equal flabbergast at contemporary domestic standards. "Now a young gentleman and lady just married require a house with six rooms, while we had no trouble, forty or fifty years ago, getting along with but one room, and to have two rooms and a kitchen was considered extravagant."[21]

In this discussion the women themselves, like the forgotten majority of poor farmers and tenants, made no appearances on the platform. But in 1879 several old women were featured in a special program and provided a revealing contrast to the point of view of the men. Collectively, they made what seemed a simple point: wives and mothers had been credited with less than they had actually contributed. A stock

speech of old settler meetings recounted the exploits of men in war, so
this year Elizabeth Lindley Harbour told of witnessing, as a girl, wom-
en's participation in the war for dispossession. She saw one woman kill
six or seven Indians who tried to invade her house, and watched another, who thought her husband had been killed and scalped, grab a
musket and bolt out the cabin door in a mad rage, firing and reloading
until a ranger dragged her back into the stockade. As Charlotte Webb
Jacobs argued when she mounted the speaker's stand, "you must know
that it took stout, hearty and resolute women to settle a wilderness
country like this was, and to buffet with the storms of life."[22]

Much of the women's commentary focused on their work in
henhouse, garden, and dairy, in households as well as in fields; but
they spent most of their allotted time reminiscing about the "forgotten
art" of fabric and clothing manufacture, a symbol of the lost world of
family work. Jacobs reminded her listeners that women of her generation "made everything that we wore." Sisters Mahala Earnest Parkinson and Sarah Earnest King recalled that "we had to raise, pick, spin,
and weave cotton to make clothes for winter and summer. That had to
be carded and spun, and when we would get enough spun and colored
to make a dress apiece, we would put it in the loom and weave it."

Simply to recall, however, was not enough. Doting on old tools and
implements had become a common ritual at the reunions; each year
old farmers passed around and laid hands on wooden plows and drinking gourds, in reverential respect for the relics of a heroic past. To the
1879 reunion women brought remains of their own. "I have some of
my towels and table cloths yet, and one sheet of my last flax spinning,"
reported Jacobs, displaying the evidence of her craft. The Earnest
sisters concluded their talk by carefully unfurling a woman's dress of
the 1820s, "the only one we have saved, it being our mother's." For
many years, the sisters told the crowd, they had "often thought and
talked of exhibiting this dress before the old settler's meetings," but
this was their first opportunity. Women sought to add their artifacts to
history's talismans, as they sought to add their experience to the history
of settlement.

What saved the testimony of these pioneer women from nostalgia
was the simultaneous expression of another sentiment that possessed
equal intensity. "The mental anguish that I suffered, tongue cannot
tell or pen describe," Maria Jaquays Lock, too feeble to speak herself,
told the 1879 reunion through the voice of a friend. Alone at home
with her children in the early 1830s, while her husband was driving a
wagon to St. Louis for supplies, she felt as "a stranger in this vast
wilderness." "There were days and weeks of agony, of fear and sus-
pense, . . . for at that time I had five little children to guard, and the

hoarse cry of the wolf was the only musical instrument Sangamon furnished to lull them to sleep." Elizabeth Harbour, summarizing her pioneer experience, told the assembled: "During the time I had many hardships, I had to weave and spin. I am nearly seventy-six years old, and have a very sick daughter at present; my mind being flustrated [*sic*] I cannot say near as much as I could otherwise. I sincerely hope no other person will ever have to pass through the many hardships which I have experienced." Women's message, then, was not quite as simple as it seemed. Women had done their part and wanted their place in pioneer history, but few would wish on their great-granddaughters the troubles they had seen.

After listening to a fusillade of Governor Palmer's backhanded praise of pioneer women at one reunion, David L. Phillips, editor of the *Journal*, mounted the platform and gave voice to the underlying tension. Palmer's "eulogy of the hard-working women of that day I most heartily endorse," declared Phillips, "because in these days there is a tendency on the part of the people to degrade the working women, to characterize the attendance to domestic duties as domestic servitude." Palmer himself acknowledged the issue at stake the next year. "Who ever knew an old settler to do his wife's milking, or to lend her any help whatever about the house?" No, he cracked, turning male privilege to his own rhetorical advantage, "they might talk now-a-days about 'women's rights,' but it took the old settlers to do justice to the question; for a striking characteristic of the old settler was an indisposition to meddle in the affairs of women, who, in *those* days, were quite secure in all their prerogatives."[23]

"Women's rights"—that was the issue, and both Palmer and Phillips seemed quite sensitive to criticisms of the drudgery imposed on farm women. The topic was still taboo when, in the years preceding the Civil War, feminists Lucy Stone and Jane Grey Swisshelm conducted Illinois lecture tours, and Olive Starr Wait attracted Springfield crowds with a series of talks on "women's rights." But by the 1870s, a discussion of the hard lives of rural women had entered the mainstream of public discourse, farm wives were writing letters to such widely distributed national women's farm magazines as *The Household* complaining of long hours and uncompensated labor, burdensome pregnancies, isolation, and insensitive husbands. The theme of women's drudgery gradually took center stage in discussions of country life and came to dominate commonplace attitudes. Despite the contention that contemporary women were indulged, the lives of most rural wives and daughters continued to be dominated by nearly ceaseless toil. During the second half of the nineteenth century, when great numbers of a farm-raised generation abandoned the countryside for the towns and cities of the Midwest, young women migrated in greater numbers than their brothers. In the voice of a Palmer or a Hay, the praise of pioneer women operated as a cover for criticism of female restlessness with a rural way of life that few older women themselves would have revived if they had had the choice. The past of the Old Settlers' Society definitely served the needs of the present.[24]

Conclusion

Sugar Creek was a settler society, a minor example of the dynamic and fearful expansion of European civilization. As such, its very foundation anticipated change and transformation—from Algonquin to Anglo-American, from subsistence to commerce, from "wilderness" to "civilization." Change, development, "improvement" were aspects of Sugar Creek's history that have continued unabated to our own time. The first generation of successful settlers had little choice but to affirm the course of development that had planted them in Sangamon soil, yet many expressed disquiet when they reflected on the consequences of change. "Civilization will continue to advance," John M. Palmer reminded the settlers of Sugar Creek, assembled in Irwin's Grove; "we can scarce conceive the progress of the next fifty years. But I do not wish to see it. I do not wish to be trampled upon by the rapidly advancing strides of civilization." At another reunion, William Herndon offered his belief that "man, the race of man, . . . has no bounds, his progress no limit. The past is nothing, the present is nothing, the great future will be all." Where would this lead? "He will master everything but the unmasterable, know everything but the unknowable. He will be free and unfettered in all the walks of life," Herndon declared, "or drench the world in blood."[1]

Herndon took an apocalyptic view. More typical, perhaps, was Edgar Lee Masters' lament a half-century later: "But ah the landscape changes! Not merely by the disappearance of a barn or a house or a

234

corncrib here and there, but by the vanishment of orchards, and strips of forest." Driving through the Sangamon countryside one afternoon, he was overcome by the effect. "I had been over this neighborhood a thousand times," he wrote, "but now the little grove by the Houghton house was no longer there, the old road had been fenced in, a new road had been made across the pasture which had belonged to my grandfather. I looked about me and did not know where I was."[2]

If the old settlers could be conjured back, they would share Masters's disorientation. Diversification long ago gave way to concentration. Farmers devote tens of thousands of dollars to highly mechanized farm equipment and plant their crops "fence post to fence post." One of the ironies of modern farming is that in the very midst of agricultural abundance it is frequently difficult to find local fresh fruits and vegetables. The interstate highway has superseded the railroad, and ease of travel has turned much of local society into an anachronism. Auburn village has fallen on hard times, shriveling while suburban shopping malls thrive. The Cumberland Presbyterian meetinghouse, St. Bernard's Catholic chapel, and other country churches have been torn down or boarded up, as the few surviving parishioners drive to worship in town or city, or watch television evangelists at home. Sugar Creek itself, now dammed and backed up nearly to the sugar grove, runs thick with silt and effluents, the timber along its banks reduced in many places to a mere thicket, in others eliminated altogether by decades of clearing. To south county commuters speeding to work in Springfield along Illinois state highway 4, the old Auburn stage road, Sugar Creek appears as little more than a distant strip of woodland bordering hundreds of rolling acres planted in corn and soybeans.

But to Paul Burtle, lifetime farmer of these lands and eighth-generation descendant of the original Catholic settlers William and Sarah Burtle, moving through that timber and over the creek still feels a bit like crossing the border from one country to another. His abiding sense of place, of neighborhood bounds, unites him with the sentiments of a distant age, in spite of an economic and social revolution that have remade the world of the settlers several times over. A certain legacy of the old traditions remains.[3]

There have been other continuities. After the Civil War, in the sacred grove along Panther Creek—no longer called Harlan's but Irwin's Grove—camp-meeting enthusiasm again shattered the silence of the forest sepulcher. Over the next quarter-century the grove provided a site for the reunions of old settlers and the "encampments" of Union veterans. Coal deposits, discovered and developed along the creek in the 1880s, drew mining families, who regularly held picnics and union rallies in the grove. Then, after the turn of the century, when the settlement of Polish mine workers reactivated long-standing anti-Catholic prejudices in the community, members of the Ku Klux Klan met at Irwin's for nighttime meetings and cross-burnings. In the early twentieth century, the descendants of James Irwin developed the grove as an amusement park for Springfield residents, who would catch the interurban trolley connecting the capital to Chatham and Auburn and spend summer evenings dancing to music from the band shell or cooling in the newly constructed swimming pool. During the prohibition years, "Irwin's Park" had a reputation as a place where folks could buy quality Canadian liquor from bootleggers on their way from Chicago to St. Louis. Like many small commercial parks, Irwin's fell on hard times after World War II, and was finally closed and abandoned. The grounds, overgrown by the encroaching forest cover, became a place of refuge for local teenagers, who congregated amid the timber to drink beer and, in more recent years, to smoke marijuana.[4]

The persistence of Irwin's Grove as a site for extraordinary community gatherings for over a century and a half may stand as a symbol of the persistence of the original settler families themselves. In the Drennan's Prairie neighborhood east of the grove, old families continued to hold substantial portions of the arable land and to participate in community institutions. From 1854 to 1913, half of the directors of the "Cherry Grove School," near Irwin's Park, were men from the Dodds, Barnes, Hutton, Irwin, and Mason families. And despite the influx of large numbers of Polish immigrants into the neighborhood to work the mines, at least a third of all the graduates of the school over the same period were descendants of original settlers. In 1914, half the land of Drennan's Prairie remained in their hands.[5]

In fact, descendants continued to play an important part in the whole community, filling, for example, nearly half of the elective offices in the four townships of upper Sugar Creek from 1861 to 1881. In the Auburn of the 1880s, descendants owned and operated a quarter of all the retail establishments, including the largest dry goods, grocery, and drug stores, a saloon, a profitable drainage tile factory, and the community's bank and newspaper. Despite the ongoing development of the countryside, despite the advent of scores of new families to farm newly opened prairie lands, by 1914 descendants with the surnames of original settlers continued to hold nearly a fifth of the one hundred square miles of upper Sugar Creek lands. As late as 1981, descendants of twenty-three of the forty-four persistent families who settled before 1840 continued to live on farms in the four contiguous townships of upper Sugar Creek and to own at least 10 percent of Sugar Creek lands.[6]

In 1817, the year of Robert Pulliam's remove to Sugar Creek, Englishman Elias Pym Fordham lived in Illinois Country. He declared himself a pessimist about the chances of planting a settled society on this frontier. "There are in England comforts, nay, sources of happiness, which will for ages be denied to these half savage countries," he wrote. Among these he counted good roads, good houses, laws well administered, and "the arts of life carried almost to perfection." The most disturbing thing about this country, Fordham noted, was that land was so cheap, even free for the using, that man's labor was too dear to be hired. Once resources began to tighten, offering remedy for this problem, "the roving spirit of the Americans" prevented society from developing as it should. "Servitude in any form is an evil," he admitted, "but the structure of civilized society is raised upon it."[7]

By the second half of the nineteenth century, the Sugar Creek community undoubtedly still lacked many of the refinements that Fordham treasured, yet the settlers had accomplished much. They had transported a traditional social order to a new environment and had progressively transformed the landscape in ways compatible with their own priorities. The "semi-barbarianism" that Fordham and others found amid the egalitarian conditions of the frontier had developed into the "civilization and refinement" of a society divided into classes of owner-operators, tenants, and hired laborers. The development of a community was not contradicted by the regular turnover in the population of the creek. The community, in fact, assured the success of the persistent and the continuity of their culture amid the flux of change. Community did not "break down" with the approach of the modern world; community, in fact, provided a means of making the transition to it. Like the society that bound the households together, cultural sentiments along the creek were essentially traditional and conservative. Family and household remained the essential social building blocks; community continued to be constructed from the relations among kinship, neighborhood, and church. The individual, the celebrated achievement of western American culture, was surely important; but it was the community along Sugar Creek which prevailed.

Notes

ABBREVIATIONS

CCC   Sangamon County Commissioners' Court

EFLS   *Early Federal Land Sales within the Present Boundaries of Sangamon County Illinois* (Springfield: SCGS, 1978)

ER   Sangamon County, County Commissioner's Court, Election Returns, 1821–65 (microfilm, ISA) reels #30/115–124

ES   John Carrol Power, assisted by Mrs. S. A. Power, *History of the Early Settlers of Sangamon County, Illinois: "Centennial Record"* (Springfield: Edwin A. Wilson, 1876)

FRF   Family Reconstitution Forms

HC   Herndon Collection, Henry E. Huntington Library, San Marino, California

HE   Newton Bateman and Paul Selby, eds., *Historical Encyclopedia of Illinois and History of Sangamon County*, 2 vols. (Chicago: Munsell Publishing Company, 1912)

HSC   *History of Sangamon County, Illinois: Together with Sketches of Its Cities, Villages and Townships, Educational, Religious, Civil, Military, and Political History; Portraits of Prominent Persons, and Biographies of Representative Citizens* (Chicago: Inter-State Publishing Company, 1881)

IRAD   Illinois Regional Archive Depository

ISA   Illinois State Archives, Springfield, Illinois

ISHL   Illinois State Historical Library, Springfield, Illinois

IW   "Illinois Women: Manuscript Letters Written by Pioneer Women of Crawford, Pike and Sangamon Counties [for the Illinois Woman's Exposition Board of the World's Columbian Exposition, Chicago, 1893]" (MSS, ISHL)

JISHS   *Journal of the Illinois State Historical Society*

Journal	*Sangamo Journal* (1832–47), *Illinois Daily Journal* (1847–60), Springfield, Illinois
MC30	Manuscript schedules of population census for Sangamon County, 1830, reprinted in *Federal Census, 1830, Sangamon County, Illinois,* comp. Ruth Z. Marko (Springfield: SCGS, n.d.)
MC40	Manuscript schedules of population census for Sangamon County, 1840, reprinted in *Federal Census, 1840, Sangamon County, Illinois,* comp. Ruth Z. Marko (Springfield: SCGS, 1980)
MC50	Manuscript schedules of population census for Sangamon County, 1850, reprinted in *Sangamon County, Illinois, 1850 Census and Mortality Schedule* (Springfield: SCGS, n.d.)
MC60	Manuscript schedules of population census for Sangamon County, 1860, reprinted in *Federal Census 1860 of Sangamon County, Illinois* (Springfield: SCGS, 1982)
PP	Joseph Wallace, *Past and Present of the City of Springfield and Sangamon County,* 2 vols. (Chicago: S. J. Clarke, 1904)
Register	*Illinois State Register* (1839–48), *Daily State Register* (1848–60), Springfield, Illinois
SCGS	Sangamon County Genealogical Society, Springfield, Illinois
SSU	Sangamon State University Archives, Springfield, Illinois
TL	Taxable Lists for Sangamon County, 1832–38 (microfilm, ISA) reel #30/157

INTRODUCTION

1. E. A. Wrigley, *An Introduction to English Historical Demography from the Sixteenth to the Nineteenth Century* (New York: Basic Books, 1966), and *Population and History* (New York: McGraw-Hill, 1969); Louis Henry, "Historical Demography," *Daedalus* (1968) 97:385–396; Peter Laslett and Richard Wall, eds., *Household and Family in Past Time* (Cambridge: Cambridge University Press, 1972). One of the best examples of the application of historical demography is John Demos, *A Little Commonwealth: Family Life in Plymouth Colony* (New York: Oxford University Press, 1970).

2. The inadequacy of demography alone is demonstrated by Philip Greven's *Four Generations: Population, Land, and Family in Colonial Andover, Massachusetts* (Ithaca, N.Y.: Cornell University Press, 1970), a study of "patriarchy" that fails to examine relations between the sexes. I discuss the problem of women's history at greater length in "History from the Inside-Out: Writing the History of Women in Rural America," *American Quarterly* (1981) 33:537–57, and in *Women and Men on the Overland Trail* (New Haven: Yale University Press, 1979). Several of the theoretical works that I find most useful are Joan Kelly-Gadol, "The Social Relations of the Sexes: Methodological Implications of Women's History," *Signs* (1976) 1:809–23; Karen Sacks, *Sisters and Wives: The Past and Future of Sexual Equality* (Westport, Conn: Greenwood Press, 1979); Michele Zimbalist Rosaldo, "The Use and Abuse of Anthropology: Reflections on Feminism and Cross-Cultural Understanding," *Signs* (1980) 5:389–417.

3. The argument for a distinctive mode of production in early America is argued in Michael Merrill, "Cash Is Good to Eat: Self-Sufficiency and Exchange in the Rural Economy of the United States," *Radical History Review* (1977) 4:42–71; Christopher Clark, "The Household Mode of Production: A Comment," ibid. (1978) 18:166–71; and James W. Wessman, "The Household Mode of Production—Another Comment," and Michael Merrill, "So What's Wrong with the 'Household Mode of Production,'" ibid. (1979–80) 22:129–46; James A. Henretta, "Families and Farms: *Mentalité* in Pre-Industrial America," *William and Mary Quarterly* (1978) 35:3–32; and Richard L. Bushman, "Family Security in the Transition from Farm to City, 1750–1850," *Journal of Family*

History (1981) 6:238–43. The counter argument for capitalist agriculture is restated persuasively in Carole Shammas, "How Self-Sufficient Was Early America?" *Journal of Interdisciplinary History* (1982) 13:247–72. Edwin B. Burrows, "The Transition Question in Early American History: A Checklist of Recent Books, Articles, and Dissertations," *Radical History Review* (1978) 18:173–90, suggests bibliography.

4. David J. Russo, *Families and Communities: A New View of American History* (Nashville, Tenn.: American Association for the Study of State and Local History, 1974), 156. I find the single best introduction to the consideration of community in American history to be Thomas Bender, *Community and Social Change in America* (New Brunswick, N.J.: Rutgers University Press, 1978). For community in the trans-Mississippi West, see Robert V. Hine, *Community on the American Frontier: Separate But Not Alone* (Norman: University of Oklahoma Press, 1980). I discuss some of the relevant sociological literature, particularly the work of rural sociologists, in "Open Country Community: Sugar Creek, Illinois, 1820–1850," in Stephen Hahn and Jonathan Prude, eds., *The Countryside in the Age of Capitalist Transformation: Essays in the Social History of Rural America* (Chapel Hill: University of North Carolina Press, 1985), a collection that samples recent work in American rural social history.

5. For the study of landscape and material culture see J. B. Jackson, *The Necessity for Ruins, and Other Topics* (Amherst: University of Massachusetts Press, 1980) and *Landscapes: Selected Writings of J. B. Jackson*, ed. Ervin H. Zabe (Amherst: University of Massachusetts Press, 1970); Donald W. Meinig, ed., *The Interpretation of Ordinary Landscapes* (New York: Oxford University Press, 1979); John F. Hart, *The Look of the Land* (Englewood Cliffs, N.J.: Prentice-Hall, 1975); Hildegard Binder Johnson, *Order upon the Land: The United States Rectangular Land Survey and the Upper Mississippi Country* (New York: Oxford University Press, 1976); Henry Glassie, *Pattern in the Material Folk Culture of the Eastern United States* (Philadelphia: University of Pennsylvania Press, 1968); and John R. Stilgoe, *Common Landscape of America, 1580–1845* (New Haven: Yale University Press, 1982).

6. I find the following local studies most helpful: Conrad M. Arensberg and S. T. Kimball, *Family and Community in Ireland*, 2d ed. (Cambridge, Mass.: Harvard University Press, 1968); W. M. Williams, *The Sociology of an English Village: Gosforth* (London: Routledge and Kegan Paul, 1956), and *A West Country Village: Ashworthy* (London: Routledge and Kegan Paul, 1962); Ronald Blythe, *Akenfield: Portrait of an English Village* (New York: Pantheon Books, 1969); Emmanuel Le Roy Ladurie, *Montaillou: The Promised Land of Error*, trans. Barbara Bray (New York: George Braziller, 1978); Pierre-Jakez Hélias, *The Horse of Pride: Life in a Breton Village* (New Haven: Yale University Press, 1978); Laurence Wylie, *Village in the Vaucluse* (Cambridge, Mass.: Harvard University Press, 1958); Kenneth Lockridge, *A New England Town: The First One Hundred Years* (New York: Norton, 1970); Robert Gross, *The Minute Men and Their World* (New York: Hill and Wang, 1976); Steven Hahn, *The Roots of Southern Populism: Yeoman Farmers and the Transformation of the Georgia Upcountry, 1850–1890* (New York: Oxford University Press, 1983).

7. Flint, quoted in R. Carlyle Buley, *The Old Northwest: Pioneer Period, 1815–1840*, 2 vols. (Bloomington: Indiana University Press, 1951), 2:542; William H. Herndon to Massachusetts Historical Society, March 29, 1842, quoted in David Donald, *Lincoln's Herndon* (New York: Alfred A. Knopf, 1948), 51.

8. George Spears to William H. Herndon, November 3, 1866, and Herndon to J. G. Holland, June 8, 1865, quoted in Donald, *Lincoln's Herndon*, 184, 174; Caroline Kirkland, "Illinois in Springtime," *Atlantic Monthly* (1858) 2:479–80.

1. THE PIONEER OF SUGAR CREEK

1. For the proceedings of the first gathering of the Old Settlers' Society and the deliberations over who settled first, see *Journal*, October 22, 1859, and *Register*, August

26, 1859. In addition to these, this account of the Pulliam family is drawn from the following sources: *ES*, 584; John Reynolds, *Pioneer History of Illinois* (Belleville, Ill.: N. A. Randall, 1852); *HSC*, 431–32, 439, 784; *History of St. Clair County, Illinois* (Philadelphia: Brink, McDonough, 1881), 51; *Combined History of Randolph, Monroe, and Perry Counties, Illinois* (Philadelphia: J. L. McDonough, 1883), 66–67; *History of Madison County, Illinois* (Edwardsville, Ill.: W. R. Brink, 1882), 81–82.

2. Reynolds, *Pioneer History*, 151, 295; H. J. Eckenrode, *List of Revolutionary Soldiers of Virginia* (n.p.: n.p., 1912), 248; *JISHS* (1915) 8:291.

3. James Hall, an Illinois "booster" who was a particularly good listener to common speech, explained the western use of the term *country:* "When we say 'this country,' we do not mean North America, nor the United States, nor any state, but a particular section of country, frequently of indefinite extent. Thus that part of Kentucky which lies south of Green River is called the *Green River Country;* a part of Illinois, lying upon the Sangamon River, is called the *Sangamon Country.* It is applied to a large region, when that region is unsettled, or has not yet been divided into districts or counties, or when those divisions are little known, and the names of them not in familiar use"; James Hall, *Letters from the West* (London: Colburn, 1828), 200–01.

4. On New Design, see Arthur C. Boggess, *The Settlement of Illinois, 1778–1830* (Chicago: Chicago Historical Society, 1908), 92, 95; *Combined History of Randolph, Monroe, and Perry Counties,* 67, 77. In the 1830s John Pulliam's youngest son, Thomas, was a principal organizer of "Pulliam Town" (renamed Fayetteville during the excitement over Lafayette's American tour), built up around the old ferry crossing; see advertisement for town lots, *Journal,* April 15, 1837.

5. *ES,* 586.

6. Ibid.

7. *Journal,* October 22, 1859; *HSC,* 439; *History of Madison County,* 81–82; Joseph Jablow, *Indians of Illinois and Indiana: Illinois, Kickapoo, and Potawatomi Indians* (New York: Garland Publishing, 1974), 343–45.

8. Lewis C. Gray, *History of Agriculture in the Southern United States to 1860,* 2 vols. (Washington, D.C.: Carnegie Institute, 1933), 1:79, 138–39; Boggess, *The Settlement of Illinois,* 130.

9. *HSC,* 432–33; "Pilgrim," in Allen D. Carden, *The Missouri Harmony, or, A Collection of Psalm and Hymn Tunes, and Anthems from Eminent Authors* (1819; reprint, Cincinnati: Phillips and Reynolds, 1844), 147, 119. On Matheny, see Donald, *Lincoln's Herndon,* 119, 172.

2. HUNTERS AND SUGAR-MAKERS

1. Edmund Flagg, *The Far West: or, A Tour beyond the Mountains* (New York: Harper and Brothers, 1838), 67. For the ecology of the Sangamon, see U.S. Department of Agriculture, Soil Conservation Service, in cooperation with the Illinois Agricultural Experiment Station, *Soil Survey of Sangamon County. Soil Report No. 111* (n.p.: n.p., 1980); University of Illinois, Agricultural Experiment Station, *Soil Report No. 4,* (Urbana, Illinois: n.p., 1912); E. M. Poggi, *The Prairie Province of Illinois: A Study of Human Adjustment to the Natural Environment. Illinois Studies in the Social Sciences* 19 (Urbana: University of Illinois Press, 1934); Donna C. Roper, *Archaeological Survey and Settlement Pattern Models in Central Illinois,* Illinois State Museum, *Scientific Papers* 14 (Kent, Ohio: Kent State University Press, 1979); E. Lucy Braun, *Deciduous Forests of Eastern North America* (Philadelphia: The Blakiston Company, 1950); J. E. Weaver, *North American Prairie* (Lincoln, Neb.: Johnson Publishing Company, 1954); Howard W. Odum and Harry Estill Moore, *American Regionalism: A Cultural-Historical Approach to National Integration* (New York: H. Holt and Company, 1938), 52–85.

2. Horace Q. Waggoner, "The Illinois Prairie Purchasing Pattern," (typescript, n.d., SSU).

3. Fredrick W. Hodge, ed., *Handbook of Indians North of Mexico*, 2 vols. (Washington, D.C.: Bureau of American Ethnology, 1907–10), 2:220; Elbert L. Little, *The Audubon Society Field Guide to North American Trees, Eastern Region* (New York: Alfred A. Knopf, 1980), 348–49; Alexander F. Chamberlain, "Algonkian Words in English," *Journal of American Folk-Lore* (1902) 15:241–69. Edgar Lee Masters, *The Sangamon* (New York: Farrar & Rinehart, 1942), is a goldmine of material on the local flora, fauna, and folks of the region.

4. Roper, *Archaeological Survey*, 68–74.

5. Howard D. Winters, "The Riverton Culture: A Second Millennium Occupation in the Central Wabash Valley," in Illinois State Museum, *Report of Investigations* 13 (Springfield: n.p., 1969); Roper, *Archaeological Survey*, 127–43; Neal Salisbury, "American Indians and American History," (unpublished essay); and Bruce E. Trigger, ed., *Handbook of North American Indians, Volume 15: Northeast* (Washington, D.C.: Smithsonian Institution, 1978).

6. Virgil J. Vogel, *Indian Place Names in Illinois, Pamphlet Series No. 4, Illinois State Historical Society* (Springfield: ISHL, 1963), 37–39; Clarence Alvord, *The Illinois Country, 1673–1818* (1918; reprint, Chicago: Loyola University Press, 1965); Emily Jane Blassingham, "The Illinois Indians, 1634–1800: A Study in Depopulation," *Ethnohistory* (1956) 3:193–224; Jablow, *Indians of Illinois and Indiana;* Hiram W. Beckwith, *The Illinois and Indiana Indians* (Chicago: Fergus Printing Company, 1884); Mary E. Good, "Guebert Site: An 18th Century Historic Kaskaskia Indian Village in Randolph County, Illinois," *Memoirs of the Central States Archaeological Societies* 2 (1972). The single best source on Kickapoo history is Arrell Morgan Gibson, *The Kickapoos: Lords of the Middle Border* (Norman: University of Oklahoma Press, 1963), a rich work to which my debt is obvious.

7. Beckwith, *The Illinois and Indiana Indians*, 117, 119, 120, 124–25; Gibson, *The Kickapoo*, 6–16, 30, 32, 39, 98f.; Jablow, *Indians of Illinois*, 58, 97, 135, 188–89, 205, 268–69; Wayne C. Temple, *Indian Villages of the Illinois Country: Historic Tribes* (Springfield: Illinois State Museum, 1958) 158–60, 164–65.

8. Hodge, ed., *Handbook*, 1:684; Trigger, ed., *Handbook*, 656; Gibson, *The Kickapoo*, 98.

9. Blassingham, "The Illinois Indians," 195–96; Harriette Simpson Arnow, *Seedtime on the Cumberland* (New York: The MacMillian Company, 1960), 122.

10. *ES*, 32–33, 424; *HSC*, 196–97; John Reynolds, *My Own Times, Embracing Also the History of My Life* (1855; reprint, Chicago: Chicago Historical Society, 1879), 54.

11. *ES*, 159, 261.

12. Helen Nearing and Scott Nearing, *The Maple Sugar Book* (New York: Schocken Books, 1970), 22–39; Henry W. Henshaw, "The Indian Origins of Maple Sugar," *American Anthropologist* (1890) 3:341–52; Alexander F. Chamberlain, "The Maple amongst the Algonkian Tribes," ibid. (1891) 4:39–43, and "Maple Sugar and the Indians," ibid., 381–83; Donald Culross Peattie, *A Natural History of Trees of Eastern and Central North America* (Boston: Houghton Mifflin, 1950), 455–58; Trigger, ed., *Handbook*, 139, 153, 226, 298, 747, 764–65, 781.

13. Jean Bernard Bossu, *Travels through that Part of North America Formerly Called Louisiana*, 2 vols. (London: T. Davis, 1771), 1:188; Joseph Francois Lafitau, *Moeurs des sauvages Ameriquains*, 2 vols. (Paris: Saugrains, 1724), 2:155; C. T. Alvord, "The Manufacture of Maple Sugar," Commissioner of Agriculture, *Report, 1862* (Washington, D.C.: Government Printing Office, 1863), 394–405; R. L. Allen, *The American Farm Book* (New York: Saxton, 1849), 221; ISHL, *Collections* (1934) 23:6, 309.

14. Braun, *Deciduous Forests*, 188–90; Nearing and Nearing, *The Sugar Maple Book*, 69–90.

15. "Food Products of the North American Indians," Commissioner of Agriculture, *Report, 1870* (Washington, D.C.: Government Printing Office, 1871), 412.

16. Grant Foreman, *The Last Trek of the Indians* (Chicago: University of Chicago Press, 1946), 92, 105; James Smith, *An Account of Remarkable Occurrences during Captivity with the Indians, 1755–59* (Philadelphia: Grigg, 1831); "Narrative of the Capture of William Biggs by the Kickapoo Indians in 1788," in ISHL, *Transactions* (1902), 7:202–15.

17. T. G. Onstot, *Pioneers of Menard and Mason Counties* (Forest City, Ill.: The Author, 1902), 234; *HSC,* 441.

18. John J. Audubon, *Delineations of American Scenery and Character,* ed. F. H. Herrick (New York: G. A. Baker and Company, 1926), 314, 316; Buley, *Old Northwest,* 1:157, 222, 224; Richard G. Lillard, *The Great Forest* (New York: Alfred A. Knopf, 1948), 91–92; Gray, *History of Agriculture in the Southern United States,* 1:5; Nearing and Nearing, *The Maple Sugar Book,* 40–66.

3. DEFENDERS OF THE MANITOU

1. Maps reprinted in Sara Jones Tucker, ed., *Indian Villages of the Illinois Country: Part One, Atlas* (Springfield: Illinois State Museum, 1942), plates 40 and 46; James H. Adams, *Illinois Place Names* (Springfield: Illinois State Historical Society, 1968).

2. Marquette, quoted in Reuben Gold Thwaites, ed., *The Jesuit Relations and Allied Documents: Travel and Explorations of the Jesuit Missionaries in New France, 1610–1791,* 73 vols. (Cleveland: Burrows Brothers, 1896–1901), 59:103.

3. Beckwith, *Indians of Indiana and Illinois,* 168; Betty Ann Dillingham, "The Oklahoma Kickapoo" (Ph.D. diss., University of Michigan, 1963), 92–95.

4. Vogel, *Indian Place Names in Illinois,* 58; "Food Products of the North American Indians"; Thomas Forsyth, "An Account of the Manners and Customs of the Sauk and Fox Nations of Indians' Traditions," in Emma Helen Blair, ed., *The Indian Tribes of the Upper Mississippi Valley and Region of the Great Lakes,* 2 vols. (Cleveland: Arthur H. Clark, 1912), 2:228.

5. Forsyth, "Account," 2:212, 216; Major Morrell Marsten to Jedidiah Morse, November 1820, reprinted in Blair, ed., *Indian Tribes,* 2:164–65; Richard K. Pope, "The Withdrawal of the Kickapoo," *The American Indian* (1958–59) 8:17; Dillingham, "The Oklahoma Kickapoo," 134–35; Felipe A. Latorre and Dolores L. Latorre, *The Mexican Kickapoo Indians* (Austin: University of Texas Press, 1976), 169f., 182; Robert E. Ritzenthaler and Fredrick A. Peterson, "The Mexican Kickapoo Indians," *Milwaukee Public Museum Publications in Anthropology* (1956) 2:59; A. Irving Hallowell, "Some Psychological Characteristics of the Northeastern Indians," in *Man in Northeastern North America,* ed. Frederick Johnson (Andover, Mass.: Robert S. Peabody Foundation, 1946), 192–225.

6. Trigger, ed., *Handbook,* 611–13; Latorre and Latorre, *The Mexican Kickapoo,* 143–51.

7. Clan leader, quoted in Dillingham, "The Oklahoma Kickapoo," 257–58; Ritzenthaler and Peterson, "The Mexican Kickapoo," 46; Latorre and Latorre, *The Mexican Kickapoo,* 354.

8. Allouez, quoted in Thwaites, ed., *Jesuit Relations,* 54:233–35; Trigger, ed., *Handbook,* 662; Ritzenthaler and Peterson, "The Mexican Kickapoo," 14–15; George R. Nielsen, *The Kickapoo People* (Phoenix, Ariz.: Indian Tribal Series, 1975), 10; James Silverberg, "The Kickapoo Indians: First One Hundred Years of White Contact in Wisconsin," *Wisconsin Archaeologist* (1957) 38:61–181, esp. 150–51; Paul Chrisler Phillips, *The Fur Trade,* 2 vols. (Norman: University of Oklahoma Press, 1961), 1:156.

9. Reynolds, *Pioneer History,* 8; Gibson, *The Kickapoo,* 17–28.

10. Ritzenthaler and Peterson, "The Mexican Kickapoo," 11–12; Trigger, ed., *Handbook,* 599; matron, quoted in Latorre and Latorre, *The Mexican Kickapoo,* 212; Dillingham, "The Oklahoma Kickapoo," 269–74.

11. Trigger, ed., *Handbook*. 662; Phillips, *The Fur Trade*, 1:501–09, 2:174–75, 362; Alvord, *The Illinois Country*, 211, 214, 401, 453; Zimi A. Enos, "The Old Indian Trail, Sangamon County, Illinois," *JISHS* (1911) 4:218–22; Archer Butler Hulbert, *Historic Highways of America*, 16 vols. (Cleveland: Arthur H. Clark Company, 1902–05), vol. 11: *Pioneer Roads*, 17, 21, and vol. 2: *Indian Thoroughfares*, passim; Solon Justus Buck, *Illinois in 1818* (Springfield: Illinois Centennial Commission, 1917), 22.

12. Hulbert, *Pioneer Roads*, 18.

4. A WAR OF EXTIRPATION

1. George Rogers Clark to George Mason, November 19, 1779, in ISHL, *Collections* (1912) 8:140–47.

2. Jablow, *Indians of Illinois*, 195; British secretary of state, quoted in Phillips, *The Fur Trade*, 1:601–02; Harrison, quoted in R. David Edmunds, *Tecumseh and the Quest for Indian Leadership* (Boston: Little, Brown and Company, 1984), 64.

3. For this quote, and this interpretation, see Reginald Horsman, "American Indian Policy in the Old Northwest, 1783–1812," *William and Mary Quarterly* (1961) 18:35–53.

4. John Woods, *Two Years Residence in the Settlement on the English Prairie, in the Illinois Country* (London: n.p., 1822), 111–12.

5. Timothy Dwight, *Travels in New England and New York, ed. Barbara Miller Solomon, 4 vols. (1821–22; reprint, Cambridge, Mass.: Harvard University Press, 1969), 2:321–22;* other quotes from Sir William Craigie and James H. Hulbert, eds., *A Dictionary of American English on Historical Principles*, 4 vols. (Chicago: University of Chicago Press, 1938–44); also see entry in *The Oxford English Dictionary*, 12 vols. (Glasgow: Oxford University Press, 1933).

6. Thomas Forsyth, quoting the Kickapoo, "Account," 2:136; Reynolds, *Pioneer History*, 117–20, 123; *Combined History of Randolph, Monroe, and Perry Counties*, 79; Beckwith, *Illinois and Indiana Indians*, 126, 133; Gibson, *The Kickapoo*, 39,41–48; Edmunds, *Tecumseh*, 30. James Hall, *Sketches of History, Life and Manners in the West*, 2 vols. (Cincinnati: Hubbard & Edmands, 1834), immortalized Moredock in "The Indian Hater," and Herman Melville satirized him in the famous chapter, "The Metaphysics of Indian Hating," in *The Confidence Man* (1857; reprint, New York: Signet, 1964).

7. Little Doe, quoted in Gibson, *The Kickapoo*, 45–47; Reynolds, *Pioneer History*, 153–54; Jablow, *Indians of Illinois*, 321; Forsyth, "Account," 2:136. For the official accounts of the 1791 raids, see *American State Papers. Indian Affairs*, 2 vols. (Washington, D.C.: Gales and Seaton, 1832–34), 1:129–35.

8. "Narrative of the Capture of William Biggs by the Kickapoo Indians in 1788," 7:209–21.

9. *United States Statutes At Large,* 17 vols. (Boston: Little, Brown and Company, 1845–73), 7:49–54, 165.

10. William Henry Harrison, *Governor's Messages and Letters*, ed. Logan Esarey, 2 vols. (Indianapolis: Indiana Historical Commission, 1922), 1:322–23; Gibson, *The Kickapoo*, 54; John Woods, *Two Year's Residence*, 106; Alvord, *The Illinois Country*, 414–15; Buck, *Illinois in 1818*, 47; Trigger, ed., *Handbook*, 599, 666, 740–41.

11. Powatomo, quoted in Gibson, *The Kickapoo*, 95–96.

12. Jablow, *Indians of Illinois*, 345–46; Gibson, *The Kickapoo*, 55–59; Harrison, *Messages*, 1:176–77.

13. Harrison, *Messages*, 1:484; Edwards quoted in Jablow, *Indians of Illinois*, 355–56, 381.

14. Harrison, *Messages*, 1:349, 417, 2:82–83. On Tecumseh and his circle, see R. David Edmunds, *The Shawnee Prophet* (Lincoln: University of Nebraska Press, 1983), and Edmunds, *Tecumseh*.

15. Reynolds, *My Own Times,* 79; Harrison, *Messages,* 2:41; Temple, *Indian Villages,* 165; Boggess, *The Settlement of Illinois,* 106–08; Gibson, *The Kickapoo,* 62–69.

16. Reynolds, *My Own Times,* 87–89; Ninian W. Edwards, *History of Illinois, from 1778 to 1833, and Life and Times of Ninian Edwards* (Springfield: Illinois State Journal, 1870), 67–72, 345; Gibson, *The Kickapoo,* 69–73.

17. Jablow, *Indians of Illinois,* 380, 384; Gibson, *The Kickapoo,* 71–74; *History of Madison County,* 81–82; Theodore C. Pease, *The Frontier State, 1818–1848* (Springfield: Illinois Centennial Commission, 1918), 160n.

18. *History of St. Clair County,* 126.

19. Robert L. Fisher, "The Treaties of Portage des Sioux," *Mississippi Valley Historical Review* (1933) 19:495–508; Temple, *Indian Villages,* 167–68; Gibson, *The Kickapoo,* 75–90.

20. *HSC,* 173, 191, 194, 455, 514, 873; Enos, "Old Indian Trail," 219–20; *ES,* 92, 671.

21. Gibson, *The Kickapoo,* 78–90, quote on 85; Temple, *Indian Villages,* 171; William Riley McLaren, "Reminiscences of Pioneer Life in Illinois" (typescript, 1916, ISHL), 10; Hall, *Sketches of History,* 2:74, 78.

22. *ES,* 312. On the Black Hawk War, see Anthony F. C. Wallace's essay in Ellen M. Whitney, ed., *The Black Hawk War* (Springfield: ISHL, 1970).

23. Cox, quoted in ISHL, *Collections* (1903) 1:218–19.

5. LAND-LOOKER

1. Abraham Lincoln, "Autobiographic Sketch" [1860], in Philip Van Doren Stern, ed., *The Life and Writings of Abraham Lincoln* (New York: The Modern Library, 1940), 604; Buley, *Old Northwest,* 1:115–23. For a general discussion of surveying in this period, see Daniel H. Calhoun, *The American Civil Engineer, 1792–1843* (Cambridge: MIT Press, 1960).

2. Surveyor-general Edwin Tiffin, quoted in Malcolm Rohrbough, *The Land Office Business: The Settlement and Administration of American Public Lands, 1789–1837* (New York: Oxford University Press, 1968), 101; C. S. Woodward, "The Public Domain, Its Surveys and Surveyors," *Michigan Pioneer and Historical Collections* (1896) 27:306–23.

3. Gibson, *The Kickapoo,* 80, 155; Rohrbough, *The Land Office Business,* 83; Stewart, *Public Land Surveys,* 130; Hervey Parke, "Reminiscence," *Michigan Pioneer and Historical Collections* (1879–80) 3:581, 589.

4. Rohrbough, *The Land Office Business,* 96, 187–90; *American State Papers. Public Lands,* 8 vols. (Washington, D.C.: Gales and Seaton, 1832–61), 3:618–20, 4:19–25; Buley, *Old Northwest,* 1:115–23; Lowell O. Steward, *Public Land Surveys: History, Instructions, Methods* (Ames, Iowa: Collegiate Press Inc., 1935), 49–50.

5. Norman J. W. Thrower, "Cadastral Survey and County Atlases of the United States," *The Cartographic Journal,* June 1972, 45; Hart, *The Look of the Land;* Johnson, *Order upon the Land;* J. B. Jackson, "The Order of a Landscape: Reason and Religion in Newtonian America," in Meinig, ed., *The Interpretation of Ordinary Landscapes.*

6. Stilgoe, *Common Landscape of America,* 99–107, esp. 104.

7. "Instructions for Deputy Surveyors by E. Tiffin," reprinted in Stewart, *Public Land Surveys,* 143–49; [Angus Lewis Langham], "Field Notes, Illinois Survey," 114:48, 60, 79, 210, 222, 270, and "Township Plats," 17:13–15, 38–40 (MSS, ISA); Stilgoe, *Common Landscape of America,* 140–45; Lillard, *The Great Forest,* 67–68; Waggoner, "The Illinois Prairie Purchasing Pattern."

8. Langham marked the location of forty-three squatters' claims with "AP" on his map, which in land-office jargon meant "applied for," indicating that these areas were preempted by settlers on the spot: [Langham], "Township Plats," 17:13–15, 38–40; notation explained in Rohrbough, *The Land Office Business,* 76. The 1820 federal census of Illinois is not precise enough in its place designations to be strictly comparable with the enumerations for successive years; but locating the names of known Sugar Creek resi-

dents of 1820 and counting the number of households between the first and last confirmed residents, suggests that fifty-two farms had been established along the upper
creek by 1820, a count reasonably close to Langham's forty-three of 1821. See the
manuscript schedules in "Federal Census, 1820: Illinois" (microfilm, National Archives
and Record Service), indexed by surname in Lowell M. Volkel and James V. Gill, comps.,
1820 Federal Census of Illinois (Thomson, Ill.: Heritage House, 1966). For the method of
determining Sugar Creek population for later censuses, see chap. 6, note 3.

Sugar Creek is composed of two principal sections: the upper creek, from its source to
its junction with Lick Creek, and the lower creek, from that point to its mouth on the
Sangamon. In the place-names of nineteenth-century Sangamon County, "Sugar Creek"
generally referred to the 100-square-mile upper section. The timber of the lower creek
formed the southern line of the prairie that included Springfield, as well as several
smaller settlements with names of their own. Because of their proximity to Springfield,
urban growth decisively affected these communities, and they have a history distinctively
different from the more isolated community of upper Sugar Creek. The landscape of the
lower creek has been dramatically reshaped by urban and suburban sprawl, interstate
highway construction, and the development of Springfield's water supply that, in the
1930s, submerged several neighborhoods beneath "Lake Springfield," created by damn-
ing the creek near its mouth on the Sangamon. The upper reach of Sugar Creek,
however, retains many of the features of its early-nineteenth-century landscape.

9. Parke, "Reminiscence," 588.

6. AMERICAN TARTARS

1. *ES*, 225; Buck, *Illinois in 1818*, 82–84; Col. Daniel M. Parkinson, "Pioneer Life in
Wisconsin," *Wisconsin Historical Collections* (1856) 2:327 [including a section on his years
in Sangamon County in the early 1820s]; Timothy Flint, *The History and Geography of the
Mississippi Valley*, 2 vols., 2d ed. (Cincinnati: E. H. Flint and L. R. Lincoln, 1833), 1:321;
"Pioneer Letters of Gersham Flagg," ISHS, *Transactions* (1910) 15:143–49.

2. Ferdinand Ernst, "Travels in Illinois in 1819," ISHS, *Transactions* (1903) 8:159,
160.

3. Henry Rowe Schoolcraft, *Travels in the Central Portions of the Mississippi Valley* (New
York: n.p., 1825), 301; *Niles Register* (1825) 29:208, cited in Boggess, *Settlement of Illinois*,
188; "Federal Census, 1820: Illinois;" *MC30-40*. Knowledge of the precise location of
many family farms (from data provided by *EFLS*, TL, probate records, and county plat
maps for 1858 and 1874) makes it possible to infer the route of the census marshal and
thus map the approximate locations of most of the residents enumerated on *MC30-60*.
(For problems with the 1820 census, and the estimates for that year, see chap. 5, note 8,
above.) This method produced the boundaries, and thus a household and population
count, for the community in each census year:

	Households	Population	Growth Rate %
1820	50 (est.)	400 (est.)	—
1830	113	894	123.5 (est.)
1840	134	991	10.9
1850	208	1319	33.1
1860	352	2134	61.8

For a discussion of this method of community reconstitution see William A. Bowen, *The
Willamette Valley: Migration and Settlement on the Oregon Frontier* (Seattle: University of
Washington Press, 1978), 97–103, and, for another example of its application, Anthony
F. C. Wallace, *Rockdale: The Growth of an American Village in the Early Industrial Revolution*
(New York: Alfred A. Knopf, 1978), 35.

4. Data on settlers' places of birth and states of origin are taken from FRF, on which I

accumulated background, genealogical, and vital statistical data on 476 women and 452 men from persistent Sugar Creek families born between 1760 and 1859 (for a definition of *persistence,* see note 14 below), using data from *MC30-60* as well as the genealogical materials in nineteenth- and early-twentieth century local histories: *ES; HSC; HE; PP;* John G. Henderson, *Early History of the "Sangamon Country"* (Davenport: Day, Egbert, & Fidlar, 1873); *Portrait and Biographical Album of Sangamon County* (Chicago: Chapman Brothers, 1891); various publications of SCGS; and miscellaneous genealogical materials in ISHL.

5. Lucy Maynard to Betsy Lincoln, February 29, 1836, and to Able Piper, December 3, 1839 (MSS, ISHL).

6. Sarah Aiken to Julia Keese, September 27, 1835 (MSS, ISHL); William Oliver, *Eight Months in Illinois* (1843; reprint, Chicago: W. M. Hill, 1924), 68. For the British origins of this speech, see entries in *The Oxford English Dictionary.* For comparison against the backgrounds of migrants for the whole state, see Buck, *Illinois in 1818,* 93–96.

7. *ES,* 76, 747; *Autobiography of Peter Cartwright* (1861; reprint, Nashville, Tenn.: Abingdon Press, n.d.), 165–66; *HSC,* 249; Boggess, *Settlement of Illinois,* 121–23; Reynolds, *My Own Times,* 153–55; Pease, *The Frontier State,* 70–90. Early nineteenth-century Americans always referred to internal American migrants as *emigrants,* thus curiously emphasizing the process of *leaving* the old home rather than *coming* to the new one. Foreign settlers, by contrast, were always *immigrants.* I have retained this usage here.

8. Simon A. O'Ferrall, *A Ramble of Six Thousand Miles through the United States of America* (London: E. Wilson, 1832), 166–67; Woods, *Two Year's Residence,* 175.

9. Pease, *The Frontier State,* 49; Moses Wadsworth, "The Sugar Creek Country in 1840 " (typescript, 1880, ISHL); *ES,* 166, 409; *MC30,* 4, 7; *MC40,* 37, 38; *MC50,* 16. For a similar view of the slavery perspectives of Southern emigrants to central Illinois, and the old Northwest generally, see Don Harrison Doyle, *The Social Order of a Frontier Community: Jacksonville, Illinois, 1825–1870* (Urbana: University of Illinois Press, 1978) 51; and Eugene H. Berwanger, *The Frontier against Slavery: Western Anti-Negro Prejudice and the Slavery Extension Controversy* (Urbana: University of Illinois Press, 1967).

10. Richard Beeman, *The Evolution of the Southern Backcountry: A Case Study of Lunenberg County, Virginia, 1746–1832* (Philadelphia: University of Pennsylvania Press, 1984), 68 and passim; Gray, *History of Agriculture in the Southern United States,* 1:120–26; Carl Bridenbaugh, "The Back Settlements," in *Myths and Realities: Societies of the Colonial South* (Baton Rouge: Louisiana State University Press, 1952), 119–96; Malcolm J. Rohrbaugh, *The Trans-Appalachian Frontier: People, Societies, and Institutions, 1775–1850* (New York: Oxford University Press, 1978); and Reginald Horsman, *The Frontier in the Formative Years: 1783–1815* (New York: Holt, Rinehart and Winston, 1970).

11. George Flower, *History of the English Settlement in Edwards County, Illinois* (Chicago: Chicago Historical Society, 1882), 29; Peck, quoted in Roy M. Robbins, *Our Landed Heritage: The Public Domain, 1776–1936* (1942; reprint, Lincoln: University of Nebraska Press, 1962), 28–29. For a discussion of frontier migration in American history, see Rohrbaugh, *Trans-Appalachian Frontier,* 157–217; Arthur H. Cole, "Cyclical and Sectional Variations in the Sale of Public Lands, 1816–1860," in Vernon Carstensen, ed., *The Public Lands* (Madison: Wisconsin University Press, 1962); Douglass C. North, "International Capital Flows and the Development of the American West," *Journal of Economic History* 16 (1956); George G. S. Murphy and Arnold Zellner, "Sequential Growth, the Labor-Safety-Valve Doctrine, and the Development of American Unionism," in Richard Hofstadter and Seymour Martin Lipset, eds., *Turner and the Sociology of the Frontier* (New York: Basic Books, 1968), 201–24; Thomas Perkins Abernathy, *From Frontier to Plantation in Tennessee: A Study in Frontier Democracy* (Chapel Hill: University of North Carolina Press, 1932).

12. Thomas Perkins Abernathy, "Kentucky," in *Three Virginia Frontiers* (Baton Rouge: Louisiana State University Press, 1940), 63–96; Gray, *History of Agriculture in the Southern*

United States, 2:861–63; Rohrbaugh, *The Trans-Appalachian Frontier*, 32, 44; Horsman, *The Frontier in the Formative Years*, 53.

13. Woods, *Two Year's Residence*, 166, 175; Mrs. K. B. Vancil, "Jonathan Vancil (John Wensel) and Some of His Descendants," in Daughters of the American Revolution, Illinois Chapter, Genealogical Collections (typescript, n.d., ISHL). Settlers' previous moves from FRF.

14. *Persistence* is here defined as the appearance of a head of household in the Sugar Creek area on two sequential federal census enumerations; persistence rates measure the proportion of the population continuing in the community ten years after enumeration. Sugar Creek crude persistence rates for each decade were 30.1 percent (1820–30), 30.5 percent (1830–40), 21.5 percent (1840–50), 22.2 percent (1850–60); Federal Census, 1820, *MC30-60*. The rigorous analysis of persistence in Hal S. Barron, *Those Who Stayed Behind: Rural Society in Nineteenth-Century New England* (Cambridge, Eng.: Cambridge University Press, 1984), in which he corrects the crude rates for estimated mortality, suggests that, so corrected, the Sugar Creek rates might be some five to ten percentage points higher. The following studies of western regions suggest the typicality of these rates of persistence in Sugar Creek: Mildred Thorne, "Population Study of an Iowa County in 1850," *Iowa Journal of History* (1959) 57:305–30; Peter Coleman, "Restless Grant County: Americans on the Move," in *The Old Northwest*, ed. Harry Scheiber (Lincoln: University of Nebraska Press, 1969); Doyle, *Social Order of a Frontier Community*, 96, 261, 262, 264; Beeman, *The Evolution of the Southern Backcountry*, 29, 67, 69; Merle Curti, *The Making of an American Community: A Case Study of Democracy in a Frontier County* (Stanford: Stanford University Press, 1959), 65–77; James C. Malin, "The Turnover of Farm Population in Kansas," *Kansas Historical Quarterly* (1935) 4:339–72. For New England comparisons, see: Robert Doherty, *Society and Power: Five New England Towns, 1800–1860* (Amherst: University of Massachusetts Press, 1977), 31; Barron, *Those Who Stayed Behind*, chap. 5; Jonathan Prude, *The Coming of Industrial Order: Town and Factory Life in Rural Massachusetts, 1810–1860* (Cambridge, Eng.: Cambridge University Press, 1983), 22, 55, 191.

15. George Flower, *The History of the English Settlement*, 67; Frederick Jackson Turner, *The Significance of the Frontier in American History* (New York: Frederick Ungar Publishing Co., 1963), 57,30.

16. William Strickland, *Observations on the Agriculture of the United States* (London: W. Bulmer, 1801), 71; Dwight, *Travels in New England and New York*, 2:321–22.

17. William Byrd, quoted in Beeman, *The Evolution of the Southern Backcountry*, 22; Edmund Burke, "Speech on Conciliation with America," [1774] in *The Works of the Right Honourable Edmund Burke*, 8 vols. (London: Bohm's British Classics, 1854), 1:472–73; Timothy Flint, *Recollections of the Last Ten Years* (Boston: Cummings, 1826), 76, 204.

18. William H. MacNeill, *The Great Frontier: Freedom and Hierarchy in Modern Times* (Princeton, N.J.: Princeton University Press, 1983), 9. For the uses of *Vandal* and *Tartar*, see Eric Partridge, *A Dictionary of Slang and Unconventional English* (New York: The Macmillan Company, 1970), as well as entries in *The Oxford English Dictionary*.

19. On the agricultural basis of the Asian migrants, for example, see Otto J. Maenchen-Helfen, *The World of the Huns: Studies in Their History and Culture* (Berkeley: University of California Press, 1973), 174–78.

20. Hall, *Sketches of History*, 2:66–67. Doyle, *The Social Order of a Frontier Community*, 12, similarly argues that, while a majority merely passed through the town, "others remained part of a stable core with deep roots in the community."

7. CUSTOMS OF ASSOCIATION

1. For background on early federal land policy, see Paul Wallace Gates, *Landlords and Tenants on the Prairie Frontier* (Ithaca, N.Y.: Cornell University Press, 1973) and Robbins, *Our Landed Heritage*.

2. Quotes from Robbins, *Our Landed Heritage*, 20, 25.

3. Buck, *Illinois in 1818*, 47–48ff.; Gates, *Landlords and Tenants*, 144.

4. *MC30; EFLS;* TL; *1835 Tax List, Sangamon County Illinois*, comps. Marilyn Wright Thomas and Hazelmae Taylor Temple (Springfield: n.p., n.d.); Gates, *Landlords and Tenants*, 112; Pease, *Frontier State*, 182. For farm-making costs, see Clarence Danhof, *Change in Agriculture: The Northern United States, 1820–1870* (Cambridge, Mass.: Harvard University Press, 1969), 115. In 1830, among the farming population of the creek, there were 55 owner-operators, and 46 squatters; 12 other heads of household showed no real property ownership, but pursued other rural occupations. For these proportions over time, see chap. 18, note 12.

5. *ES*, 183, 564; *HSC*, 432, 784. Pulliam's son Martin remembered his father moving the family into a nearby cabin built and then abandoned by "old man Shellhouse," but since the Shellhouse family did not move to Sugar Creek until 1830 he must have been mistaken; in 1820 Robert built a second, more substantial cabin, later occupied by the Shellhouse family. *Journal*, October 22, 1859; *ES*, 645.

6. Enos, May 26, 1826, quoted in Paul Angle, *"Here I Have Lived": A History of Lincoln's Springfield, 1821–1865* (New Brunswick, N.J.: Rutgers University Press, 1935), 9n.; Wisconsin quote in Stephen Thernstrom, *A History of the American People*, 2 vols. (San Diego: Harcourt, Brace, Jovanovich, 1984), 1:263; Reynolds, *My Own Times*, 156.

7. For each persistent head of household, I used local histories and genealogies to reconstruct emigrant parties. In addition, for each head of household appearing on the Sugar Creek enumerations in *MC30-60*, I checked the entire county enumeration for similar surnames, defining families with "kin connection" as those sharing surnames with at least two other county households. Of the 113 heads of household on the 1830 enumeration, 50 (44.3 percent) had such kin connection; but of the 40 heads of household on that census who persisted through 1840, fully 33 (82.5 percent) had kin connection. These proportions held steady over the entire period under study: of the 190 heads of household who persisted through at least two federal enumerations, 87.9 percent had kin connection within the county, but of the 617 heads who appeared only once only 31.0 percent did.

Doyle, *The Social Order of a Frontier Community*, 267, found that 28 percent of the "nondependent" population had related households in Morgan County, Illinois, in 1850, 35 percent in 1860. Hahn, *Roots of Southern Populism*, 53n., found that 35 percent of his Georgia yeomen were similarly related in 1850. Prude, *The Coming of Industrial Order*, 8, 278n., found that 21 percent of the heads in his southeastern Massachusetts towns were related in 1810. The method used in this and these other studies is imperfect: it counts as kin, unrelated families with the same surname and undercounts relatives with different surnames. Nevertheless, it provides a sense of the importance of kinship to patterns of persistence. For further discussion of kinship and community in Sugar Creek, see chap. 15, especially note 3.

8. *ES*, 262–64, 319, 369, and *HSC*, 796, 873. Sites of settler's claims drawn from *EFLS*.

9. William Faux, *Memorable Days in America* (London: W. Simpkin and R. Marshall, 1823), 315; Gray, *History of Agriculture in the Southern United States*, 2:867.

10. *ES*, 123–24, 393–94, 425, 559–60, 590–91, 745; *HSC*, 746–47, 760, 769; *PP*, 330–33, 1065–69; Charles L. Patton, "The Chronicles of the American Lineage of the Pattons" (typescript, 1954, ISHL); *MC30-40; EFLS*.

11. *ES*, 75–76, 299–302, 498–99; *HSC*, 136–37, 745, 763–64, 786, 789, 795–96; *PP*, 575–76; "Fletcher" vertical file, and "Fletcher Family Papers" (MSS, ISHL).

12. *ES*, 194–95; 462–64, 530, 547–48; *HSC*, 772, 797, 839; *PP*, 981–82.

13. *ES*, 257–60, 750–51; *HSC*, 241–43.

14. *ES*, 564–65.

8. WITH MILK AND HONEY FLOW

1. Bryant, quoted in Masters, *The Sangamon*, 20–21; *HSC*, 178, 195.

2. *HSC*, 178; *ES*, 300; DeWitt Smith, "Agriculture—Farming Lands," in *HE*, 2:778. "Took to the timber" was a common expression in central Illinois, meaning to flee from danger; W. H. Milburn, *The Lance, Cross and Canoe* (New York: N. D. Thompson, 1892), 668.

3. *HSC*, 749.

4. Hall, *Letters from the West*, 348; Arnow, *Seedtime on the Cumberland*, 247; Caleb Atwater, 1818, quoted in Stilgoe, *Common Landscape*, 148.

5. Quotes in Alvord, *The Illinois Country*, 390, 415.

6. *ES*, 163.

7. *HSC*, 785.

8. Ibid.

9. *ES*, 477.

10. McLaren, "Reminiscences of Pioneer Life in Illinois," 25; Robert L. Wilson to William H. Herndon, February 10, 1866, HC; *HSC*, 178.

11. Elizabeth McDowell Hill, in IW; Flint, *The History and Geography of the Mississippi Valley*, 1:321.

12. John Mason Peck, *A Guide for Emigrants, Containing Sketches of Illinois, Missouri, and the Adjacent Parts* (Boston: Lincoln and Edmands, 1831), 171; Patrick Shirreff, *A Tour Through North America* (Edinburgh: Oliver & Boyd, 1835), 249; Allan G. Bogue, *From Prairie to Corn Belt* (Chicago: University of Chicago Press, 1963), 106–11, 225–28; Alan Kraus, "Sangamon County Hogs, 1830–1860" (typescript, 1973, SSU). The counts of farm animals in this discussion are computed from the county-level statistics in U.S., Census Office, *Compendium of the Enumeration and Statistics of the United States . . . from the Returns of the Sixth Census* (Washington: Thomas Allen, 1841), 84–87.

13. John Bradbury, *Travels in the Interior of America in the Year 1809, 1810, and 1811* (London: Sherwood, Neely, and Jones, 1817), 308–09; Flint, *The History and Geography of the Mississippi Valley*, 1:321; Gray, *History of Agriculture in the Southern United States*, 1:204–05; Buley, *Old Northwest*, 1:190.

14. Jones, *Illinois and the West*, 212–13; Peck, *A Guide for Emigrants*, 161–65; Reynolds, *My Own Times*, 54; *HSC*, 175; *ES*, 70.

15. Population figures from Lewis C. Beck, *A Gazetteer of the States of Illinois and Missouri* (Albany, N.Y.: Webster, 1823), 72, and *Compendium of the . . . Sixth Census*, 86; Benjamin Harding, *A Tour Through the Western Country, A.D. 1818 & 1819* (New London: Samuel Green, 1819), 9; Robert L. Wilson to William H. Herndon, February 10, 1866, HC; Shirreff, *A Tour through North America*, 249–50.

16. Purchases by soil type calculated with the aid of *Soil Survey of Sangamon County*, which includes overlays of soil type on detailed aerial photographs; Waggoner, "Illinois Prairie Purchasing Pattern"; and *EFLS*. Among the many references to these neighborhoods in the documents of the CCC see, e.g., Minutes, A:3–9, B:31–33.

17. Charles L. Patton, *The Chronicle of the American Lineage of the Pattons* (Springfield: The Author, 1954), 92–93; *PP*, 1065–66.

18. *ES*, 70–71, 659; *HSC*, 749, 791; *HE*, 1:632; Mrs. Anthony W. Sale, "The Old Mills of Sangamon County," *JISHS* (1926) 18:1056–58; Elizabeth Wier and Edward Hawes, "Mills and Mining in the Clayville Area," (typescript, n.d., SSU).

19. Petition of Robert Crow, September 1825, CCC, Proceedings Files, Box 1; R. B. Rutledge to William Herndon, n.d., HC; Masters, *The Sangamon*, 186; *HSC*, 177, 749, 791, 792.

20. *ES*, 94; Wadsworth, "Sugar Creek Country in 1840," 10.

21. CCC, Minutes, C:57; Petition of Jacob Rauch, March 1830, CCC, Proceedings Files, Box 2; *ES*, 595–97; Eileen Gochanour graciously let me use her material on the Rauch family.

22. Rebecca Burlend, *A True Picture of Emigration,* ed. Milo Milton Quaife (1848; reprint, New York: The Citadel Press 1968), 131–32.

23. Sugar Creek farm size from TL; county-level agricultural statistics in *Compendium of the . . . Sixth Census,* 84–87; *Journal,* October 22, 1859.

24. Mary Jane Drennan Hazlett, in IW; Wadsworth, "The Sugar Creek Country in 1840," 10; *ES,* 645; H. W. Price, "Shelter Forms in the Sangamo Country to 1850" (typescript, n.d., SSU).

25. Glassie, *Pattern in the Material Folk Culture of the Eastern United States,* 88–99, 157; Harold Shurtleff, *The Log Cabin Myth: A Study of the Early Dwellings of the English Colonists of North America* (Cambridge, Mass.: Harvard University Press, 1939); Fred Kniffen and Henry Glassie, "Building in Wood in the Eastern United States, *The Geographical Review* (1966) 56:65; E. Estyn Evans, "Cultural Relics of the Ulster-Scots in the Old West of North America," *Ulster Folklife* (1965) 11:33–38, and "The Scotch-Irish: Their Cultural Adaptation and Heritage in the American Old West," in *Essays in Scotch-Irish History,* ed. E. R. R. Green (London: Routledge & Kegan Paul, 1969), 69–86; Edgar W. Martin, *The Standard of Living in 1860: American Consumption Levels on the Eve of the Civil War* (Chicago: University of Chicago Press, 1942), 136–37.

26. Jones, *Illinois and the West,* 171; *HSC,* 452; Hulbert, *Pioneer Roads,* 44.

27. *HSC,* 174–78.

28. Morris Birkbeck, "Observations of an English Immigrant in 1817," in *Pictures of Illinois One Hundred Years Ago,* ed. Milo Milton Quaife (Chicago: R. R. Donnelley & Sons, 1918), 17–18; Alexis de Tocqueville, *Journey to America,* ed. J. P. Mayer (1835; reprint, Garden City, N.Y.: Anchor Books, 1971), 361.

29. Hall, *Sketches of History,* 2:69.

30. *HSC,* 178; Reynolds, *My Own Times,* 151; Washington, quoted in Henry Nash Smith, *Virgin Land: The American West as Symbol and Myth* (Cambridge, Mass.: Harvard University Press, 1970), 203; "Canaan," in Allan D. Carden, *The Missouri Harmony,* 36.

31. Virgil Vogel, "Indian Place Names in Illinois, *JISHS* (1962) 55:405–07, calls the Reynolds translation "romantic nonsense," although it continues to be used by modern historians such as Oscar and Lilian Handlin in *Abraham Lincoln and the Union* (Boston: Little, Brown, 1980), 19.

32. Gershom Flagg, "Pioneer Letters," in ISHS, *Transactions* (1910) 15:58; David Thomas, *Travels through the Western Country in the Summer of 1816* (Auburn, N.Y.: D. Rumsey, 1819), 206.

9. TOTALLY AND FOREVER DISSOLVED

1. Elizabeth Drennan v. Joseph Drennan, December 1836 and March 1837, Sangamon County, Office of Circuit Clerk, Circuit Court Case Files, Box 9 (MSS, IRAD/SSU); *ES,* 267–68, 612, 670–71, and *HSC,* 164, 409. *Encient* is an antiquated legal term for "pregnant."

2. For Sangamon County marriages see *Marriage Records, Sangamon County, Illinois, 1821–1860,* 4 vols. (Springfield: SCGS, n.d.).

3. Ruth B. Shofield and Elizabeth McDowell Hill, in IW; *HSC,* 65–66; Reynolds, *My Own Times,* 41; Charles James Fox Clarke, "Letters," *JISHS* 22 (1930); Charles Beneulyn Johnson, *Illinois in the Fifties* (Champaign, Ill.: Flanigan-Pearson, 1918); Francis Grierson, *The Valley of Shadows* (1909; reprint, Boston: Houghton Mifflin Company, 1948); and Federal Writers Project, "Illinois Materials—Folklore," Box 104 (MSS, ISHL).

4. "Wedlock," in Emmanuel Hertz, ed., *The Hidden Lincoln: From the Letters and Papers*

of William H. Herndon (New York: Viking Press, 1938), 294–95, and George Pullen Jackson, *Down-East Spirituals and Others* (New York: J. J. Augustin, 1939), 76–78.

5. Schofield, in IW; Kate W. Keller and Ralph Sweet, *A Choice Selection of American Country Dances of the Revolutionary Era (1775–1795)* (New York: Country Dance and Song Society of America, 1975); Thornton Hagert, "Instrumental Dance Music 1780s–1920s," liner notes in *Come and Trip It: Instrumental Dance Music 1780s–1920s*, New World Records-293 (New York: Recorded Anthology of American Music, 1978).

6. Charles James Fox Clark, quoted in Benjamin Thomas, *Lincoln's New Salem*, rev. ed. (New York: Alfred A. Knopf, 1954), 41; Grierson, *The Valley of Shadows*, 110; *HSC*, 66.

7. *HSC*, 181. In the twenty unindexed boxes of materials that constitute the entire run of case files for the Sangamon County circuit court before 1860, I found Sugar Creek residents (those enumerated in *MC30-60*) involved in only the three divorce cases discussed here. The state legislature also granted divorces, but none to Sugar Creek residents. Earl Schenck Miers, ed., *Lincoln Day by Day: A Chronology, 1809–1865*, 3 vols. (Washington, D.C.: United States, Lincoln Sesquicentennial Commission, 1960), suggests the frequency of divorce cases on the court dockets of central Illinois. National data from United States Bureau of the Census, *Historical Statistics of the United States, Colonial Times to 1970* (Washington, D.C.: Government Printing Office, 1976), 10, 15, 64, and Carl Degler, *At Odds: Women and the Family in America from the Revolution to the Present* (New York: Oxford University Press, 1980), 165.

8. Elijah A. West v. Elizabeth West, August and November 1853, Circuit Court Case Files, Box 17.

9. Mary Ann Pulliam v. Thomas J. Pulliam, June 1854, Circuit Court Case Files, Box 17; *ES*, 451, 585.

10. The proportion of households composed of families (married couples or kin of at least two generations) was 88.8 percent (in 1830), 95.9 percent (1840), 90.2 percent (1850), 93.3 percent (1860); sex ratios of adults (aged sixteen to fifty-nine) for the same years were 111 men for every 100 women (1830), 108 (1840), 126 (1850), 144 (1860): *MC30-60*. Doyle similarly concludes that the population of Morgan County, Illinois, immediately west of Sangamon County, "consisted of a base of family units, not just lone individuals," and provides comparable data in *Social Order of a Frontier Community*, 110 and passim. For the increasing number of single men in the late 1840s and the 1850s, see chap. 18.

11. Quote from Le Roy Ladurie, *Montaillou*, 49.

10. IN SICKNESS AND IN HEALTH

1. Marsh, quoted in Carl Sandburg, *Abraham Lincoln: The Prairie Years* (1925; reprint, San Diego, Calif.: Harvest/Harcourt Brace Jovanovich, 1982), 71. Total completed fertility for the cohort of women born from 1770 to 1809 and surviving through age forty-five was 8.2 (N = 158), for women born from 1810 to 1849, 5.9 (N = 224). The vital statistics in this chapter are derived from a sample of 476 women and 452 men of Sugar Creek, born from 1770 to 1849, drawn from FRF.

2. Degler, *At Odds*, 6–7; Robert V. Wells, "Women's Lives Transformed: Demographic and Family Patterns in America, 1600–1970," in Carol Ruth Berkin and Mary Beth Norton, eds., *Women of America: A History* (Boston: Houghton Mifflin Company, 1979), 16–33. Also see Robert V. Wells, *Revolutions in Americans' Lives: A Demographic Perspective on the History of Americans, Their Families, and Their Society* (Westport, Conn.: Greenwood Press, 1982). The average age of marriage for the cohort of women born from 1770 to 1809 was 19.4, for the cohort born from 1810 to 1849, 21.3.

3. The Sugar Creek fertility ratio (the number of children under ten to every thousand women aged sixteen to forty-five) was 2,452 (in 1830), 2,228 (1840), 2.082 (1850),

and 1,939 (1860): *MC30–60*. By comparison, for the northern backcountry as a whole, the ratio stood at 2,550 (1830) and 2,091 (1840); in Oneida County, New York, it was 942 (1830), 822 (1840), and 809 (1850); in Chelsea, Vermont, it was 1200 (1840). Figures taken from James E. Davis, *Frontier America, 1800–1840: A Comparative Demographic Analysis of the Frontier Process* (Glendale: Arthur H. Clark Co., 1977), 169; Mary P. Ryan, *Cradle of the Middle Class: The Family in Oneida County, New York, 1790–1865* (Cambridge, England: Cambridge University Press, 1981), 249; Barron, *Those Who Stayed Behind*, 26.

4. *ES*, 393–94, 254.

5. *ES*, 123, 137, 172, 256, 268, 299, 300, 477, 548, 586, 750, 751; *HSC*, 440; song from T. C. Blake, *The Preacher's Hand-Book: A Guide in the Discharge of Ministerial Duties* (Nashville, Tenn.: 68 Union Street, 1880), 130, used by Cumberland Presbyterians, an important sect in Sugar Creek. See chap. 16.

6. *Journal*, July and August, 1832; "Mortality Schedules," *MC50* and *MC60*.

7. Francis Trollope, *Domestic Manners of the Americans*, ed. Donald Smalley (1832; reprint, New York: Knopf, 1949), 117; Reynolds, *My Own Times*, 44; Erwin C. Ackerknecht, *Malaria in the Upper Mississippi Valley, 1706–1900* (Baltimore: n.p., 1945); Frederick F. Cartwright, *Disease and History* (New York: Thomas Y. Crowell Company, 1972), 141–44.

8. Thomas L. McKenney, *Memoirs, Official and Personal* (New York: Paine and Burgess, 1846), 137–38; *HSC*, 476; medical authority, quoted in Ackerknecht, *Malaria in the Upper Mississippi Valley*, 16.

9. Schoolcraft, *Travels in the Central Portions of the Mississippi Valley*, 204.

10. Buley, *Old Northwest*, chap. 5.

11. *Journal*, December 28, 1833; Lucius H. Zeuch, *History of Medical Practice in Illinois*, 2 vols. (Chicago: Illinois State Medical Society, 1919), 1:312, 392–93; *ES*, 649–50. The "p.m." after Squire Fletcher's name stands for "post master."

12. Elizabeth McDowell Hill, in IW; Federal Writers Project, "Illinois Materials— Folklore," Box 105 (MSS, ISHL).

13. Hall, *Letters from the West*, 340; Ackerknecht, *Malaria in the Upper Mississippi Valley*, 99–125; Caroline Kirkland, *A New Home, or Life in the Clearings*, ed. John Nerber (1843; reprint, New York: G. P. Putnam's Sons, 1953), 97, 201–02.

14. Kirkland, *A New Home*, 204; Hall, *Letters from the West*, 344–45; Wayland D. Hand, "Folk Medical Magic and Symbolism in the West," in *Forms upon the Frontier: Folklife and Folk Arts in the United States*, ed. Austin Fife, Alta Fife, and Henry H. Glassie (Logan: Utah State University, 1969), 103–04, 106, 107ff.; Buley, *Old Northwest*, 1:283–94.

15. For "quilling," see Buley, *Old Northwest*, 1:309. An unusually complete record of an Illinois midwife in the 1840s is documented in the record-book of Sarah Jackson Hymer (MSS, ISHL). On childbirth in general, see Catherine M. Scholten, *Childbearing in American Society, 1650–1850* (New York: New York University Press, 1985).

16. *Historical Statistics of the United States*, 57; by 1970, this maternal death rate had been reduced over 95 percent.

17. Poem, quoted in *ES*, 643; Carlinville doctor, quoted in Isaac D. Rawlings, *The Rise and Fall of Disease in Illinois* (Springfield: State Department of Public Health, 1927), 87. Since the enumerations of death on the "Mortality Schedules" in *MC50* and *MC60* were notoriously undercounted, they cannot be reliably used to calculate general or age-specific death rates but can suggest the proportion of deaths by age and specific causes of death. The rough estimates of fetal and infant mortality and the statistics for Massachusetts mortality are drawn from the available data in *Historical Statistics of the United States*, 57, 63. In the United States in 1970, the national fetal mortality rate was 14 per 1,000 live births, the infant mortality rate 35 per 1,000, and infant death only 6.5 percent of the total number of deaths, with children from one to five adding only .2 percent more.

18. *The Journals of Washington Irving*, ed. William P. Trent and George S. Hellman, 3 vols. (Boston: Bibliophile Society, 1919), 3:116. Age structure computed from *MC30;* United States data taken from *Historical Statistics of the United States*, 16.

11. RAISING HOGS AND CHILDREN

1. Morris Birkbeck, "Observations of an English Immigrant in 1817," 22; James Hall, "Notes on Illinois," *Illinois Monthly Magazine* (1830–31) 1:126; McLaren, "Reminiscences of Pioneer Life in Illinois," 25; *HSC*, 175; Smith, "Agriculture—Farming Lands," in *HE*, 2:779. The conclusion about farm tools is from an analysis of the estate inventories in the probate files of sixteen Sugar Creek heads of household before 1840. Probate records dating before 1849 are in the Office of Circuit Clerk, Sangamon County Courthouse; for a guide through 1835 see "Early Probate Records of Sangamon County, Illinois. Nos. 1– 55," in Daughters of the American Revolution, Illinois Chapter, Genealogical Collections, 4 (typescript, n.d., ISHL) and Hazlemae Taylor Temple and Marilyn Wright Thomas, comps., *Probate Records: Sangamon County Illinois (1827–1835)* (Thompson, Ill.: Heritage House, 1975). The Illinois constitution of 1848 created a new set of county probate courts; their records are most conveniently consulted through the use of the Fee Books (1849–29), Office of Probate Court, 29 vols. (MSS, IRAD/SSU).

2. Timothy Flint, *A Condensed Geography and History of the Western States* (Cincinnati: E. H. Flint, 1833), 398; Parkinson, "Pioneer Life in Wisconsin," 2:326–27; *HE*, 2:984; *ES*, 738.

3. Federal Writers Project, "Illinois Materials—Folklore," Boxes 101 and 104; Nicholas P. Hardeman, *Shucks, Shocks, and Hominy Blocks: Corn as a Way of Life in Pioneer America* (Baton Rouge: Louisiana State University Press, 1981), 70; Hall, *Letters*, 345; Sandburg, *Lincoln*, 65.

4. Richard Lyle Power, *Planting Corn Belt Culture: The Impress of the Upland Southerner and Yankee on the Old Northwest* (Indianapolis: Indiana Historical Society, 1953), 161–62; Christiana Holmes Tillson, *A Woman's Story of Pioneer Illinois* (Chicago: Lakeside Press, 1919), 81–82; Grierson, *The Valley of Shadows*, 41, 42, 44–45; Dennis Hanks to William H. Herndon, March 22, 1866, HC.

5. Hanks to Herndon, January 26, 1866, HC; Buck, *Illinois in 1818*, 130; modal farm size in Sugar Creek from the 1838 tax list in TL. Unfortunately, farm-by-farm agricultural statistics are available only for 1850 and 1860, so county-wide averages must suffice here. Averages were computed by dividing the estimated number of Sangamon County farms (derived by hand-counting all households outside Springfield on *MC40*) into the aggregate county agricultural statistics published in *Compendium of the . . . Sixth Census*, 299–301. I do not mean to imply here that the individual farm household was entirely self-sufficient, but will argue in chapter 11 that the community achieved a form of self-sufficiency. Hahn, *The Roots of Southern Populism*, 142, calls the productive strategy of small to mid-sized farmers "security first."

6. Hanks to Herndon, March 22, 1866, HC; Charles Watts to Edward Watts, Greenfield, Illinois, June 20, 1841 (MSS, ISHL).

7. Shirreff, *A Tour through North America*, 250, 450; *Marriage Records, Sangamon County, Illinois* 1 (1821–35); *MC30; Journal*, June 15, 1853.

8. Lucinda Casteen to Mary Peters, November 22, 1834 (MSS, ISHL).

9. Flint, *Recollections*, 250; Casteen to Peters, November 23, 1833.

10. William Cooper Howells, *Recollections of Life in Ohio, from 1813 to 1840* (Cincinnati: Robert Clarke Co., 1895), 157; Elias Pym Fordham, *Personal Narrative of Travels in Virginia, Pennsylvania, Ohio, Indiana, Kentucky; and of a Residence in the Illinois Territory: 1817– 1818*, ed. Fredrick A. Ogg (Cleveland: Arthur H. Clark, 1906), 120.

11. McLaren, "Reminiscences of Pioneer Life in Illinois;" Casteen to Peters, October 16, 1836.

12. *ES*, 488; Burlend, *A True Picture of Emigration*, 89–92; *HSC*, 68; Paul G. Brewster, "Specimens of Folklore from Southern Indiana," *Folk-Lore* (1936) 47:365; Vance Randolph, "Nudity and Planting Customs," in Tristram P. Coffin and Hennig Cohen, eds., *Folklore in America* (New York: Doubleday & Co., 1966), 138–39; Albert D. Richardson, *Beyond the Mississippi* (Hartford, Conn.: American Publishing Co., 1867), 223.

13. *ES*, 661, 97.

14. On the economic development of Springfield, see Angle, *"Here I Have Lived"*, 41–48.

15. *ES*, 105.

16. Wadsworth, "Sugar Creek Country in 1840," 17–18; *ES*, 141, 66–67.

17. *ES*, 140, 242, 300, 451, 463, 474, 478; William Brown, *America: A Four Year's Residence* (Leeds, Eng.: privately printed, 1849), 48.

18. Sarah Elizabeth Smith Connett and Elizabeth McDowell Hill, in IW; statistics computed from 1850 federal census of agriculture (microfilm, ISA), reel #31/4.

19. Mrs. Andrew McCormick in IW [punctuation added]; *HSC*, 188; Casteen to Peters, November 22, 1834; Lucy Maynard to Sibil Piper, December 25, 1844 (MSS, ISHL). For a study of women in one "butter belt," see Joan M. Jensen, *Loosening the Bonds: Mid-Atlantic Farm Women, 1750–1850* (New Haven: Yale University Press, 1986).

20. *HSC*, 398; *Michigan Pioneer and Historical Collections* (1897–98) 28:405, and (1912) 38:369; Dennis Hanks, interviewed by Erastus Wright, January 26, 1866, HC.

21. *ES*, 229, 477, 500, 568–69, 758, 732; *EFLS*, 41.

22. TL; H. C. Whitley and S. B. Wheelock, *Plat Map of Sangamon County* (St. Louis: Whitley and Wheelock, 1858), copy in ISHL; *EFLS*.

23. Sir William Blackstone, *Commentaries on the Laws of England*, 2 vols. (Oxford: Clarendon Press, 1765–69), 1:442; Lincoln, "Announcement of Political Views," [1836] in Stern, ed., *Life and Writings*, 225; *Revised Statutes of Illinois* (1845), chap. 34; *Statutes of Illinois* (1869), chap. 69.

24. File 403, Probate Records, Office of Circuit Clerk, Sangamon County Courthouse; Sangamon County, Office of Probate Court, Will Record (MSS, IRAD/SSU), 1:256–57. This Elijah West was the father of Elijah A. West who petitioned for divorce; see chap. 9.

25. *Revised Statutes of Illinois* (1845), 546, 306; Robert T. Lawley, "Estate Inventories—Complete or Incomplete?" (typescript, n.d., SSU).

26. Nancy M. Moore to "dear children," March 17, 1862 (MSS, ISHL); File 86, Probate Records, Office of Circuit Clerk, Sangamon County Courthouse; Fletcher v. Fletcher, Circuit Court Case Files, Box 13; Will Record, 2:243–44; Fletcher Family Papers (MSS, ISHL).

27. *EFLS*, 4, 37, 75; Power, *ES*, 159–60, 766.

28. William A. McElvain v. James McElvain et al., March 1856, Circuit Court Case Files, Box 18. Hahn, *The Roots of Southern Populism*, 77–79, similarly finds that fathers willed real property to sons, cash or chattel property to daughters.

29. File 403, Probate Records, Office of Circuit Clerk, Sangamon County Courthouse.

30. Fordham, *Personal Narrative*, 121.

12. SHE DRAINED HERSELF TO GIVE THEM LIFE

1. Herndon, quoted in Hertz, *Hidden Lincoln*, 170; for other details about prostitutes, promiscuous farmer's daughters, and general bawdiness on the circuit, see 233–34, 246–47, 259, 284, 307, 371.

2. Trollope, *Domestic Manners of the Americans*, 118; James Fenimore Cooper, *Notions of the Americans*, 2 vols. (London: Henry Colbun, 1828) 2:257.

3. Trollope, *Domestic Manners*, 49, 117; Margaret Fuller, *Summer on the Lakes, in 1843*

(Boston: Charles C. Little and James Brown, 1844), 116–17; Clarke, quoted in Thomas, *Lincoln's New Salem,* 33.

4. Harriet Martineau, *Society in America,* 3 vols. (London: Saunders and Otley, 1837), 2:101; Mary Jane Hazlett Drennan, in IW; Trollope, *Domestic Manners,* 49; Tillson, *A Woman's Story of Pioneer Illinois,* 144.

5. Trollope, *Domestic Manners,* 118; Martineau, *Society in America,* 3:120, 130. Nancy Cott, *The Bonds of Womanhood: "Woman's Sphere in New England, 1790–1830"* (New Haven: Yale University Press, 1977), argues that the development of a separate women's culture provided the basis for an independent women's understanding of the world and, ultimately, a critique in the service of their own liberation. Such social perspective was made possible because of the space created by late marriage in nineteenth-century New England but was more difficult in the West with its patterns of early marriage.

6. Justice of Peace Court, Legal Papers in People v. Thomas Edwards (MSS, ISHL); Trollope, *Domestic Manners,* 429.

7. Tillson, *A Woman's Story of Pioneer Illinois,* 63, 59, 102; Reynolds, quoted in Donald F. Tingley, "Anti-Intellectualism on the Illinois Frontier," in Robert P. Sutton, ed., *The Prairie State: A Documentary History of Illinois, Colonial Years to 1860* (Grand Rapids, Mich.: Eerdmans, 1976), 184; Trollope, *Domestic Manners,* 117.

8. French explorer, quoted in Beckwith, *Indians of Indiana and Illinois,* 168; Reynolds, *Pioneer History,* 235; Thomas Jefferson, *Notes on the State of Virginia,* ed. William Peden (1781; reprint, Chapel Hill; University of North Carolina Press, 1955), 60.

9. Trollope, *Domestic Manners,* 156–57; Birkbeck, "Observations of an English Immigrant in 1817," 12–13.

10. Ritzenthaler and Peterson, "The Mexican Kickapoo Indians," 36, 64–81; Latorre and Latorre, *The Mexican Kickapoo Indians,* 214; Sarah M. Worthington, "Stories of Pioneer Mothers of Illinois" (MSS, ISHL), 4.

11. Philip Vincent, *A True Relation of the Late Battle Fought in New England* (1638), quoted in Richard Drinnan, *Facing West: The Metaphysics of Indian-Hating and Empire-Building* (Minneapolis: University of Minnesota Press, 1980), 50; Nancy Folbe, "Patriarchy and Capitalism in New England, 1620–1900" (Ph.D. diss., University of Massachusetts, 1979), 95 and passim; Rae Lesser Blumbert, "Fairy Tales and Facts: Economy, Family, Fertility and the Female," in Irene Tinker et al., eds., *Women and World Development* (New York: Praeger, 1976), 11–21; Elizabeth Fisher, *Women's Creation: Sexual Evolution and the Shaping of Society* (Garden City, N.Y.: Anchor, 1979), part 5; Linda Gordon, *Woman's Body, Woman's Right: A Social History of Birth Control in America* (New York: Grossman/Viking, 1976), chaps. 1 and 2.

12. Forsyth, "Account," 2:218; see also chap. 3, above.

13. Benjamin Wadsworth, *The Well-Ordered Family* (Boston: B. Green, 1712), 29, 35; Elizabeth Fries Ellet, *Pioneer Women of the West* (New York: C. Scribner, 1852), 35.

14. Forsyth, "Account," 2:215; Dillingham, "The Oklahoma Kickapoo," 128–29; Latorre and Latorre, *The Mexican Kickapoo,* 35–38, 141, 149–50, 188, 190–91, 194–95; Ritzenthaler and Peterson, "The Mexican Kickapoo," 15, 81–88.

15. Toasts, quoted in Angle, *"Here I Have Lived,"* 29.

16. Kirkland, *A New Home,* 106–07; Grierson, *Valley of Shadows,* 112; John Drury, diary (MSS, ISHL).

17. Dennis Hanks, interviewed by Erastus Wright, June 8, 1865, HC; Simone de Beauvoir, *The Second Sex* (New York: Bantam Books, 1961), 100–01, 119.

18. Alexis De Tocqueville, *Journey to America,* 364–65.

13. A SCENE TO ROUSE THEIR PASSIONS

1. *Journal,* March 10, 1838.
2. *Journal,* April 7, 1838.

3. *ES*, 467–69, 576–77, 592–93; *HSC*, 830, 833, 914–16. Among persistent families, 9 percent were emigrants from northeastern states. In 1850, when the census enumeration included place of birth for the first time, 17.0 percent of household heads born outside the Midwest came from the Northeast. Their proportion increased slightly to 17.7 percent in 1860. *MC50-60*. For more on "Yankees" in Sugar Creek, see chap. 17.

4. *ES*, 770, 788; *HSC*, 444–45, 792; Samuel Williams, "Old Settlers. Incidents and Items of Frontier Life," in *Snow Birds: Poll Books of Sangamo County, 1821–1830* (Springfield: SCGS, 1983), 142–43.

5. *HSC*, 447–48, 996. Wright's brother Erastus also taught school in the county and in the 1830s became the first county school commissioner.

6. *HE*, 2:633; *HSC*, 176, 996; Kunigunde Duncan and D. E. Nickols, *Mentor Graham: The Man Who Taught Lincoln* (Chicago: University of Chicago Press, 1944), 21; Samuel Haycraft to William Herndon, n.d., HC; Noah Webster, "Lessons of easy words, to teach children to read, and to know their duty," in *The American Spelling Book* (1810; reprint, Wells River, Vt.: Ira White, 1843), 46.

7. *HSC*, 996.

8. Quote in Charles Fayette McGlashan, *History of the Donner Party. A Tragedy of the Sierras* (Truckee, Calif.: Crowley & McGlashan, 1879), 117–18; *ES*, 608, and *HSC*, 246.

9. Commissioner's report reprinted in *HE*, 2:796; also see the report in *Register*, December 13, 1860; Wadsworth, "Sugar Creek Country in 1840," 15; teacher contract in Willis F. Berry, "Memoranda Book, 1837–1858" (MSS, ISHL); teacher salaries and records of the township school trustees in "Sangamon County School Commissioners Quarterly Reports" (MSS, ISHL); county and statewide figures in W. L. Pillsbury, "Early Education in Illinois," in *Sixteenth Biennial Report of the Superintendent of Public Instruction* (Springfield: H. W. Rokker, 1886), civ–cciii.

10. Membership of township trustee committees in CCC, Proceedings File, Box 1, undated materials (MSS, SSU/IRAD), and CCC, Minutes (transcript, SSU/IRAD), 40 (see, for example, an accounting of one year's income from the leasing the school lands of township 14/5 in book "C," December 3, 1832); Samuel Willard, "A Brief History of Early Education In Illinois," in *Fifteenth Biennial Report of the Superintendent of Public Instruction of the State of Illinois* (Springfield: H. W. Rokker, 1884); Robert G. Bone, "Education in Illinois before 1857," *JISHS* 50 (1957); Charles B. Johnson, "The Subscription School and the Seminary in Pioneer Days," in ISHS, *Transactions* 32 (1925); and Duncan and Nickols, *Mentor Graham*, 91, 94–95, 130, and passim.

11. "Meeting at Sugar Creek," *Journal*, March 12, 1832; Wayne C. Temple, of the Illinois State Archive, provided me with the data on section sixteen sales for townships missing from records transcribed in *EFLS*.

12. *HSC*, 188; "Sangamon County School Commissioners Quarterly Reports," extant for intermittent quarters for the period 1837–44.

13. Edith Drennan Sprinkell, comp., "Records of Some Early Churches in Sangamon County, Illinois. Sugar Creek Congregation of the Cumberland Presbyterian Church, 1825 to 1870," in Daughters of the American Revolution, Illinois Chapter, Genealogical Collections (typescript, 1928, ISHL), 1–16.

14. *Journal*, February 3, 1838; *HSC*, 251, 914; Sandburg, *The Prairie Years*, 117; *ES*, 577–78, 714. Lincoln's "Lyceum Address" [1838] in Stern, ed., *Life and Writings*, 231–41.

15. "Sangamon County School Commissioner's Quarterly Reports," March 1840; *ES*, 469, 593; *HSC*, 830; George E. Caldwell, comp., *Chatham United Presbyterian Church* (Williamsville, Ill.: SCGS, 1971), 5.

14. GOOD NEIGHBORSHIP

1. Frederick Jackson Turner, *The Significance of the Frontier in American History*, 51, and *The Frontier in American History* (New York: Henry Holt and Co., 1920), 107, 342, 344;

Mody C. Boatright, "The Myth of Frontier Individualism," in Richard Hofstadter and Seymour Martin Lipset, eds., *Turner and the Sociology of the Frontier* (New York: Basic Books, 1968), 43–64.

2. Hall, *Sketches of History,* 2:70; Kirkland, *A New Home,* 301, 303; George Flower, *The Errors of Emigrants* (London: n.p., 1841), 35; John Bradbury, "Illinois on the Eve of Statehood," in Sutton, ed., *The Prairie State,* 134.

3. According to his biographer, Turner missed much of the collective aspect of the frontier experience because he used "logic and imagination rather than evidence" to demonstrate the impact of frontier individualism on the American character; Ray Allen Billington, *Frederick Jackson Turner: Historian, Scholar, Teacher* (New York: Oxford University Press, 1973), 199.

4. Calculated from listings of Sugar Creek real property on 1838 tax list in TL. For more on wealth distribution, see chap. 18, esp. note 11.

5. Oliver, *Eight Months in Illinois,* 241; Lillard, *The Great Forest,* 157–75. On the importance of rural exchange networks, see the works cited in introduction, note 3, as well as Christopher Clark, "The Household Economy, Market Exchange and the Rise of Capitalism in the Connecticut Valley, 1800–1860," *Journal of Social History* (1979) 13:169–90; Prude, *The Coming of Industrial Order;* and Hahn, *Roots of Southern Populism.*

6. Wadsworth, "Sugar Creek Country in 1840," 11; Shirreff, *A Tour through North America,* 446; Burlend, *A True Picture of Emigration,* 75–76; Buley, *Old Northwest,* 1:190; Gray, *The History of Agriculture in the Southern United States,* 1:205; Gates, *Landlords and Tenants,* 198; Hahn, *Roots of Southern Populism,* 60, 243.

7. Ford, quoted in Pease, *Frontier State,* 385; *HSC,* 451.

8. Parkinson, "Pioneer Life in Wisconsin," 327; John Regan, *The Western Wilds of America, or, Backwoods and Prairies; and Scenes in the Valley of the Mississippi* 2d ed. (Edinburgh: John Menzies and W. P. Nimmo, 1859), 62–63; Elizabeth F. C. Ellet, *Summer Rambles in the West* (New York: J. C. Riker, 1853), 221.

9. Kirkland, *A New Home,* 104, 241, 301; Trollope, *Domestic Manners of the Americans,* 120; Charles J. Latrobe, *The Rambler in North America,* 2 vols. (New York: R. B. Seeley & W. Burnside, 1835), 2:136. On reciprocity, in addition to the studies cited in note 5 above, see Michael Taylor, *Community, Anarchy and Liberty* (Cambridge: Cambridge University Press, 1982), 28–29, 38, 53, 69–71, 82–91.

10. *HSC,* 182; Willis Berry, Memoranda Book, 1837–58 (MSS, ISHL); Eddin Lewis accounts, included in Job Fletcher, Jr., Account Book, 1848–63 (MSS, ISHL). "The accommodating nature of debtor-creditor relationships helped to modify the harshness of rural inequality: accounts often ran for years before the debt was settled, partially settled, or forgiven;" Bettye Hobbs Pruitt, "Self-Sufficiency and the Agricultural Economy of Eighteenth-Century Massachusetts," *William and Mary Quarterly* (1984) 41:353.

11. John Smith, Account Book (MSS, ISHL); Lemira Gillet, "Reminiscences of Pioneer Life in Springfield and Logan County Illinois" (typescript, 1901, ISHL), 2; Buck, *Illinois in 1818,* 130; Kirkland, *A New Home,* 176; Wier and Hawes, "Mills and Mining in the Clayville Area;" *HSC,* 749, 791; Sale, "The Old Mills of Sangamon County," 1056–1058.

12. Lucy Maynard to Libbit and Able Piper, December 3, 1839 and July 15, 1840 (MSS, ISHL); Prude, *The Coming of Industrial Order,* 11–12; Winifred B. Rothenbert, "A Price Index for Rural Massachusetts, 1750–1855," *Journal of Economic History* 39 (1979).

13. *HSC,* 443; Rutledge, quoted in Hertz, ed., *Hidden Lincoln,* 316; Elizabeth McDowell Hill, in IW; Everett N. Dick, *The Dixie Frontier* (New York: Alfred A. Knopf, 1948), 126–31.

14. Oliver, *Eight Months in Illinois,* 235; Regan, *The Western Wilds,* 315; *ES,* 429–30; Glassie, *Pattern in the Material Folk Culture of the Eastern United States,* 156–57; Price, "Shelter Forms in the Sangamo Country to 1850."

15. Albert Shaw, "Local Government in Illinois," in Herbert Baxter Adams, ed., *Johns*

Hopkins University Studies in Historical and Political Science (Baltimore: The Johns Hopkins University, 1883), 3:5–19; Robert M. Ireland, *The County Courts in Antebellum Kentucky* (Lexington: University Press of Kentucky, 1972); Rohrbough, *The Trans-Appalachian Frontier,* 119–22; Conrad M. Arensberg, "American Communities," *American Anthropologist* (1955) 57:1143–62.

16. Robert Murray Haig, *A History of the General Property Tax in Illinois. University of Illinois Studies in the Social Sciences* (Urbana: University of Illinois, 1914), 3:52–53, 121, and passim; *ES,* 30–38; *HSC,* 49–51, 282–83; Angle, *"Here I Have Lived";* Taylor, *Community, Anarchy and Liberty,* chaps. 1 and 2.

17. CCC, Minutes, A:3–9, 10, B:31–33, 97; Buck, *Illinois in 1818,* 124; Pease, *Frontier State,* 41; Haig, *Tax in Illinois,* 52–53.

18. "Micajah Organ, Supervisor of Road District," in CCC, Proceedings Files, Box 1, file 1.

19. Coles, quoted in Haig, *Tax in Illinois,* 28; "David Drennan, Application for Pauper," December 1839, CCC, Proceedings Files; Box 2, but see also the various documents on this case throughout the 1840s, including CCC, Minutes, E:4, 7, 14–15; "James Burtle & Geo W. Parkinson, Report of Elizabeth Hartsock," December 1850, CCC, Proceedings Files, Box 5.

20. "Indenture of Serepta Parker with Peter Gates," October 18, 1842, "Jacob Shutt, Bond," June 1851, in CCC, Proceedings Files, Box 3; *ES,* 475; *Register,* July 6, 1859.

21. *HSC,* 996; *JISHS* (1911) 3:23; Pease, *Frontier State,* 40–41. For a general discussion of the history of the America militia, see Walter Millis, *Arms and Men. A Study of American Military History* (New York: G. P. Putnam's Sons, 1956).

22. William J. Butler, "Indian and Mexican Wars," in *HE* 2:905; CCC, June 5, 1821, Minutes, A:5; "Militia Election, House of John Taylor," June 23, 1821, in ER, reel #30/115; reprinted in *Snow Birds,* 5.

23. "Sugar Creek District. A Poll Book of and Election at the Home of Samuel Wycoffs," August 6, 1827 and "Returns of an election in Sugar Creek," August 1, 1831, in ER, reel #30/115; *Journal,* June 20, 1835; *HSC,* 175.

24. Ford, *History of Illinois,* 104–05.

25. Quotes from legislative debate, in Buck, *Illinois in 1818,* 259–60; Samuel Willard, "Personal Reminiscences of Life in Illinois, 1830–1850," ISHL, *Transactions,* (1906) 11:76. Viva voce voting had first been instituted in 1821, repealed in 1823, then reinstituted by popular demand in 1829: Pease, *The Frontier State,* 39; Donald, *Lincoln's Herndon,* 25. John Michael Rozett, "The Social Bases of Party Conflict in the Age of Jackson: Individual Voting Behavior in Greene County, Illinois, 1838–1848" (Ph.D. diss., University of Michigan, 1974), 5, suggests that "the widespread illiteracy in early Illinois, with the attendant possibility of fraud, encouraged the use of viva voce voting instead of a written ballot system." For a discussion of voting patterns and politics in Sugar Creek, see chaps. 15, 18, and 20 below.

26. Pease, *Frontier State,* 38; *Journal,* August 8, 1835; *ES,* 302, 564. Most of the poll books for justice of the peace elections are not extant, but see "Returns of an election in Sugar Creek," August 1, 1831, in ER, reel #30/115.

27. Grierson, *Valley of Shadows,* 170; "Law," quoted in Reagan, *Western Wilds,* 97; *ES,* 576, 665, 681. For the local justice system, see Val C. Simhauser, "Simple Justice: A Study of Sangamon County Justices of the Peace, 1858–1860," (typescript, SSU); and, for comparison, John R. Wunder, *Inferior Courts, Superior Justice: A History of the Justices of the Peace on the Northwest Frontier, 1853–1889* (Westport, Conn.: Greenwood Press, 1979).

15. OPEN-COUNTRY CONNEXIONS

1. Reynolds, *Pioneer History,* 100; Kenneth Lockridge, *A New England Town: The First Hundred Years* (New York: W. W. Norton & Company, 1970), 168, 172.

2. R. B. Rutledge to William Herndon, n.d., HC.

3. Forty-four "original settler families" (families who settled before 1840 and counted at least one household in *MC30-60*) represented 60.3 percent of all households in 1840, 33.7 percent in 1850, 30.2 percent in 1860. The proportion of Sugar Creek households sharing surnames with at least two others was 17.7 percent in 1830, 35.3 percent in 1860. Data from *MC30-60*. Methods of measuring the importance of kinship in historical communities have not yet been standardized, but for other studies, see Beeman, *Evolution of the Southern Backcountry;* Barron, *Those Who Stayed Behind;* Doyle, *The Social Order of a Frontier Community;* Robert Alsop Riley, "Kinship Patterns in Londonderry, Vermont, 1772–1900: An Intergenerational Perspective of Changing Family Relationships" (Ph.D. diss., University of Massachusetts, 1980).

4. Out of the 250 marriages of second-generation original settler family members (for whom spouses could be identified by name), 69.9 percent were to individuals who had resided in the community through at least two census enumerations; comparable statistics for the third generation are 56.1 percent of 157 marriages. In the first generation, 39.0 percent of men and 46.6 percent of women married within the group of forty-four families itself; in the second generation, the rates were 25.9 percent and 33.3 percent for men and women, respectively. Sibling-exchange marriage constituted 19.2 percent of all marriages within original settler families before 1860. Data from FRF. For the sibling-exchange marriages mentioned in the text see *ES*, 123, 138–40, 194–95, 299, 380–81, 498–99, 462–63, 590–91, 595–97.

For the same marriage pattern, see Peter Dobkin Hall, "Marital Selection and Business in Massachusetts Merchant Families, 1700–1900," in Michael Gordon, ed., *The American Family in Social-Historical Perspective*, 2d ed. (New York: St. Martin's Press, 1978), 101–14; Leonore Davidoff and Catherine Hall, "Marriage as an Enterprise: The English Middle Class in Town and Countryside, 1780 to 1850," (paper delivered at the annual meeting of the American Historical Association, 1982); and Elmora Messer Matthews, *Neighbor and Kin: Life in a Tennessee Ridge Community* (Nashville: Vanderbilt University Press, 1965), 35, who quotes a mother as saying that "my three daughters married Ed's three sons; ain't nothin' that brings a family together like that."

5. In 1838, members of original settlers families owned 87.0 percent of lands privately held in the district of upper Sugar Creek; in 1858, members from these same families held 78.5 percent of the timber and margin land and 37.6 percent of the prairie, for a total of 50.7 percent of the entire 100 square mile drainage of the upper creek. Data from the 1838 tax list in TL, and from Whitley and Wheelock, *Plat Map* [1858].

6. For similar findings for other areas of antebellum Illinois see Doyle, *The Social Order of a Frontier Community*, and Richard S. Alcorn, "Leadership and Stability in Mid-Nineteenth Century America: A Case Study of an Illinois Town," *Journal of American History* (1974–75) 61:685–702.

7. ER, reel #30/115, reprinted in *Snow Birds*, 18–24, 46–54; Theodore Calvin Pease, ed., *Illinois Election Returns, 1818–1848*, in ISHL, *Collections* (1923), 18:189, 198, 229, 239. On politics before the Jacksonian period see Buck, *Illinois in 1818;* Pease, *The Frontier State;* Pease, *The Story of Illinois*, 69–70; and Richard Jensen, *Illinois: A Bicentennial History* (New York: W. W. Norton, 1976), 27.

8. *Snow Birds*, 40; *HSC*, 522.

9. *Journal*, April 12, May 17, May 25, and August 25, 1832. On the Illinois Whigs, see Pease, *The Frontier State*, and, on Whigs in general, Daniel Walker Howe, *The Political Culture of the American Whigs* (Chicago: University of Chicago Press, 1979).

10. ER, reel #30/115.

11. *Journal*, July 16, 1834; ER, reel #30/116.

12. Arguments in this and the following paragraph are supported by an analysis of individual citizens' votes recorded in the poll books through 1848, an artifact of the system of viva voce voting. Transient electors (voters appearing on just one or none of the

censuses, *MC30-50*) voted 61.0 percent Democrat in both elections; electors from the forty-four original settler families voted 61.4 percent Whig in 1836, 53.7 percent Whig in 1838. In 1838, 70.8 percent of the voters with no property enumerated on the tax list of that year voted for Democratic candidates; propertied electors voted 73.3 percent for Whigs, and the tendency to vote for Whig candidates rose as wealth in real property increased. Calculated from tabulations of individual votes on the Sugar Creek poll books for 1836 and 1838, in ER, reels #30/115, 116, from 1838 tax list in TL, and *MC30-50*. For a discussion of politics through the 1850s, see chap. 19, below.

13. Wadsworth, "The Sugar Creek Country in 1840," 17–19, and *HSC*, 174–78; kin connections from *ES*, 97, 234–35, 276–77, 362, 476–77, 745–46.

14. Moses G. Wadsworth, autobiographical sketch in "Wadsworth" (vertical files, ISHL); "Moses Wadsworth and Hannah Stevens. Their Ancestral Lines and Their Descendants" (typescript, n.d., ISHL); Moses G. Wadsworth to Henry Bailey, August 18, 1861 (MSS, ISHL); *Journal*, May 13, 1857. For studies of the place of kinship in the construction of community, in addition to those cited in introduction, note 6, see Matthews, *Neighbor and Kin*, and F. Carlene Bryant, *We're All Kin: A Cultural Study of a Mountain Neighborhood* (Knoxville: University of Tennessee Press, 1981). See also discussion of the development of this perspective in studies of rural community in Faragher, "Open Country Community."

15. George L. Hicks, *Appalachian Valley* (New York: Holt, Rinehart and Winston, 1976), 35; for persistence by sex, see Faragher, "Open Country Community," table 6. Of 165 couples from persistent families who married and continued to reside in Sugar Creek from 1819 to 1860, 69 (42 percent) lived near the wife's kin, 79 (48 percent) near the husband's, and 17 (10 percent) near both sets of kin; data from FRF.

16. Benjamin Thomas, *Lincoln's New Salem*, 41.

17. Nathan Dillon, "Early History of Northern and Middle Illinois," in *Register*, June 30, 1854; Roy P. Basler et al., eds., *The Collected Works of Abraham Lincoln*, 9 vols. (New Brunswick, N.J.: Rutgers University Press, 1953–55), 1:272; *Journal*, April 12, 1832; *HSC*, 49, 443, 526, 693, 996; *ES*, 173, 477, 500; McLaren, "Reminiscences of Pioneer Life in Illinois", 50, 53; CCC, Minute Books, A:13, 94, B:10–11, C:93; Reynolds, *My Own Times*, 49; Elizabeth Crawford to William Herndon, February 21, 1866, HC.

18. Milburn, *Lance, Cross and Canoe*, 668; *HSC*, 178, 203; Donald F. Tingley, "Anti-Intellectualism on the Illinois Frontier," in Sutton, ed., *The Prairie State*, 185–86; *Register*, October 15, 1841; McLaren, "Reminiscences of Pioneer Life in Illinois," 50.

19. Kirkland, *A New Home*, 215, 230, 280.

20. *HSC*, 92, 94.

21. *HSC*, 996; Jensen, *Illinois*, 7; Simhauser, "Simple Justice: A Study of Sangamon County Justices of the Peace."

22. James Haines, "Social Life and Scenes in the Early Settlement at Central Illinois," ISHS, *Transactions* (1905) 10:52; Fuller, *Summer on the Lakes*, 117; Charles M. Baker, "Pioneer History of Walworth County," *Report and Collections of the State Historical Society of Wisconsin* (1869–72) 6:470.

23. May, quoted in Angle, *"Here I Have Lived"*, 61–62; *Journal*, April 7, 1838.

24. Raymond Williams, *The Long Revolution* (New York: Columbia University Press, 1961), 72–100, discusses the possible relationships of community.

25. Wadsworth, "The Sugar Creek Country in 1840," 19.

16. THE COMMUNITY OF FEELING

1. *HSC*, 793; *HE*, 867; Joseph J. Thompson, *Diocese of Springfield in Illinois: Diamond Jubilee History* (Springfield: Diocese of Springfield, 1927), 231–32.

2. St. John the Baptist Catholic Church, Springfield, "Register: Liber Baptizatorium, Liber Matrimonorium, Liber Defunitorium, 1843–1858" (MSS, Regional Diocese, Cathedral of the Immaculate Conception, Springfield), in which itinerant priests recorded their activities. Burial lists compiled by Dr. Floyd S. Barringer (typescript, n.d., Lincoln Room, Springfield Public Library) and those in *The Cemeteries of Auburn Township* (Springfield: SCGS, 1980) guided my exploration of Sugar Creek cemeteries.

3. *ES*, 125–26, 162–63, 273, 326–27, 466, 549, 657–58, 795; *PP*, 2:416, 1052–55; *MC50-60;* Conlan, in St. John the Baptist, "Register."

4. Joseph Burtle v. John Thomas Burtle et al., March 1853, Sangamon County, Office of Circuit Court, Case Files, Box 16; Office of Probate Court, Will Record, 1:230–31, 2:237–38, and Minute Book, February 11, 1851 (MSS, IRAD/SSU); *Journal*, April 21, 1851; federal census of agriculture, 1850 and 1860 (microfilm, ISA), reels #31/4 and 31/10, respectively.

5. *ES*, 125–26, 795; *HSC*, 793.

6. Herndon, quoted in Hertz, ed., *The Hidden Lincoln*, 173; Doyle, *The Social Order of a Frontier Community*, 27; ER, reel #30/120.

7. *HSC*, 748–49, 752–56, 792–93, 829–33, 976–77; *Methodist Church, Auburn* (Williamsville, Ill.: SCGS, n.d.); William Royal [Methodist circuit rider], Papers, 1823–70 (MSS, ISHL), file 1; Sangamon County Circuit, Methodist Episcopal Church, Minute Book of Quarterly Meeting, 1837 (MSS, ISHL); George E. Caldwell, comp., *Cumberland Presbyterian Church of Auburn, Illinois* (Williamsville, Ill.: SCGS, 1971); Sprinkell, comp., "Sugar Creek Congregation of the Cumberland Presbyterian Church," 1–16; Cumberland Presbyterian Church, Synod of Sangamon, Minutes, October 1865–October 1885 (MSS, ISHL); Mrs. John Handlin, "A Brief History of the First Baptist Church of Auburn, Illinois 1843–1943," *The Circuit Rider [Quarterly of the SCGS]* 9 (2):51–52; Sangamon Association of Regular Predestinarian Baptists, Minutes, 1823–82 (MSS, ISHL).

8. *The Autobiography of Peter Cartwright*, 236. For studies of protestantism in the American West, see John B. Boles, *The Great Revival, 1787–1805: The Origins of the Southern Evangelical Mind* (Lexington: University Press of Kentucky, 1972); Dickson D. Bruce, *And They All Sang Hallelujah: Plain-Folk Camp-Meeting Religion, 1800–1845* (Knoxville: University of Tennessee Press, 1974); William G. McLoughlin, *Revivals, Awakenings, and Reform: An Essay on Religion and Social Change in America, 1607–1977* (Chicago: University of Chicago Press, 1978); and Sidney Ahlstrom, *A Religious History of the American People* (New Haven: Yale University Press, 1972), chap. 27.

9. Thomas Ford, *A History of Illinois from Its Commencement as a State in 1818 to 1847*, 2 vols. (Chicago: The Lakeside Press, 1945; first published 1854), 1:38–39; *HSC*, 828.

10. *HSC*, 996; Rev. J. B. Logan, *The History of the Cumberland Presbyterian Church in Illinois* (Alton, Ill.: Perrin and Smith, 1878), 74, 109, 181–183; Ben M. Barrus, *A People Called Cumberland Presbyterians* (Memphis, Tenn.: Frontier Press, 1972), 206; Sprinkell, comp., "Sugar Creek Congregation of the Cumberland Presbyterian Church."

11. Logan, *The History of the Cumberland Presbyterian Church in Illinois*, 41, 48–49.

12. Charles A. Johnson, *The Frontier Camp Meeting* (Dallas: Southern Methodist University Press, 1955).

13. Bayard Rush Hall, *The New Purchase, or Seven and a Half Years in the West*, 2 vols. (New York: D. Appleton, 1843), 1:369; Ferdinand C. Lane, *The Story of Trees* (Garden City, N.Y.: Doubleday, 1952), 84–86; Gwen Kennedy Neville, "Kinfolks and the Covenant: Ethnic Community among Southern Presbyterians," in John W. Bennett, ed., *The New Ethnicity: Perspectives from Ethnology* (St. Paul, Minn.: West Publishing Co., 1975), 26; Moritz Busch, *Travels Between the Hudson and the Mississippi, 1851–1852*, ed. and trans. Norman Binger (Lexington: University Press of Kentucky, 1971), 182, 185; Sarah Margaret Fuller, "Summer on the Lakes in 1843," in Paul Angle, ed., *Prairie State: Impressions*

of Illinois, 1673–1967, By Travelers and Other Observers (Chicago: University of Chicago, 1968), 217, 9.

14. Rev. B. W. Gorham, *Camp Meeting Manual, A Practical Book for the Camp Ground* (Boston: H. V. Degen, 1854), 17, and passim; [Charles Wesley], "Vernon," in *The Missouri Harmony*, 55.

15. Burlend, *True Picture of Emigration*, 144–45; Tillson, *Woman's Story of Pioneer Illinois*, 80; Milburn, *Lance, Cross and Canoe*, 669; Regan, *Western Wilds*, 187.

16. Timothy Flint, "Religious Character of the Western People," *Western Monthly Review* (1827–28) 1:270; Nathan L. Gerrard, "Churches of the Stationary Poor in Southern Appalachia," in John D. Photiadis and Harry K. Schwarzweller, eds., *Change in Rural Appalachia: Implications for Action Programs* (Philadelphia: University of Pennsylvania Press, 1970), 109; Buley, *Old Northwest*, 2:459; *HSC*, 68. Donald G. Mathews suggests interpreting the camp meeting as a community organizing process in "The Second Great Awakening as an Organizing Process, 1780–1830," *American Quarterly* (1969) 21:23–43; also see McLoughlin, *Revivals*, 102ff., 132.

17. *HSC*, 878–79, 451; *ES*, 659; Royal, Papers, file 1; Sangamon County Circuit, Methodist Episcopal Church, Minute Book of Quarterly Meeting, 1837; *Journal*, August 28, 1840.

18. *HSC*, 176, 182, 451.

19. D. Turnham to Herndon, December 30, 1865, HC. On the religious music of the West, see George Pullen Jackson, *White Spirituals of the Southern Uplands* (Chapel Hill: University of North Carolina Press, 1933), and Daniel Kingman, *American Music: A Panorama* (New York: Schirmer Books, 1979), part 2.

20. "Old Hundreth" and "Captain Kidd," in *The Missouri Harmony*, 24, 57; Johnson, *Illinois in the Fifties*, 68–73; Alan Lomax, *Folk Songs of North America in the English Language* (Garden City, N.Y.: Doubleday and Co., 1960), 7, 15, 66, 70. On the persistence of the reformed tradition, the conservatism of revivalism, and the essential similarity among the western denominations, see Ahlstrom, *Religious History of the American People*, 131–32, 326–27, 381, 453; and Boles, *The Great Revival*, 129ff.

21. [Isaac Watts], "Funeral Thought," in *The Missouri Harmony*, 57, 64; John A. Lomax and Alan Lomax, *Folk Song U.S.A.: The 111 Best American Ballads* (1947; reprint, New York: New American Library, 1975), 415; *Preacher's Hand-Book*, 129–30; Ahlstrom, *Religious History of the American People*, 438–39.

22. John Ross to an unidentified recipient, April 7, 1861, "Stewart Family Papers" (MSS, ISHL).

23. Sprinkell, comp., "Sugar Creek Congregation of the Cumberland Presbyterian Church," 3–6; George Caldwell, comp., "Chatham Methodist Church, 1836–1936" (typescript, n.d., Lincoln Room, Springfield Public Library), 1.

24. Richard Beard, quoted in Logan, *Cumberland Presbyterian Church in Illinois*, 136–37; *HE*, 2:633; Oliver, *Eight Months in Illinois*, 122–23; Trollope, *Domestic Manners*, 156–57.

25. Sprinkell, comp., "Sugar Creek Congregation," 6; Masters, *The Sangamon*, 122; William H. Herndon to Truman H. Bartlett, October 1887, in Hertz, ed., *The Hidden Lincoln*, 208.

26. Reynolds, *My Own Times*, 14; "Rockingham" and "Whitestown," in *The Missouri Harmony*, 39, 119.

27. *HSC*, 68–69.

28. Masters, *The Sangamon*, 124.

29. George Flower, *The Errors of Emigrants*, 35.

30. Proportions from lists of church affiliates in the sources cited in note 7, above, checked against the enumeration of household heads on *MC40*. 79 of the 134 heads were affiliated with the six Protestant congregations, 12 with the Catholic church.

17. IT ANSWERS WELL FOR A VILLAGE

1. This account of the Wadsworths is drawn from [Mary Wadsworth Jones], "Moses Wadsworth and Hannah Stevens. Their Ancestral Lines and Their Descendants," (typescript, 1941, ISHL); Moses G. Wadsworth: "Auburn," in *Sangamon County Gazetteer* (Springfield: John C. W. Bailey, 1866), 13–16; Wadsworth, "The Sugar Creek Country in 1840"; Wadsworth, "Auburn and Vicinity Forty Years Ago," in *HSC,* 174–79; *HSC,* 750–52; "Moses Goodwin Wadsworth" (typescript, 1905, ISHL); "Wadsworth" (vertical file, ISHL).

2. *ES,* 276–77; *PP,* 823–24; *EFLS,* 4; 1838 tax list in TL; Wadsworth, "The Sugar Creek Country in 1840," 6–7.

3. Buley, *Old Northwest,* 2:147; Gates, *Landlords and Tenants,* 56, 113–14, 149; Pease, *Frontier State,* 175–77; *Register,* April 29, 1836; Waggoner, "The Illinois Prairie Purchasing Pattern;" *EFLS.*

4. Illinois investor, quoted in Douglas R. McManis, *The Initial Evaluation and Utilization of the Illinois Prairies, 1815–1840* (Chicago: University of Chicago Press, 1964), 87; *HSC,* 750, 792, 830, 854, 864, 875–76, 914, 920, 932, 940, 963, 1047.

5. *HSC,* 751; William Swaney and David Eastman documents, in Sangamon County, Office of Circuit Court, Case Files, Boxes 13 and 14.

6. Wadsworth, "The Sugar Creek Country in 1840," 7; *PP,* 283; *MC40-50.*

7. Masters, *The Sangamon,* 191; *HSC,* 792.

8. CCC, Minutes, A:3–9; Pease, *Frontier State,* 10; John Leslie Tevebaugh, "Frontier Mail: Illinois, 1800–1830," (M.A. thesis, University of Illinois, 1952), 83, 101; *Journal,* January 26 and May 18, 1833, and January 11, 1834; John Mason Peck, *A Guide for Emigrants, Containing Sketches of Illinois, Missouri, and the Adjacent Parts* (Boston: Lincoln and Edmands, 1831), 298.

9. John Mason Peck, *The Traveller's Directory for Illinois* (New York: Colton, 1839), 207–208; Wadsworth, "The Sugar Creek Country in 1840," 6; *HSC,* 177; "William Caldwell, Report," in CCC, Proceedings Files, Box 2; Daniel Wadsworth to Abraham Lincoln, January 25, 1848, quoted in Don E. Fehrenbacher, "The Post Office in Illinois Politics," *JISHL* 46 (1953), 62n.

10. *HSC,* 178–79; *MC40.*

11. Road petition, 1838, CCC, Proceedings Files, Box 2.

12. *Beck's Gazetteer of Illinois and Missouri* (1823), quoted in *HE,* 2:617; Angle, *"Here I Have Lived,"* 54–55, 144–48; *Charter of the Chicago and Mississippi Rail Road Company, Originally Incorporated by the Name of the Alton and Sangamon Railroad Company* (New York: William C. Bryant & Co., 1854), 3, 11; *HSC,* 751–52.

13. *HSC,* 751–52; Wadsworth, "The Sugar Creek Country in 1840," 6; *Journal,* January 19, 1854.

14. For typical accidents see: *Journal,* July 19 and November 1, 1853, June 28, 1854, and August 25, 1855; the Chatham girl's death was reported on July 10, 1855; *Register,* October 17 and November 9, 1853, January 30, 1855. On Irwin see *HSC,* 839–40.

15. Wadsworth, "Auburn," 14; MC60.

16. *HSC,* 1029; *Private Laws of the State of Illinois,* 2 vols. (Springfield: Boke and Phillips, 1865), 2:362–69.

18. LANDLORDS AND TENANTS

1. Unless otherwise specified, the analysis in this chapter is based on population data from *MC30-60;* farming data from the manuscript schedules of the federal census of agriculture for Sangamon County, 1850 and 1860 (microfilm, ISA), reels #31/4 and #31/10, respectively; ownership data in federal land sale records provided by the Illinois

State Archives as well as *EFLS; 1835 Tax List;* TL; and Whitley and Wheelock, *Plat Map* [1858].

2. *ES*, 584–86; *Journal,* October 22, 1859.

3. *EFLS,* 12; Sangamon County, Circuit Court, Case Files, Boxes 1 and 5; Circuit Court, Record, B:118, 146–47, 148, 149–150, 154; Circuit Court, Judgement Docket, A:section "P"; CCC, Minutes, C:158; "R. Pulliam to James Mason: Deed," in Sangamon and Logan County, Miscellaneous County Documents, file 1 (MSS, ISHL); *Journal,* August 18, 1832.

4. Circuit Court, Case Files, Boxes 4 and 8; Circuit Court, Record, C:84, 136, 224–25.

5. Circuit Court, Case Files, Boxes 8 and 9.

6. *ES*, 586; *Journal,* October 22, 1859.

7. Gates, *Landlords and Tenants,* 55–60.

8. On nonresident speculators in central Illinois and Sugar Creek, see Gates, *Landlords and Tenants,* 77, 78, 151, 246; residents from *MC30-50;* purchases from *EFLS.*

9. *HSC,* 178; Gates, *Landlords and Tenants,* 101, 243, 246–47. For numbers of owners and nonowners, see note 12 below.

10. Percentage of nonresident ownership calculated from Whitley and Wheelock, *Plat Map* [1858].

11. Distribution of wealth in real property calculated from 1838 tax list in TL, and Whitley and Wheelock, *Plat Map* [1858]:

Wealth fifths	1838	1858
top	42.5	50.3
2d	21.8	24.0
3d	15.3	13.3
4th	10.6	7.3
5th	9.7	4.7

12. Rental agreement, 1843, in Willis F. Berry, Memoranda Book, 1837–58 (MSS, ISHL); Caird, quoted in Gates, *Landlords and Tenants,* 308, see also 63–64, 242; Regan, *Western Wilds,* 351. Although the federal census did not separately identify tenants until 1880, tenant heads of household are shown on the 1850 agricultural schedules as operating farms without any enumerated acreage; in 1860 they are shown as operating farms on the agricultural schedules but are listed as having no real property on the population schedules. Heads of household who were agricultural laborers were listed as farmers on the population schedules, but not listed on the agricultural schedules. In addition to these censuses, the following data are derived from TL; *EFLS; ES; HSC:*

	1830	1840	1850	1860
Owner-operators	55	66	128	189
Nonowners	46	53	—	—
Tenants	—	—	20	87
Laborers	—	—	44	40
Other occupations	12	15	16	35
Total	113	134	208	351

13. *MC60,* 70–75, and the corresponding 1860 agricultural schedules.

14. *MC60,* 45–47, 60–63, and the corresponding 1860 agricultural schedules.

15. *MC60,* 69–70, 52, 62, 47–48.

16. Seventy-three road petitions from Sugar Creek residents in CCC, Proceedings Files, passim.

17. Survey of the signers of twelve road petitions dating before 1845 and sixty-one thereafter; Pease, *Frontier State*, 41; Haig, *Tax in Illinois*, 53.

18. "Pet for Road Leading from Springfield to Auburn," June 1846; "Report of Road," June 1856; "No. 50. Mr Lockridge's Petition," September 1859, all in CCC, Proceedings Files, Boxes 3 and 5.

19. "James Patton & others, Pet to change Alton & Springfield Road," March 1851, in CCC, Proceedings Files, Box 4.

20. "Josiah Lord, Pet for Road" June 1851, in CCC, Proceedings Files, Box 4.

21. Glassie, *Patterns in the Material Folk Culture of the Eastern United States*, 49, 99–100; Price, "Shelter Forms in the Sangamo Country," and Bill Smith, "Barns" (typescript, n.d., SSU).

22. Martin, *The Standard of Living in 1860*, 136–37.

23. *Land Limitation and Homestead Exemption* (n.p.: n.p., n.d. [1846]), broadside in ISA; Wentworth, quoted in Cole, *The Era of the Civil War*, 89.

24. *Journal*, March 13, July 3, 1840; *Register*, October 15, 1841, June 30, 1852, September 6, 1858, July 31, 1860; *HSC*, 205, 251; Charles Manfred Thompson, *The Illinois Whigs before 1846*, in *University of Illinois Studies in the Social Sciences* (Urbana: University of Illinois Press, 1915), 4:68.

25. *Journal*, February 16, 1839. 80.0 percent of 60 Sugar Creek electors who voted in seven elections from 1836 to 1848 consistently voted the party ticket; 58.3 percent were Whigs, 41.7 percent Democrats. Poll books of elections from 1836 to 1848 in ER, reels #30/115–19. Doyle, *The Social Order of a Frontier Community*, 171, similarly notes that in Morgan County, Illinois, from 1836 to 1872, "regardless of the shifts in issues and candidates, the voting patterns remained steady;" and Rozett, "The Social Basis of Party Conflict," 30, concludes that party loyalty "appears to have been the rule of partisans of both sides" in Greene County.

Individual votes for the presidential of election of 1840 were stratified with data from the 1838 tax list; votes for the election of 1848, with property data in the population and agricultural schedules of the census of 1850. Rozett finds that in Greene County, southeast of Sugar Creek, 67 percent of the poorest fourth of the population voted Democratic, 63 percent of the middle half, and only 46 percent of the richest fourth. "An unmistakable affinity was especially apparent," he writes, "for lower class yeomen to prefer the Democratic party and for upper class non-farmers to opt for Wiggery." He is at pains, however, to insist that "neither party could lay exclusive claim to the allegiance of one class," that "the two parties, in spite of very suggestive and distinct tendencies, did not behave in a rigorous economic fashion, each party harboring many exceptions to any general economic rule of voting behavior." Wealth and class certainly do not explain all—who but simplistic determinists ever supposed they did—but even in Rozett's work, despite his disclaimers, they explain much. "Social Basis of Party Conflict," 91f., 94, 128–32.

26. Rozett, "Social Basis of Party Conflict," 234, contrary to these findings, produces evidence that "this did not happen in Greene County."

27. *Register*, February 21 and April 6, 1853, June 12, 1854.

28. *Register*, March 9, 1852, August 7 and October 3, 1854.

29. *Journal*, July 2, 1841, April 1 and October 7, 1842; *HSC*, 205; *Register*, March 15, 1844.

30. Sangamon County Temperance Union Society, Records, 1847–50 (MSS, ISHL), 4, 6–10, 26–27, and later section, unpaginated.

31. *Journal*, June 17, 1847; Sangamon County Temperance Union Society, Records, 10, and later section, unpaginated.

32. *Journal*, September 27, 1848; Sangamon County Temperance Union Society, Records, later section, unpaginated. Howe, *The Political Culture of the American Whigs*, is

helpful on the connections between Whig politics and evangelical religion and provides a good review of recent historical work stressing the importance of "ethnocultural" factors like religion in determining party identity.

33. Cole, *Era of the Civil War,* 207, 210; Reynolds, *My Own Times,* 49.

34. "Job Fletcher Jun & W. A. Lockridge. Pet for Cart Way," April 6, 1847; this, and all further road petitions cited in this chapter, in CCC, Proceedings Files, Box 3.

35. "Gilbert Dodds. Remonstrance Against Cart Way," April 9, 1847, and "J. A. Ball & Wm Chambers. Report of Cart Way," no date; "Job Fletcher & others petition for County Road," June 23, 1847.

36. Quotes from Fletcher's trial, in Sprinkell, comp., "Sugar Creek Congregation of the Cumberland Presbyterian Church," 6–11.

37. "Arthur Ledle, Eddin Lewis—Report of road—Accepted & Entered," September 8, 1847; *ES,* 257.

19. CONSERVATIVE CHANGE

1. Unless otherwise noted, this account of the Eddin Lewis family is based on probate documents and the standard family history sources: Sangamon County, Office of Probate Court, Will Record, 1:125–28, and Probate Court, Minutes, 1849–52, February 6, April 1, August 13, September 23, and October 7, 1850; February 8 and June 16, 1851 (MSS, IRAD/SSU); "The Estate of Eddin Lewis [1851]," in Fletcher Family Papers (MSS, ISHL) and Eddin Lewis's accounts for 1847–50, included in Job Fletcher, Jr., Account Book (MSS, ISHL); *ES,* 452–53; *PP,* 1386–89; *EFLS,* 11. See *MC50,* 207, for the cause of Lewis's death.

2. Sangamon County Temperance Union, Records, later section, unpaginated; *Journal,* March 3, 1840, October 29, 1842, February 22, March 21, 1844, March 5, 1846, April 13 and 27, 1848.

3. *Journal,* August 6, 1856; *Register,* September 20, 1860; Sangamon County, Office of Probate Court, Estate Inventory Record, 1:33–41 (MSS, IRAD/SSU). Figures here and elsewhere in this chapter on the state of agriculture in 1849–50 and 1859–60 are taken from the agricultural schedules of the federal census for Sangamon County, 1850 and 1860. All changes in values are adjusted for price inflation, using rates in *Historical Statistics of the United States,* 211–12.

4. Figures here and in the following discussion are computed from analysis of the 1838 tax list in TL, and Whitley and Wheelock, *Plat Map* [1858].

5. For sources of fertility statistics see chap. 10, note 1. Richard A. Easterlin, "Factors in the Decline of Farm Family Fertility in the United States: Some Preliminary Research Results," *Journal of American History* (1976) 63:600–12, finds a similar relationship between lower completed fertility and the earlier cessation of child bearing, as do Nancy Osterud and John Fulton, "Family Limitation and Age at Marriage: Fertility Decline in Sturbridge, Massachusetts 1730–1850," *Population Studies* (1976) 30:481–94.

6. Figures in this and the next paragraph computed from aggregate data for Sugar Creek are compiled from *MC30-60;* see chap. 10, note 3 above. For a general discussion of family limitation in the nineteenth century see Degler, *At Odds,* chaps. 8 and 9.

7. *Register,* July 1, 1856, and December 28, 1857.

8. Drake quoted in Everett N. Dick, *The Dixie Frontier* (New York: Alfred A. Knopf, 1948), 104; *HSC,* 176.

9. Robert Patterson, "Early Society in Southern Illinois," *Fergus Historical Series* 14:109; Elizabeth McDowell Hill, in IW.

10. Hill, in IW. For some suggestions about the persistent patterns of rural women's labor, see Edgar Schmiedeler, *The Industrial Revolution and the Home: A Comparative Study of Family Life in Country Town and City* (Washington, D.C.: n.p., 1927); Carl Hamilton, *In No Time At All* (Ames, Iowa: Iowa State University Press, 1975); Joan Jensen, *With These*

Hands: Women Working the Land (Old Westbury, N.Y.: Feminist Press, 1980); Norman Juster, *So Sweet to Labor: Rural Women in America, 1865–1895* (New York: Viking, 1979).

11. Philemon Stout, Jr., Diaries, 1860–1907 (MSS, ISHL). This account is based on diaries for 1860–61, as well as *MC50-60* and agricultural schedules of the 1850 and 1860 census. For background see *ES*, 690–93; *PP*, 671–72; 1028–34, 1423–24; Littleton Porter Bradley, comp., *Some Stout Families of Central Illinois* (St. Louis: the author, 1972):8–21; *HSC*, 776–77, 801.

12. *PP*, 1033, 1034; Gates, *Landlords and Tenants*, 313. Land holdings calculated from Whitley and Wheelock, *Plat Map* [1858]; *Illustrated Atlas Map of Sangamon County, Illinois* (Springfield: Brink, McCormick & Co., 1874), 25, 30, 31; and *PP*, 1033.

13. *Register*, July 31, 1860; *Journal*, September 4 and 24, 1860.

14. This, and the following two paragraphs, are based on accounts in the *Register*, January 19 and May 11, 12, 14, 1860; and *HSC*, 525.

15. Doyle, *The Social Order of a Frontier Community*, 177, argues that the presence of women at political rallys in Jacksonville, first noted in the 1850s, was a deliberate effort to control and refine what were previously rough-and-tumble masculine affairs.

20. THE REMNANT OF THAT PIONEER BAND

1. *Journal*, March 1, April 12, July 8, 1851, and March 14, 1856; *Register*, January 1 and October 9, 1858; *Alton Courier*, February 22, 1854, quoted in Cole, *The Era of the Civil War*, 49; *MC60*.

2. *Journal*, September 1 and October 6, 1856; *Register*, September 1, 1856 and November 6, 1857. The poll books of the elections of 1854–60 are in ER, reel #30/120–22.

3. *HSC*, 261. *Register*, July 14, 1858, lists Fletcher, Burtle, and Gatton on Stephen Douglas's "Committee of Reception." For Democratic rhetoric see, e.g., *Register*, July 18, 1856 and July 14, 1858. Survey of Democratic percentages from ER, reel #30/115–24, et seq. Since the Illinois constitution of 1848 abolished viva voce voting and instituted the secret ballot, it is impossible to examine systematically the changing allegiances of individuals after that date.

4. *Journal*, July 7, 1856, and October 6, 1857; *Register*, June 28, 1858.

5. *Register*, June 23 and November 11, 1853, January 10, April 11, May 30, and June 30, 1854; *Journal*, May 7, 8, 9, and June 1, 1857.

6. *Journal*, May 26 and October 20, 1859; *Register*, May 27 and August 26, 1859.

7. Analysis of the petitioners drawn from *MC60, ES, HSC*, and *Journal*, August 5 and 22, 1849.

8. *Register*, January 17, 1854.

9. *HSC*, 123, 463–64.

10. My argument here is indebted to George B. Forgie, *Patricide in the House Divided: A Psychological Interpretation of Lincoln and His Age* (New York: W. W. Norton & Company, 1979).

11. The following account of the 1859 reunion is based on the report in the *Journal*, October 22, 1859, and the *Register*, October 21, 1859; a shorter version is reprinted in *HSC*, 432–39. Local planning for the event is reported in *Register*, September 29 and October 11, 1859.

12. The conversion is mentioned in *ES*, 586.

13. Militia lists by townships, 1861 (MSS, ISHL), compiled by each township assessor, provide a master list of eligible men to check against the rosters of Sangamon County regiments in *HSC*, 365–415. Brief histories of the regiments are appended to these rosters, but my discussion draws from the fuller regimental histories in Frederick H. Dyer, *A Compendium of the War of the Rebellion* (Des Moines: Dyer Publishing Company, 1908).

14. Moses G. Wadsworth to Henry Bailey, August 18, 1861 (MSS, ISHL); casualities taken from *HSC*, 416–22, and from family accounts in *ES*.

15. *HSC*, 194.

16. *ES*, 107–08, 300, 453, 585. For a fictional treatment of the story in the next paragraph, see MacKinlay Kantor, *Andersonville* (Cleveland: World Publishing Company, 1955), 478.

17. "Committee on Statistics of the Church and the State of Religion," Cumberland Presbyterian Church, Synod of Sangamon, Minutes, October 1865–October 1885 (MSS, ISHL), 7–8.

18. *HSC*, 448–51, 454, 465–66.

19. *ES*, 13, 4; *HSC*, 65, 457.

20. *HSC*, 464, 68.

21. *HSC*, 451, 452, 453, 454.

22. The women's presentations are reprinted in a special section of *HSC*, 187–94.

23. *HSC*, 454–55.

24. *Journal*, January 24, 1853; *Register*, December 30, 1853, and February 2, 1855; Cole, *The Era of the Civil War*, 212. For reprints of letters published in *The Household*, see Juster, *So Sweet To Labor*. Greater rates of migration for country women are discussed in Bengt Ankarloo, "Agriculture and Women's Work: Directions of Change in the West, 1700–1900," *Journal of Family History* (1979) 4:118–19; E. C. Young, *The Movement of Farm Population* (Ithaca, N.Y.: Cornell University Agricultural Experimental Station, 1924), 16, 21; Carle C. Zimmerman, "The Migration to Towns and Cities," *American Journal of Sociology* (1926–27) 32:452; Walter F. Wilcox, "The Distribution of Sexes in the United States in 1890," *American Journal of Sociology* (1895) 1:725–37.

CONCLUSION

1. *HSC*, 453, 457.

2. Masters, *The Sangamon*, 87.

3. Interview with Paul Burtle, Auburn, Illinois, June 1981.

4. Interviews with Walter Burtle, Father James Kondrath, and John Knoefel, Auburn and Springfield, Illinois, June 1981.

5. *History Cherry Grove School, 1854–1913* (Auburn, Ill.: Cherry Grove School Board, 1913), copy in the possession of Walter Burtle. Property ownership calculated from *Plat Book of Sangamon County, Illinois* (Springfield: Sangamon County Abstract Co., 1914), 54, 82, reprinted in *Combined Atlases of Sangamon County, Illinois, 1874, 1894, 1914* (Evansville, Ind.: Whipporwill Publications, n.d.). Without doubt, the figures in this and the next paragraph underestimate descendants' holdings, since many have not retained the original patrilineal surnames.

6. *HSC*, 750, 758, 793–94, 830, 977–78. In 1914, same-surname descendants owned 19.3 percent of the 100-square-mile drainage of upper Sugar Creek, in 1981, 10.0 percent; *Plat Book* [1914], 54, 62, 70, 82; *Land Atlas and Plat Book, Sangamon County, Illinois, 1981* (Rockford, Ill.: Rockford Map Publishers, 1981), 9. 10, 14, 15. Residence taken from *Official 1980 Sangamon County, Illinois Rural Resident Directory* (Boulder, Colo.: Directory Service Company, 1980).

7. Fordham, *Personal Narrative*, 124–25, 210–11, 227, 228–29.

Index

Women (*continued*)
214; and ownership, 105–06; and law,
106; and public culture, 111–12, 151–
55, 214; and scolding, 116–17; rights,
232
Wood River, Ill., 5, 7, 23, 30, 31, 32, 33,
44, 56, 57
Woods, John, quoted, 26, 48, 50

Worthington, Sarah, quoted, 114
Wright, Charles, 124, 220
Wright, Erastus, 34, 124, 219–20
Wrightsman, Christian, 202
Wycoff, Samuel, 140

Yankees, 45–46, 123, 124, 129, 258n
Young America, 220–22